THE
VENTURE CAPITAL
HANDBOOK

THE
VENTURE CAPITAL

HANDBOOK

Editors

WILLIAM D. BYGRAVE

MICHAEL HAY

JOS B. PEETERS

FINANCIAL TIMES
Prentice Hall

PEARSON EDUCATION LIMITED

Head Office:
Edinburgh Gate
Harlow CM20 2JE
Tel: +44 (0)1279 623623
Fax: +44 (0)1279 431059

London Office:
128 Long Acre, London WC2E 9AN
Tel: +44 (0)171 447 2000
Fax: +44 (0)171 240 5771
Website: www.business-minds.com

First published in Great Britain 1999

ISBN 0 273 63899 8

British Library Cataloguing in Publication Data
A CIP catalogue record for this book can be obtained from the British Library.

10 9 8 7 6 5 4 3 2 1

Typeset by Northern Phototypesetting Co. Ltd, Bolton.
Printed and bound in Great Britain by Biddles Ltd, Guildford and King's Lynn.

The Publishers' policy is to use paper manufactured from sustainable forests.

ABOUT THE EDITORS

William D. Bygrave, MA, D.Phil. (Oxon.), MBA, DBA, is the Frederic C. Hamilton Professor for Free Enterprise and Director of the Center for Entrepreneurial Studies at Babson College, Visiting Professor at INSEAD (The European Institute of Business Administration), Special Professor at the University of Nottingham, and Visiting Professor at the London Business School.

As an academic, he teaches and researches entrepreneurship, especially financing of start-up and growing ventures. He spent the 1992–3 academic year at INSEAD where he introduced an MBA course Entrepreneurial Finance and lead a Pan-European team from eight nations that studies entrepreneurs' attitudes toward realizing value and harvesting their companies. One of the outcomes of that research was the initiative that led to the founding of EASDAQ.

He is author of *Venture Capital at the Crossroads*, with Jeffry Timmons; and editor of *The Portable MBA in Entrepreneurship*, *Frontiers of Entrepreneurship Research* and *Entrepreneurship Theory and Practice*. He has served on the review boards of three entrepreneurship journals. He was director of the annual Babson College – Kauffman Foundation Entrepreneurship Research Conference in 1994 and 1995.

As a practitioner, William D. Bygrave founded a Route 128 venture-capital-backed high-tech company, managed a division of a NYSE-listed high-tech company, co-founded a pharmaceutical database company, and was a member of the investment committee of a venture capital firm.

Michael Hay is Director of the Foundation for Entrepreneurial Management and an Associate Professor of Strategic and International Management at London Business School. He is Associate Dean of the Sloan Programme. He joined the faculty in 1987 having previously spent ten years in academic publishing principally with Blackwell where he was deputy managing director of Blackwell Publishers and chairman/chief executive of Marston Book Services. He is a founder director of two venture-capital-backed companies, Cherwell Scientific and Imparta Limited.

Michael Hay has undertaken assignments for a number of major international companies including British Airways, 3M and United News & Media both in the UK and USA. He has also worked as a consultant for the United Nations on welfare in Eastern Europe.

He is author of *The Strategy Handbook*, with Peter Williamson, and *Realizing Investment* Value with William D. Bygrave and Jos B. Peeters. Most recently, he has co-authored with Steven Abbott *Investing for the Future: New Firm Funding in Germany, Japan, the UK and USA*.

 **Jos B. Peeters** holds a Ph.D. in Physics from the University of Louvain. He was co-founder and first chairman of the Belgian Venturing Association. He has been a member of the board of EVCA, the European Venture Capital Association, and was chairman of the association in 1989–90.

He is founder and managing director of Capricorn Venture Partners NV, a Belgian-based venture capital advisory company specializing in early stage, technology-based growth companies. He is also co-founder and chairman of Quartz Capital Partners Ltd, a London-based integrated investment banking firm focusing on technology and life sciences companies. He is chairman of Quest for Growth NV, a technology-oriented investment fund quoted on the Brussels Stock Exchange. He is a co-founder and vice-chairman of EASDAQ SA, the pan-European stock market for growth companies.

CONTENTS

In memory of Richard A. Onians

The plan to do a Venture Capital Handbook, where professionals from the venture capital industry share some of their valuable lessons with colleagues, newcomers and outsiders to this profession, was a project that exited Dick Onians enormously. Dick was one of these great human beings who was always concerned in creating an environment in which there would be more opportunity for everybody to flourish.

Not surprisingly, he was one of the driving forces behind the establishment of the European Venture Capital Association, a club that was meant to build contacts between the emerging venture capitalists in Europe in the early 1980s. He served on its first Board of Directors and was Chairman in 1985–6. When we invited him to author an introduction he enthusiastically accepted. Unfortunately his sudden illness interfered with this plan. With Dick, the European Venture Capital Industry lost one of its founding fathers and one of its respected leaders. We are dedicating the *Venture Capital Handbook* to his memory and have substituted the introduction that was never written by an extract from a lecture that Dick delivered to the Royal Society of Arts in London in January 1995. The full text of this lecture was published in the *RSA Journal* of May 1995.

'Making small fortunes; success factors in starting businesses'

The purpose of this lecture is to attempt to identify a few investment criteria which if applied, can improve the success rate of new business creation. I intend to confine my remarks only to those incipient businesses which are private and have the potential to be world class. The characteristics of these businesses are internationally competent management, globally attractive products or services, and sustainable international cost advantage.

Most Western governments in the past 15 years have watched with increasing concern the downsizing and retrenchment of the large multinational companies as smaller businesses have pioneered new technologies and markets and provided all the growth in new employment. It is not particularly original therefore to say that an important burden for growth lies with the owners and managers of new world class businesses. I am proposing that we need a better understanding of the how we can make [these] incipient, potentially world class businesses succeed.

Over the past ten years, Barings has been involved in reviewing or advising on more than 10,000 requests for start-up or early stage equity capital in more than 20 countries. Investment has been made in fewer than 2 per cent of the businesses.

Of those businesses 20 per cent have been within a company that failed. All equity capital was thus lost. Another 20 per cent have developed into substantial, profitable and independently sustainable businesses exploiting international markets. The balance of 60 per cent have made their way with varying degrees of success. Their likely destiny is to be acquired by a larger company for whom they represent a piece of a strategic mosaic. Some merge with small competitors, the resulting larger businesses increasing their market clout. Some regress to being life-style businesses for a small group of owner-managers.

This portfolio balance is fairly typical of most providers of star-up capital. Losses on the failed companies are limited to the amount of equity capital provided. The improvement in value of the winners will be a pleasing multiple of invested capital. In fact, the upside potential of these successful equity positions is theoretically infinite. A multiple of ten times ones investment in five years is not unusual and multiples of 25 times within ten years are not so rare. In the USA, multiples of more than 100 times are not so rare, either. For a provider of private equity to exceed a return on capital employed expected from the FTSE or Dow Jones over a seven year period (say 15 per cent per year) it only needs to have 20 per cent of its capital employed at a multiple of ten times, merely redeem its invested capital in the middle 60 per cent of cases, and can afford to write-off the balance of 20 per cent. Success financially therefore requires that at least one, but not necessarily more than three, start-ups out of ten build significant shareholder value. But financial success is a result not an explanation of performance. It also does not embrace the full scope of the wealth created.... It is critically important to know which characteristics of start-up businesses foretell and warrant success so that money and other resources can be increasingly channelled to those most likely to succeed. And ... to identify which characteristics particularly apply to incipient world class businesses.

In an attempt to learn some of these lessons, I have conducted a personal review of 20 start-ups to which I have had personal exposure in the last ten years. I have taken from an international portfolio the ten that failed most spectacularly and the ten most rewarding and attempted an objective assessment of the causes of failure or success on a case by case basis.

Firstly, some information about the businesses. Of the ten successes, two are British, one is Italian, one is Scandinavian, one is American, one is German while four are French. Six of the businesses were dependent for their success on techno-logical development while four are happy to use state-of-art. Four of the businesses are in data and/or image development, analysis and communication, two are in innovative engineering, two are media businesses and two were start-ups in financial services. All the businesses can truly be classified as world class.

The ten failed start-ups, on the other hand, were all based in the UK. Seven of the failed businesses were dependant on new technology developments to become viable whereas only six of the successes were so dependant. I do not consider this a significant difference although speed and efficiency of technological devel-opment is a factor that we will explore later. The sector mix of the businesses also does not appear to be significant in explaining differences between failure and success. Of the ten failures, four businesses were involved in data development, analysis and communication, three in innovative engineering, two were media businesses and one was in consumer marketing. Of the ten failed companies that were either voluntarily or involuntarily liquidated, in only three cases does the business no longer exist at all. In the other seven cases, the businesses have survived the demise of their respective companies. To provide a roll call – three are now owned and operated by other British companies, one is owned and operated by its bank, two were handed back to the entrepreneurs to operate as life style businesses and one was sold to an American entrepreneur who moved the business to California which is the centre of gravity of its market. Therefore, while the equity holders and some creditors have taken write-offs, while some egos have been severely bruised, many new business concepts and technologies are still being exploited and some rewarding and intellectually challenging jobs still being performed.

I now return to my main theme – the main causes of success or failure. These are, of course, both legion and complex. However, experience tells us that there are six broad groupings under which all the important causes will fall:

1. An ability to analyse and exploit a market.
2. An ability to develop, communicate and implement a realistic strategy for the business.
3. An ability to manage technology or product development programmes in an efficient and timely fashion.
4. An ability to attract sufficient capital on affordable terms and with a strategically compatible time horizon.
5. An ability to install, interpret and act upon reliable management information systems and controls.
6. An ability to recruit, build and continuously motivate a competent and experienced work force within the immediate financial capacity of the business.

Firstly, the marketplace. There are two market-related capabilities a business needs to succeed. An ability to know the market and an ability to exploit it. In our sample of 20 businesses, with one exception, the failures either did an acceptable job of analysing their opportunity or failed for other reasons before we could find out whether they had. Overall, with the benefit of hindsight, we can say that the opportunity did exist as evidenced by the fact that the market is currently being served by those self same businesses under different owners or by erstwhile potential competitors. Of the ten successful start-ups, eight clearly defined their opportunity well, one did not but stumbled by blind luck into another market and succeeded despite itself. The tenth never had a chance to demonstrate its prowess at market analysis as the business was sold to a potential American competitor at a substantial profit for its original shareholders before it had recorded its first sale. I recognise that it is such 'quick-buck' tactics that gets venture capitalists a bad name but as one of my favourite clients – a very wealthy self-made American often says: 'I've never knowingly lost by taking a quick profit.'

The other main marketing skill needed is the ability to sell – to complete transactions with customers. Five of the failed businesses were never able to demonstrate their transaction capabilities because they never developed that far as businesses. Three did demonstrate more than adequate competence but failed for other reasons. Only in two cases can one say that incompetence in closing sales was a major contributor to their demise. Where the successful companies are concerned, nine of them have significant selling abilities and only one, the 'quick-buck' provider, never had a chance to make a single sale before it was sold on. An overall conclusion can, therefore, be drawn that lack of marketing ability need not be fatal but its presence will contribute to success.

The second of our causes to examine is that of development, communication and implementation of a realistic strategy for the business. As the key facet of business strategy is the positioning of the business within a chosen marketplace; an inability to define market opportunity will reduce strategic effectiveness and vice versa. It is not, therefore, unrelated to the marketing issues we have already addressed.

Despite their failure to remain independent businesses, five of our ten problem children had devised strategies that with hindsight, were workable. The evidence is that their strategies are currently being implemented either by them under different ownership or by others. The other five, however, demonstrably got it wrong. On the other hand, our prodigies seem to have got it right ten times out of ten. A realistic strategy always accompanies success but frequently can also be a fellow traveller of failure. Expressed another way, in our experience developing an appropriate strategy for a business is usually accomplished. Failure is only rarely caused by a misguided strategy.

New world class businesses should be, and are normally, innovating. During the initial period of the start-up, therefore, management is often preoccupied with the development and optimisation of a new technology, product or service which will eventually become the main revenue earner for the business. An ability to manage this development process within agreed resources and time scales is therefore a third cause of success or failure of a start-up.

For small businesses attempting to grow on the back of a new technological development, getting the timing right is often more important than living within the resource budget. With technology now developing at an exponential rate and accelerating the changes in customer needs in most markets, even a quarters delay in getting a new product into position can destroy the wealth creating potential of a business. Ironically, the market analysis and chosen strategy can remain totally valid – the rub is that the delay in having the product available clears the way for those most secretive of people – potential competitors.

How did our 20 fledgling role models cope with product development? Of the disasters, only two met the timing required by their own development plans – the other eight missed by significant margins. They either ran out of money, enthusiasm or some other vital fluid or took so long that they were pre-empted or invalidated by parallel events. Interestingly, three of them were ahead of their time so while they could have been ready for the market, the market was not ready for them.

Even our success candidates failed to meet their development phase targets in four cases out of ten. In three of those cases the delay or additional costs incurred did not affect the ability to succeed because they were already so far ahead of the competition, time was on their side. In the other case, they inadvertently discovered an easier way to make money than persisting with an expensive, complicated and highly speculative project. Strategic conviction combined with tactical flexibility are the hallmarks of a true entrepreneur.

So far we have considered marketing, strategic positioning and late product development as causes of success or failure of incipient businesses. In my opinion, while they are important, they are subsidiary to those causes that are resource related – specifically the resources of people, information and, money. While it may not be immediately obvious there is, in our experience, evidence of symbiosis, for good or evil, in the conditions under which financial and human resources are recruited and employed.

I will begin by discussing how outside money most frequently becomes available for start-up businesses. There are three possibilities – to borrow, to accept equity capital in return for shares, or a combination of the two. For the purpose of this discussion I am ignoring the traders options of using the working capital of suppliers and customers on a back-to-back basis. Where equity is concerned, I would include so-called 'quasi-equity' which normally comes in the form of long-term loan stock, usually convertible into ordinary shares and usually with deferred interest payments. This money almost always comes from investment funds, high net worth individuals or families or corporations but very rarely from commercial banks. Borrowed money, on the other hand, almost always comes from commercial banks, is secured, if only on debtors/receivables, and always carries with it a commercial rate of interest on a 'pay-as-you-go' basis. Also, borrowings of this nature are almost always redeemable on call thus further weakening the balance sheet of the enterprise.

The question is, then, which source, or combination of sources of capital is most appropriate to any start-up business – and particularly a business which may need a sturdy balance sheet to attack world markets? [Often,] the tendency…is for entrepreneurs to use banks as their preferred source of start-up funds. The reasoning appears to be as follows:

- By working with borrowed money, management can retain a larger share of the equity – indeed, ideally keep 100 per cent. Thus by remaining the dominant owners, management can award themselves salaries, perquisites, bonuses, pensions, and eventually, dividends with no deference to other shareholders or their board representatives.
- Also, by remaining the dominant owners, management think they will reap the lion's share of any growth in asset value should the business eventually be sold to a third party. They know exactly what their money is costing them. The cost of equity on the other hand is speculative – difficult to calculate in advance.
- It is less complicated and distracting to deal with one source of capital and everyone needs a banker in any case.

The illogicalities of a debt-dominated strategy are:

- Firstly, in the initial start-up stage, when the business has no revenue and no earnings, the only security available to the bank will be any fixed assets or any intellectual property. For the bank, this represents an above average risk which will be reflected in the interest rate they have to charge.
- Secondly, even when the business has generated revenue but still has no earnings (and this is normally true for the first three years of a business and can last up to ten years for businesses employing very exotic technologies) the bank interest is being paid largely out of borrowings. Paradoxically, the cost of servicing the financial needs of the business then inhibits the progress of the business towards breakeven and profitability.
- Thirdly, the ability of the business to attract new equity capital is severely inhibited. The thought of shareholders funds being used to repay short-term debt (and particularly to subsidise interest payments with no earnings coverage) most certainly discourages new equity except under swingeing terms for management including drastic dilution.

Borrowing as a dominant source of start-up financing is symptomatic of what I call 'incomism'. Incomism – as opposed to capitalism – demands an instant result even if it requires the future to be mortgaged, significantly scaled down, or delayed. The entrepreneur who borrows heavily wants a standard of living reflective of business success – now – before it has been demonstrated. The bank that lends wants a commercially competitive return on its exposure – now – regardless of the financial health of the business. Management also, by keeping the equity closed think they are keeping for themselves a higher percentage of the longer-term asset value of the business. Also, because of the lack of outside shareholders, management will also constitute the board – a board that will thus talk to itself. But this enables them to avoid applying many aspects of good corporate governance. It also probably necessitates the use of more consultants than other businesses. Consultants to small businesses can be just another breed of incomists – rarely prepared to have even a part of their compensation based on long-term results.

In very simple terms, the result of incomism is under capitalisation of new businesses during their most critical stages of development. Let me now revert to our case histories to see if incomist entrepreneurs – high debt, high expense, low equity – outperform or underperform capitalist entrepreneurs who go for high dependence on shareowners funds. You will not be surprised to know that nine out of the ten businesses were very highly dependent on short-term debt. Management and friends had maintained a dominant position and had been generally unwelcoming to new equity which might have saved them. In five of the cases, it was their so-called friends, the bankers, who pulled the proverbial rug from under them and dictated over the heads of management and other shareholders the terms and conditions for the demise of their businesses.

Our ten successful start-ups behave in a much more capitalist fashion. Eight out of the ten do not have and have never had, any loans requiring short-term servicing or redemption options. They can, in fact, be considered debt-free businesses. The two that have been borrowers, did so to meet specific short-term needs and have since repaid the debts incurred. In all cases, the entrepreneurial management has taken a long term view of their businesses prospects and needs and, more importantly, their personal prospects and needs. They have accepted significant equity dilution in return for a solid balance sheet. They have exhibited confidence in their ability to build a significant international business where 10 per cent of the equity in absolute terms may eventually be worth more than 100 per cent of an undercapitalised, underperforming enterprise.

Their proactive strategy of attracting external sources of equity has also enabled them to be selective as to the sources of that equity and to have a strong bargaining position during determination of business valuation. The most favoured sources of equity for any business – but particularly new businesses – are those that bring with them expertise, contacts and other resources that can complement management's own arsenal. An astute entrepreneur can not only attract new investors of equity capital on favourable terms but can also put together a formidable board of directors at very little, if any, additional cost to the business.

Boards comprised of representatives of shareholders who, among them, have a controlling interest in a business can also provide objective insights on specific management issues – particularly financial control and forecasting realism. Another issue they can help with is management compensation practices but I will revert to that a little later.

One of the hidden costs of this spread sheet era we now live in is the apparent inability of many younger people – and particularly financially educated younger people – to estimate or overlay computed numbers, with reasoned judgements and experience. Computer programmes are increasingly credited with an ability to validate – not just manipulate – input. Increasingly frequently business plans and financial forecasts represent well organized fantasies – mathematically pristine but managerially impossible. Preparing a financial forecast manually demands an ability to do mental arithmetic and, to save unnecessary effort, an ability to apply, continuously, the test of reasonableness to the results of ones calculations.

In the case of five of our failed start-ups, lack of numeracy or numerical judgement played an important part in their demise. In all of the successful businesses an ability to make a realistic assessment of financial needs and expectations made a critical contribution. The role of the non-executive directors in reviewing the monthly or quarterly figures and applying objective and experienced judgements helped management to question the validity of their immaculately prepared spreadsheets. This is an excellent mechanism by which management credibility can be tested and good management should welcome it.

This brings me to the last and most critical cause of success or failure that I promised to address – the quality of the management team and its remuneration. When entrepreneurs create businesses, for themselves they must address at least two questions.

- Firstly, how am I going to support myself financially in the initial unprofitable trading period?

- Secondly, who, if anyone, should I choose to share the management burden, to complement my skills and experience, and to commiserate or celebrate with on a daily basis?

The answer to the first question depends, of course, on whether we are dealing with an incomist or a capitalist – an opportunist or a builder of a world class business. The three factors the capitalist entrepreneur would realistically ignore are: (1) what they were paid in their last job, (2) what the market would normally pay for someone with their skills and experience, and (3) any reward specifically compensating for the extraordinary risk of a start-up.

The three factors which a wise capitalist entrepreneur would take into account are: (1) what the business can afford in the immediate future, (2) what level of compensation will enable them to meet their minimum financial and social commitments in the period before the business is consistently profitable, and (3) what is their estimate of the net present value of their equity share (or their share options) in the 5th or 10th year and is that, combined with the proposed short-term package, adequately motivating. Compensation, in all businesses, is a leadership issue. The compensation practices of top management must be perceived by all other employees to be appropriate to the circumstances of the business at the time. If those at the top are ostentatiously working to create future value, others will follow especially if employee stock options are widely distributed.

In our little sample of 20 start-ups, the ten successful businesses are dominated by those who took a long-term capitalist or asset building point of view. Eight of the ten cut their short term compensation cloth to meet the immediate resources of the business. They lived on less than their market value. The two that did not, ironically, were the two teams managing the financial services businesses. Of the unsuccessful businesses only three top management groups had a thoughtfully constrained attitude to their own compensation, the other seven being somewhere on a scale between Oliver Twist and the reputed practices of chief executives of privatised utilities.

Finally, do entrepreneurs need soulmates to share the burden of management? All the evidence says that they do. We also have evidence that prima donnas rarely succeed in building a sustainable business. In four of our failed start-ups the seeds of destruction were sown and reaped by the founder of the business. In eight of our successes a tightknit, self-selected, complementary management team has taken each business from milestone to milestone. Most often it is two people, occasionally three or four. Rarely more than four. They do not have to be at the same level in the management hierarchy but it is rare for more than one level of management to separate them.

A new set of guidelines for entrepreneurs wishing to build new internationally competitive enterprises … is now needed. Based on my experience in recent years those guidelines should be:

- Concentrate on building a durable business – not managing a company. Companies are the preoccupation of lawyers, accountants and bankers – all fee driven, all incomists. Customers, suppliers, employees, shareholders and society at large prefer to relate to businesses because they satisfy needs, possess character, and express themselves through people and products – not legal agreements, forms and tax returns.

- Be bold – go for a global opportunity immediately. Develop a global strategy, and resource the business development programme appropriately.
- Raise all required finance in the form of equity or quasi equity sufficient to take the business well beyond the stage of steady cash generation. Incur no short-term or commercial debt until interest payments can be extravagantly covered by earnings.
- Shop internationally for capital. Select your shareholders based on their ability to contribute to long term world-class performance because of their global knowledge, expertise and contact networks.
- Use your shareowner base to convene an internationally experienced board of directors dominated by non-executives. Do not be afraid to use foreigners. Foreigners can be knowledgeable, smart and even nice to know. They are also less expensive than UK non-executives.
- Routinely involve selected non-executive directors in financial planning and forecasting as well as short- and long-term compensation issues. This way you may only make a fool of yourself in the board room – not in public.

In summary, what Europe needs immediately is more boldly managed, more robustly financed, more internationally aggressive, start-ups which build on the ability to innovate. We must create, build and sustain a continuously evolving array of world-class businesses exploiting global markets.

ACKNOWLEDGEMENTS

This book represents the culmination of a number of years of chasing of very busy people, who are full of goodwill but whose agenda is dominated with the next deal, the late report to investors or a board room crisis to mend.

Firstly, we are deeply appreciative of Dr Mariëtte E. Roodenburg. When working at the European Venture Capital Assocation's programme for developing Venture Capital in Central & Eastern Europe she produced an internal *Private Equity Guidebook* sponsored by the Phare project of the European Commission. It was her perseverance that got most of the authors to contribute their agreed chapters, and it was this work that laid the foundation for the *Venture Capital Handbook*.

Secondly, we are grateful for the time and effort that Ms Helena Yli-Renko has put in to completing the final version of this book. Not only did she make a major contribution in the form of the two chapters that provide an overview of the European Venture Capital Industry, but she was also crucial in putting all the final details in place.

Finally, as you read through the chapters, many practitioners have contributed to the genesis of this book. We would like to thank all of them for their insights and knowledge, which they share in our continuing education in venture capital.

1

EUROPEAN VENTURE CAPITAL – AN OVERVIEW

Helena Yli-Renko and Michael Hay
London Business School

Introduction

Market size and growth

The European venture capital landscape

Sources of venture capital fund investment

Investment patterns in Europe

Exit mechanisms

Performance

Trends and outlook

Helena Yli-Renko is a Research Fellow at London Business School's Foundation for Entrepreneurial Management. She received her Master of Science and Licentiate in Technology degrees from Helsinki University of Technology, and is currently finishing her Doctoral dissertation. Previously, Helena Yli-Renko has worked as an Associate Consultant in a Finnish management consultancy and as a University Lecturer at the Institute of Strategy and International Business at Helsinki University of Technology. She has taught courses in strategy, new venture financing and marketing.

Helena Yli-Renko's research interests include the growth dynamics of new, technology-based companies, innovation and technology management, venture capital, and the interorganizational relationships of entrepreneurial firms. The topic of her Doctoral dissertation is 'The Growth of Technology-Intensive New Firms: A Relational, Knowledge-Based Perspective'. Her research work has won best paper awards at the International Council for Small Business (ICSB) conferences in Stockholm and San Francisco and the Entrepreneurship Development conference in Singapore. Her articles have been published in *Small Business Economics*, *Research Policy*, *Journal of Enterprising Culture* and *Entrepreneurship & Regional Development*.

Michael Hay, Ph.D., is Director of the Foundation for Entrepreneurial Management and an Associate Professor of Strategic and International Management at London Business School. He is Associate Dean of the Sloan Programme. He joined the faculty in 1987 having previously spent ten years in academic publishing, principally with Blackwell where he was deputy managing director of Blackwell Publishers and chairman/chief executive of Marston Book Services. He is a founder Director of two venture-capital-backed companies, Cherwell Scientific and Imparta Limited.

Michael Hay has undertaken assignments for a number of major international companies including British Airways, 3M and United News & Media both in the UK and USA. He has also worked as a consultant for the United Nations on welfare in Eastern Europe.

He is author of *The Strategy Handbook*, with Peter Williamson, and *Realizing Investment Value* with William D. Bygrave and Jos B. Peeters. Most recently, he has co-authored with Steven Abbott *Investing for the Future: New Firm Funding in Germany, Japan, the UK and USA*.

INTRODUCTION

The purpose of this chapter is to create an overall understanding of the European venture capital industry. In line with European common practice, we use the term venture capital in its broad meaning, referring to all forms of private equity. The term thus encompasses both 'traditional' venture capital, such as seed and start-up financing, and 'merchant' or 'development' capital, such as later stage financing and management buyouts.

In order to give the reader an overview of European venture capital, we address the following questions:

- How has the venture capital industry in Europe developed in recent years and how will it continue to develop in the future? Which factors influence this development?

- How do the European countries compare in terms of the size and growth of their venture capital industries?

- What are the sources for the funds invested in European venture capital?

- What are the investment patterns of venture capital disbursement, in terms of e.g. venture stage, industry sectors, investment size?

- What exit mechanisms are used and what levels of return are achieved?

In our analysis, we draw mostly on data collected and assembled by the European Venture Capital Association (EVCA). The discussion covers the 17 Western European countries, which are surveyed by EVCA each year.[1] The survey does not cover informal venture capital ('business angels') or the debt financing of deals.

MARKET SIZE AND GROWTH

Much of the European venture capital industry was formed during a period of rapid growth commencing at the beginning of the 1980s. This was very recently compared to the USA, where formal venture capital investment was introduced soon after the Second World War. During the 1990s, the rapid growth in Europe has accelerated. As Fig. 1.1 shows, the total size of the European venture capital investment portfolio increased threefold, from ECU 9.5 billion in 1988 to 32.8

billion in 1997. Looking at Fig. 1.2, we can see that growth was particularly rapid in 1997 – the annual amount of new funds raised exceeded ECU 20 billion. This figure represents an all-time high, more than twice the 1996 figure of 7.96 billion. Much of the phenomenal growth in 1997 was due to the wrapping up of several very large pan-European buyout vehicles.

The level of disbursement, or investment into deals, has naturally reflected the amount of new funds raised. Disbursement grew significantly in 1997, reaching ECU 9.7 billion. The total number of investments made by European venture capitalists in 1997 was 6,252. As Fig. 1.2 illustrates, disbursement has not kept up with the accelerated inflow of new capital. The overall liquidity of venture capital funds is very high – the amount of capital estimated by EVCA to be still available for investment at year end was ECU 14.1 billion in 1997, compared with ECU 8.3 billion in 1996.

The total number of venture capital executives in Europe was 3,150 in 1997, with only a slight increase from the 1996 figure of 2,937. This indicates that, to a high extent, growth is the result of a core group of firms bringing larger and larger funds to the market. Naturally, the recent high-profile successes in the industry attract an increasing number of new players, as well, but it will take many years for these new firms to be able to raise larger funds and have a significant impact on the industry as a whole.

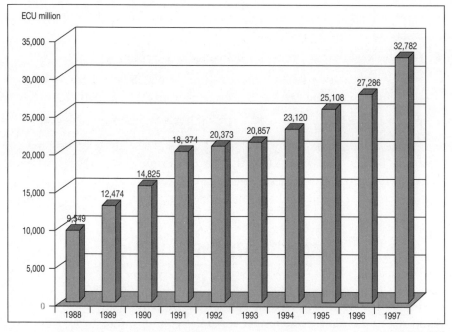

Source: EVCA

Fig. 1.1 ♦ Total size of the European venture capital investment portfolio, calculated as portfolio at cost – net of divestment

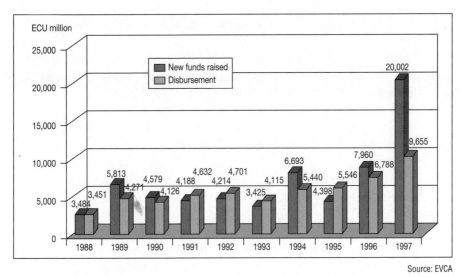

Source: EVCA

Fig. 1.2 ♦ Annual amount of new funds raised and annual disbursement of funds in Europe from 1988 to 1997

The growth prospects for European venture capital are positive in the long term. A slow-down in European fund-raising may be seen in the 1998–9 statistics, reflecting the record amount of new funds raised in 1997, of which a large proportion was still available for investment at year end 1997. On the other hand, the introduction of the Euro in 1999 is likely to provide a further boost to the European market, facilitating cross-border institutional investments. Another development in the European venture capital industry is the introduction of more funds-of-funds, which are likely to attract more small-scale investors into the market.

The political and fiscal environment in Europe is generally becoming more attractive to venture capital, as most governments are increasingly concerned with promoting the growth of small and medium-sized enterprises (SMEs). Several governments have introduced tax and other incentives in order to encourage investment in venture capital and thus improve the availability of funding for SMEs. Also the European Commission has introduced schemes to promote venture capital.[2]

The fluctuations that the public markets have experienced as a result of the Asian and Russian economic crises and the uncertain situation in Latin America are likely to have mixed effects on the venture capital industry. On one hand, problems in public markets will make exits through initial public offerings (IPOs) more difficult and have a negative influence on the performance of funds. On the other hand, problems with public markets could divert a wave of capital into the private market.

THE EUROPEAN VENTURE CAPITAL LANDSCAPE

The European venture capital industry varies greatly across the European countries in terms of size and development stage. Some markets, such as the UK, the Netherlands and France, are traditionally more 'equity-minded', and tend to have more developed venture capital markets than the more 'debt-minded' markets such as, for example, Germany or Italy. European countries also vary in the degree to which the cultural and political environment encourages entrepreneurship. This is reflected in varying legal and fiscal conditions, which differ across countries in the degree to which they promote venture capital investment.

The introduction of the single currency, a common fiscal policy and the continued harmonization of regulations in Europe will naturally have a diminishing effect on the national differences in the venture capital industry. Also, the European Commission is increasingly promoting pan-European schemes to encourage venture capital investment, particularly in the early investment stages.

The general trend in Europe is towards larger funds and more pan-European and multi-country funds, usually focusing on the later investment stages. This development has been influenced by the fact that many institutional investors, particularly large pension funds within and outside Europe, have a high minimum participation rate while also insisting on relatively low individual participation. In order to attract these investors, funds need to set a correspondingly large minimum fund size to ensure that individual investors do not feel exposed. Therefore, venture capital funds are increasingly adopting a cross-national, pan-European, or even global focus, and thus contributing to the increasing integration of the European venture capital market.

Figure 1.3 compares the size of the venture capital portfolios in European countries. As can be seen, the UK is by far the dominant market, representing 45 per cent of the European venture capital portfolio. France and Germany are the next largest markets, with portfolios representing 15 per cent and 12 per cent of the European total.

Much of the recent record growth of the industry has been concentrated in the UK and Germany (Fig. 1.4). New funds raised in the UK accounted for 61 per cent of total new funds raised in Europe in 1997, compared with 47 per cent in 1996. The German proportion was 13 per cent in 1997, compared with just 4 per cent in 1996. The increase in the UK is likely to be heavily inflated by the UK being a centre for pan-European fundraising. The disbursement statistics in Fig. 1.4 support this – the UK accounted for 46 per cent of total disbursement in 1997, with only a slight increase from 44 per cent in 1996.

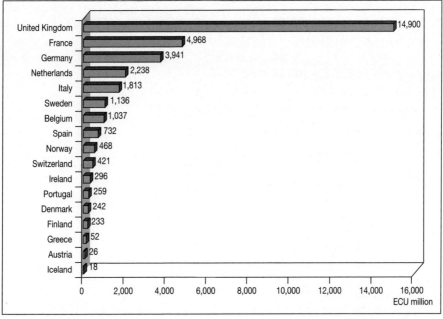

Fig. 1.3 ♦ Size of the venture capital portfolios in European countries in 1997, calculated as portfolio at cost – net of divestment

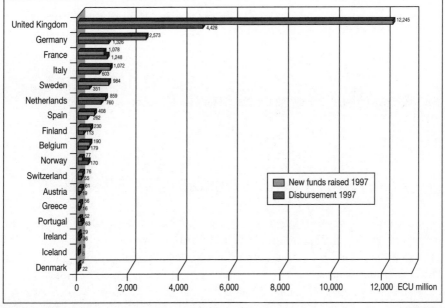

Fig. 1.4 ♦ New venture capital funds raised and disbursement in European countries in 1997

In order to get a better picture of the comparative size of the venture capital industries in European countries, Fig. 1.5 compares the annual amount of venture capital investments to the gross domestic product in each country. As can be seen, the UK ranks first in Europe with 0.39 per cent. The UK is followed by the Netherlands, Sweden, Norway and Finland. These smaller countries thus have proportionately larger venture capital industries than France, Germany and Italy, which are major markets when measured in absolute terms.

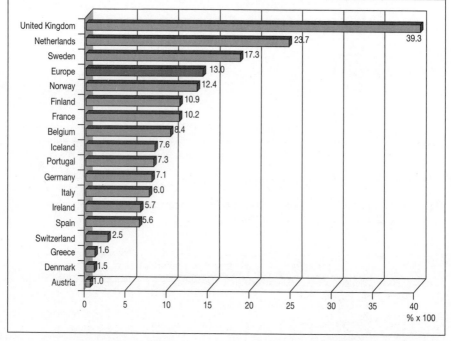

Source: EVCA

Fig. 1.5 ◆ Venture capital investment as percentage (× 100) of gross domestic product in European countries in 1997

SOURCES OF VENTURE CAPITAL FUND INVESTMENT

Figure 1.6 illustrates the sources of venture capital investment in Europe. The major sources of funds are banks, pension funds and insurance companies. The increase in pension fund and insurance fund investment is quite recent. In 1993, bank investment was still nearly twice as large as that by pension funds.

What is notable is the rise of the corporate investor. Corporate investment increased eightfold from ECU 278 million in 1996 to ECU 2.3 billion in 1997, from just 4 per cent of total investment in 1996 to 11 per cent in 1997. Many technology companies, in particular, are investing in venture capital funds specializing in new, technology-based firms. For example, Microsoft has been a recent founding investor in one European fund, as have many European telecommunications conglomerates. Investing in technology funds gives the companies not only high returns, but also access to new technologies.

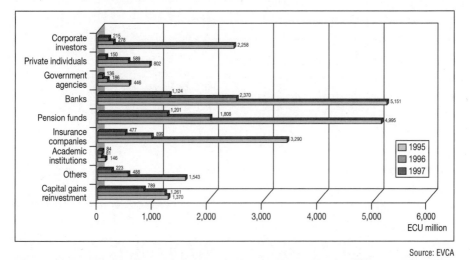

Source: EVCA

Fig. 1.6 ♦ Sources of venture capital fund investments by type of investor from 1995 to 1997

As Fig. 1.7 illustrates, there has been a significant increase in non-domestic fundraising in recent years. European, cross-borders investments increased from 7 per cent in 1993 to 17 per cent in 1997, and non-European funding increased from 12 per cent in 1993 to 34 per cent in 1997. By non-European funding we mean funding from outside the 17 Western European countries included in the EVCA survey. For the first time, in 1997 more than 50 per cent of total funds raised in Europe came from non-domestic sources.

In 1997, a third of the total capital committed had non-European sources. This represents an explosive increase from 1996, when only 17 per cent of new funds came from outside Europe. Much of this growth can be accounted to the increase in European investment by US pension funds, which also explains the rapid growth in the amount of capital invested by pension funds, which we noted in Fig. 1.6. The significant increase in non-domestic funding is largely concentrated in the UK, which, as mentioned above, is the main centre for pan-European funding. In most other European markets, domestic fundraising is still dominant, although decreasing in proportion.

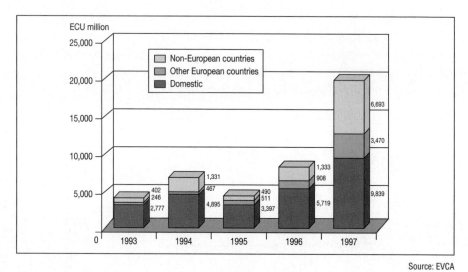

Source: EVCA

Fig. 1.7 ♦ Sources of venture capital fund investments by geographic origin from 1993 to 1997

INVESTMENT PATTERNS IN EUROPE

Funding stage and size of investments

There has been little change in the distribution of investments by funding stage during the 1990s. In terms of the amount of money invested, buyouts continue to dominate European venture capital disbursement (Fig. 1.8). Buyouts[3] offer easier and faster opportunities to achieve returns than the earlier stages of funding. The average holding period for buyout investments is three to four years, compared with over seven years for early-stage investments. Also, buyouts require less 'hands-on' participation from the venture capitalist.

Buyout investments consist of a relatively small number of very large deals. The average deal size in buyouts was over ECU 6 million in 1997. Looking at Fig. 1.9, we see that measured by the number of companies invested in, the classical venture capital investments in seed, start-up and expansion represent over two thirds of total investments. Naturally, these investments are much smaller in size, averaging ECU 0.4 million per company for seed financing, ECU 0.7 million for start-ups and ECU 1.4 million for expansion financing in 1997.

Of the 4,762 companies which received European venture capital investment in 1997, 67 per cent received venture capital backing for the first time. The remaining 33 per cent of companies received follow-on investments. The ratio between initial and follow-on investments has remained relatively unchanged in the 1990s, at over 60 per cent, with a slight increase in 1997.

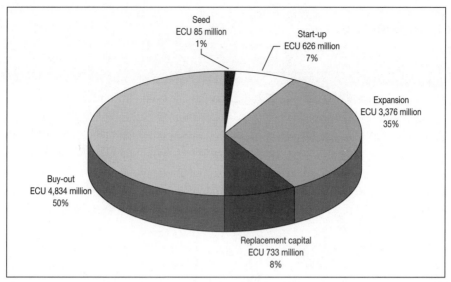

Source: EVCA

Fig. 1.8 ♦ Disbursement by stage of investment in 1997, according to amount invested

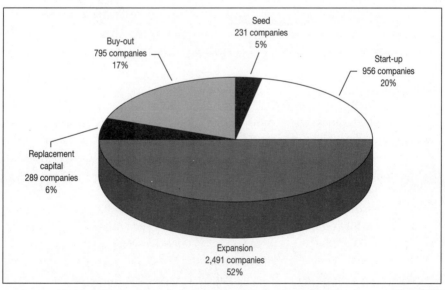

Source: EVCA

Fig. 1.9 ♦ Disbursement by stage of investment in 1997, according to number of companies invested in

Figure 1.10 illustrates the distribution of investments by the number of employees in the companies invested in. In line with Figs 1.8 and 1.9, in terms of value, large companies dominate investments. In terms of the number of investments, however, we see that firms with under 100 employees accounted for as much as 62 per cent of total investments. There have been no significant changes in this distribution in recent years.

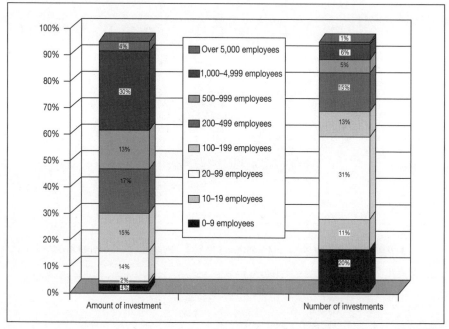

Source: EVCA

Fig. 1.10 ♦ Disbursement by the number of employees in the companies invested in, 1997

Figure 1.11 illustrates a recent trend in the European venture capital industry – an increase in average deal size. Especially buyouts have become larger, doubling in size from 1994 to 1997. Also other types of investments have shown increases in average deal size.

There are significant differences between the European countries regarding the stages of investment. Among the major markets, the Netherlands and Germany have had the highest levels of early stage investment, with seed and start-up investments accounting for 20 per cent and 15 per cent of total disbursements in 1997, respectively. The UK and Sweden had the lowest percentages of early stage investments in 1997, 2 per cent and 1 per cent. Expansion capital is dominant in Germany, while buyouts account for the majority of UK disbursement. It is expected that buyout investment in Continental Europe will increase as a result of increased corporate divestments, succession issues facing medium-sized family-owned businesses, and the ongoing privatization process taking place in many economies in order to reduce budget deficits for the monetary union.

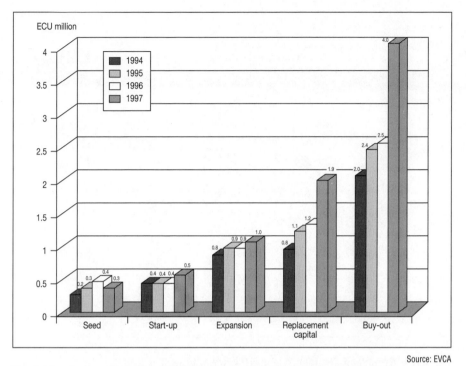

Source: EVCA

Fig. 1.11 ♦ Average size of investment by stage of investment from 1994 to 1997

Geographic breakdown of investments

The majority of venture capital investments in Europe are domestic, although there has been an increase in investments to other European countries and outside Europe (Fig. 1.12). In 1997, domestic investments accounted for 80 per cent of the total amount of investments. Investments to other European countries represented 17 per cent; and non-European investments only 3 per cent of the total. These figures are a bit misleading, as they do not include disbursements by offices of European venture capital companies that are based outside Europe. This will underestimate the proportion of non-European investments.

The rapid increase in investments to other European countries indicates that Europe is becoming more and more an integrated market. We are also seeing within Europe an increase in the importance of regional markets, which share a common language and cultural base, such as the German-speaking region and the Scandinavian countries. As Fig. 1.12 illustrates, investments to other European countries grew from just 7 per cent of total investments in 1993 to 17 per cent in 1997. This trend is expected to accelerate, especially with the introduction of the Euro.

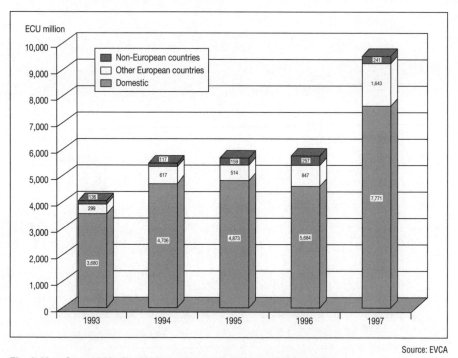

Source: EVCA

Fig. 1.12 ♦ Geographic distribution of investments from 1993 to 1997

Industry sectors receiving venture capital investment

Figure 1.13 shows the amount disbursed to various industry sectors from 1995 to 1997. Consumer-related products and services are the single largest sector attracting venture capital investment in Europe, accounting for 27 per cent of total investment in 1997. Although the individual technology sectors are comparably small, when combined, they account for over one quarter of total investments. Altogether ECU 2.6 billion was invested in 1,869 technology companies in 1997. The combined technology-based sectors (broadly defined here as including information and communications technologies, medical, health and biotechnology, energy technology, industrial automation, other electronics, and chemicals and materials) have increased their share from 21 per cent of total investment in 1993 to 28 per cent in 1997. This trend is similar to the long-term trend in the USA, where investment into technology-based sectors has been steadily increasing.

Europe is seeing growth in the number of science parks and 'silicon valleys' – concentrations of new, technology-based firms, research and development (R&D) divisions of large firms, research institutions – in various parts of Europe. Usually, these concentrations develop around a leading university. Examples of European technology clusters include the biotechnology concentration in Cambridge, the

'Silicon Glen' in Scotland, and the telecommunications concentrations in Sophia Antipolis near Nice and in Oulu, in Northern Finland. Increasingly, these regions are also centres for early-stage venture capital activity. The growing number of new, technology-based firms is reflected into the venture capital industry as increasing opportunities in early-stage technology investments. The increasing early-stage venture capital activity, in turn, improves the funding possibilities of new, technology-based firms, facilitating their formation and growth.

The development of 'hotbeds' of new, technology-based firms and venture capital to the level of dynamism present in the Silicon Valley will, however, take decades. After 30 years of development, Cambridge is only just getting there. Most of the European technology clusters are still dominated by the R&D divisions of major corporations, not young start-ups. The European technology concentrations need to gain momentum in order to become true melting pots of new, technology-based firms, venture capitalists, technology experts, lawyers, real estate agents, researchers, accountants and anybody else who can participate in the entrepreneurial process.

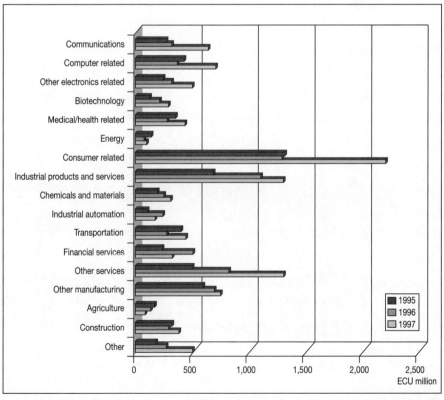

Source: EVCA

Fig. 1.13 ♦ Industry sectors receiving venture capital funding in Europe from 1995 to 1997

EXIT MECHANISMS

The information collected by EVCA for its annual survey maps exits, or divestments, is according to the cost of the original investment, without taking into
account any growth or decline in the value of the investment. The figures do not,
therefore, reflect the actual amounts received by venture capital funds in the exits.
Rather, they are meant for tracking changes in the portfolio of investments in
Europe. The information does, however, give some indication of the relative
importance of various exit mechanisms. Pricing of exits and the true rates of
return for various exit mechanisms will be discussed later in this book.

Trade sales are the dominant exit mechanism in Europe. As Fig. 1.14 illustrates,
they accounted for nearly half, 49 per cent (ECU 2.8 billion) of total divestment at
cost and 33 per cent of the total number of divestments in 1997. Public offerings[4]
accounted for 9 per cent of total divestment at cost and 15 per cent of the total
number of divestments in 1997. Although the number of public offerings dropped
slightly, from 416 in 1996 to 391 in 1997, the amount divested in this way
increased by 13 per cent. The category 'other' covers such exit mechanisms as
management buy-backs and sale of quoted equity.

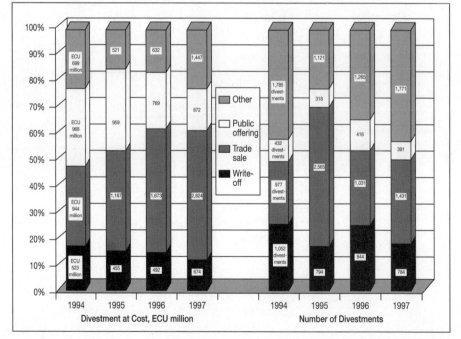

Source: EVCA

**Fig. 1.14 ♦ Divestment by exit mechanism from 1994 to 1997, in terms of the amount divested
(ECU million at cost of investment) and in terms of the number of divestments**

The UK has traditionally had the most accessible stock markets in Europe. The London Off-Exchange facility (OFEX) was started in 1991 to enable the London Stock Exchange member firms to deal in the securities of unlisted and unquoted companies. More recently, the listing rules of the London Stock Exchange were changed to facilitate the listing of loss-making research-intensive companies, especially in the life sciences sector. In 1995, the Alternative Investment Market (AIM) was established, enabling small, young and growing companies to raise finance. The AIM is regulated by the London Stock Exchange.

In recent years, several new stock markets have been established in Europe in order to facilitate the flotation of small and medium-sized high growth companies. The European Association of Securities Dealers Automated Quotation (EASDAQ), a pan-European, screen-based stock market was launched in November 1996, with the goals of establishing a European version of the National Association of Securities Dealers Automated Quotation (Nasdaq). By the end of September 1998, 37 companies with a total market capitalization of approximately ECU 9.5 billion were listed on EASDAQ. Several European stock exchanges have established specific trading segments for small and medium-sized high growth companies. The Paris Stock Exchange opened Le Nouveau Marché, Frankfurt opened Neuer Markt, Brussels the EURO.NM Brussels, and Amsterdam the NMAX. Recently, these trading segments were combined to form the EURO.NM market, in order to compete with EASDAQ. By the end of September 1998, 138 companies were listed on EURO.NM, with a total market capitalization of ECU 22.2 billion.

Despite the recent developments, the possibilities for IPOs in Europe are still far behind those of the USA. In Europe, it can take from one to four decades after founding for a company to be listed on a stock exchange. In the USA, new companies can go public on the Nasdaq in a few years after creation. Also, on average, IPOs on Nasdaq tend to raise ten times more capital than their European equivalents. The lack of a liquid, pan-European, price-driven (rather than offer-driven) stock market for young, growing businesses in Europe is a structural weakness of the European venture capital industry.

PERFORMANCE

The *Investment Benchmark Report*, published by Venture Economics and Bannock Consulting in early 1998, analyzed the performance of 202 European venture capital funds, which had been formed between 1980 and 1992.[5] The study found that compared with other asset classes, European venture capital investments have performed well. As Fig. 1.15 illustrates, the pooled net return to investors (IRR) of the surveyed venture capital funds, from inception to year-end 1996, was 20.1 per cent. This was higher than the performance of the Cazenove Rosenberg small business index, the ECU Bond Index and the Datastream Europe Equity

Index. Of course, the pooled IRR varies greatly between funds specializing in different investment stages. The performance of buyout funds has been strong, 17.8 per cent, exceeded only by the generalist funds (which do not have a specific stage focus), at 22.4 per cent.

Figure 1.16 illustrates the performance of the upper quartile of the funds included in the performance survey. Comparing Figs 1.15 and 1.16, we see that the performance of early-stage investments reflects their high-risk profile. Overall, they performed poorly compared with other asset classes, but in the upper quartile, they achieved high returns. The recent performance of these funds has been improving, reflecting the ongoing development of the IPO markets in Europe, especially in technology sectors, as well as the growing experience of the managers of these funds. In 1996, European early-stage funds returned a spectacular 47.7 per cent.

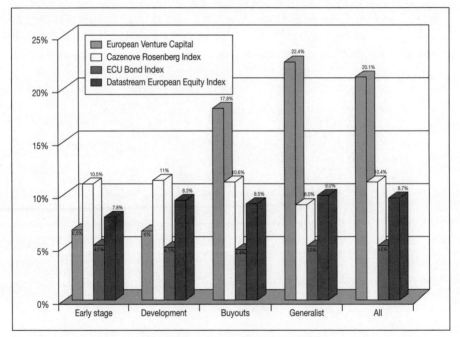

Source: *Venture Economics and* ECVA; *177 funds included in the statistics. Note: there is one very large evergreen fund in the generalist category*

Fig. 1.15 ♦ Performance of European venture capital funds compared with other asset classes, cumulative net IRRs from inception to year-end 1996

The overall returns of European venture capital investments are encouraging, with buyouts continuing to perform strongly and early-stage funds showing great potential. The recent stock market fluctuations will naturally have an impact on returns. In the short term, flotations are likely to be postponed. But more important for the long-term development of IPO markets is the structural development taking place in European stock markets.

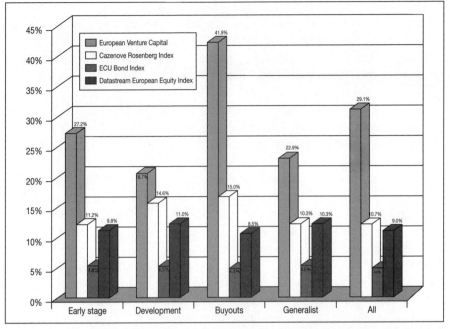

Source: *Venture Economics and* EVCA; *50 funds included in the statistics*

Fig. 1.16 ♦ Upper quartile performance of European venture capital compared with other asset classes, cumulative net IRRs from inception to year-end 1996

The performance results indicate that the European venture capital industry is not only growing in volume, but developing in quality as well. Facing increased competition for deals, venture capitalists are focusing on actively managing their investments, bringing greater specialist knowledge and more value-added into them.

TRENDS AND OUTLOOK

Venture capital is, clearly, a growing business throughout Europe. New funds are flowing into the industry from both domestic and foreign sources. Pension funds and insurance funds are growing steadily in Europe, providing a deeper future pool of venture capital in Europe. The growth in the number of funds-of-funds will attract more individual investors into the venture capital market. The tidal wave of capital from the USA has so far been targeted mainly at the European buyout market, and may spread to the other investment stages as the number of opportunities increases.

There has been a lot of discussion on whether the European venture capital industry is going to change structurally towards the US model, which is more focused on early-stage investment. In Europe, the buyout market has offered, and continues to offer, investment opportunities from which returns can be achieved more easily and faster than from early-stage investments. The buyout sector will maintain its importance, with growth being driven by opportunities in the medium-sized companies in, for example, Germany and the Netherlands.

In the long term, it is likely that early-stage investment will increase in importance in Europe. The national governments and the European Commission are increasingly aware of the role of venture capital in facilitating the establishment and growth of SMEs, and thereby in creating employment and economic growth. But it will take a long time for early-stage investment to reach the American level. The growth of 'hotbeds' of new, technology-based firms and venture capital such as the Silicon Valley takes decades.

There are still many regulatory, fiscal and cultural barriers hindering the growth of venture capital, particularly early-stage investment. There is no harmonized structure for venture capital funds in Europe, which would enable funds to raise capital easily in other European countries. Accounting rules vary from country to country, making it difficult for companies to seek cross-border issues of shares. Taxation of venture capital funds and capital gains varies greatly between European countries. Only recently have some countries introduced tax incentives to encourage venture capital investment. Europe also lacks an entrepreneurial culture, which would favour risk taking and wealth creation. Again, it takes a long time to address the regulatory and fiscal problems, and for attitudes towards entrepreneurship to change, but we are seeing development in the right direction.

The current fragmentation of the European stock markets is likely to be reduced, as the stock exchanges increase their co-operation. The development of a large, pan-European, liquid stock exchange comparable to Nasdaq is a requirement for the long-term development of European venture capital. This could take place either through the EASDAQ gaining momentum or through the consolidation of the national markets in the EURO.NM network. The improving possibilities for IPOs in Europe will lead to an increase in exits through public offerings. As a result, the proportion of trade sales may decrease in the future.

The Euro will have a significant positive influence on the development of the European venture capital industry. A single currency will facilitate the emergence of more pan-European financial instruments and lead, over time, towards more harmonized conditions in financial markets. The removal of exchange risks and currency matching requirements will create more freedom for cross-border investments by institutional investors, enhancing the liquidity of the European venture capital market.

As a conclusion, the outlook for European venture capital is highly positive. Development is taking place on all fronts. New funds are rolling in. Investment opportunities in both the buyout and early-stage sectors are increasing. Fiscal and legal conditions are improving. It is becoming easier to exit through IPOs. High rates of return are achieved. While there is still a lot of room for development, the basic elements of a flourishing venture capital industry seem to be getting into place.

European venture capital at a glance

Market size and growth

◆ Industry developed through rapid growth in early 1980s; growth accelerated in 1990s.

◆ Total European investment portfolio in 1997: ECU 32.8 billion; the amount of new funds raised: ECU 20 billion; annual disbursement: ECU 9.7 billion.

◆ The UK alone represents 45 per cent of European venture capital portfolio; France and Germany are the next largest markets.

Sources of capital

◆ Banks, pension funds and insurance companies are the main sources of capital; the latter two have increased their share mainly due to investors from the USA.

◆ Investment by corporate investors is increasing.

◆ Non-domestic fundraising has grown rapidly; in 1997, over 50 per cent of total new funds came from non-domestic sources.

Disbursement patterns

◆ Buyouts have traditionally dominated, and continue to dominate, European venture capital in terms of the amounts invested.

◆ Expansion capital accounted for 50 per cent of the number of companies invested in 1997; seed and start-up deals accounted for 25 per cent.

◆ Nearly two thirds of the number of investments in 1997 went into companies with fewer than 100 employees.

◆ Average deal size has been steadily increasing, especially in the later stages of funding.

◆ The consumer-related sector and industrial products and services receive most investments; the combined technology sectors accounted for 28 per cent of total investment in 1997.

Exits and performance

◆ Trade sales are the most important exit route in Europe.

◆ IPO opportunities have improved with the establishment of EASDAQ and EURO.NM.

◆ Performance of European venture capital has been strong and is expected to remain at a high level.

▶

▶

Key trends

♦ Increasing internationalization: larger pan-European buyout funds and more transnational early stage funds, increasingly non-domestic fund-raising.

♦ Increasing specialization of early-stage investment according to region or industry sector.

♦ Euro expected to have a positive effect, facilitating cross-border investments.

♦ Development of a large, pan-European liquid stock market.

♦ Regional high technology concentrations are developing around Europe.

Notes

1. The 17 countries included in the analysis are: Austria, Belgium, Denmark, Finland, France, Germany, Greece, Iceland, Ireland, Italy, the Netherlands, Norway, Portugal, Spain, Sweden, Switzerland and the United Kingdom.

2. For example, the European Commission has launched the European Seed Capital Scheme, as well as provided support for the establishment of the European Association of Securities Dealers Automated Quotation (EASDAQ), a European capital market for high-growth SMEs.

3. In line with common practice, we use the term 'buyout' to denote both management buyouts and management buy-ins.

4. We use the terms 'public offering' and 'IPO', initial public offering, interchangeably. The EVCA statistics do not monitor whether an exit taking place through a public offering is, in fact, an initial public offering or a new offering by an already publicly listed company. However, the majority of venture capital exits through public offerings are IPOs.

5. It should be noted that over half, 106, of the 202 funds included in the study concentrate on investing in the UK.

THE MAJOR
EUROPEAN VENTURE
CAPITAL MARKETS

Helena Yli-Renko and Michael Hay
London Business School

Introduction

Venture capital funding in the UK

Venture capital funding in France

Venture capital funding in Germany

Venture capital funding in the Netherlands

Venture capital funding in Italy

Dimensions of national differences

Helena Yli-Renko is a Research Fellow at London Business School's Foundation for Entrepreneurial Management. She received her Master of Science and Licentiate in Technology degrees from Helsinki University of Technology, and is currently finishing her Doctoral dissertation. Previously, Helena Yli-Renko has worked as an Associate Consultant in a Finnish management consultancy and as a University Lecturer at the Institute of Strategy and International Business at Helsinki University of Technology. She has taught courses in strategy, new venture financing and marketing.

Helena Yli-Renko's research interests include the growth dynamics of new, technology-based companies, innovation and technology management, venture capital, and the interorganizational relationships of entrepreneurial firms. The topic of her Doctoral dissertation is 'The Growth of Technology-Intensive New Firms: A Relational, Knowledge-Based Perspective'. Her research work has won best paper awards at the International Council for Small Business (ICSB) conferences in Stockholm and San Francisco and the Entrepreneurship Development conference in Singapore. Her articles have been published in *Small Business Economics*, *Research Policy*, *Journal of Enterprising Culture* and *Entrepreneurship & Regional Development*.

Michael Hay, Ph.D., is Director of the Foundation for Entrepreneurial Management and an Associate Professor of Strategic and International Management at London Business School. He is Associate Dean of the Sloan Programme. He joined the faculty in 1987 having previously spent ten years in academic publishing, principally with Blackwell where he was deputy managing director of Blackwell Publishers and chairman/chief executive of Marston Book Services. He is a founder Director of two venture-capital-backed companies, Cherwell Scientific and Imparta Limited.

Michael Hay has undertaken assignments for a number of major international companies including British Airways, 3M and United News & Media both in the UK and USA. He has also worked as a consultant for the United Nations on welfare in Eastern Europe.

He is author of *The Strategy Handbook*, with Peter Williamson, and *Realizing Investment Value* with William D. Bygrave and Jos B. Peeters. Most recently, he has co-authored with Steven Abbott *Investing for the Future: New Firm Funding in Germany, Japan, the UK and USA*.

INTRODUCTION

Whereas the previous chapter was an overview of the European venture capital industry as a whole, this chapter focuses on the major national venture capital markets in Europe. Our approach is twofold: we aim at creating an understanding of each of the major markets individually, as well as giving the reader an awareness of the similarities and differences between the markets.

First, we individually discuss the five largest venture capital markets in Europe, namely the UK, Germany, France, the Netherlands and Italy. We shall look at the national characteristics of the industry and its development in each of the five countries. We shall briefly review the fiscal and legal conditions, the sources of funds, the disbursement patterns and the exit mechanisms used in each of the five countries. We shall also look at the available performance figures, and draw conclusions regarding the trends and outlook for the venture capital industry in each of the countries.

Then, in the final part of the chapter, we shall analyze the dimensions of national differences of venture capital markets. We shall compare and contrast the most important characteristics of the five national markets discussed previously. In our analysis, we draw mostly on data collected and assembled by the European Venture Capital Association (EVCA) and by the national venture capital associations in each of the countries.

VENTURE CAPITAL FUNDING IN THE UK

Market size and development

The UK has the largest venture capital industry in Europe, both in terms of absolute size and in relation to GDP. Globally, only the USA has a larger venture capital industry than the UK. At the end of 1997, the UK investment portfolio of ECU 14.9 billion represented as much as 45 per cent of the total European venture capital portfolio.

The UK venture capital industry became established as a formally distinct industry during the latter part of the 1970s. Throughout most of the 1980s, the industry experienced rapid growth and development, becoming the second largest in the world. This growth was fuelled by the strong performance of the economy, improvement in the entrepreneurial environment under the Thatcher government, and the establishment of a secondary stock market. In the early 1990s, the industry experienced a period of consolidation and slow growth, indicating that it had reached maturity. The annual number of deals remained at a constant level, and fundraising suffered due to the recession and the cyclical nature of fundraising. Since then, however, the UK venture capital industry seems to have started a new phase of rapid growth. The improvement in the economy, successful realizations of venture capital investments, and increasing international venture capital activity were among the factors contributing to this new growth.

The UK is the centre for the recent explosive growth in fundraising in Europe. In 1997, the ECU 12.2 billion raised in the UK represented 61 per cent of total new funds in Europe. As Fig. 2.1 illustrates, the amount of new funds increased threefold from the 1996 figure of ECU 4.4 billion. This surge can be partly attributed to some very large pan-European buyout funds. Other factors include the strong past performance of venture capital firms, and the overall increase in pan-European and global fundraising and investment, for which the UK is an important centre.

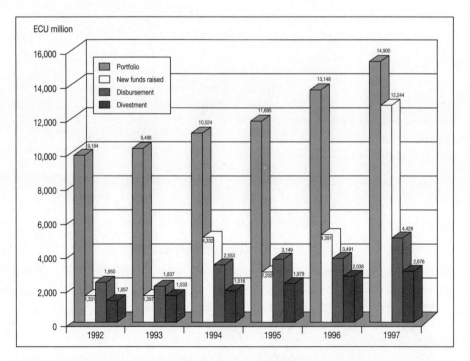

Source: EVCA

Fig. 2.1 ♦ Development of the UK venture capital industry from 1992 to 1997 in terms of portfolio at cost, new funds raised, disbursement and divestment

Also disbursement has grown at an accelerated pace. The ECU 4.4 billion invested into 1,090 companies in 1997 represents a 27 per cent increase in the amount invested from 1996. Comparing disbursement and new funds raised in 1997, we see that a significant amount of capital remained available for investment at the end of the year, about ECU 8.7 billion.

The British Venture Capital Association (BVCA), founded in 1983, represents the majority of venture capital providers in the UK. According to its estimate, there were 889 full-time venture capital executives in the UK in 1997. Most of the investment in the UK takes place through firms which manage independent venture capital funds and investment trusts.

Legal and fiscal environment

The top marginal rate of personal income tax in the UK is 40 per cent, the same rate as for capital gains. This level of capital gains tax is the highest in Europe. However, in terms of the investment vehicles available for venture capital investors and the tax advantages associated with these, the legal and fiscal conditions in the UK are highly favourable.

For institutional investors, the most common investment vehicles are private equity funds. These funds are usually structured as limited partnerships, allowing tax-exempt investors such as pension funds to receive investment gains free of tax. Both private and institutional investors may invest in venture capital and development capital investment trusts. For individual private investors, there are two government programmes which encourage investment into unquoted companies by offering tax reliefs: the Enterprise Investment Scheme (EIS) and Venture Capital Trusts (VCTs).

The Enterprise Investment Scheme was established in 1994 to provide tax relief for individuals who subscribe for ordinary shares in companies fulfilling certain criteria. For example, the company must be unquoted (although companies listed on the London Off-Exchange facility (OFEX) or the Alternative Investment Market (AIM) do qualify), carry out its trade mainly in the UK, be an independent company (not a subsidiary), and its activities must fall within certain restrictions. In the year in which the shares are issued, the investor may claim a reduction in income tax for an amount equal to 20 per cent of the investment, and a deferral of gains on any asset where the disposal was within a certain period before or after the EIS investment. Any gains realized on the sale of EIS shares after a minimum of five years are tax free. If EIS shares are disposed of at a loss at any time, the loss is deductible from either the investor's capital gains tax or income tax. EIS funds are a common investment vehicle. Individual investors invest in the fund and the managers of the fund, as nominees of the participants, subscribe for shares in qualifying companies, spreading the risk of individual investors over several companies.

Venture Capital Trusts were introduced in 1995. They differ from EIS funds in that they are quoted investment trust companies. VCTs offer a spread of investments, both equity and loans, into smaller unlisted companies. VCTs must fulfil a number of requirements under the Financial Services Act and Stock Exchange listing rules. Approved VCTs are exempt from corporation tax on investment gains. Individual investors investing in VCTs can claim the same initial tax reduction and deferral of tax on capital gains as with EIS. Any gain on the sale of VCT shares is tax free at any time, and dividends paid by a VCT to individuals are tax free up to £100,000 a year.

In addition to the EIS and VCTs, the government has also introduced the Reinvestment Relief, which offers, under certain conditions, indefinite deferral of tax on that part of a gain which is invested in ordinary shares in a qualified, unquoted trading company.

In a recent report by the Working Group on the Financing of High Technology Businesses, sponsored by Her Majesty's Treasury, recommendations are presented for government actions in the next budget to encourage investment in early-stage technology-based companies. These recommendations include, for example, the establishment of specific Technology VCTs and significant changes in the taxation of capital gains.

Sources of new funds

In terms of the amount of new funds invested, institutional investors clearly dominate the UK venture capital industry. Pension funds are the most substantial and stable source of capital. Between 1993 and 1997, their proportion of total new funds has consistently been between 30 per cent and 45 per cent. Insurance companies and banks are other main sources of capital, accounting for 21 per cent and 16 per cent of total funds in 1997, respectively. Both of these groups increased their share in 1997. The increase in UK insurance company investment in 1997 is likely to have been facilitated by changes which have taken place in the past few years in the insurance company regulations on valuing venture capital investments. Investment by corporate investors surged from ECU 168 million (4 per cent) in 1996 to ECU 1.5 billion (13 per cent) in 1997. Private individuals, government agencies and academic institutions remain marginal sources of new funds, although the amounts invested by these groups grew significantly from 1996 to 1997.

Most of the record increase in new funds in 1997 came from abroad. Well over half, or 59 per cent of new funds came from abroad in 1997, compared with 36 per cent in 1996. The current level of foreign funding in the UK is the second highest in Europe. Only Sweden has a higher proportion of foreign funds at 65 per cent.

Other Western European countries accounted for 12 per cent of new funds raised in the UK in 1997. Non-European sources made up nearly half, 47 per cent, of total new funds. Not surprisingly, the USA is the main non-European source of capital. As mentioned earlier, the high proportion of foreign funds in the UK is partly due to the fact that many venture capital companies use the UK as a centre for pan-European or global fundraising.

Disbursement patterns

Figure 2.2 illustrates disbursement according to the stage of investment in 1997. Management buyouts[1] and buy-ins accounted for nearly two thirds, or 65 per cent of total investment. Their share of total investment decreased from 72 per cent in 1996, which was the highest level during the past decade. Expansion deals are most important in terms of the number of investments made, accounting for 50 per cent of the total number of deals and 24 per cent of the total amount invested in 1997.

With buyout funds accounting for the majority of new funds raised, this segment of the venture capital market is very well funded for the foreseeable future. The market is very competitive, even overheated at the moment. Prices are driven up, and as a result there are increased efforts by venture capital companies to specialize and innovate, leading to further evolution and development of the market. Venture capital companies are also increasingly looking for investment opportunities abroad. In recent years, the trend has been towards larger buyouts with decline in the smaller (under £1 million) buyout market.

Start-up and seed investments are at a comparatively low level in the UK. Only 148 start-up and six seed investments were made in 1997. They accounted for a mere 2 per cent of the total amount invested and 9 per cent of the number of deals. This low level of early-stage activity is at least partly explained by the difficulties in fundraising that some of the smaller UK venture capital firms focusing on the smaller early-stage and high-technology end of the market have been experiencing in previous years. Recently, the positive influence of the EIS and VCT schemes has been noticed. The absolute amount invested into start-ups doubled from 1996 to 1997 and the number of investments grew by 19 per cent. This development is expected to continue.

In all investment stages, deal sizes in the UK are, on average, larger than in most other European countries. In 1997, the average deal size for seed investments was ECU 0.9 million, for start-up investments ECU 0.6 million, and for expansion stage investments 1.3 ECU million. Replacement capital deals and buyouts were significantly larger, averaging ECU 3.2 million and ECU 5.0 million, respectively.

Of the total number of investments in 1997, 68 per cent were initial venture capital investments into 'new opportunities', with the remainder being follow-up investments into companies which already had venture capital backing.

The proportion of investments made into companies outside the UK increased significantly in 1997. Previously, domestic investment has accounted for at least

80–90 per cent of the total. In 1997, 74 per cent of the total amount of investment was domestic, with other Western European countries accounting for 24 per cent and other countries for the remaining 2 per cent. In terms of the number of deals, however, domestic deals accounted for 89 per cent of the total number of investments. These figures indicate that the non-domestic investments are, on average, relatively large deals. We should again note that the EVCA figures do not include investment activities of the foreign subsidiaries of venture capital companies, and are therefore understating the extent of overseas investment activity.

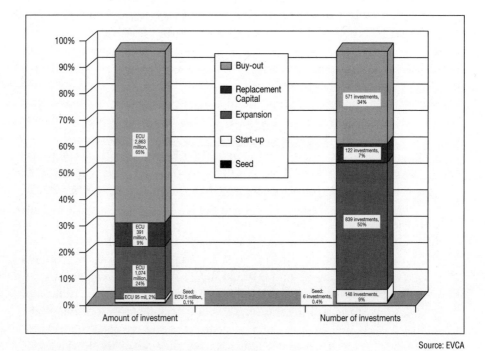

Source: EVCA

Fig. 2.2 ♦ Disbursement by stage in the UK in 1997

In terms of regional distribution within the UK, the South East of England, including the Greater London area, is by far the most active for venture capital investment. Scotland, the North West and West Midlands are the next most active regions, measured as the number of companies backed by venture capital.

Figure 2.3 illustrates the sectoral distribution of venture capital investments in the UK from 1993 to 1997. The consumer-related sector is the single most dominant sector. It accounted for 30 per cent of the total amount invested in 1997. Industrial products and services and the category 'other services' each accounted for more than 10 per cent. 'Other services' include, for example, engineering, consulting, advertising and distribution.

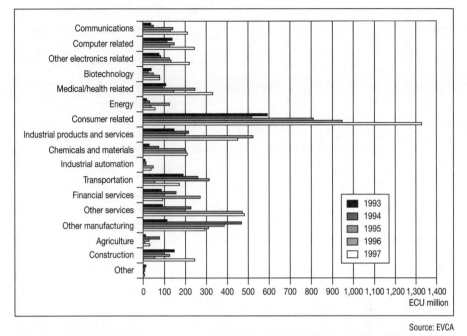

Source: EVCA

Fig. 2.3 ♦ Sectors receiving venture capital investment in the UK from 1993 to 1997

Investment into technology-based companies is at a relatively high level in the UK. In 1997, the combined technology sectors (including information and communications technologies, medical, health and biotechnology, energy technology, industrial automation, other electronics, and chemicals and materials) accounted for roughly one third of investment, both in terms of the amount invested (30 per cent) and in terms of the number of investments (36 per cent). There has been significant growth in investment to these sectors. In 1997, a record amount of ECU 1.3 billion was invested into 601 technology companies, compared with ECU 452 million into 528 companies in 1993. Many new venture capital funds specializing in technology sectors have been raised. The factors underlying this growth include the improved flotation opportunities on the LSE, AIM, Nasdaq and EASDAQ, and the recent improved returns on investments in technology-based companies.

Exit mechanisms and performance

Trade sales remain the most important exit route in the UK. In 1997, the 546 divestments through trade sale accounted for 50 per cent of total divestment at cost and 33 per cent of the total number of divestments.

The UK has the highest level of exits through public offerings in Europe in absolute terms. In 1997, 129 exits from investments in 71 companies were made

31

through public offerings. The total value at cost of these was ECU 399 million. Public offerings accounted for 15 per cent of divestment at cost and 8 per cent of the total number of divestments. The possibilities for flotation in the UK are the best in Europe. The OFEX was started in 1991 to enable the London Stock Exchange member firms to deal in the securities of unlisted and unquoted companies. More recently, the listing rules of the London Stock Exchange were changed to facilitate the listing of loss-making technology-based companies particularly in the biosciences sector. In 1995, the Alternative Investment Market (AIM) was established for small, young and growing companies.

In 1997, there were 58 IPOs of venture-backed companies on the London Stock Exchange, 18 on the AIM, as well as some others on the OFEX, EASDAQ and Nasdaq. The number and value at cost of public offerings decreased in 1996 and 1997 from higher levels in 1995 and 1994. These record levels can be attributed to the changing of the listing rules of the LSE and to the opening of the AIM, which naturally induced a wave of IPOs. In early 1998, IPO activity was at a normal level, but the stock market turmoil caused by the economic crises in Asia and Russia and the financial unrest in Latin America led to many IPOs being postponed, leaving a backlog of IPOs to take place in the near future.

In 1997, there was a significant increase in divestment through management-buy-backs and the sale of quoted equity (included in the category 'other means of divestment' which accounted for 24 per cent of divestment in 1997). The increase in the sale of quoted equity is natural as venture capital companies make further divestments from companies which have floated in the preceding years, when the level of IPO activity was high. Although not included in the statistics, there has also been an increase in fund-to-fund sales, due to the stock market fluctuations. For example, limited life funds, if unable to exit through flotations, or smaller funds looking to quit the market, will sell their investments to larger funds in more liquid positions and with longer-term investment horizons. In 1997, write-offs accounted for 11 per cent of divestment at cost. The proportion of write-offs has remained at this level in recent years.

Figure 2.4 compares the performance of UK venture capital funds to the performance of UK pension funds, the FTSE 100 index and the FTSE small cap index over three, five and ten years until year end 1997. The statistics are based on a study published by the British Venture Capital Association, WM Company and Crossroads Management (UK) Ltd. As we can see, UK venture capital funds have performed strongly. On the three-year and five-year time horizons, all types of venture capital funds outperformed the comparators by a substantial margin.

The ten-year pooled net internal rate of return (IIR) for all venture capital funds combined was 14.6 per cent compared with 13.3 per cent for pension funds, 16.7 per cent for the FTSE 100, and 12.4 per cent for the FTSE small cap. Large management buyout (MBO) funds performed strongly, generating an IRR of 19.7 per cent. Early-stage and development funds did not do as well, with IRRs of under 10 per cent.

Naturally, the latter figures mask more variation, due to the higher risk associated with these stages of investment. The ten-year figures also include a number of old, poorly performing early-stage vehicles of management groups which have since dropped out of the market.

In the future, the growing competition and higher prices in the buy-out sector are likely to have a negative effect on returns. However, the performance of buy-out funds would have to drop radically to be below the comparators. The earlier stage investments, on the other hand, are showing improving performance.

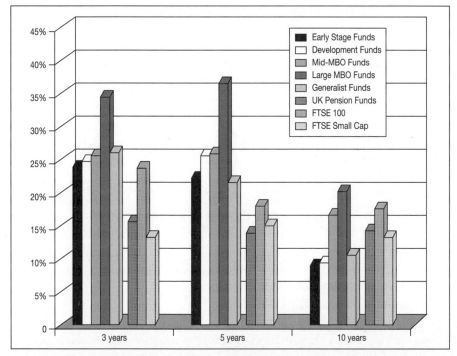

Source: BVCA *and WM Company; 152 funds included in statistics*

Fig. 2.4 ♦ Performance of UK venture capital funds and comparators, pooled net IRR for three, five and ten years until year end 1997

A recent survey by the BVCA[2] studied the economic impact of venture capital in the UK. The survey found that venture-capital-backed companies create a significant amount of jobs and boost the economy through high growth. An estimated 1 million people were employed by venture-capital-backed companies in the UK and a further 0.5 million overseas in 1998. The average annual growth rate in employment in these companies was 15 per cent in the four year period from 1990/1 to 1994/5. The national growth rate is less than 1 per cent per year. The venture-capital-backed companies also increased their sales, profits, exports and investment at a faster rate than companies in general. The study also found that the majority of venture-capital-backed companies felt they benefited from the participation of venture capitalists, by receiving advice on strategic and financial matters.

Outlook

The UK venture capital industry is experiencing a fundraising boom, as massive increases in foreign funding, particularly from the USA, have taken place. The current liquidity situation is good, but there is not an oversupply of capital on the UK market in general. Disbursement is increasingly taking place elsewhere in Europe, as the UK is functioning as the main centre for pan-European fundraising and investment. Also, the record amount of funds raised in 1997 have been invested over several years.

The buyout market may suffer from the present overheating, as competition is driving prices up. Growth will continue in early-stage and technology investments, encouraged by the EIS and VCT schemes. Further increase in average deal sizes across all investment stages is likely.

The flow of fresh money from the USA, as well as from domestic investors, the favourable legal and fiscal conditions, and the liquid IPO markets are among the factors which will ensure that the UK remains the flagship of European venture capital also in the future.

UK venture capital at a glance

Market size and development

- ◆ Largest venture capital market in Europe and second largest in the world; investment portfolio ECU 14.9 billion in 1997.

- ◆ New phase of rapid growth started in mid-1990s; a record amount of new funds, ECU 12.2 billion, raised in 1997.

- ◆ Most investment activity takes place through independent venture capital funds and investment trusts; available variety of investment vehicles provides tax advantages for both institutional and individual investors.

- ◆ The UK is the main centre for pan-European fund-raising and disbursement.

Sources of capital

- ◆ Most of the record increase in new funds came from abroad, mainly the USA; in 1997, over half, 59 per cent, of new funds was raised abroad.

- ◆ Pension funds, insurance companies and banks are the main sources of new funds.

Disbursement patterns

- ◆ Disbursement into companies outside the UK is increasing; in 1997, 26 per cent of investments were made overseas, mainly in other European countries.

- Buyouts dominate disbursement in terms of value, accounting for 65 per cent of investment in 1997.

- Half of deals made in 1997 were expansion investments.

- Early-stage investment is at a comparatively low level, but increasing; the EIS and VCT schemes have a positive influence.

- Consumer goods and services is dominant sector receiving investment.

- Investment into technology sectors is increasing rapidly; in 1997, 36 per cent of investments were into technology sectors.

Exits and performance

- Trade sales remain most important exit route.

- IPO possibilities in the UK are the best in Europe; level of IPO activity is relatively high.

- Performance has been strong; funds have outperformed comparators in three- and five-year statistics.

Key trends

- The buyout market may be overheating; competition is driving prices up.

- The size of deals is increasing.

- Growth in early-stage and technology investments continues.

- Increasing internationalization in fundraising and disbursement.

VENTURE CAPITAL FUNDING IN FRANCE

Market size and development

The French venture capital industry is the second largest in Europe in terms of the absolute size of the investment portfolio, and sixth in proportion to GDP. In recent years, France has not seen the rapid growth that many other European countries have experienced. As Fig. 2.5 illustrates, growth seems to have plateaued, indicating that France is a rather mature venture capital market. In 1997, the overall venture capital portfolio grew only 1.6 per cent to ECU 5.0 billion and the amount of new funds raised increased by a modest 4.5 per cent to ECU 1.08 billion. Disbursement grew more significantly, by 44 per cent to ECU 1.2 billion. France was the only one of the major European markets where disbursement exceeded the amount of total funds raised in 1997.

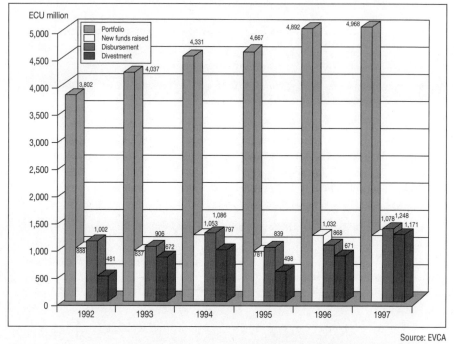

Source: EVCA

Fig. 2.5 ♦ Development of the French venture capital industry from 1992 to 1997 in terms of portfolio at cost, new funds raised, disbursement and divestment

The French association of venture capital companies (Association Française des Investisseurs en Capital (AFIC)) estimates that there were 643 full-time venture capital executives in France in 1997. The French banks continue to dominate the industry, investing either via dedicated subsidiaries or by sponsoring external funds. In recent years, many of the smaller funds have been consolidated, which has resulted in an increase in fund size.

The French venture capital industry is more domestic in nature than European venture capital in general. The majority of funds are raised in France and invested in French companies. In 1997, 86 per cent of new funds were domestic, with only 3 per cent coming from other European countries and 11 per cent from non-European sources. Of total disbursement in 1997, 93 per cent was domestic, 3 per cent went into other European countries, and 4 per cent outside Europe. France has not experienced the recent growth in non-domestic funding and disbursement which has been typical in Europe in general.

The comparative insularity of the French venture capital industry may be due to cultural and language barriers, with international institutions preferring 'Anglo-Saxon' practices. Also, the poor past performance of some French funds and the small size of France-specific vehicles may have deterred foreign investors. We must note, however, that France is one of the top target markets for the large pan-European funds raised in the UK.

Legal and fiscal environment

The venture capital process in France became more organized in the mid-1990s, when two formalized structures were established for venture capital companies. These structures are the Sociétés de Capital Risque (SCRs) and the Fonds Commun Placement à Risque (FCPRs).

In order to promote venture capital investments, there are a number of specific incentives in French tax legislation for both individual and corporate investors, making the fiscal environment favourable for the venture capital industry. Under certain conditions, SCRs and FCPRs are exempt from tax, and shareholders are only taxed on distributed profits and capital gains.

Aiming at further encouraging individuals to invest in venture capital, a third form of venture capital company was recently introduced, the Fonds Commun de Placement Innovation (FCPIs). An FCPI is an FCPR which has invested at least 60 per cent of its assets in unquoted technology-based companies. Companies qualify as 'technology-based' if their level of research expenses is sufficiently high. Individual investors in FCPIs are entitled to a tax reduction equal to 25 per cent of the amount invested, if certain conditions are met. For example, the shares have to be held for a minimum of five years.

Sources of new funds

As a relatively mature venture capital market, the share of capital gains available for reinvestment is comparatively high in France, accounting for 40 per cent of total new funds in 1997. In line with the overall trend in Europe, the proportion of bank funding has decreased, from 41 per cent in 1996 to 35 per cent in 1997. At the same time, corporate investments have grown significantly, from just 3 per cent in 1996 to 17 per cent in 1997. It is expected that investment by insurance companies, which accounted for only 3 per cent of total funds in 1997, will increase significantly in the near future, as legal restrictions on life insurance fund managers in France have recently been relaxed, allowing life insurance funds to invest in private equity vehicles and directly in non-listed companies. Pension fund investment in France has historically been marginal. In 1997, pension funds accounted for only 3 per cent of total new funds. Due to the restructuring of the French pension system, from pay-as-you-go to funded pensions, investments by pensions funds into venture capital are expected to grow dramatically.

Disbursement patterns

In 1997, a total of 1,090 companies received financing from French venture capital. Of these, 63 per cent received venture capital backing for the first time. The remaining 37 per cent of companies received follow-on investments.

Figure 2.6 illustrates the distribution of disbursement according to the stage of investment in 1997. Buyouts and expansion capital account for the majority of investments. Especially the larger buyout market is flourishing at present, which will most likely increase the interest of foreign investors in the French market.

The French venture capital industry has historically placed greater emphasis on early-stage investment than many other European countries such as, for example, the UK. In recent years, there has been growth in start-up investments, from ECU 15 million (2 per cent of total amount invested) in 1993 to ECU 89 million (7 per cent) in 1997. In terms of the number of investments, start-up deals accounted for nearly 16 per cent of the total in 1997, reflecting the smaller size of these deals. In 1997, the average start-up investment size was ECU 0.4 million, compared with ECU 2.3 million for buyouts, ECU 0.9 million for replacement deals, ECU 0.6 million for expansion, and ECU 0.1 million for seed investments. In all of the categories, deal sizes are considerably smaller in France than in Europe overall, reflecting the high proportion of domestic deals. In 1997, however, the size of French buyout deals grew significantly.

Nearly 60 per cent of investments in 1997 were into companies with fewer than 100 employees, but these deals accounted for only 19 per cent of total disbursement. In sharp contrast to this, the later-stage deals into large companies with 1,000 to 5,000 employees accounted for only 6 per cent of completed deals but received 46 per cent of total disbursement.

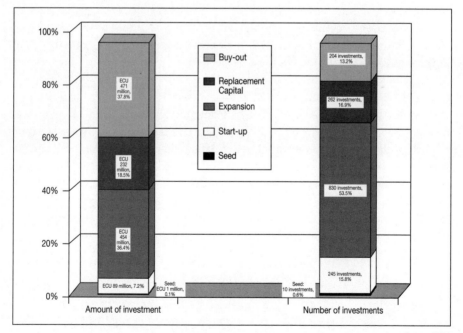

Source: EVCA

Fig. 2.6 ◆ Disbursement by stage in France in 1997

Figure 2.7 illustrates the sectoral distribution of venture capital investments in France from 1993 to 1997. The consumer-related sector and industrial products and services have traditionally received the most investments. In 1997, there was a significant increase in the category 'other services', which includes e.g. engineering, consulting and distribution.

The combined technology sectors (including information and communications technologies, medical, health and biotechnology, energy technology, industrial automation, other electronics, and chemicals and materials) accounted for 21 per cent of the total amount of investment and as much as 38 per cent of the total number of investments in 1997, indicating that a significant proportion of the smaller seed and start-up deals are made into new, technology-based companies. The amount invested in technology sectors grew from ECU 160 million in 1993 to ECU 260 million in 1997. In recent years, French venture capital funds have increasingly specialized in particular industry sectors, including many of the technology sectors.

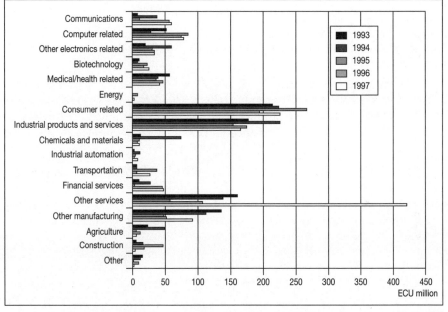

Source: EVCA

Fig. 2.7 ♦ Sectors receiving venture capital investment in France from 1993 to 1997

Exit mechanisms and performance

The trade sale is the most significant exit route in France. In 1997, trade sales accounted for 56 per cent of total divestment at cost and 40 per cent of the total number of divestments in 1997. There has been a significant increase in the amount divested by trade sales, from ECU 383 million in 1993 to ECU 660 million in 1997. The level of IPO divestment in France is the second highest in Europe, exceeded only by the UK. The recent increase in IPO divestment clearly reflects the beneficial effect of the Nouveau Marché of the Paris Stock Exchange, as well as Europe's other new stock markets. In 1997, public offerings accounted for 13 per cent of total divestment at cost and 28 per cent of the total number of divestments. The number of IPOs decreased from 126 in 1996 to 101 in 1997, but the average size of an IPO at cost increased from ECU 0.8 million to ECU 2.2 million. Other means of divestment and write-offs accounted for 13 per cent and 12 per cent of the amount of divestment in 1997.

Figure 2.8 illustrates the results of a performance survey of French venture capital funds carried out by the French Venture Capital Association AFIC and Ernst & Young. Forty-eight venture capital companies operating in France participated in the study. Please note that as the French survey uses *gross* IRR as the performance measure, the results are not directly comparable with the *net* IRR figures for Europe and the UK, which we have discussed earlier.

The ten-year (from 1988 to 1997) pooled gross IRR on realized investments for all venture capital funds combined was 15.9 per cent. For the five years until the end of 1997, the figure was slightly lower, 14.9 per cent. In both the ten-year and five-year periods, buy-out funds performed significantly better than early-stage or development funds.

Looking at the one-year figures for 1996 and 1997, we see that buy-out funds, which reached record performances in 1996, showed a lower rate of return in 1997 at 17.8 per cent. Early-stage and development funds performed very poorly in 1996, but improved their performance in 1997 to reach very high gross IRRs of 31.1 per cent and 26.6 per cent, respectively. The strong performance of these funds in 1997 will have had a significant positive effect on the ten-year and five-year figures. Although little can be inferred from comparing the performance figures for just two consecutive years, there do seem to be indications that the performance of early-stage and development funds is improving.

Outlook

Despite the slow-down in the growth of domestic fund-raising, the future for the French venture capital market looks promising. The future growth and development of the industry depends to a large degree on whether France can attract a substantial inflow of foreign funds.

The recent growth in the buy-out sector suggests that there are increasing opportunities for pan-European investors in the French market. Although not yet evident in the present statistics, growth in foreign fundraising is likely to take place, following the general European trend. Also the shift from an industry dominated by captive venture capital funds towards more independent or semi-captive players, as well as the recent improvements in performance are likely to have a positive effect on the development of the French venture capital industry.

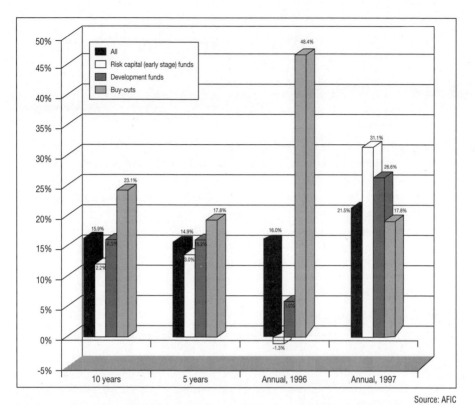

Source: AFIC

Fig. 2.8 ♦ Performance of French venture capital funds; gross IRRs for the ten year and five year periods until year end 1997, and the annual IRRs for 1996 and 1997

French venture capital at a glance

Market size and development

◆ France is the second largest venture capital market in Europe with an investment portfolio of ECU 4.97 billion in 1997.

◆ Market growth has been slower and more stable in recent years than in most other European countries.

◆ In 1997, there were 643 venture capital executives in France.

◆ France is the most domestic market in Europe in terms of both fundraising and disbursement.

Sources of capital

◆ As a mature market, capital gains account for a large proportion of new funds, 40 per cent in 1997.

41

♦ Banks and, to an increasing degree, corporate investors, are the other main sources of new funds.

Disbursement patterns

♦ Investments most often made into management buyouts or into expanding companies.

♦ Early-stage investing increased its proportion of total disbursement in 1993–7.

♦ Most investments are made into small companies; in 1997, 60 per cent of investments into companies with fewer than 100 employees.

♦ The consumer-related sector as well as industrial products and services are the main industry sectors receiving investments.

♦ Notable growth in disbursement into technology-based sectors; in 1997 they accounted for 21 per cent of total investment and 38 per cent of the total number of investments.

Exits and performance

♦ Trade sales are the dominant exit mechanism.

♦ The level of IPO divestment in the second highest in Europe (after the UK).

Key trends

♦ A shift from captive venture capital funds towards independent and semi-captive organizations.

♦ Increasing specialization of venture capital funds according to stage, sector or region.

♦ Growing importance of buy-out sector.

♦ Increase in foreign funds invested into France.

VENTURE CAPITAL FUNDING IN GERMANY

Market size and development

The German venture capital industry is, at the moment, the fastest growing venture capital market in Europe after the UK. In 1997, the industry was the third largest in Europe, following the UK and France, with an investment portfolio of ECU 3.9 billion. Relative to the size of the economy, however, the German venture capital industry is still somewhat underdeveloped, ranking tenth in Europe.

The industry has been growing at a steady rate throughout the 1990s. This growth saw a tremendous acceleration in 1997. As Fig. 2.9 illustrates, the amount of new funds raised grew from ECU 330 million in 1996 to ECU 2.6 billion in 1997. Disbursement grew significantly, as well, from ECU 695 million to ECU 1.3 billion. As these figures indicate, money is flowing into the industry faster than new deals. The number of venture capital companies operating in Germany is increasing. Many new early-stage funds are being established and more and more venture capital companies from elsewhere in Europe and from the USA are setting up offices in Germany. The result is increased competition, which seems to be driving up the prices of deals.

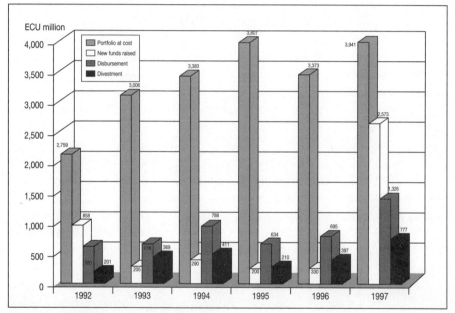

Source: EVCA

Fig. 2.9 ◆ Development of the German venture capital industry from 1992 to 1997 in terms of portfolio at cost, new funds raised, disbursement and divestment

The main organization for German venture capital funds is the Bundesverband Deutscher Kapitalbeteiligungsgesellschaften (BVK) (the German Venture Capital Association). The BVK had 115 members in November 1998. In addition to these companies, there were approximately 80 venture capital companies in Germany which were not members. The majority of the non-members are very small, regional companies founded in 1997 or 1998, most often captives or semi-captives of savings banks. The BVK estimates that there were about 530 full-time venture capital executives in Germany in 1997.

Legal and fiscal environment

Growth in the German venture capital industry has been partly driven by developments in legal and fiscal conditions. The political attitude in Germany has been very favourable towards venture capital. A number of government and Länder schemes have been established to promote venture capital investment. The Beteiligungskapital für Technologieunternehmen (BTU) aims at increasing investment in young, technology-based companies. Under the BTU programme, the Deutsche Ausgleichsbank, a government-owned bank that subsidizes businesses, runs a scheme called the 'Technology Participation Society' or TBG. This society finances new, technology-based firms by offering a mark for every mark invested by private investors. The German government also provides partial re-financing for venture capital companies investing in new, fast-growing companies and guarantees for investors that if a company goes broke, their investments will be protected.

Some legal and tax regulations were modified in 1997, to provide more favourable conditions for venture capital operators by liberalizing regulations and creating tax incentives. For example, capital gains realized by Unternehmensbeteiligungsgesellschaften, or venture capital companies, on the sale of shares of companies are not subject to income tax or trade tax, if the proceeds of such a sale are reinvested within four years.

There are also specific incentives to encourage venture capital investment in the new Länder of Eastern Germany. The Beteiligungsfond Ost is a special fund for refinancing investment in Eastern Germany. Realized capital gains are also exempt from taxation if the proceeds are invested into small and medium sized enterprises (SMEs) registered in the Eastern Länder. In 1997, the new Länder of the eastern part of Germany accounted for approximately 17 per cent of the total venture capital investment portfolio and 16 per cent of total disbursement.

After the new Social Democratic government came into power in late 1998, there have been some references in the media to government intentions to cut some of the current tax incentives. There are concerns in the German venture capital community that the new government may not be as favourable towards the industry as the old one was.

Sources of new funds

Banks have traditionally been the single largest source of new funds in Germany. They have strengthened their position slightly in recent years, from 52 per cent of total funds in 1993 to 58 per cent in 1997. The dominant position of banks is explained by the fact that most German venture capital funds are captive or semi-captive funds associated with the banking sector, and to a lesser degree with the insurance sector.

Even though the amount of new funds increased eightfold from 1996 to 1997, the proportions of various sources remained largely unchanged. Explosive growth took place in all categories of investors. All of the funds invested by pension funds, 12 per cent of total new funds in 1997, came from abroad, as there are no pension funds as yet in Germany. Insurance companies accounted for 11 per cent. Corporations are starting to invest not only through their internal vehicles, but also into 'outside' venture capital companies. Corporate investors accounted for 7 per cent of new funds in 1997. Private individuals and government agencies accounted for 6 per cent and 5 per cent of new funds in 1997, respectively. Unlike the statistics for the other countries, the German statistics do not monitor realized capital gains available for reinvestment.

Much of the record growth in new funds raised in 1997 came from non-domestic sources. The proportion of domestic funding, which had been between 67 per cent and 78 per cent from 1992 to 1996, fell to 60 per cent in 1997. A significant increase in funds from other European countries took place, from 15 per cent in 1992 to 34 per cent in 1997. The proportion of non-European funding decreased from the highest value of 17 per cent in 1994 to only 6 per cent in 1997. However, this statistic is misleading, as the funds invested by local German offices of foreign venture capital companies are included in the statistic for domestic funds. Therefore, the proportion of non-domestic funding in Germany is, in reality, even higher than the statistics suggest.

Disbursement patterns

In 1997, a total of 958 companies received financing by German venture capital. Of these, 69 per cent were new opportunities, that is, the companies were receiving venture capital backing for the first time. The remaining 31 per cent of companies received follow-on investments. The proportion of investment into new opportunities has remained at approximately the same level throughout the 1990s.

Figure 2.10 illustrates the distribution of disbursement according to the stage of investment in 1997. Expansion capital has been and remains dominant both in terms of the amount invested (ECU 650 million in 1997) and the number of investments (503 in 1997). The value of buy-outs increased threefold from ECU 150 million in 1996 to ECU 476 million in 1997, a jump from 21 per cent of total investment in 1996 to 36 per cent in 1997. Also the number of buy-outs increased, from 61 to 107. The growth in buyout investment has been accredited to the succession problems facing many family-owned medium-sized companies, which were founded after the Second World War.

Early-stage investment is growing. The effects of government incentives, the improved opportunities for young companies to float on stock markets, as well as the changing attitudes of entrepreneurs – more positive towards outside equity

45

finance – can be felt as a recent heating-up of the early-stage market. Many venture capital funds are specializing according to investment stage, with an increasing number of early-stage funds competing for deals.

According to the German Venture Capital Association, growth in early-stage investments will continue at least throughout 1999. As early-stage investments increase their proportion of total disbursement, expansion capital will probably decrease in importance, with buyouts maintaining their share.

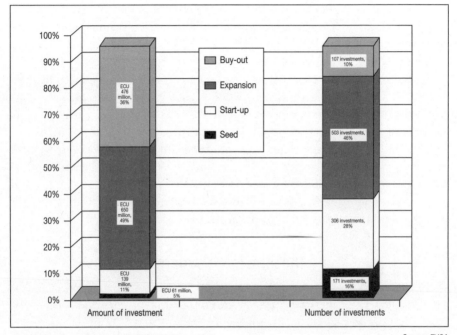

Source: EVCA

Fig. 2.10 ♦ Disbursement by stage in Germany in 1997

Figure 2.11 illustrates the sectoral distribution of venture capital investments in Germany from 1993 to 1997. Industrial products and services have traditionally received the most investments, and they remain dominant. Within this sector, products and services related to mechanical engineering accounted for roughly two thirds of investment and pulp and paper products and services for one third in 1997. The significant increase in 1997 in the category 'other', which includes energy, mining, utilities and conglomerates, is most probably due to a small number of very large buyout deals.

The combined technology sectors (communications, computer-related, other electronics, medical/biotechnology, and chemicals and materials) accounted for 31 per cent of the total amount of investment and as much as 43 per cent of the total number of investments in 1997, indicating that a significant proportion of the smaller seed and start-up deals are made into new, technology-based companies. There has been explosive growth in technology investments over the past five years. In 1993, these investments accounted for only 16 per cent of the total amount of investment and 20 per cent of the number of deals. The amount invested in technology sectors grew fourfold from ECU 96 million in 1993 to ECU 413 million in 1997.

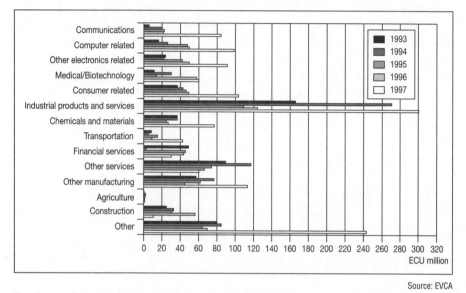

Source: EVCA

Fig. 2.11 ♦ Sectors receiving venture capital investment in Germany from 1993 to 1997

Exit mechanisms and performance

The most common methods for exits in Germany are trade sales and management-buy-backs. Trade sales accounted for 35 per cent of the total amount divested in 1997 and 20 per cent of the number of divestments. Management-buy-backs are included in the category 'other means', which accounted for 47 per cent of the amount divested and 54 per cent of the number of divestments in 1997. The number of exits through public offerings was still at a low level in 1997 – only 20 exits through public offerings took place. The establishing of the 'Neuer Markt' in Frankfurt in March 1997 enables young, fast-growing companies to float more easily. The Neuer Markt is part of the EURO.NM network. Its impact will most likely be seen as a significant increase in the number of IPOs in the 1998 statistics.

The German Venture Capital Association does not collect official performance data, but according to an unofficial estimate based on a small sample, German funds were, on average, generating net IRRs in the range of 17 to 18 per cent in 1997. With the improved possibilities for IPO exits, these rates are likely to be around 22 to 23 per cent in 1998 and 1999.

Outlook

Germany has been referred to as the 'sleeping giant' of European venture capital. Now it seems that the giant has woken up. Large amounts of fresh money are flowing into the industry, inducing an intense, almost euphoric atmosphere. Several favourable factors, including increasing deal opportunities in both early stage financing and MBOs, the government's supportive attitude, and the rapid increase in foreign funds, have been the main drivers for growth.

There are no signs that this growth would slow down in the short term. On the contrary, the German Venture Capital Association predicts that the amount of new funds will again reach a new record in the 1998 statistics and continue to grow through 1999 as well. Competition in the market will increase further, and funds will continue to specialize into particular stages, sectors or regions. At the present rate of growth, Germany may bypass France as Europe's second largest market already in the 1998 statistics. In the long term, the actions of the new Social Democratic government as well as the developments taking place on the European level will have an impact on the development of the German venture capital industry.

German venture capital at a glance

Market size and development

◆ Third largest market in Europe in 1997 with an investment portfolio of ECU 3.9 billion.

◆ Fastest growing market in Europe; the amount of new funds raised in 1997 was ECU 2.6 billion.

◆ Approximately 200 venture capital companies in Germany at end of year 1998.

◆ Majority of German venture capital funds are affiliated with the banking and insurance sectors; banks are the main source of new capital.

◆ A high proportion of new funds come from non-domestic sources, 40 per cent in 1997.

◆ An increasing number of foreign venture capital companies are setting up offices in Germany.

Disbursement patterns

◆ Expansion capital remains most important investment stage both in terms of value and number of investments.

◆ The buyout sector is growing rapidly.

◆ Early-stage investment is at a very high level and growing; 42 per cent of companies receiving investment in 1997 were in the seed or start-up phase.

◆ Industrial products and services, especially the mechanical engineering and pulp and paper sectors receive the most investments.

◆ Explosive growth in technology investment: from 16 per cent of total investment in 1993 to 31 per cent in 1997.

Exits and performance

◆ Trade sales and management-buy-backs are the dominant exit mechanisms.

◆ In 1997, IPOs were at a very low level; the establishing of the Neuer Markt in Frankfurt in March 1997 will lead to an increased number of exits through IPOs.

◆ According to an estimate by the German Venture Capital Association, German venture capital funds generated, on average, net IRRs between 17 and 18 per cent in 1997.

Key trends

◆ The 'sleeping giant' of European venture capital has woken up – rapid growth will continue.

◆ Growth particularly in early-stage investments and the buyout sector.

◆ Competition in the market will continue to increase in the near future.

◆ Increasing internationalization of fundraising and disbursement.

VENTURE CAPITAL FUNDING IN THE NETHERLANDS

Market size and development

The venture capital industry in the Netherlands is the fourth largest in Europe with a total investment portfolio of ECU 2.2 billion in 1997. In relation to the size of the economy, the Dutch venture capital industry is the second largest in Europe.

The industry developed comparatively early in the Netherlands, and is therefore a rather mature and competitive market. The first Dutch venture capital company was started soon after the Second World War, but the significant growth in the industry took place in the 1980s, when the government took measures to encourage early-stage investments. For example, the government covered half of any losses incurred in early-stage investment. In 1995, this scheme was abolished, as the industry was considered to have reached maturity. As a result, there was a short-term negative impact on early-stage investments, but in the long term, the venture capital market became more effective, requiring venture capitalists to carry out better due diligence and risk management.

Traditionally, the public sector dominated Dutch venture capital. But since a shift in the early 1990s, the private sector has carried out the majority of investment activity. An increase in the number and variety of private venture capital companies operating in the market was followed by a period of consolidation through mergers and acquisitions. At the moment the market is quite stable in terms of the major players. The Dutch Venture Capital Association (Nederlandse Vereniging van Participatiemaatschappijen (NVP)) estimates that there were 145 venture capital executives in the Netherlands in 1997 and approximately 60 venture capital companies at the end of 1998.

The transition to private venture capital companies has brought with it a new phase of rapid growth for the industry, following several years of slower growth. As can be seen in Fig. 2.12, the amount of new funds raised increased significantly from 1995 to 1996. The record level of new funds in 1996, ECU 1.4 billion, was the result of rigorous fundraising efforts after the liquidity problems which many funds suffered in 1995. Also, a significant proportion of the 1996 growth can be accounted to one major venture capital company raising a very large amount of capital. Although the amount of new funds fell in 1997, it still remained at a relatively high level at ECU 859 million.

Disbursement has grown steadily in the last few years, reaching an all-time high of ECU 760 million in 1997. It is estimated that ECU 452 million was still available for investment at the end of 1997. According to the Dutch Venture Capital Association, the present liquidity situation is good, and due to improving performance figures, venture capital companies will not have trouble raising new capital in the near future.

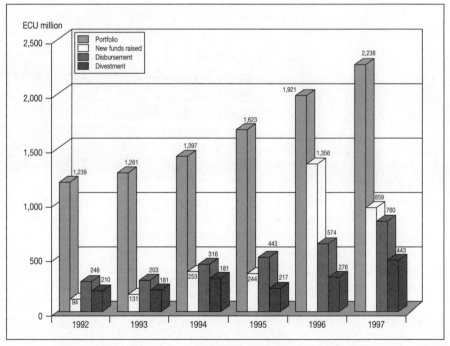

Source: EVCA

Fig. 2.12 ♦ Development of the Dutch venture capital industry from 1992 to 1997 in terms of portfolio at cost, new funds raised, disbursement and divestment

Legal and fiscal environment

The most common legal forms for venture capital funds in the Netherlands are the public limited liability company (NV) and the private limited liability company (BV). Both are subject to corporate income tax. Dividends received and capital gains on shares in other companies may be exempt from corporation tax, if certain criteria are met (for example, at least 5 per cent shareholding). Otherwise, dividends and capital gains are subject to 25 per cent withholding taxes. Venture capital companies are, in many cases, able to reduce the effect of corporate income tax and withholding tax by selecting certain kinds of structures between them and the companies they have ownership in.

The personal tax rates are relatively high in the Netherlands, but the government tries to encourage investment through a number of incentives. The 'Aunt Agatha rule' allows a certain higher level of interest to be exempt from income tax by individuals investing in start-ups over an eight year period. Losses in that period are tax deductible up to Fl50,000. Venture capital funds with a minimum of 70 per cent of their portfolio invested in start-up companies are allowed to take tax deductible losses once the value falls below the original cost. In addition to these tax incentives, the government also specifically encourages technology-oriented start-up funds. The Ministry of Economic Affairs may contribute up to 25 per cent of total capital into these funds, if certain criteria are met.

Sources of new funds

As a mature venture capital market, the proportion of realized capital gains has been high in the Netherlands, over 40 per cent in 1995. As the amount of new funds surged in 1996, the proportion of capital gains dropped accordingly. In 1997, capital gains accounted for 25 per cent of new funds. Banks have mainly accounted for the recent growth in new funds. In 1997, they committed 40 per cent of total new funds. The proportion of bank funding is likely to remain at a high level, as many venture capital companies are 'captive' funds affiliated with banks. Pension funds and insurance companies are the other principal sources of capital in the Netherlands, accounting for 24 per cent and 7 per cent in 1997, respectively. The Dutch Venture Capital Association does not collect data on corporate investors. There is some corporate venturing in the Netherlands, but it is only a minor source of new funds for the venture capital industry.

The majority of new funds are raised within the Netherlands. In 1997, domestic funds accounted for 79 per cent of total new funds, with the remainder coming from other European countries. The highest level of foreign funding was in 1996, when 67 per cent of funds were domestic and 33 per cent from elsewhere in Europe.

Disbursement patterns

In 1997, a total of 360 companies received Dutch venture capital financing. Of these, 61 per cent were 'new opportunities', or companies receiving venture capital backing for the first time. The remainder were follow-on investments into companies which already had venture capital backing.

Figure 2.13 illustrates the distribution of disbursement according to the stage of investment in 1997. Expansion capital is the largest investment category, both in terms of the amount invested and the number of deals. In 1997, the 210 expansion investments worth ECU 311 million accounted for 41 per cent of total investment volume and 49 per cent of deals. Management buyouts accounted for 39 per cent of volume and 22 per cent of deals.

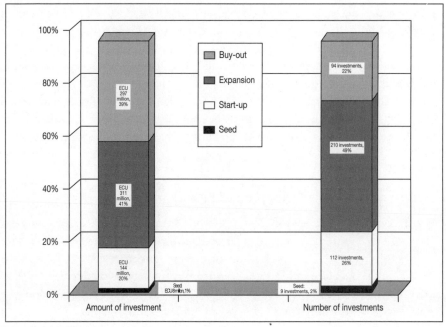

Source: EVCA

Fig. 2.13 ♦ Disbursement by stage in the Netherlands in 1997

The level of start-up investment in the Netherlands is the highest of the major markets in Europe. Only Greece and Iceland have proportionately higher levels. In 1997, 112 start-up deals worth ECU 144 million were completed in the Netherlands. They accounted for 20 per cent of the amount of investment and 26 per cent of the total number of deals.

The Dutch Venture Capital Association expects buyouts to increase their proportion of investment, as middle-sized, family-owned companies of the 'baby boom' generation face succession problems. Start-up investments will continue to grow in absolute terms, but will probably not increase their share of total investments.

There has been increasing specialization of Dutch venture capital funds into particular stages of investment or certain industry sectors. This more narrow focus has led to regional expansion, both in the Netherlands and abroad, as venture capitalists have to go further to find suitable investment opportunities. Some firms have chosen regional specialization, usually within the Netherlands, instead of a stage or industry focus. These are often smaller, locally operating venture capital companies.

The majority of investments are still made into companies within the Netherlands, although, in line with the general trend in Europe, the proportion of domestic investment has decreased. In 1993, 92 per cent of the total amount invested went into companies in the Netherlands. In 1997, this figure was 70 per cent. In 1997, 25 per cent of total investment went into other European countries and 5 per cent outside Western Europe. This represents a shift from 1996, when European and non-European investment accounted for 13 per cent each.

Figure 2.14 illustrates the sectoral distribution of investments from 1993 to 1997. Investments are spread across industry sectors more evenly than in most other European countries. In 1997, the most important sectors receiving investment were industrial products and services and the consumer-related sector, as well as the category 'other', which includes mining, utilities and conglomerates.

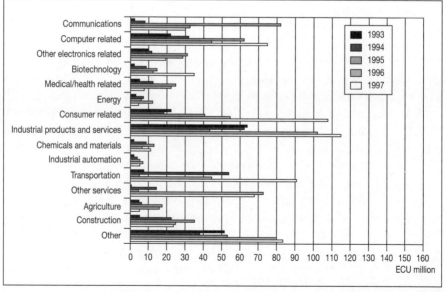

Source: EVCA

Fig. 2.14 ♦ Sectors receiving venture capital investment in the Netherlands from 1993 to 1997

Investment into technology-based companies is at a high level in the Netherlands. As Fig. 2.14 illustrates, most of the technology sectors (including information and communications technologies, medical, health and biotechnology, energy technology, industrial automation, other electronics, and chemicals and materials) saw significant growth from 1993 to 1997. In 1993, only ECU 49 million was invested into 124 technology-based companies. In 1997, the combined technology sectors accounted for ECU 191 million, or 25 per cent of the total amount invested. The 172 technology-based companies into which investments were made accounted for as much as 41 per cent of the total number of companies invested in, indicating that a significant proportion of the smaller start-up investments were made into technology-based firms.

At the present time, 12 Dutch venture capital companies are participating in financing business incubator centres for technology-based start-up companies, especially in the IT sector. The first of these so-called Twinning Centres has been opened in Eindhoven, with two others to follow. Projects such as these will probably encourage further growth in the venture capital funding of early-stage technology companies.

Exit mechanisms and performance

Mergers and acquisitions (i.e. trade sales) are the most common methods of divestment in the Netherlands, accounting for 36 per cent of divestment at cost in 1997. Investments in 40 companies were exited by IPO in 1997, a slight decrease from the 47 companies in 1996. The value at cost of public offerings was 20 per cent of total divestment. The first half of 1998 was also active in terms of IPOs, but slowed down considerably during the second half, as a result of the fluctuations in the stock markets following the economic crises in Asia and Russia. The level of write-offs has been relatively high in the Netherlands, but has decreased from 22 per cent of divestment at cost and 38 per cent of deals in 1993 to 14 per cent of divestment and 16 per cent of deals in 1997.

The Nieuwe Markt Amsterdam (NMAX), which belongs to the EURO.NM network, has improved the possibilities for flotation significantly, as the listing rules are not as strict as on the main stock exchange. Many of the recent exits through public offerings took place on the NMAX and a few on Nasdaq.

Figure 2.15 illustrates the performance of Dutch venture capital by investment stage. The statistics are based on a survey carried out by NVP. Please note that as the NVP survey uses *gross* IRR as the performance measure, the results are not directly comparable with the *net* IRR figures for Europe and the UK.

Buyouts have performed the strongest, with a gross IRR of 22 per cent on investments realized between 1987 and 1996. Also bridge finance has generated a high level of returns at 19 per cent. Early- and later-stage venture capital have not performed as well. Especially early-stage investments have fared badly, with a realized IRR of –1 per cent for the ten-year period from 1987 to 1996. We must note, however, that there is likely to be more variation in the performance figures of early-stage venture capital than in the other categories, as a result of the higher risk associated with these investments. Also, until 1995, the government covered half of any losses incurred in early-stage investments. Thus the returns for early-stage investors have been better than what the negative IRR suggests. The unrealized IRR of 7 per cent at the end of 1996 suggests that the performance of early-stage investments is improving. Further improvement is expected, as venture capitalists carry out better due diligence and get more actively involved in their investments as losses are no longer protected by the government.

As a whole, Dutch venture capital is underperforming compared with the general European level and compared to other asset classes in the Netherlands. The quoted market would have given investors an average rate of return of 16 per cent during the period from 1987 to 1996, compared with the 13 per cent of

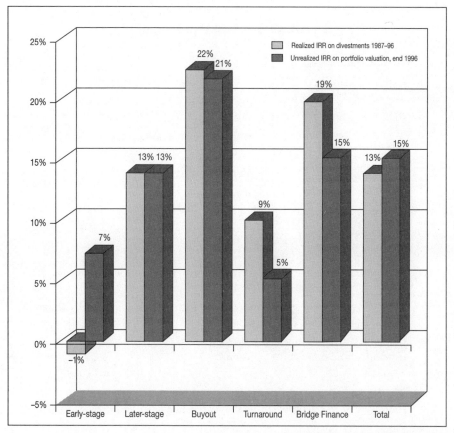

Source: NVP

Fig. 2.15 ◆ Performance of Dutch venture capital funds in terms of realized gross IRR from 1987 to 1996 and unrealized gross IRR at year end 1996

venture capital (including all stages). Of course, some venture capital firms in the Netherlands are performing strongly, as are some industry sectors. For example, investments in automation and computer companies outperformed all other sectors, generating an average gross IRR of 32 per cent.

Outlook

The future looks promising for Dutch venture capital. The current liquidity situation is good, and no shortage of new funds is expected in the near future. Both the buyout market and early-stage investing are growing. With the consolidation and increasing specialization of venture capital companies, we will hopefully see improved rates of return, which will, in turn, encourage further growth of the industry.

Dutch venture capital at a glance

Market development

♦ Fourth largest venture capital market in Europe; investment portfolio ECU 2.2 billion in 1997.

♦ Until the early 1990s, the public sector dominated the industry.

♦ A shift took place, with an increase in the number and variety of private venture capital companies, followed by consolidation through a series of mergers and acquisitions.

♦ Following several years of slower growth, a new phase of rapid growth started in 1996.

♦ Approximately 60 venture capital companies in the Netherlands at the end of 1998.

Sources of capital

♦ Banks are the main source of new funds; many venture capital companies affiliated with banking sector.

♦ As a more mature market, realized capital gains are an important source of capital; pension funds and insurance companies are the other main sources.

♦ Domestic funds account for majority of new capital, 79 per cent in 1997; remainder from other European countries.

Disbursement patterns

♦ Majority of investments are made into the Netherlands, 92 per cent in 1997.

♦ Nearly half of investments are made in the expansion stage.

- ◆ Early-stage investment is at a high level; in 1997, seed and start-up deals accounted for 21 per cent of the total amount invested and 28 per cent of deals.

- ◆ Investments are spread across industry sectors more evenly than in most other European countries; industrial products and services, the consumer-related sector, transportation, 'other services', and the technology sectors all receive significant amounts of investment.

- ◆ Investment into technology sectors has grown rapidly and reached a very high level; in 1997, 41 per cent of companies receiving investment were in technology sectors.

Exits and performance

- ◆ Trade sales are the main exit route.

- ◆ Number of IPOs increased significantly in 1996 and 1997.

- ◆ Performance has been lower than in Europe in general; early-stage funds especially have performed poorly.

Key trends

- ◆ Venture capital funds will continue to specialize by investment stages, industry sectors or regions.

- ◆ No shortage of new funds is expected as performance levels are improving.

- ◆ The buyout sector will increase in size and relative importance.

- ◆ Early-stage investing will continue to grow, maintaining its relative importance.

VENTURE CAPITAL FUNDING IN ITALY

Market size and development

At the end of 1997, the Italian venture capital investment portfolio was the fifth largest in Europe, with ECU 1.8 billion invested in 819 companies. In proportion to the size of the economy, which is the third largest in the world, the industry is still rather underdeveloped. The Italian venture capital industry ranks only 11th of the 17 Western European countries.

Traditionally, Italian venture capital has been dominated by bank-affiliated organizations receiving their funds from banks and the public sector. In recent years, however, many new players, both international and domestic, have entered the market, leading to rapid growth in 1996 and 1997. As Fig. 2.16 illustrates, the amount of new funds more than doubled from ECU 291 million in 1995 to ECU 738 million in 1996, and then grew by 45 per cent to ECU 1.1 billion in 1997.

Disbursement has grown significantly, as well, but has not kept up with the rapid inflow of new funds. An estimated ECU 777 million was still available for investment at year end 1997.

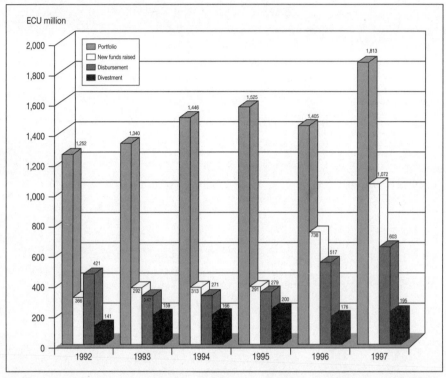

Source: EVCA

Fig. 2.16 ◆ Development of the Italian venture capital industry from 1992 to 1997 in terms of portfolio at cost, new funds raised, disbursement and divestment

The Italian Venture Capital Association (Associazione Italiana degli Investitori Istitutionali nel Capitale di Rischio (AIFI)) estimates that there were 229 venture capital executives in Italy in 1997. This figure has doubled from the 1993 estimate of 109 executives.

Legal and fiscal environment

There are no particular fiscal incentives for venture capital investments in Italy, but there is a wide range of general incentives to encourage investments, exports, reorganization of industrial enterprises and regional development. For example, long-term loans are provided to certain financial investors in order to finance up to 50 per cent of the acquisition of minority share holdings in small and medium-sized enterprises.

Corporate income tax regulations were significantly reformed in 1998 to enhance the capitalization of companies. These reforms include a reduction of the total corporate income tax rate, with specific additional benefits for companies that are going to be quoted on the Italian Stock Exchange. This 'Super DIT' (Dual Income Tax) legislation was expected to provide significant encouragement for venture capital, but has so far had little effect.

A new law for company reorganization and capital gains taxation is particularly relevant for the venture capital industry, as it affects the taxation of the sales of participations in controlled or affiliated companies. A new substitute tax of 27 per cent may be applied, at the taxpayer's discretion, to capital gain realized from the sale of such participations, providing they have been owned for at least three years. Investment funds are subject to a substitute tax at a rate of 12.5 per cent calculated on the mathematical difference between the net value of the fund at the end of the year (including distributions and reimbursement made during the year) and the net value at the beginning of the year.

According to AIFI, in addition to the above-mentioned tax legislation reforms, a strong fiscal stimulus would be needed to encourage the venture capital market in Italy, particularly in the smaller, early-stage end of the market.

Sources of new funds

Most of the significant growth in the inflow of new funds in 1997 came from abroad. While domestic capital accounted for 86 per cent of total new funds in 1996, in 1997 its proportion was less than half, 47 per cent. Other European countries represented 24 per cent and non-European countries 29 per cent of new funds in 1997. The current level of foreign funding in Italy is among the highest in Europe, exceeded only in the UK, Sweden and Greece. The amount of capital committed by domestic sources actually decreased by 26 per cent from 1996 to 1997.

The surge in foreign funding in 1997 reflects the fact that Italy is one of the target markets for funds which are pan-European or global in nature. The small group of domestic players on the market has generated good returns in past years, which has attracted international investors. Also, as a less developed market, Italy is less competitive than some of the more developed, 'over-crowded' markets. However, with the growing number of new foreign and domestic players on the market, competition for deals is increasing also in Italy.

Banks remain the single largest source of new funds, accounting for 47 per cent of total new funds in 1997. Investment by pension funds increased sharply from ECU 19 million in 1996 to ECU 134 million in 1997 (12 per cent of total new funds), entirely as a result of foreign pension funds investing in the market. Also domestic pension funds, which have only been established in recent years, are starting to develop to the stage where they can consider investing in venture capital, but it is likely to take several years before they will be a major source of capital for the Italian venture capital industry. Private individuals accounted for 10 per cent of new funds in 1997, and capital gains for 17 per cent. Corporate investors and insurance companies are marginal sources of new funds in Italy.

Disbursement patterns

Disbursement is very domestic in focus. In 1997, 82 per cent of the total value of investment went into 200 companies in Italy. Investments into nine companies in other European countries accounted for the remaining 18 per cent. These proportions have remained largely unchanged over recent years.

Of the 209 companies receiving investment in 1997, 80 per cent received venture capital backing for the first time. The proportion of initial investments is relatively higher in Italy than in the other major European markets.

Figure 2.17 illustrates the distribution of disbursement by the type of venture capital investor in 1997. In terms of investment volume, international investors are the largest group, representing 30 per cent of market value with a total investment of ECU 183 million in 1997. Most of these funds are newcomers to the Italian market. They typically focus on large buyout deals, where 'financial muscle' is more important than local knowledge. In terms of the number of deals, international investors were involved in only 16 per cent of all investments in 1997, reflecting their focus on the large end of the market.

Domestic banks and bank-related vehicles, which have traditionally dominated the market, were the second most active group, with a total investment of ECU 169 million in 1997, representing 28 per cent of market value and 22 per cent of the total number of deals. The domestic banks have better access to and more involvement in the Italian middle market, focusing on smaller buyouts, expansion investments and replacement capital deals. Public sector investors and the Italian co-operative sector are most active in seed and start-up financing.

Looking at Fig. 2.18, we see that buyouts represented 32 per cent of the total amount of investment and 12 per cent of the number of deals in 1997. Start-up deals accounted for 39 per cent of the number of investments but only 12 per cent of investment volume. No stable trends can be identified regarding recent changes in the stage distribution of investments, apart from an increase in the proportion of replacement capital from 13 per cent of total investment in 1993 to 29 per cent in 1997.

The average size of start-up deals was rather small, only ECU 0.8 million, compared with ECU 1.9 million for expansion investments, ECU 5.5 million for replacement capital, and ECU 7.2 million for buyouts. Italian replacement capital and buyout deals are, on average, larger than in the other major European markets. The small size of start-up deals indicates that the European trend towards larger early-stage deals has not yet been felt in Italy.

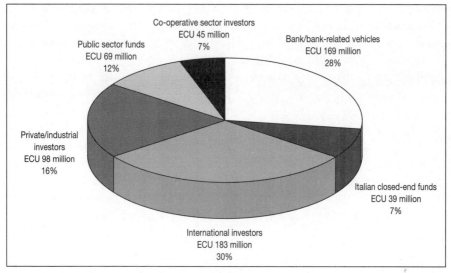

Source: AIFI

Fig. 2.17 ◆ Distribution of disbursement by venture capital investor type in Italy in 1997

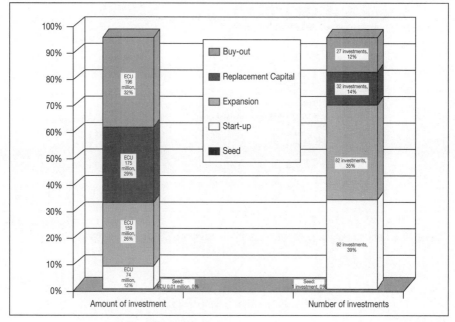

Source: EVCA

Fig. 2.18 ◆ Disbursement by stage in Italy in 1997

Figure 2.19 illustrates the sectoral distribution of venture capital investments in Italy from 1993 to 1997. Most investment has been received by the consumer-related sector, financial and other services, industrial products and services, and the category 'other manufacturing', which includes the textile industry.

Compared with other European markets, the level of investment into technology-based companies is rather low in Italy. In 1997, the combined technology sectors (including information and communications technologies, medical, health and biotechnology, energy technology, industrial automation, other electronics, and chemicals and materials) accounted for ECU 52 million, or 9 per cent of the total amount of investment. The 31 deals made into these sectors represented 13 per cent of the total number of investments. Contrary to the general trend in Europe, the proportion of technology investments in Italy has decreased. In 1993 they accounted for 15 per cent of the total amount of investment.

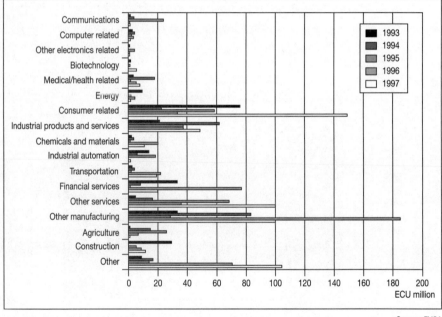

Source: EVCA

Fig. 2.19 ♦ Sectors receiving venture capital investment in Italy from 1993 to 1997

Exit mechanisms and performance

Trade sales are the most important exit route in Italy. They represented 66 per cent of divestment at cost, or ECU 129 million, in 1997. In terms of the number of divestments, the 74 trade sales represented 59 per cent of all divestments. The level of write-offs in Italy was the lowest in Europe in 1997. The proportion of write-offs of the total value of divestments at cost was only 1 per cent in 1997. Most of the write-offs were start-up investments.

Regarding exits through public offerings, the Italian market has started more or less from scratch in recent years. In 1997, only four exits through IPOs took place, compared with ten in 1996 and seven in 1995. The Italian Stock Exchange has gone through significant reforms, and is considering the launch of a special market for small and medium-sized companies, which could join the EURO.NM network.

The Italian Venture Capital Association (AIFI) reported that Italian venture capital funds performed strongly from 1986 to 1996. They generated an average 31.2 per cent gross IRR on realized investments in this ten-year period. Please note that this figure is not directly comparable with the European and UK performance figures, as it is measured as *gross*, not *net*, IRR.

Outlook

The Italian venture capital market has gained momentum as the amount of new funds has rapidly increased since 1996. Similarly to the UK, Italy has seen a rapid surge in foreign funds flowing into the market both from other European countries and from outside Europe. An increasing number of international venture capital companies have entered or are entering the Italian market, most often focusing on the buyout sector. Also the number of domestic players is rapidly growing. It seems that the dynamism brought by the international players is spreading to other segments of the market, as well.

According to the Italian Venture Capital Association, further fiscal incentives from the government would be needed to give a significant thrust to the early-stage sector in particular. The development of the Italian Stock Exchange is important in order to facilitate IPO exits.

Italy can be described as an exciting and innovative venture capital market, with plenty of unrealized potential. Growth will continue as the opportunities to exploit this potential continue to improve and both international and domestic investors take advantage of these opportunities.

Italian venture capital at a glance

Market development

- ◆ Fifth largest market in Europe; investment portfolio ECU 1.8 billion in 1997.
- ◆ Industry still underdeveloped relative to the size of the economy.
- ◆ Rapid growth since 1996; new domestic and international players coming to the market at a fast pace.
- ◆ International venture capital companies dominate the buyout sector; domestic banks focus on the middle market; other public and private sector investors are prominent in early-stage investing.

Sources of capital

- ◆ Domestic funds accounted for less than half, 47 per cent, of new funds in 1997.
- ◆ Both non-European funding and funding from other European countries are at a high level.
- ◆ Domestic banks and foreign pension funds are the main sources of new capital; also the amount of capital gains available for reinvestment and investment by private individuals are at a comparatively high level.

Disbursement patterns

- ◆ The vast majority of investments are made into companies in Italy.
- ◆ Proportion of early-stage investments is among highest in Europe; these investments tend to be rather small.
- ◆ Main industry sectors: the consumer-related sector, financial and other services, industrial products and services, and the textile sector.
- ◆ Technology investment at a very low level; contrary to the general trend in Europe, the level of technology investment has decreased in recent years.

Exits and performance

- ◆ Trade sales are the dominant exit mechanism; they accounted for two thirds of divestment in 1997.
- ◆ Least developed IPO market of the main European markets; only four exits through IPO took place in 1997.
- ◆ Average gross IRR for realized investments of Italian venture capital funds in 1986–96 was 31.2 per cent.

Key trends

- ◆ Rapid growth continues as foreign funds flow into the Italian market; the buyout sector remains the main focus of international players.
- ◆ Competition increases as a result of the growing number of players on the market.
- ◆ Development of the Italian Stock Exchange will lead to better exit opportunities.

DIMENSIONS OF NATIONAL DIFFERENCES

In the previous sections, we have individually discussed the venture capital industries in the UK, Germany, France, the Netherlands and Italy. It is clear that these national markets share a lot of characteristics and that they are increasingly becoming part of an integrated European venture capital market. But there are vital differences between the countries, as well. In this section, we shall contrast and compare the most important aspects of venture capital in the five national markets.

Market size and growth

Figure 2.20 compares the size of the five national venture capital markets in terms of the size of the investment portfolio, amount of new funds raised, and disbursement in 1997. As we have noted earlier, the UK is by far the largest venture capital market in Europe. It is also the fastest growing in terms of the amount of new funds raised.

A key point to note is that in the UK in 1997, the amount of new funds raised was nearly three times as large as disbursement. Also in Germany the amount of

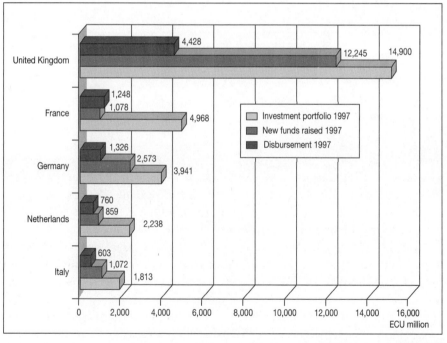

Source: EVCA

Fig. 2.20 ♦ Market sizes: comparison of the five national markets in terms of investment portfolio, new funds raised and disbursement in 1997

65

new funds significantly exceeded disbursement. In the 1998 statistics, therefore, we are likely to see a surge in disbursement, as the funds still available at year end 1997 will have been invested. Also, a significant proportion of these funds will have been invested abroad, as the UK and Germany are the main pan-European fundraising centres.

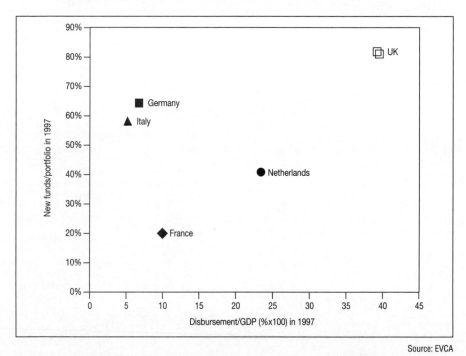

Fig. 2.21 ◆ Comparison of the major European markets in terms of relative size (x-axis) and growth rate (y-axis)

Figure 2.21 compares the five national venture capital industries in terms of their size in proportion to the economy and their growth rate in 1997. On the x-axis is the amount of disbursement in 1997 as percentage of GDP. On the y-axis, as our measure of growth rate, is the amount of new funds raised as a percentage of the total investment portfolio in each country in 1997.

In Italy and Germany, the industry is still rather underdeveloped in relation to the size of the economies, but the present growth rate in these countries is very high. In the Netherlands, the industry is further developed in terms of size, and still growing quite rapidly. Of the five national markets, France has the slowest growth rate. The industry in France is marginally larger in relation to GDP than in Germany or Italy. And as we have already seen, the UK has the largest market size as well as the fastest growth.

Figure 2.21 above is a snapshot of the present situation. But how does the growth of the five markets compare over a five year period? Figure 2.22 illustrates the growth rate of each of the markets from 1993 to 1997. As a measure of growth, we again use the ratio: new funds/portfolio size in each year.

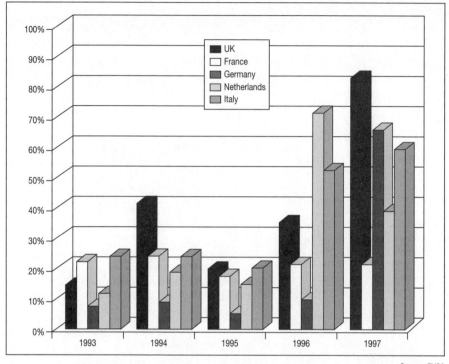

Source: EVCA

Fig. 2.22 ♦ Growth rate measured as the proportion of new funds of the investment portfolio in a country each year, 1993–7

The UK has seen fluctuations in the rate of growth, probably due to fundraising cycles, with an enormous surge in 1997. In Italy, growth accelerated in 1996, and continued to increase in 1997. The Netherlands saw a surge in 1996, and growth in 1997 was still rapid, although it decreased from the record level of 1996. Rapid growth in Germany started only in 1997, later than in the other markets. France has not seen the high growth levels of the other countries – the French growth rate has remained rather stable in the five-year period. We should again note that the growth rates in the UK and Germany are inflated by funds being raised for pan-European investment.

Sources of new funds

Figure 2.23 compares the five major European markets in terms of the distribution of new funds according to source in 1997. As we can see, banks are a major source of funds in all of the markets, but they are most prominent in Germany, the Netherlands and Italy. France is peculiar in that the proportion of capital gains available for reinvestment is significantly higher than in the other countries. This is explained by France's lower growth rate in terms of the amount of new funds raised.

Pension funds and insurance companies are the most important sources of capital in the UK. They are significant and growing sources also in the Netherlands and to a lesser degree in Germany and Italy. A high proportion of new funds raised from pension funds and insurance companies is coming from the USA.

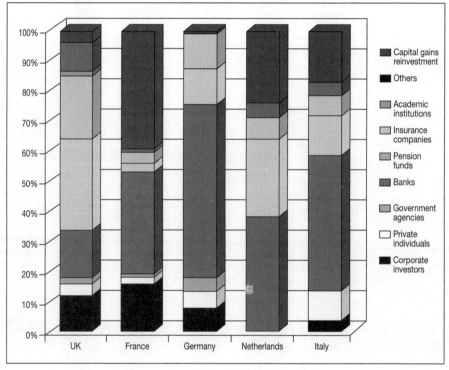

Source: EVCA

Fig. 2.23 ♦ **Distribution of new funds according to source in 1997**

The general trend is towards more foreign funds flowing into the European national markets. But the countries vary a great deal in the degree to which this shift from domestic to foreign funding has so far taken place. Figure 2.24 illustrates the geographic breakdown of new funds in each of the five national markets in 1997.

The UK is clearly the main centre for non-European fundraising, with 47 per cent of new funds coming from non-European sources. Especially investors from the USA have traditionally tended to approach Continental Europe via the UK. Germany, Italy and the Netherlands have a high proportion of funds coming in from other European countries. The UK is an important source of these funds. France is by far the most domestic market, with 86 per cent of funds still being raised domestically. As mentioned earlier, this is probably due to cultural and language barriers, as well as the small size and poor past performance of some French investment vehicles.

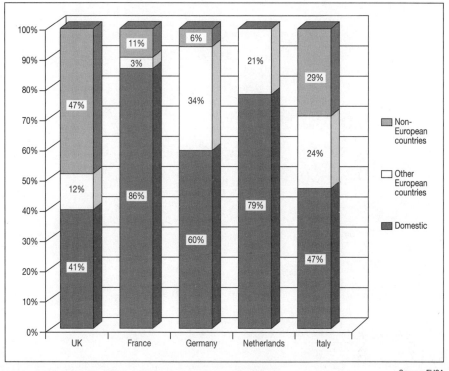

Source: EVCA

Fig. 2.24 ♦ Geographic breakdown of new funds in 1997

Disbursement patterns

The majority of funds in all of the national markets is disbursed domestically. As Fig. 2.25 illustrates, the Netherlands and the UK have the lowest proportions of domestic investment at 70 per cent and 74 per cent, respectively. In both of these countries, the industry is well-developed and the current situation is very competitive. As a result, venture capital companies are increasingly looking for investment opportunities abroad.

Germany and France still invest as much as 93 per cent of funds domestically. In Germany, the industry is at an earlier development stage, with domestic deal opportunities increasing rapidly. With the surge in new funds in 1997, foreign investments by German venture capital companies are likely to increase in the near future, particularly into Eastern Europe. In France, where the amount of new funds has been growing at a slower, more stable rate, there has not yet been a trend towards increasing investments abroad, either. Italy has proportionately more foreign investment than France or Germany. We must remember, however, that the 18 per cent of Italian investment which went into other European countries in 1997 went into only nine companies.

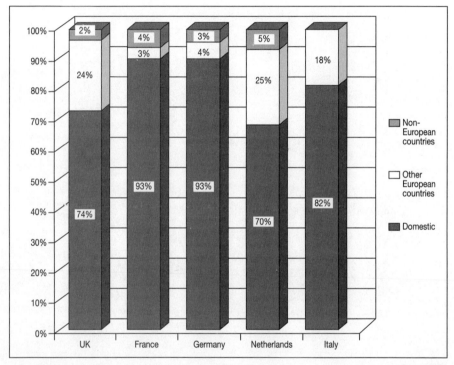

Source: EVCA

Fig. 2.25 ♦ Geographic breakdown of investments in 1997

Figure 2.26 compares the number of companies receiving venture capital funding according to investment stage in 1997. In all five markets, investments are most often made into companies seeking to expand their operations, for example, for increasing production capacity, for product or market development, or to provide additional working capital.

Surprisingly, the total number of companies receiving investment in 1997 was the same for the UK and France, 1090. The German figure was only slightly smaller, 958. This is remarkable considering that the total amount of disbursement in the UK was nearly four times larger than in France or Germany. The explanation lies partly in the high proportion of management buyouts and buy-ins in the UK,

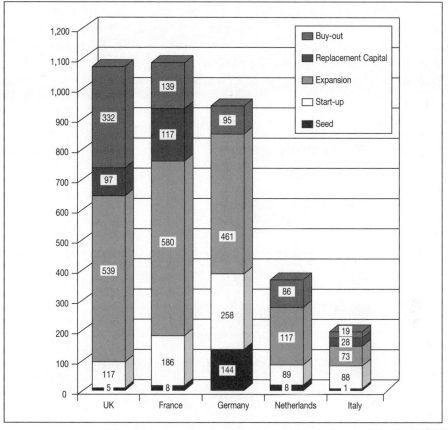

Source: EVCA

Fig. 2.26 ◆ Funding stage: distribution of investments according to stage, measured as the number of companies receiving investment in 1997

and also in the greater average deal sizes in the UK across all investment stages. National differences in deal sizes are discussed in more detail below.

Measured in absolute terms, Germany has by far the highest level of early-stage investment activity, with 144 companies receiving seed investments and 258 receiving start-up investments in 1997. France is second with eight seed and 286 start-up companies.

Figure 2.27 compares the five countries in terms of the proportion of companies receiving early stage investment as a percentage of the total number of companies receiving investment. In Italy and Germany, over 40 per cent of companies receiving investment were in the seed or start-up stage, followed by the Netherlands with 27 per cent. France and the UK had the lowest relative levels of early stage investments at 18 per cent and 11 per cent, respectively.

Figure 2.28 compares the average deal size, measured as the amount invested in a company, in each funding stage in the five national markets. The UK and Italy have the largest investment sizes in the buyout, replacement capital and expansion markets. Please note that Germany and the Netherlands do not collect data for replacement capital. In the Netherlands, start-up deals tend to be significantly larger than in the other countries. Seed financing deals in the UK and the Netherlands are much larger than in the other countries.

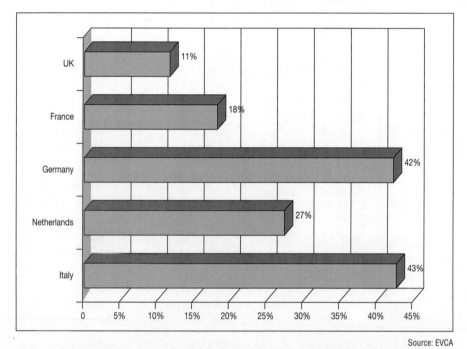

Source: EVCA

Fig. 2.27 ◆ Early stage investments: proportion of companies receiving seed and start-up investments as a percentage of the total number of companies receiving investment in 1997

In terms of the main industry sectors into which investments are made, the consumer-related sector, industrial products and services, as well as the categories 'other manufacturing', 'other services' and 'other' (which includes mining, utilities and conglomerates), were prominent sectors between 1993 and 1997 in all of the markets. The proportion of consumer goods and services has been particularly high in the UK. In Italy, the category 'other manufacturing', which includes the textile industry, and the financial services sector have been important. The Netherlands has had the most balanced distribution of investments across a variety of sectors.

Figure 2.29 illustrates the amount invested in the combined technology sectors (including communications, the computer-related sector, other electronics, biotechnology, medical/health related technology, energy, and chemicals and materials) from 1993 to 1997 in the five markets. Germany, the UK and the Netherlands have

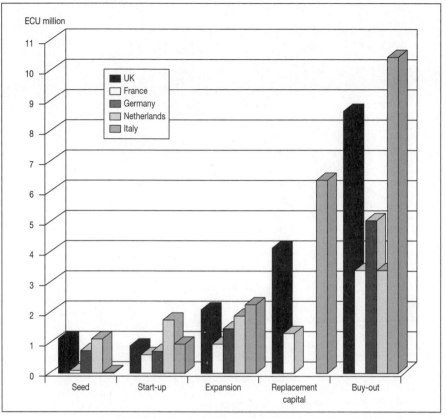

Source: EVCA

Fig. 2.28 ◆ Comparison of the five national markets in terms of the size of the average investment into a company according to the stage of investment in 1997

seen rapid growth in technology investments in the five-year period. In France and Italy there has only been marginal growth in these sectors.

Figure 2.30 depicts the development of technology investment as a percentage of total investment over the five-year period from 1993 to 1997 in each of the five countries. Germany has shown the most consistent growth in technology investment, from 16 per cent in 1993 to 31 per cent in 1997. The Netherlands had a record high in 1995, 54 per cent, but dropped in the following years, to 25 per cent in 1997. The UK has fluctuated between 19 per cent and 31 per cent in the five-year period. Technology investment in France grew from 18 per cent in 1993 to 28 per cent in 1996, but dropped again to 21 per cent in 1997. Italy has remained at a significantly lower level of technology investment throughout the five-year period. In 1997, only 9 per cent of Italian investment went into the combined technology sectors. Naturally, the level of technology investment in each country reflects the importance of technology sectors in the economy in general.

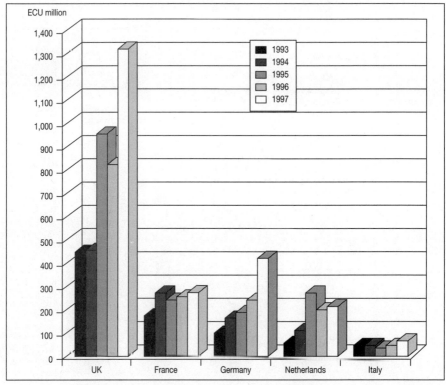

Source: EVCA

Fig. 2.29 ♦ Technology investment: amount of investment into the combined technology sectors from 1993 to 1997 in the five countries, ECU million

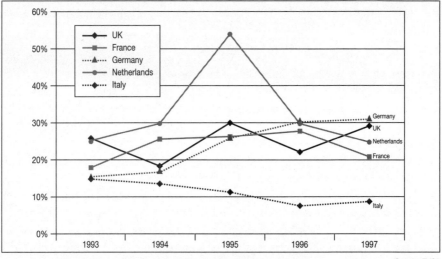

Source: EVCA

Fig. 2.30 ♦ Technology investment: investment into technology sectors as a percentage of total investment from 1993 to 1997 in the five countries

Exit mechanisms and performance

Figure 2.31 compares the five national markets in terms of the exit mechanisms used. Trade sales are the single most important exit mechanism in all five countries. Management-buy-backs (included in the category 'other') are most important in Germany and the Netherlands. The proportion of public offerings varies between 10 per cent and 20 per cent of divestment at cost in all of the markets, excluding Germany, where IPOs accounted for only 3 per cent of divestment in 1997.

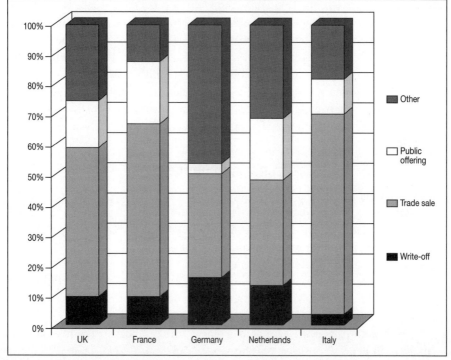

Source: EVCA

Fig. 2.31 ◆ Exits: Distribution of divestment at cost according to exit mechanism in the five national markets in 1997

Comparable performance statistics are not available for all of the five markets. We shall summarize the performance statistics for the five countries in any case. According to the UK study, venture capital funds generated a pooled net IRR of 15 per cent in the ten-year period from 1986 to 1996. This level of performance was higher than, for example, the returns generated by UK pension funds. In the same period, Dutch venture capital funds generated a pooled *gross* IRR of 13 per cent, which was lower than the 16 per cent achieved by quoted equities in the Netherlands. French venture capital funds performed somewhat better than their Dutch counterparts, generating a 16 per cent pooled gross IRR from 1986 to 1996. The

Italian Venture Capital Association reported that Italian funds performed strongly from 1986 to 1996, generating a pooled gross IRR of as much as 31 per cent.

The French, Dutch and UK studies all found that buyout funds were performing better than early-stage or development funds. This is not surprising considering that buyouts have much shorter investment periods, are much less risky, and require less 'hands-on' management from venture capitalists. Early-stage funds were, in aggregate, the worst performers in all three countries. Especially the Dutch and French early-stage funds fared badly in the ten-year period from 1986 to 1996.

Performance levels seem to have improved in recent years. The unrealized gross IRR at year end 1996 in the Netherlands was 15 per cent. The UK reported a pooled net IRR of 21 per cent in 1997. The corresponding figure for Germany was 17–18 per cent, according to an unofficial estimate by the German Venture Capital Association. In France, the pooled gross IRR in 1997 was 22 per cent. In all of these countries, the improved performance of early-stage funds in particular is driving up the overall performance figures. In general, the better IPO possibilities, the growing expertise of fund managers, and the increasing number of deal opportunities have been the main factors leading to the improved performance of early-stage funds.

Trends and outlook

The key trends are similar across the five national markets, reflecting broader European development patterns rather than national trends. Rapid growth is taking place mainly in the buyout and early-stage sectors. Particularly the UK is experiencing overheating of the buyout sector. Both fundraising and investment activity are becoming increasingly international. This trend is apparent in all of the markets with the exception of France, which has so far remained more isolated than the other markets. Venture capital funds are becoming more specialized according to regions, industries or investment stages.

As for European venture capital as a whole, the outlook for the five national markets is, in general, positive. No shortage of new funds is expected. IPO opportunities are improving with the development of European small-cap markets. With the introduction of the Euro and the growing efforts to harmonize fiscal and legal conditions, it is likely that the national markets will increasingly become part of a truly pan-European, flourishing venture capital industry.

National comparisons at a glance

Market size and development

◆ The UK is the largest and fastest growing venture capital market in Europe.

◆ The UK, Germany, Italy and the Netherlands have all experienced a fundraising boom in 1996 and/or 1997; growth in France has been slower and more stable.

◆ Banks are a major source of capital in all of the markets.

◆ Insurance companies and pension funds are most important in the UK; capital gains reinvestment is a major source in France.

◆ Highest levels of corporate investment are in the UK and France.

◆ The UK is the main centre for non-European fundraising.

◆ Germany, the Netherlands and Italy receive a high proportion of new capital from other Western-European countries – the UK is an important source of these funds.

◆ The French venture capital market is the most domestic in nature.

Disbursement patterns

◆ Expansion funding is the most common investment stage in all of the markets.

◆ The UK has the highest proportion of management buyouts and buy-ins.

◆ Early-stage investment is highest in Germany and Italy, lowest in the UK.

◆ Technology investment is highest in the UK and Germany, lowest in Italy.

◆ Deals tend to be larger in the UK across all investment stages; Dutch early stage investments and Italian later stage deals are comparatively large.

Exits and performance

◆ Trade sales are the dominant exit mechanism in all of the markets.

◆ Management-buy-backs are more significant in Germany than the other markets; Germany has the lowest level of IPOs.

◆ The possibilities for IPOs are historically best in the UK and have improved in the other countries, as a result of the establishment of the new stock markets for young growth companies.

◆ Performance of venture capital funds in all of the national markets has improved in recent years.

Key trends

◆ Key trends are similar across the markets.

◆ Rapid growth in early-stage investing and in the buyout market.

◆ Increasing internationalization both in terms of fundraising and investment, can be seen so far in all of the markets except France.

Notes

1. In line with common practice, we use the term "buyout" to denote both management buyouts and management buy-ins.
2. British Venture Capital Association and Coopers & Lybrand (1998) *The Economic Impact of Venture Capital in the UK*.

3

STRUCTURING VENTURE CAPITAL FUNDS FOR INVESTMENT: THE LEGAL DIMENSION

Jonathan Blake
S. J. Berwin & Co.

 **Jonathan Blake** is a partner with S. J. Berwin & Co. where he is the head of the private equity group in the corporate finance department. He advises private equity funds, investing institutions and management teams on management buyouts, venture and development capital investments and related taxation issues. He also advises venture capital fund managers in many countries in Europe and elsewhere on the structuring of venture capital funds and management companies.

He is a member of the taxation committee and a former council member of the British Venture Capital Association in which capacity he has been closely involved with the development of the Venture Capital Trust proposals with the Inland Revenue and the Treasury. He was previously responsible for negotiating with the Inland Revenue and Department of Trade and Industry, an agreed statement and guidelines on the use of limited partnerships as venture capital investment funds. He is also chairman of the tax and legal subcommittee of the European Venture Capital Association in which capacity he has produced and edited several publications on venture capital related matters across Europe. He is the author of a book entitled *AIM and EASDAQ – The New Enterprise Markets* published by FT Law and Tax.

INTRODUCTION

Many taxation and legal issues arise in relation to the structuring of venture capital funds for investments. There are no easy answers and the optimum structure will depend on the requirements of structures of the individual investors and the country or countries in which the investments are to be made and from which a fund is to be managed.

This chapter therefore gives general guidance as to the issues which need to be considered in structuring funds for investment, but cannot be taken as advice in relation to any specific case as this will always depend on the individual circumstances.

COMMERCIAL STRUCTURES

Quite apart from legal and tax constraints, there are a number of ways in which a fund may need to be structured from a commercial point of view.

Self-liquidating fund

The most typical commercial structure for a venture capital fund is the limited life self-liquidating fund, often structured as a limited partnership. Here a number of investors, which are usually institutions, commit to advance up to a certain amount to the fund during its lifetime. Commitments are drawn down as funds are needed to make investments or to pay costs, expenses or management charges, and usually relatively little is left drawn down but uncommitted. Funds are dispersed in making investments immediately following drawdown. When investments are sold, or when interest or dividends are received, these are distributed to investors as soon as practicable. Thus the fund is self-liquidating as the underlying investments are realized. Proceeds of sale are not reinvested. Instead the manager raises a new fund once a fund is substantially invested which is approximately every two to three years. In addition to this, the fund usually has a limited life of approximately ten years, in which time the objective is for the manager to have realized all investments.

Evergreen fund

In contrast to the self-liquidating fund, some funds do not automatically distribute dividends and proceeds of realization of investments but instead reinvest them in further investments. This may go on either for ever or until a pre-agreed liquidation date. Sometimes it is agreed that a resolution will be put to the participants of the fund to consider liquidation after a set number of years. While this prevents the fund manager having to raise new funds every three years or so, it also means that investors will not be able to realize their investments out of the proceeds of the underlying investments themselves and instead will only be able to realize their investments by selling the entire interest in the fund or by waiting until its liquidation date. For this reason, many such funds are often quoted on a stock exchange. One problem that often arises here is that the price at which shares in an investment fund stand on the market is often at a discount to the net asset value.

For some investors, the existence of a quote is essential if they are to be able to put a proper value on their investment in the fund at all. This may be the case with some insurance companies, pension funds or other institutions from certain countries which are required by law to maintain solvency margins and therefore to value their assets on the basis of solvency. In the USA and the UK, at least, it does not normally appear necessary for the fund to have a quote.

Club/parallel investment arrangements

Some arrangements are not structured as funds at all but instead are merely investment clubs or a series of parallel management agreements between investors and a particular fund manager. Under these the fund manager agrees to make investments on behalf of the investor directly in the underlying companies. This clearly has the advantage of simplicity in terms of the documentation with investors, but because there is no entity constituting the fund it is more difficult for the manager to keep control of the assets, and it is more difficult to manage the process where there are many investors.

Non-discretionary funds

All the above have assumed that the fund manager will have discretion over the funds being managed. In some cases, particularly where one is simply dealing with parallel investment management agreements, discretion in relation to the making of investments is left to the client.

Funds for individuals

Other considerations such as taxation or regulatory issues sometimes arise when structuring funds for investment by individuals. Often these need to be structured as quoted companies.

Fund or holding company

In some cases, it is not entirely clear whether one is really looking at a fund which is designed to make and dispose of investments with a view to realizing the capital profit from the sale of investments individually, or whether what is being done is to build a holding company which will retain investments or will instead realize itself by an initial public offering (IPO) on the stock exchange. In some cases the manager may wish to retain flexibility as to whether the objective is to realize individual investments or whether it is to retain them and create marketable securities in the vehicle itself.

A simple fund structure

Figure 3.1 illustrates a simple structure applicable to most funds.

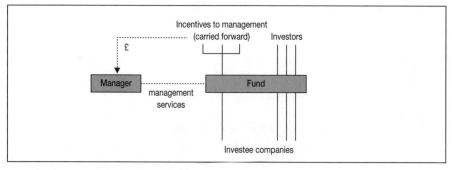

Fig. 3.1 ♦ Simple fund structure applicable to most funds

Normally the fund is just a pool of cash which is managed by a separate manager, and the manager will be owned either by a financial institution or by the executives of the manager itself. The fund is owned by its investors, who hold shares, units or limited partnership interests in the fund (depending on the structure). The fund then in turn invests money in investee companies. There is usually a carried interest in favour of the manager or its executives, and this is often structured as an interest in the fund itself.

OBJECTIVES

In structuring a venture capital fund, the manager or promoter will have in mind a number of objectives.

Limited liability

Investors will want to see their liability for their investment in the fund limited to the amount of their investment, as they will not be playing an active part in the management of the investments.

Avoiding an additional level of tax

The key requirement is to avoid tax being payable once by the fund when it receives a dividend or interest from investee companies or realizes a capital gain and again by investors when they realize their investment in the fund. For this reason the fund normally needs to be exempt or transparent to tax. A common principle is that an investor should be no worse off than it would have been had it made an investment directly. In some cases, it is possible to be more ambitious than this and to create a situation where an investor is better off by investing through a fund than it would have been had it invested directly.

Suitability for all kinds of investors

It is normally desirable to have a single fund structure for all types of investors, whether they be exempt pension funds, insurance companies, banks, industrial or trading companies or private individuals, coming from whatever jurisdiction. This will not always be possible because of conflicting taxation, regulatory and commercial requirements, but it is an ideal to aim for.

Where it is not possible, one can either make an arrangement so that investors of a particular category would invest in a feeder fund, which in turn would invest in the main fund structure; or one could arrange a parallel fund structure which would make investments and sell them alongside the principal fund and be managed in common with it. Alternatively, investors for whom no fund structure is appropriate may be invited to co-invest alongside the fund, perhaps through the use of the same nominee company which holds the shares for the fund and on the basis that investors have no discretion over such shares but merely follow the fund.

Tax efficient management charge

If possible, the management charge should be structured so as to minimize the impact of irrecoverable value added tax on the fund. In addition, to the extent that the fund receives income and capital profits which are applied in payment of the management charge, neither the fund itself nor the investors should be taxed on profits.

Tax efficient carried interest

The carried interest is normally structured as an interest in the fund itself, although it could be structured as a bonus management charge. On the one hand, the fund should be tax efficient for the fund itself, so that, as with the management charge, the fund does not suffer irrecoverable VAT, and profits earned with the fund which are applied towards the carried interest are not taxed in the hands of the fund or investors; on the other hand, it should also be tax efficient for the individuals or the management company receiving it. This can best be achieved by making the carried interest a capital interest in the fund itself.

Marketable to suitable investors

Many countries have marketing laws along the lines of the UK Financial Services Act or the US Securities Acts which restrict the marketing of funds depending on their structures and depending on the investors they are seeking to attract. Since the restrictions vary for different types of reasons, a structure will need to be chosen which permits marketing to the investors being targeted. This is particularly the case where the fund is to be marketed to private individuals.

Simplicity of administration

The structure should be simple to operate to the extent that this is consistent with the objectives above, and if it is inconsistent one will need to consider carefully whether it is more important to have a structure which is simple to operate or one which meets all those objectives. For example, use is often made of fund structures resident in a country where little or no tax is payable and this entails the need to hold meetings of the fund outside the country where the investment executives carry on business and also to have documents signed abroad.

TYPICAL TERMS AND CONDITIONS

Term

A typical term is eight to ten years with provision for an extension of two to three years, often requiring the consent of 75 per cent of investors.

Management charge

This is usually up to 2.5 per cent per annum of the committed capital for the fund, and often more for funds. Sometimes the management charge is index linked. However, for larger funds it is often appropriate for the figure of 2.5 per cent to be reduced.

Sometimes there is a commitment period (*see* Drawdowns and distributions, below), after which the percentage rate decreases, and the percentage rate applies to the amount drawn down at the end of the commitment period (possibly plus a provision to follow-on investments). In addition, there is usually provision for the management charge to reduce according to the cost of investments which are realized and distributed.

Drawdowns and distributions

Increasingly, funds provide for drawdowns to be made on an 'as needed' basis. However, some funds which have commitment periods only allow drawdowns for investment to be made in, say, the first five years of the life of the fund. Thereafter only a percentage, say, 25 per cent of initial commitments, may be drawn down and only for follow-on investments.

Most funds provide for all income and capital to be distributed as soon as possible after receipt, although sometimes income is distributed only once or twice a year. Under limited partnership structures, partners are liable to tax on their income and gains as if they receive them at the time when the fund received the income or gain.

Many funds have provisions for underwriting or bridging investments so that if a realization takes place within six months of an investment, the amount realized does not need to be distributed and can be reapplied in making new investments. Alternatively, the proceeds are distributed but are available for recall.

Management company/general partner

Most funds allow a majority of, say, 75 per cent of investors to remove the manager/general partner at any time, but if that removal is without cause (that is, in the absence of negligence or reckless disregard of duties or default), compensation equal to two or three years' management charge is payable. Some funds provide for investors also to have the right of termination by 75 per cent vote if the key people involved in the manager/general partner leave.

Fees and expenses

Most funds allow organizational expenses up to, say, 1 per cent of the fund, to be borne by the fund at the outset. In many cases, however, placing fees may not be borne by the fund and many investors, particularly US ones, do not think it is right that they should bear any part of the placing fees.

Certain ongoing expenses of running the fund are borne by the fund. These would include audit fees and the costs of any investor committee. However, investors are increasingly requiring all other expenses to be borne out of the management charge, although this may depend on the type of fund under consideration. Usually the fund's costs of making an investment are borne by the investee company. The question arises whether any amount not borne by an investee company should be borne by the fund or by the manager out of the management charge. Likewise there is an issue as to who should bear the cost of abortive investments: many investors require this to be borne by the manager, although there is an argument that this would make the manager too cautious. This may not be appropriate for a small fund with high costs.

Similar issues arise with regard to fees received. These may include directors' fees, underwriting fees paid by the company, syndication fees paid by the company or by third-party investors, broken deal fees paid by the company (in respect of deals which do not proceed) and arrangement fees. Again, there are differences between funds as to which of such fees go to the manager and which go to the fund, but investors are increasingly requiring such fees to be paid into the fund except, perhaps, directors' fees, syndication fees so far as they relate to bringing in third-party investors, broken deal fees to the extent that they are matched by abort costs paid by the manager and corporate finance fees entered into on an arm's length basis. Here too the economics of the fund manager need to be taken into account and it is more likely that, for a small fund with high costs, the fees can be retained by the manager as opposed to larger buyout funds.

Carried interest

Most funds provide for a carried interest of, typically, 20 per cent of the gains and income realized by the fund. Most carried interests are on a 'fund as a whole' basis so that the carried interest only applies once investors have received the whole of their investment in the fund plus the hurdle. Some carried interests are on a 'deal-by-deal' basis so that the carried interest is payable if the rate of return on any deal exceeds the hurdle but, usually carried interests which are on a deal-by-deal basis often require unrealized investments to be valued and not be below cost before carried interest can be paid out. Some require the amount to be paid into escrow until the results on a 'fund as a whole' basis are known: in this latter case it is often better to go for a 'fund as a whole' basis as it is more tax efficient.

Usually the carried interest is subject to a hurdle of, say, 10 per cent so that it only applies once investors have received a 10 per cent rate of return on their investment. There are many different types of hurdle. Some funds have stepped carried interests so that the amount of the carried interest depends on the internal rate of return (IRR). Thus, for example, there might be a 15 per cent carried interest on a 10 per cent IRR and a 20 per cent carried interest on a 15 per cent IRR.

In many cases the hurdle is subject to a right of catch-up for the holders of the carried interest so that realizations are applied first to the investors until they have received their initial investment in the fund plus a hurdle. Then all realizations are applied to the holders of the carried interest until they have 'caught up' on the hurdle, so that by the end of the catch-up period they have 20 per cent of all sums distributed in excess of the original investment by investors. Thereafter all realizations are shared in the proportion 80:20.

Many investors require at least 50 per cent and sometimes at least 75 per cent of the carried interest to be in the hands of individual members of the management team rather than the management company or its controlling group. Usually there are also leaver and joiner provisions as between the members of the management team to ensure that if members of the management team leave they have to give up part of their carried interest depending on the circumstances (for instance, whether they are good or bad leavers and the length of time

87

they have been there), and to ensure that carried interest is made available for new members of the management team who may join. Investors are not normally party to these leaver and joiner arrangements.

Increasingly there are provisions for the carried interest to be reduced or be subject to capping if the manager/general partner is removed.

For English tax purposes there is an advantage in allocating all gains to investors while proceeds of realization are paid to them (that is, until the carried interest cuts in): otherwise the holders of the carried interest will be liable to tax on the gains allocated to them even though there may be a restriction on distribution until the carried interest cuts in. This involves a reallocation of such gains once the carried interest does become payable.

STRUCTURING VENTURE CAPITAL FUNDS

The main issue which arises in structuring venture capital funds is to avoid the additional layer of taxation (often called the 'double charge') which would arise if investors simply invested in a company which in turn made investments in the desired investee companies. Tax would then arise both on the sale by the fund company of its interests in the investee companies and again on the distribution of those gains to investors or on the disposal by investors of their interests in the fund company. Also, in most jurisdictions the distribution of proceeds of sale of individual investments during the life of the fund will be treated as a dividend rather than a partial realization of capital, thus converting a capital gain which arises on the sale of an investment at a profit into income. Although there are certain investors such as Continental European companies for whom this can be an advantage, a general principle in structuring venture capital funds is that most investors will be best served by a structure under which they will be in a similar position by investing through the fund as they would have been in by investing directly into the investee companies (or at least no worse off). Occasionally some structures can result in certain investors being better off than they would have been had they invested directly, but this usually entails a structure which is not so widely acceptable.

Two types of structures avoid the double charge to taxation: exempt (or non-transparent) structures and transparent structures, and these are discussed below. Another major tax constraint in structuring venture capital funds arises from the fact that certain countries impose a charge to capital gains tax on sales of shares by non-residents. This charge is usually removed where the non-resident investor is resident in a country which has a double tax treaty with the country in which the investment is made. Where there is a non-transparent structure, it will be important that the country of the non-transparent structure has such a double tax treaty. It is, however, relatively rare for countries both to have double tax treaties and to be low tax jurisdictions. Where the structure is transparent, it will be important that the country where the investment is made recognizes the transparency of the transparent structure and that each investor's country has a double tax treaty with the country concerned.

Finally, it will usually be necessary to conduct the affairs of the fund in such a way as to avoid there being a permanent establishment in the country concerned, as this will make it more likely that tax will be payable there. These points are discussed below.

Non-transparent structures

In an exempt non-transparent structure, gains made by the fund suffer no tax in the fund and tax only arises on the distribution of profits to investors. This usually involves the use of a company situated in a tax haven (such as the Channel Islands) or a country providing a specific exemption from tax on capital gains and possibly income (for instance the Dutch BV (private limited liability company) with the participation privilege, the UK investment trust and the French Sociétés de Capital Risque (SCR)). Four possible problems arise as follows.

◆ Where the fund is situated in a tax haven, there is unlikely to be a double tax treaty between the country of residence of the fund and that of the investee companies (or, indeed, of the investors). Thus, depending on whether the country of residence of the investee company charges non-resident investors to capital gains tax in the absence of an applicable double tax treaty or imposes high withholding taxes on income or capital gains (which would normally be reduced by the application of a double tax treaty), there may be a significant tax cost.

◆ Even where the fund is situated in a country which does have the benefit of double tax treaties, there will often be withholding tax on distributions to investors.

◆ Distributions to investors during the life of the fund, or even on its termination, may be taxed as income rather than as capital gains, which may cause a problem for some investors.

◆ An investor's country of residence may have legislation along the lines of the US passive foreign investment company (PFIC) legislation or the UK offshore fund legislation, which may have an adverse effect.

Transparent structures

In transparent structures, such as limited partnerships, investors are liable to tax on the disposal of an investment by the fund, on their share of the profit whether or not it is distributed to them. A structure which is fully tax transparent will result in each investor being treated as if it had made a proportionate investment in each underlying investee company and as if all income and profits from an investee company allocated to it through the fund was derived directly from that investee company. This will therefore avoid a double charge to tax while at the same time preserving the investor's ability to apply the benefit of any double tax treaty between its country of residence and the country of residence of the investee company.

There will be a question for each relevant country as to whether the transparency of the particular structure is recognized in that country, and this sometimes creates a problem. Even where transparency is recognized, care needs to be taken to ensure that the fund itself does not cause investors to be treated as carrying on business in another country through a permanent establishment, thus becoming liable to tax in that country at a higher rate than the one applicable in their own country. Special care is required in obtaining local advice when planning a fund for investment in a particular jurisdiction.

Double tax treaties

Certain countries impose a charge of capital gains tax on sales by non-residents which is removed if the non-resident comes from a country which has a double tax treaty with the country concerned – it is necessary to choose a country which has both low tax and a good network of double tax treaties. Obviously this is quite rare, but possibilities include Holland, Luxembourg and Cyprus. The difficulty which then arises is that in both cases the use of a company can transform capital gains into income, and in the case of Holland, this may be subject to high withholding taxes on distribution to foreign residents (subject to reduction where double tax rates apply). By contrast, the use of a transparent structure such as a limited partnership should preserve the ability to claim the benefit of double tax treaties between the country of the investor and the country in which the investment is made, while at the same time preserving the capital gains tax treatment of profits on the disposal of investments.

Permanent establishment

Whether the structure being used is transparent or non-transparent, it will be important to ensure that it does not operate through a permanent establishment in the country where it is investing, if that is a country where the presence of a permanent establishment might lead to taxation there without the possibility of a release through a double tax treaty. In such cases, the funds must be managed from outside – in a country where the presence of a permanent establishment would not create adverse tax consequences. Such countries would include the Channel Islands, although they might also include the UK and Holland. Where the investment process involves a team which is operating in a country where a permanent establishment is to be avoided, such a team's function must be limited to the provision of advice to a foreign manager, with actual investment and divestment decisions being taken in the country of the manager – as would, in many cases, the actual signing of investment and divestment agreements. This is a matter over which a great deal of care needs to be taken and for which local advice will be necessary.

At the same time it would be important to avoid or minimize value added tax on the management charge or on any fee charged by local advisers to the manager. This is usually best achieved by situating the manager in a non-VAT country such as one of the Channel Islands. Any fees then charged by advisers or other suppliers of services to the manager would also be outside the scope of VAT but with full input recovery so that attributable VAT inputs might still be recoverable.

TYPICAL LEGAL STRUCTURES

Many different types of legal structure have been used for private equity investment. Many of these have been discussed in this chapter but they include the following.

Transparent structures

Limited partnership

The main transparent structure is the limited partnership, which can be formed under the laws of England, the Channel Islands, Delaware or various tax havens such as the Cayman Islands or Bermuda. These are extremely flexible structures and particularly suitable for self-liquidating funds. The main issues which arise are that some countries do not regard them as transparent and that they cannot (at least without considerable difficulty) be quoted on a stock exchange.

Parallel investment

This has been discussed above.

Non-transparent structures

UK investment trust

This is a UK investment company which is resident in the UK and whose shares are quoted on the stock exchange. It enjoys exemption from UK tax on capital gains provided it complies with certain requirements.

Jersey companies

These are many other tax haven companies which can be used and can be quoted. The main issue which arises is that they do not benefit from double tax treaties and in order to invest in some countries they would need to act through intermediate companies if they are to avoid local taxation being imposed.

Dutch BV

A Dutch BV enjoys the participation privilege whereby no tax is payable in Holland provided it owns more than 5 per cent of the shares in underlying companies. However, there is withholding tax on distributions out of Holland. Distributions (even on a liquidation) are treated as income rather than capital gains.

Others

The main non-transparent structures are as above, but a number of other structures involve Malta, Luxembourg or Madeira and may also be worth considering.

US INVESTORS

Many funds for investment in private equity will want to target US investors, many of which will be tax exempt. Such US investors have a number of requirements which will need to be included, including the following.

Partnership

If the investment is through a partnership it is important that it qualifies as a partnership for US tax purposes. The rules on this are becoming easier to comply with but certain US partners require the general partner to have an interest in the fund of approximately 1 per cent of commitments, and a number of other tests need to be checked.

Employee Retirement Income Security Act (ERISA)

Where US pension funds invest in a fund in which more than 25 per cent of the interests are held by pension funds (including non-US pension funds), it is necessary for the fund to qualify as a 'venture capital operating company'. Broadly, for this to be the case, the fund needs to have management rights in at least 50 per cent (by acquisition cost) of its investments. If the fund has a right to appoint a director to the board of the investee company, that will be sufficient, but other rights without the right to appoint a director can also constitute management rights for this purpose.

Unrelated Business Taxable Income (UBTI)

Again, US tax exempt investors will want to ensure that the fund does not receive UBTI. Thus, if the fund receives trading income directly rather than just investment income, this could be treated as UBTI. Another way in which UBTI can arise (which is not obvious) is that if the fund borrows to make investments, then dividends and capital proceeds from that investment can be treated as UBTI in certain circumstances.

Investment Companies Act

A number of detailed disclosures will need to be given both by US and non-US investors in a fund.

Controlled Foreign Corporation (CFC)

If more than 50 per cent of the interests in the fund are held by US holders then the fund could be treated as a CFC, and if it then has a controlling stake in companies in which it invests, they will be treated as CFCs which give rise to certain filling and taxation requirements on US investors.

CONCLUSION

In conclusion therefore, the choice of structure will depend partly on the country or countries in which the investments are to be made, partly on the tax position of the carried interest holders and partly on the specific backgrounds and requirements of investors in the fund. In most cases, a limited partnership appears to be the most flexible structure, but it is always necessary to take good up-to-date advice.

FUND-RAISING

AND

INVESTOR RELATIONS

Janet Brooks
ECI Ventures

Introduction
Targeting the investor
Identifying investor requirements
Launching the fund
Investor relations
Conclusion

Janet Brooks is a director of ECI Ventures, where she has responsibility for fundraising, investor relations and deal flow marketing. Founded in 1976, ECI Ventures is one of the oldest and most experienced private equity groups in the UK. It specializes in mid-sized buyouts, buy-ins and business development transactions requiring total financing of up to £40 million. ECI Ventures currently manages private equity funds with a capital base of £240 million. Its most recent fund, ECI 6, closed in April 1998 having raised £106 million from institutional and private investors in the UK, USA, continental Europe, Far East and Middle East.

Janet Brooks joined ECI Ventures in 1992, having previously been an investment manager at VenCap International, managing a portfolio of private equity funds on behalf of several institutional investors. Prior to that, she worked at Charterhouse Investment Management and Andersen Consulting. She holds an MA from Cambridge University and an MBA from INSEAD.

INTRODUCTION

Marketing venture capital funds

In the increasingly competitive venture capital markets of the late 1990s, venture capital managers are having to become ever more sophisticated and professional in the ways that they raise funds and manage relations with investors. Effective marketing and communications have now become essential for a venture capital manager to attract, retain and expand the range of its investors. This means that to be successful, management needs a firm commitment to selling itself through sound analysis and convincing argument at all stages of the funding cycle, from the first decision to launch a fund to the design of a follow-up fund. This chapter looks at this process in four parts: targeting the investor; identifying investor requirements; launching the fund; and investor relations.

TARGETING THE INVESTOR

The nature of venture capital means that it is likely to appeal only to a certain type of investor. Its illiquidity and high perceived risk mean that investors have to have substantial assets and be looking to the long term. As new investment opportunities open up through globalization, competition for funds is intensifying. Long before the launch of a fund, thorough research of investment markets is required to identify and understand the needs of potential investors.

Investors have a range of reasons for choosing venture capital, including the following as the most important.

◆ *High returns* This is the most commonly heard reason for investing in venture capital. Expectations have subsided from the early days when annual returns of 30 per cent were often quoted. While a few investors are still looking for returns of 20 to 25 per cent, most would be happy with a consistent 15 to 20 per cent per annum. Investors now tend to compare venture capital returns with quoted companies, adding a premium for the additional perceived risk.

◆ *Diversification* High exposure to the stock market, particularly in the UK and the USA, has led investors to consider alternative investments which have a low correlation with the quoted investments. Unquoted private equity investments have been shown to fulfil this need.

◆ *Long-term horizon* By nature, unquoted investments are illiquid and as such they attract a premium return. They are therefore suitable for investors who have long-term liabilities such as pension funds.

◆ *Research and development* In its original form of investing in early stage and technology-related companies, venture capital could give large corporations a relatively cheap way of accessing new ideas in the market. This is less the case today as venture capital has shifted to financing later stage companies and buyout transactions.

◆ *Employment* Small companies have proved very successful in generating employment in recent years, and this can prove a compelling reason for some investors, particularly government-related bodies. Although the pursuit of social goals could appear at odds with the traditional obligations of institutional investors such as pension funds to maximize financial returns, many investors will look at locally targeted venture capital funds in the hope of securing social and economic, as well as financial, returns.

On the other hand, set against these positive reasons for investing in venture capital, investors see a range of potential problems.

◆ *Lack of management resources* Selecting and carrying out due diligence on funds is very time consuming, as is the post-investment monitoring. For institutions who are allocating only a small portion of their assets to venture capital, it may be difficult to justify the personnel required in terms of the additional returns expected.

◆ *Inadequate benchmarks* Historically, it has been difficult to assess either the performance of funds over time or their relative performance against other funds. This has been a serious problem for institutions who mainly deal with quoted stock although recent moves by the European Venture Capital Association (EVCA) to produce industry statistics may lessen this in the future.

◆ *Illiquidity* This is a deterrent, especially to smaller investors with less certain liabilities. However, the rise of institutions willing to purchase secondary positions in venture funds, albeit at a discount to net asset value, has lessened this as a problem today.

At the same time, different types of investors – institutional, corporate and private – can have quite distinctive needs, which have to be taken into account during fund-raising. Across Europe, banks followed by pension funds and insurance companies have been the largest investors in venture capital if reinvested capital gains are put to one side (Fig. 4.1). This breakdown gives a somewhat misleading impression, since many banks only invest via their own venture capital subsidiaries. Looking at the funding sources for independent funds alone, statistics from the UK show pension funds in a predominant position (Fig. 4.2), and this is echoed in the USA. Leading categories of investors can be summarized as follows.

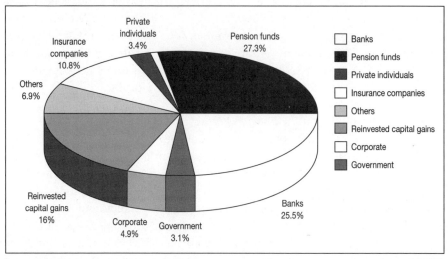

Source: EVCA 1995

Fig. 4.1 ◆ Who invests in venture capital?

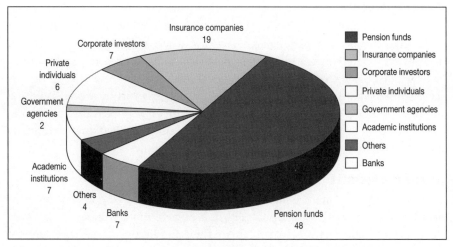

Source: British Venture Capital Association (average of 1993, 1994 and 1995)

Fig. 4.2 ◆ Money raised by independent funds in the UK by category of investor

Pension funds

Pension funds have long been the largest investors in independent venture capital funds in both the UK and the USA. While they are not so dominant in the rest of Europe, their importance is likely to grow over the next decade. Pension funds generally have long-term liabilities and limited requirements for liquidity, making venture capital an attractive option. The growth in pension fund assets world-wide since 1970 (from US$250 billion to US$3.5 trillion in the USA alone) makes this the core funding source for venture capital, and to date US pension funds have invested over US$20 billion in venture capital funds. Private equity has now been established as an asset class by pension funds, and US funds in particular are seeking to diversify their venture capital investments globally.

Insurance companies

As the major money managers in most countries, insurance companies have tended to invest in venture capital as an extension of their equity investment departments. The uncertain nature of their liabilities has meant that they have tended to be a more volatile group of investors than pension funds. Many a venture capital company has got close to receiving a large amount of funding from an insurance company only to be told that the latest hurricane has put a stop on all new investment. In addition, in many countries, including the USA and UK, certain restrictions are put on insurance companies regarding the way in which they value holdings in venture capital funds and these may be a disincentive to investment.

Corporate investors

Venture capital has also been used as a way for large corporations to engage in technology prospecting, gaining access to innovation, with a possibility of future acquisition. Some corporations, such as Shell Oil, have used in-house venture capital units, while others which have a wider field of interest, such as Monsanto, have chosen to invest via funds. This second strategy has, however, been less prevalent in the UK than in the USA. Corporate investors in venture capital may have tighter investment criteria and demand more detailed information on portfolio companies than is the norm for institutional investors.

Government agencies

Traditionally important, the public sector now represents a very small proportion of UK investment in venture capital. The bulk of government interest comes from local government agencies, which focus their funding on regionally targeted investments. Elsewhere in Europe the proportion from government-related bodies tends to be higher, and the European Bank for Reconstruction and Development alone has committed significant funding to the sector in Central and Eastern Europe over the last few years.

Private individuals

Private investors are a rare but potentially important category of investor. Most venture funds have been structured for institutional investors, typically with a £1 million minimum investment, keeping out all but the very wealthy. However, a few groups in the USA and Europe have chosen to specifically target private individuals as the benefits of quick internal decision making and more stable investment policies may outweigh the costs associated with a large number of small investors.

In the USA, the investor breakdown is similar, but with the addition of endowments, foundations and advisers or 'gatekeepers', who also play a significant role. All the major US universities have endowments, which for some can be sizeable: 15 universities have endowments worth more than US$1 billion, with Harvard reaching US$11 billion. These endowments have even longer and more certain liabilities than pension funds, and are now moving to invest globally. Charitable foundations are smaller, but some have proved important investors in venture capital and together with endowments provided 12 per cent of the money going into private equity funds in the USA in 1994.

Gatekeepers are financial intermediaries, representing mainly institutions with capital to invest. Large investment consultancies and managers in the USA often have units dedicated to private equity investments, while the number of independent venture capital specialists has grown substantially over the last few years. Their room for discretion varies considerably from a purely advisory relationship at one extreme, to the management of a 'fund-of-funds' with complete discretion over investments, at the other.

While the domestic market is always likely to be the largest source of finance for venture capital funds, the effect of global financial liberalization and increasing investor sophistication is expanding the number of investment markets from

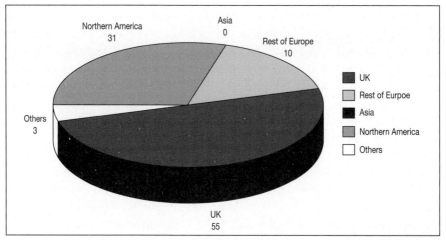

Source: BVCA (average of 1993, 1994 and 1995)

Fig. 4.3 ◆ Money raised by independent funds in the UK by source country

which venture capitalists can raise money. In the UK, for example, 45 per cent of investment in independent funds now comes from outside the UK, the bulk from North America (Fig. 4.3).

A decision to attract international capital will have significant implications for fund-raising. The costs and scope of marketing will be increased, and extra effort will be required to understand the culture and dynamics of different financial markets. This said, a firm foothold in the domestic market is a prerequisite for convincing international investors.

IDENTIFYING INVESTOR REQUIREMENTS

Investors interested in venture capital now have a wide range of funds to choose from. A persuasive package, based around the core information memorandum, is required to convince investors of the relative merits of a particular fund. Six main issues will influence their decision: the quality of the market analysis; the focus of the investment strategy; the composition of the management team; the company's track record; the structure of the fund; and the detailed terms and conditions.

Market analysis

At the macro-economic level, the investor needs to be able to determine that companies suitable for investment exist, that the risk of adverse political change is low and that there are options for realizing investments ('exit routes') and returning the capital to investors. While these issues are all out of the fund's direct control, the venture capitalist needs to be able to demonstrate that a broad range of investment opportunities are available where external funding would be acceptable and desirable. Investors may be particularly attracted to new market areas which offer the prospect for rapid economic growth and allow strategic research and development. Funds in Central and Eastern Europe may be able to benefit from this desire, and if this rationale is strong enough, investors may be prepared to make allowances in other areas such as track record and exit mechanisms. Foreign investors in particular need to be reassured about the risks of any possible change of government over the life of the fund, and informed of the prospects for price and currency stability so that value is maintained. A sophisticated capital market is essential to allow venture capitalists to exit their investments at reasonable valuations. While a thriving stock market for young growth companies (such as NASDAQ in the USA) is obviously beneficial, it is not a necessity. In many countries, including the UK and Germany, trade sales are the main way in which venture capitalists realize their investments. A good mergers and acquisition environment is therefore paramount.

Investors also look for evidence of an enterprise economy. This involves questions of business tradition and entrepreneurial spirit, as well as positive regulatory and tax structures. These are all factors that can encourage or discourage potential entrepreneurs to set up on their own. It is often argued that the reason why the German venture capital market did not develop as quickly as other markets is because of a cultural aversion of entrepreneurs to having outside shareholders. High capital gains taxation in other countries may also mean that managers could prefer to continue to earn a salary rather than risk security for capital growth.

Investment strategy

If an investor has decided to invest in a particular country or area, then the next major choice is to assess the compelling investment strategies presented by different funds. This is where the venture company needs to spell out its 'unique selling points' in terms of investment stage and sector, deal flow, decision-making and management approach.

A critical question for many investors is the fund's target stage and sectors for investment. Here, the fund has to make a persuasive case for its decisions. These can be as varied as specializing in early stage companies or in large buyouts, concentrating on making investments in a particular industry (such as biotechnology or media) or acting as a generalist, investing in all sectors and all stages of development. There are rarely any right or wrong answers to these questions but investors will expect to see a logical explanation of why the types of investments have been chosen.

Investors also like to see a proactive marketing strategy with regard to attracting investment deals ('deal flow'). Although many markets have gone through periods where demand for venture capital far outstrips supply – such as in the UK in the mid-1980s – investors will still want evidence that firms are hunting for the best deals. Arrangements can vary between sourcing investments directly, using intermediaries or building on previous investments. Investors are keen to ensure that the fund is not too dependent either on a single deal source or on a high level of deals sourced from other venture capital firms.

How the firm intends to conduct its due diligence on potential investments also receives attention from investors – especially those investing internationally. Investors need to see that it is possible both to conduct reference checks on individuals and to get an accurate financial picture of a potential investment.

The issue of whether the fund intends to have a hands-on or passive approach to managing its investments can also prove important for investors. At one extreme is the 'hands-on' or active approach, where a representative of the venture company will sit on the board of the company and will maintain a close dialogue with the company on all major operational and strategic issues. At the other extreme are passive investors whose role is limited to acting as a financial watchdog, ensuring that returns are meeting expectations. The stage and sector of the investment affects the management style considerably. Investors can be concerned with the resource implications of adopting an active management style, as time spent on portfolio company boards will reduce the ability of team members to make new investments.

The structure of investments is another key determinant. Some funds will only invest where they can take a majority holding of 51 per cent or more; others may take only minority positions. Where funds are in a minority situation, investors will want to see safeguards established, both in terms of rights to appoint a director and to receive management information, as well as restrictions on the management of the company in terms of asset sales and the issue of further shares. At the heart of these concerns is the importance investors attach to being able to achieve a profitable exit from an investment within the desired time-scale.

The manager's internal decision-making process should be of interest to investors. Investors like to be able to evaluate the relative contributions of all the members of a venture team and in order to do this they need to understand the process by which potential investments are evaluated and decisions reached. In general, investors prefer structures that promote a cohesive team rather than those which could provoke conflicts of interest among team members.

The weight that investors give to each of these issues varies considerably, and it is wise to learn the pet likes and dislikes of key investor groups. Ultimately, it is up to the manager to demonstrate that the fund's strategy makes sense and is more likely to succeed than those of the competition.

Management team

Many investors argue that the management team is the most important criterion for judging whether to support a fund. While track record is undoubtedly the best measure of a team (see below), there are a number of issues relating to the composition of the team itself that need to be communicated. The size of the team needs to be right for the fund: investors would be unhappy to see a team of two raising £500 million. Even if the fund were only planning to make five investments of £100 million each, something might happen to one of those people. But investors would be even more concerned if they were planning to make 50 investments of £10 million each and sit on the boards of all of them. In that case there would be serious concern that the money would not be invested within the required time period.

Previous venture capital experience is perhaps one of the most required skills in the team, preferably in the fund's target area. However, it is not impossible to raise a fund without direct experience, and funds can successfully argue that other skills, such as industrial management or financial expertise, are a prerequisite because of their particular investment strategy. In fact many investors prefer to see a team with interdisciplinary skills, especially in a generalist fund, so that team members are more likely to spot trends and opportunities in the market rather than to stick slavishly to an existing strategy.

The ability to add value is a hard quality to define. In essence, it means that investors want the team to include individuals who have had experience beyond simply carrying out transactions. The main difference between corporate finance professionals and venture capitalists is that the latter have to live with their trans-actions for a long period – frequently five years or more – and then successfully realize them. As a result, the fund needs to show that it can add value at every step, from the time of the initial transaction, during the life of the investment and at exit.

If investors are making a long-term investment in a fund, they will expect to see a similar long-term commitment from the venture capitalists. Low turnover of senior staff is critical for investor confidence. Equally, for small teams where the older members are nearing retirement, investors will require that plans have been made for adequate succession. A related point is the pattern of incentives for the team. Investors expect to see that the team's financial motivation is aligned with its own interest and will probably want to see the majority of the carried interest going directly to members through an appropriate vesting schedule.

Track record

Track record sets a benchmark for investor expectations of future returns. For first-time funds, this can be one of the major obstacles to overcome, since many investors understandably prefer to focus on groups with a demonstrated track record, where the team have worked together previously and have raised prior funds with similar investment strategies. In the USA, however, there has been something of a renaissance for first-time funds as investors have begun to experience succession problems in established firms. Some investors are also prepared to sponsor new venture capital groups in order to get a better deal on terms and conditions.

Greater creativity is certainly required to attract investors if the venture firm is without a track record, either individually or as a team. This can mean raising money on a deal-by-deal basis, or through a co-investment club, which has the disadvantages of not allowing the venture firm total discretion and being admin-istratively burdensome. Some funds have started by raising small amounts through close contacts and then going to the wider institutional market only when they have completed some investments, thus giving potential investors some basis on which to make a judgement.

For those groups who can show a track record, investors will apply several criteria, including the level of historic returns, the amount of money repaid to investors and the spread of returns. Investors are looking for consistent returns over time and where benchmarks exist, they would like to see funds having achieved above median performance. In nearly all cases, investors will judge a fund's performance by looking at its net internal rate of return (*see* below).

Internal rates of return

An internal rate of return (IRR) is defined as that rate of discount which equates the present value of the cash outflows with the present value of the cash inflows from an investment. The IRR has been used in the USA for many years and has become the performance standard for European venture capital funds. There are three acceptable IRR measures, as outlined by EVCA in its 'performance measurement principle', and they all have their different uses: thus a fund could correctly have 'an IRR' of 42 per cent, 29 per cent and 17 per cent all at the same time.

Gross IRR on realized investments

This measures the return only for those investments which have actually been realized. The advantage is that it does not depend on subjective carrying valuations. The disadvantage is that if it is used part way through a fund's life, it will not necessarily be a guide to the performance of the fund at the end of its life, as good investments tend to mature quickly, while poorly performing companies may have only been written down rather than written off and so may be excluded.

Gross IRR on all investments

This attempts to measure the performance of realized and unrealized investments. With the adoption of EVCA valuation guidelines by most funds, this measure is now more comparable across funds and, if the valuations are accurate, should provide a reasonable guide to final performance. However, it does not reflect the return that investors see as it takes no account of the costs of the fund.

Net IRR to the funder

This measures the actual return for investors, across all investments, after having accounted for management fees and carried interest paid to the venture fund managers. Depending on the cost structure of the fund, the net IRR can be a significantly lower number than the gross IRR on either realized or all investments.

While net IRRs are the most important measure of performance, investors will often additionally look at the multiple of cost that the fund has returned to investors. This may be important where a good IRR has been produced because of significant realizations happening early in the fund's life. In this case, investors may prefer a slightly lower IRR together with a higher multiple of cost. Investors also prefer a fund with a good spread of reasonable successes, rather than a fund which has performed well purely due to the stellar success of one company. This

type of performance may be based too much on luck, and be impossible to repli-
cate in the future.

Structure of the fund

Taking care of the details of tax and fund structure can be important to help investors
who are convinced of the strategy and the management team take the next step
towards financing a fund. The main goal is to avoid the additional costs that could
arise through a poorly structured fund, whether these be tax or administrative
charges. In the worst case a poor choice of structure may lead to double taxation –
once when the fund sells an investment, and again when the gains are paid out to
investors, with the latter payment treated as income rather than capital gain. In
nearly all cases investors need to see that the structure is tax transparent, low cost and
easy to administer and that it meets any particular legal restrictions which they as
investors operate under.

There are two tax-efficient structures which venture firms have tended to use:
funds based in tax havens and limited partnerships. If the venture company is registered in a tax haven (such as the Netherlands Antilles), gains made by the fund when
realizing investments do not suffer tax, and a tax liability only arises when the money
is paid out to investors. The limited partnership is truly transparent because it treats
investors in the fund as if they were direct investors in the portfolio company, with a
liability to tax arising when a disposal occurs, whether or not it is distributed.

Clearly, tax efficiency for investors has to be weighed against management
efficiency for the fund and so there are some other issues to consider. Rather than
the team being employed directly by the fund, for example, the establishment of
a separate management company can provide the best mechanism for a
management charge and incentive arrangement.

If the fund is hoping to attract international investors, this may bring a whole
range of specific tax and other legal issues – such as the Erisa legislation governing US
pension funds. While it is advisable to consider these issues up front, legal advice is
expensive and should be minimized until a closing on the fund is imminent.

Terms and conditions

Venture firms would like to believe that investors are keen to invest in their fund
because of its strategy and ability to produce good returns. However, if the terms
and conditions are not in line with investors' expectations, they will often not
invest – regardless of how much they like the fund. Many items make up the
complete set of terms and conditions and some of the detail may vary considerably between funds, especially if they are targeting different types of investment
(Table 4.1). The following are some of the most important and sometimes
contentious issues.

Table 4.1 ♦ Terms and conditions

	Fund A	Fund B
Status	Independent, UK	Independent, USA
Investment focus	Large buyouts over £20 million, primarily UK	Early stage, medical and high tech US west coast
Size of fund	£200 million	US$65 million
Structure	UK limited partnership	US limited partnership
Minimum investment from a single investor	£1 million	US$2 million
Term	8 years plus 2 years extension	10 years plus 3 years extension
Investment period	Up to 5 years	Not more than one third of committed capital to be called in each of first two years
Management fee	1.25 per cent of commitments during investment period, reducing to 0.5 per cent from year 5	2.5 per cent of commitments, reduced by 10 per cent p.a. from year 6
Other fees	Directors fees to the manager	All fees to the fund
Carried interest	20 per cent	20 per cent
Preferred return	10 per cent with catch-up	None
Calls	14 days notice	15 days notice
Distributions	As soon as possible	As soon as possible
Investment restrictions	Minimum investment £5 million; not more than 15 per cent of committed capital in one investment	Typical range US$2–3 million
New fund restrictions	No new fund to be raised until the earlier of 5 years from closing or 75 per cent invested	Not stated in document
Marketing period	9 months after first close	Not stated in document

Fund size

Investors generally prefer what is called a closed end fund. This means that once closed, the fund cannot increase in size. The amount of money that a fund targets depends on several things, including the size of the team and the number and sizes of investments that it is planning to make. There are also several investor-related points to consider when setting a target size for the fund. Investors will generally be happy to see a rise in the larger size compared to previous funds managed, but not by too great a factor as they may doubt the team's ability to invest that amount of money unless the investment strategy has changed significantly. Investors are always concerned that funds' targets are set too high, with the manager being motivated by the larger fee income that comes with a larger fund (the management fee is frequently based on the level of committed rather than invested capital). At the same time, venture firms may need to set a reasonably high target to attract larger investors. Many of the large US investors will not invest less than US$10 million per fund, but they do not want to hold more than say 10 per cent of the fund. This leads to a minimum fund size of US$100 million.

Whatever target size is set, care should be taken in looking at the minimum fund size that is acceptable. Venture firms need to ensure that at that level management fees will be sufficient to remunerate staff and pay operating costs. Cutting back too far will ultimately affect returns and the firm's ability to raise future finance.

Fund term

Traditional venture fund structures in the USA and UK have been for a limited life with an undertaking to repay investors' capital within a set period. The standard term has been for ten years, envisaging an investment period over four years and a further six years to mature and exit the last investments. Some buyout funds, which have tended to require a shorter period for realizing their investments, have more recently opted for an eight year life. The fund's legal agreements will generally allow for an extension of perhaps two years to cater for investments which have not been realized during the life of the fund; however the management fee for this period will normally be very unattractive.

Management fee

In the relatively easy fund-raising climate of the 1980s, a flat fee of 2.5 per cent of committed capital was very much the norm for funds in both the UK and USA. In the late 1990s investor pressure means that the majority of new funds are having to accept a much lower fee. Investors are unhappy to see the management fee as a profit centre because they believe it distorts the incentive arrangements of the carried interest. In addition, many funds are using a 'variable' management fee, as investors are keen to see that the fee earned relates to the amount of work involved rather than just the size of the fund.

Fees are generally now tapered at the end of a fund's life (say from year 5) to reflect the fact that as investments are realized, less time is being spent on the fund by the management team. This may also coincide with the team raising a follow-on fund. The tapering is generally effected in one of two ways, either by keeping the notional rate the same but reducing the base on which it is applied – for example by taking out the cost of realized and liquidated investments – or second, by reducing the fee rate by set amounts each year.

Fees may also be tapered at the beginning of a fund's life to reflect the fact that it takes several years to invest all of the committed capital. This type of arrangement is more appropriate for second or later funds since the group will not have the initial heavy start-up costs associated with raising a first-time fund.

With tapering arrangements, investors will be concerned about the average fee. The acceptable level of this is hard to determine as it will often relate to the size of the fund and the area in which it invests. For very large buyout funds, the average rate may be as low as 1.5 per cent of committed capital. However, for small funds investing in resource-intensive technology deals, for example, it may be over 2.5 per cent.

Carried interest

For the venture capitalist, the main incentive to achieve high returns and the primary source of profit lies in the carried interest. This is normally defined as a proportion of the fund's overall profit; traditionally 80 per cent of the profit on the fund was split between the investors, with the manages receiving the remaining 20 per cent. For investors who are used to investing in venture capital funds, this structure is acceptable. For first-time investors who are more familiar with quoted markets, this incentive arrangement requires some explanation.

Preferred return

Investors are concerned to overcome the perceived inequity where fund managers receive a fixed proportion of profit regardless of whether returns to investors have met expectations. Preferred returns are used to ensure that the venture capitalist only becomes entitled to a share of profits once investors have received a reasonable rate of return on their investment (this is sometimes also called a 'hurdle'). Preferred returns can be set as fixed, floating or stepped rate. Fixed rates are generally set at between 8 per cent and 12 per cent. Floating rates may be linked to returns on government bonds or a relevant stock market index. A stepped return allows the manager to increase his or her share of profits as the investors' rate of return increases. An additional device is to introduce a catch-up, which means that when the fund has achieved the preferred return, the management becomes eligible for its carried interest on all of the fund's gains. Without a catch-up, the preferred return is a true hurdle, and the management only shares in those gains made subsequent to the achievement of the hurdle rate of return.

Not all funds need to include a preferred return, however. Firms with a good track record can often dispense with them. For example, in the USA, top quartile performers are often so oversubscribed from investors that they do not need to negotiate preferred returns to capture investor interest. In addition, the type of investment will influence investor requirements for preferred return clauses. Buyout funds are seen by investors as less risky and so investors believe there should be some guaranteed level of return. By contrast, the risk associated with early stage investments means that managers should avoid having to commit to a set level of return. Indeed, the imposition of a preferred return may even backfire: managers of funds with mediocre performance may become demotivated if they feel they will not reach the preferred return and thus not receive any carried interest.

Capital calls

In the early 1980s it was not uncommon for a venture fund manager to draw down all the committed capital from investors in one tranche at the start of the fund. However, funds take around four years to become fully invested. Unless interest rates are exceptionally high, money sitting on deposit at the bank will drag down the net IRR of the fund. With improvements in telecommunications, it has now become common practice to call money from investors in small tranches at perhaps only two weeks' notice.

Distributions

The same considerations have to be borne in mind when dealing with the distribution of realization proceeds to investors. Failure to pay out proceeds promptly will negatively affect the IRR and so distributions should be made as frequently as possible.

Reinvestment of capital

In fixed life funds, investors are generally opposed to the reinvestment of capital. Even when an investment is held for only one year and then sold, the money must be paid out to investors. This can cause practical problems for funds since it may prove impossible to fully invest all the committed capital; amounts for fees need to be kept aside, as do resources for follow-on investments. But even if the money is never invested, if it is called, investors need to see a return on it.

Increasing investor power has allowed investors to force a hard bargain on all these items in recent years. Venture firms need therefore to look critically at their strengths and weaknesses, and look for ways to present a balanced and attractive package. Funds can explore different options for their investment strategy, seeking out areas currently undersupplied by venture capital: this will be attractive for investors, since experience has shown that a surfeit of funds drives funds to invest in marginal deals, thereby reducing returns. A critical look at the management team from the investors' perspective can also lead to useful changes, and perhaps provisional appointments could be made dependent on achieving the funding in order to round out the team. Finally, terms and conditions can be fine-tuned, making trade-offs between carried interest, preferred returns and management fees in order to produce a package that is acceptable to the majority of investors.

LAUNCHING THE FUND

Targeting potential investors and identifying their requirements are only preparations for the intensive task of actually launching the fund. The core marketing document is the information memorandum, which needs to be prepared, circulated and then followed up aggressively by the venture firm. The fund-raising process can involve marketing tours, one-to-one meetings with potential investors, answering due diligence enquiries and organizing meetings between interested investors and portfolio companies and the rest of the team. In all, the whole process from the launch of the fund to the final closing can easily take 12–18 months.

Initial soundings

Early investor research is essential both to gauge overall appetite and trends in the venture capital market and also to gain feedback from investors on the attractiveness of the funding proposal. Key potential investors can be sounded out using a short introductory document outlining the investment strategy, the team and some indications about fund structure. Asking for comments and suggestions can be a good way of starting a dialogue with potential investors and gaining useful market intelligence. But don't expect to receive a consensus of opinion from different types of investors: concentrate on pulling out the key themes and issues.

Preparing the information memorandum

The information memorandum or placing document for the fund needs to be clear, concise and easy to use, while at the same time selling both the skills of the team and the investment strategy of the fund. There is no set presentational structure for the memorandum. However, it is worth remembering that it must outshine the many similar documents that land on major investors' desks each week. In terms of content, the document should essentially cover all the investor requirements outlined in the section on identifying investor requirements above. It may be broken into several sections, such as:

◆ *management summary* – containing the highlights of the fund in an easy-to-read form

◆ *the opportunity* – covering market conditions and investment strategy

◆ *the team* – detailing past experience of all team members

◆ *the investment process* – describing the decision-making procedures

◆ *track record* – giving details of past performance

◆ *legal and tax* – covering the structure and operation of the fund.

Given that the fund-raising process is often lengthy, there is a strong likelihood that the document will need updating during the process. This may be to include more recent performance information or to reflect changes in terms and conditions agreed as part of the early negotiation process. Either way, it is often best to state that the early versions are drafts and only to publish the final document towards the end of the marketing process.

Marketing the fund

After the information memorandum is written, the decision when to launch the fund becomes one of timing. Considerations include the general economic environment, investor appetite and the amount of liquidity left in the firm's earlier funds. While the manager wants to be distinctive, there are rare occasions when there can be advantages to following a similar group of funds to the market. The launch of '1992' funds in the late 1980s is a prime example of funds designed to appeal to US investor desires to take advantage of the European Community's single market programme. Riding waves such as these still requires skill and timing, particularly to ensure that the launch does not come too late, after investors have turned their attention to other investment opportunities or regions.

Once the decision to go ahead has been taken, the tough selling period commences. The starting point should be to win interest and backing from local investors before going further afield. International investors will often need to see strong local support for a fund before taking it seriously.

A number of marketing options are available, ranging from sending the information memorandum cold to investors and then following up, through to contacting potential investors first to prequalify them before sending the document. Different investors will have different ways of responding to new funds. Some will prefer to meet team members for a presentation on the highlights of the fund, while others will refuse to meet until they have seen the marketing document and prequalified the fund. Whichever method is used, it is critical to follow up quickly after meetings with potential investors in order to maintain the dialogue and prevent the fund from slipping to the bottom of the investor's pile. Additional information, meetings with the rest of the team and visits to portfolio companies should be offered as ways of furthering the process. Due diligence requests should also be elicited from investors at this stage in the proceedings to avoid them arriving very late in the process.

A 'soft circle' is formed as investors give indications of their positive interest in the fund. The firm can then turn to the legal details, circulating these to investors for comments and feedback. The 'hard circle' emerges when verbal commitments to invest have been made and these open the way for the first close once the fund's minimum target level has been achieved. A closing allows the fund to secure the funding committed to date and to start investing. It can also be used to encourage other investors to accelerate their decision making. But the timing of the first close has to be well chosen, as there is normally only a limited period after the first close within which to complete the marketing and hold the final close.

The marketing process is time and resource intensive. Recently, increasing numbers of funds have turned to placement agents as an alternative to building up internal marketing capacity. Placement agents represent people trying to raise capital and have excellent networks of contacts in investing institutions. Many of the major agents are located in the USA, comprising both subsidiaries of investment banks and independent individuals. Firms need to weigh up carefully the pros and cons of placement agents on a clear cost-benefit basis. Agents can be expensive, charging around 2 per cent of the capital they raise; in most cases, this fee is not chargeable to the fund. Furthermore, the manager will not learn from the marketing exercise, and will face the same problem when seeking to raise a subsequent fund. Set against this, placement agents can provide a range of services, including helping to structure the fund and put together the information memorandum, organizing investor meetings and handling follow-up calls. Placement agents can appeal especially to funds that are short of time or resources, or which lack basic knowledge of the potential investors.

INVESTOR RELATIONS

Venture fund managers are now, rather belatedly, paying more attention to communicating progress and performance to their investors. Building good working relationships with investors is more than simply a legal or financial obligation, it is in the firm's long-term self-interest. Indeed, there are few legal requirements for reporting performance to investors beyond the audited annual financial statement. Yet many funds are now producing much greater amounts of written information – both formal reports and informal mailings – as well as hosting a range of investor meetings to build up relationships. In the increasingly competitive markets for venture capital, venture firms realize that not only is it much easier to raise future funds from existing investors – saving considerable cost and effort – but new investors may require references from existing investors before committing themselves. Investor loyalty is thus a valuable asset for a firm, one that needs to be carefully cultivated through a programme of communications, based on regular reports and meetings.

How to communicate

Investor reports
Alongside the standard annual report, semi-annual and quarterly reports are becoming increasingly common. To be useful for investors, three key issues need to be addressed: content, timeliness and consistency.

Reports should include the highlights for the period, updates on each investment in the portfolio, explanations of any changes in progress or valuation, an account of fund performance and unaudited financial statements, including individual capital accounts. Trade-offs invariably need to be made between detail, ease of use and cost, and the style of reporting should therefore be worked out carefully with the investors in a particular fund.

For investors used to investing in quoted markets, where they can receive valuation data almost instantaneously, the timeliness of venture fund reports is an issue. Some investors are now cracking down on poor reporting. AT&T, for example, which has venture capital investments in over 150 partnerships, has measured the receipt of their fund reports. Just over half of their quarterly reports arrive within 45 days of the end of the reporting period. The earliest arrive in two weeks, but the latest take five months. AT&T has now set a target of receiving quarterly reports within 30 days and annual reports (not including audited numbers) within 45 days of the end of the period.

Consistent information is vital to allows investors to assess performance accurately over time and against other funds and asset classes. The progress of portfolio companies should therefore be measured against both the most recent budget and the plan at the time the investment was made. There are also increasing investor pressures for reports to include indications of ultimate expected returns on portfolio investments in addition to the current valuation.

On top of this necessarily formal reporting format, many funds are now using informal mailings as an alternative method of keeping investors up to date with news and progress. This can involve sending out recent press coverage of the fund and portfolio companies or circulating investor newsletters. Newsletters are, however, only feasible for larger firms who need to reach a wide and disparate investor base.

Investor meetings

Many funds hold annual investor meetings which follow a fairly standard format. Members of the team give presentations on the progress of the fund during the year and outline any changes affecting the team. This is followed by presentations by chief executive officers (CEOs) of several of the portfolio companies. Although from the point of view of the fund manager this is an efficient way of verbally updating all the investors in a fund at the same time, for investors, with mounting demands on their time, it is becoming increasingly difficult to attend for the time required. Funds need to be able to offer more tailored programmes for investors on a one-to-one basis, either in addition to or instead of the annual meetings. These private meetings also have the advantage of allowing the investor to ask questions which would not be raised at open meetings, and allow for a greater depth of examination of the portfolio companies.

Investor committees

Most funds are structured to include an investor committee or advisory board. This can be used by the fund as a more select form of communication, this time drawing on the investors. The committee may meet once or twice a year to discuss issues concerning the fund and, given the increasing importance of valuations and performance measurement, there is a trend towards the committee also being used to consider valuations policy. The manager needs to consider membership strategically, and to resist just including the largest investors. Committee membership can help to develop a closer relationship with knowledgeable investors, who may be able to apply their experience to sensitive issues such as conflicts of interest. Provision of a seat on the committee may also be a good way of getting to know an investor new to venture capital.

What to communicate

Investors require up-to-date information on both the firm and the fund, and give priority to six main issues: management changes, strategic shifts, deal flow, new investments, realizations and performance.

Management changes

Though investors like to believe that they are investing in venture capital firms, in reality they are relying on a number of key individuals. If one of those should leave, for whatever reason, it may unsettle investors. Management moves should be communicated promptly to investors to prevent friction emerging if they learn of any change through the markets or the press.

Strategy

Although the investment strategy is normally laid out in the information memorandum, a fund may still have a fair degree of flexibility over the areas it invests in. It is certainly worth indicating to investors any shifts in strategy, however slight, and describing the rationale (for example, changes in the overall economic climate).

Deal flow

The quantity and quality of deal flow that is being seen by the fund is both an indication of the firm's marketing success and an indication of the general level of activity in the market. Investors rarely need to know the details on specific potential investments considered, but they do like to have a feel for the general environment in which the fund is operating.

New investments

Investors need basic details such as when an investment was made, how much the fund invested, as well as the rationale and the team's plans for adding value. Some funds go as far as circulating the entire internal investment paper. A one-page summary, provided it is distributed in a timely manner, is usually sufficient.

Realizations

Funds usually concentrate on telling investors the good news of profitable realizations. Investors frequently also want to know about the companies which have not done well and to understand the reasons.

Performance data

Investors have to receive both valuation information for the individual holdings in the fund, and fund-level information so that they can value their overall portfolio of funds and also make comparisons between funds during their life.

Many funds now ensure that investors receive this information on a quarterly basis. However, production of reports with that frequency is a time-consuming task and does require dedicated resources within the team. An alternative is to produce less frequent reports, but to circulate news on new investments and realizations as they occur during the year.

CONCLUSION

Looking ahead, the opportunities for raising European venture capital funds will grow as institutionally managed assets expand and allocations to venture capital are raised both domestically and internationally. But competition is also intensifying. Thus, while institutional assets are growing, the actual number of investing institutions remains fairly static, so the audience for venture capital is likely to remain limited. Competition will also come from other investment products offering high returns (notably property and emerging equity markets), as well as private equity opportunities in ever more distant parts of the globe. Effective marketing and communications attuned to the needs of investors will thus become evermore crucial to success in this competitive world.

Firms have had to respond by giving more senior management time and resources to the marketing function. There has been a realization that it is never too early to start talking to the people who could provide the money that will enable the firm to prosper. Teams are concentrating on improving their selling skills so that they can better promote both themselves and their product, recognizing that investors have a steadily increasing choice of places and types of investment. And firms are paying more attention to investor needs than ever before to ensure that once they gain investors, they do not lose them.

DEAL GENERATION

Jos B. Peeters
Capricorn Venture Partners NV

Introduction

Marketing venture capital

Key messages

Methods of communication

Sources of deals

Deal flow management

Conclusion

Appendix 1

Appendix 2

Jos B. Peeters holds a Ph.D. in Physics from the University of Louvain. He was co-founder and first chairman of the Belgian Venturing Association. He has been a member of the board of EVCA, the European Venture Capital Association, and was chairman of the association in 1989–90.

He is founder and managing director of Capricorn Venture Partners NV, a Belgian-based venture capital advisory company specializing in early stage, technology-based growth companies. He is also co-founder and chairman of Quartz Capital Partners Ltd, a London-based integrated investment banking firm focussing on technology and life sciences companies. He is chairman of Quest for Growth NV, a technology-oriented investment fund quoted on the Brussels Stock Exchange. He is a co-founder and vice-chairman of EASDAQ SA, the pan-European stock market for growth companies.

INTRODUCTION

The deal flow; the number of investment opportunities which a venture capitalist gets to see per unit of time is like the pulse rate of a sportsmen. It is a health indicator of the economic environment in which the venture capitalist is operating. A large number of investment opportunities means a great deal of entrepreneurial activity. It is usually an indicator of the overall economic dynamics of a given geographical area and an early warning signal for economic recessions and booms. In times of economic optimism more individuals are prepared to take a risk and venture into unknown horizons, whereas in times of depression, the number of new initiatives is significantly down.

To venture capitalists the deal flow is the supply of raw material out of which they are going to select the limited number of entrepreneurs with whom they are going to ride a good part of their route to wealth or poverty. Without the supply of deals they have no investment business. To prospective investors the ability of the venture capitalist to generate deal flow is one of the main evaluation criteria and between venture capitalists the question 'How is the deal flow' is a standard phrase for inquiring about the health of a colleague.

In order to get their hands on interesting investment opportunities, venture capitalists have three options. They can sit and wait in their offices and see what comes through the door; they can take a pro-active approach, identifying targets and going after them; or they can build a network of referrals, individuals and organizations that will direct entrepreneurs in their direction. Most venture capitalists will use a mixture of these three approaches. Only a few houses will refuse direct inquiries, but a referred opportunity has a much higher probability of leading to an investment. Whichever their main approach to deal flow generation, venture capitalists will have to build their own image in the market and create awareness of their services with their target customers. This process is basically no different from the marketing of other specialist financial services and comes in the sophisticated category of business-to-business marketing of services.

MARKETING VENTURE CAPITAL

Money is money, is money: nothing is less true in the venture capital world. Venture capital organizations differ considerably in investment objectives, industry, stage and geographical preferences, and style of operating. Entrepreneurs and intermediaries are often not very adept at defining the financial needs of their company, both in amount and particularly in terms of the type of financial instrument that would suit them best. Venture capitalists too often take it for granted that equity is a well-understood concept and assume that money is an easy product to sell. Experience proves the contrary. Providing venture capital is a sophisticated financial service and for an organization to be successful a great deal of reflection on its marketing approach is crucial. According to Peter Drucker[1] marketing requires separate work and a distinct group of activities. But it is, first, a central dimension of the entire business. It is the whole business seen from the point of view of its final result, that is, from the customer's point of view. It asks, 'What does the customer want to buy?' It does not say, 'This is what our product or service does.'

This attitude is particularly difficult to achieve when the product one provides is a type of financing which is in short supply and which the entrepreneur perceives as the key missing ingredient, the means to make dreams come true. This problem is made worse by the fact that venture capitalists see the investors whose money they manage as their real customers and the entrepreneurs in which they invest as the unfortunate product. A venture capitalist is a financial intermediary: there are customers on the supply side, but also on the demand side. A single-sided approach which considers only the investors as customers can lead to arrogance towards the entrepreneurs and a cut-off of the vital supply of investment opportunities. Both in the USA and in Europe venture capitalists have learned that as venture capital markets develop, as new and larger funds are raised, competition heats up. It is necessary then not only to be able to raise money and to be fast on one's feet, but also to have an image in the market which appeals to the entrepreneurs.

In his book *Venture Capital*[2] David Silver describes how in 1981 the Microsoft Corporation in Bellevue, Washington, was visited by 24 different venture capital funds each offering venture capital. Microsoft at that time was a highly successful computer software company which had annualized sales of $7.5 million and pre-tax profits of about $3 million. Bill Gates, the company's founder, told the venture capitalists that the company did not need venture capital, but would accept $1 million in exchange for 5 per cent of Microsoft's common stock from the venture capital fund which agreed to work the hardest to help Microsoft grow into a professionally managed growth company. The race was on and was eventually won by Technology Venture Investors of Menlo Park, California, which agreed to work closely with middle management to assist them in developing professional managerial skills.

As illustrated above the venture capitalist has to build an image and communicate what services are being provided in order to be a party to the best investment opportunities. This marketing strategy should not be an afterthought, but should form an intrinsic part of the venture capital business and be supported by the key decision makers in the venture capital organization.

KEY MESSAGES

The marketing efforts of a venture capital organization should focus on communicating three areas: investment strategy, reputation and value added services.

Investment strategy

The investment strategy of a venture capital fund is usually well defined in its prospectus or in its charter. Features which are important to position a fund relative to its competitors include stage of investment – early stage and start-ups versus development capital or management buyouts and buy-ins; industry sector specialization or generalists; regional, national or continental constraints; and size of preferred investments. 3i in the UK promotes itself as a one-stop window for all private equity requirements. Atlas Venture positions itself as the US-European expert in IT and life science investments. Capricorn Venture Partners is known as an early stage technology investor. The more focused a strategy is, the easier it is to convey the message, and the more efficiently its target audience can be addressed.

Reputation

The venture capitalist becomes a partner with the entrepreneurs, gaining access to privileged information and often having an influence on strategic decisions of the company. Professional reputation is one of the main criteria persuading entrepreneurs to come your way. Reputation is established partly by word of mouth and so is difficult to control. Impressions of your behaviour and attitudes as a venture capitalist in negotiations and board meetings can travel faster than light in small markets. Particular attention should be given to the confidentiality with which information is treated and the integrity displayed in difficult circumstances. To build your image, information on successful past investments, examples of stock market introductions, curricula vitae of the investing partners and the identities of the major investors in the fund can be used in publications. But what others write and say will always have more impact than what you write yourself about your way of working and your track record.

Value added service

As illustrated by the example of Microsoft, most entrepreneurs are looking for more than money when they approach a venture capital organization. The experience of growing successful companies, access to international networks of information and people, increased credibility of the investee company, the professionalism and independence of the board of directors, the recruitment of additional members to the team or the provision of specific *ad hoc* skills are the venture capital qualities searched for. MTI Managers, for example, has specialized in early stage investments in the UK and provides a very hands-on support whereby one or more of its executives spend several days a week at the premises of the company in various part-time executive roles.

METHODS OF COMMUNICATION

In business-to-business communications one has to combine mass media communications which are used to build general awareness and name recognition with specific, very focused communication to reach the entrepreneurs in the target group.

Advertising

Advertising the services of your venture capital fund in financial newspapers and magazines and in specialist publications is a good way of positioning your fund and creating awareness with a larger audience. In a competitive market such as the UK management buyout market, advertisement has become a common practice. Publications such as *Investors Chronicle* and the *Monthly Buyout Monitor* depend on the advertisement income of the large buyout funds. The *Financial Times* will have the occasional one-page ad for one or other major player, and no closing of a significant transaction will go without the publication of a dedicated tombstone in the financial press.

Advertisement space is expensive and any public relations expert will convince you that one-shot campaigns are not effective, but that you need repeated exposure. The result is that advertising comes at significant costs and the impact on deal flow is difficult to measure. In my own experience I saw very few business plans come in as an immediate response to an advertising campaign, but these campaigns were important to build our image and make a much broader referral network aware of our existence. In the early days at BeneVent Management I wanted to induce executives of multinational companies to start their own businesses and seek the required funding with us. From my own experience I knew that coming back late at night from some meeting abroad was when I most hated the idea that all this effort in my own time was building somebody else's company and not my own. So I hired space on two billboards along the travelator in Brussels airport and placed an aggressive message 'Mind your own business! We invest' on an eye-catching cartoon. For the three years that the billboard was there we have not been able to trace five requests for investment to that advertisement. However, years later when I was introduced to a vice-president of a Fortune 500 company in the USA his instant reaction was 'BeneVent from the board at Brussels airport'. So at least our name was known.

Interviews

Press articles and interviews are not only free of charge, they are much more powerful in communicating your key messages and in generating response from entrepreneurs and intermediaries than advertisements. What others and particularly entrepreneurs with whom you have worked tell about you has a significant impact on your reputation as a venture capitalist. However, these messages are difficult or impossible to control. Because of their impact and the lack of control over them, they have to be handled with absolute care. For senior executives in a venture capital organization a media training is no luxury and even small organizations might benefit from the public relations services of a local independent adviser. Public relations and contacts with journalists have to be built when they are not needed. When you find yourself suddenly in the middle of a controversy being fought out in public, it is too late to start building contacts.

Although attention from the press for venture capital activities goes through ups and downs, it seems a favourite subject in most countries. The problem is more often to avoid premature or undesired disclosures than to get coverage for stories. When a journalist becomes aware of an imminent transaction, you don't necessarily want details which are still being negotiated to be published, and you don't want to alert your competitors before the deal is signed and sealed.

Important to deal flow generation are stories about new investments made and successful stock market introductions. An entrepreneur relates easily to the situation of a colleague. The example of a transaction can appeal to other entrepreneurs and often acts as the incentive to approach you. The visible involvement of Baring Venture Partners as an early investor in Gemplus has brought dozens of deals relating to smart cards to them. Equally the successful investment and NASDAQ IPO of Business Objects has flooded Atlas Venture with investment opportunities relating to object-oriented software applications.

But just as one can benefit from success stories, so one can suffer from failures or bad relationships. As a certain percentage of venture capital investments are bound to turn sour, it is dangerous to associate too strongly with investee companies. In the late 1980s Super Club NV in Belgium seemed to become a supersuccess story. The company was posting double-digit growth numbers each month and was attracting investors from all over the world at ever increasing valuations. All the venture capitalists and investment banks involved used the story to underline their competence and genius. However, when the company hit turbulent waters and capsized amid allegations of malpractice the impact on the early investors was disastrous. The problems at Super Club were by then largely outside the influence of the venture capitalists, but the impact on their image was such that their deal flow came to a grinding stop.

Printed material

Most used in the form of printed material are company brochures, annual reports and newsletters. The quality of material, the choice of graphics and the creativity of the presentation will help to portray an image of professionalism and reliability. It is important to develop a corporate style and image and to apply it consistently from letterheads and business cards to printed brochures and newsletters. The quality of the way in which an organization presents itself helps to establish it as a credible business partner. In the intangible world of financial services this is especially important.

Some of the documents produced to inform the investors in the funds can be designed in such a way that they can be used for a wider audience. Annual reports and newsletters can include stories of successful investments and profitable exits. Large as well as small organizations are circulating such documents to a wider group of fellow venture capitalists, referral networks and entrepreneurs. Good examples of these are the newsletters of Euroventures and Atlas Venture and the annual reports of NIB in the Netherlands and GIMV in Belgium.

Internet

The World Wide Web offers new and unprecedented convenience in distributing information. Most of the web users are young and computer literate, and an unusually high percentage of entrepreneurs inside and outside the IT business are frequent users of the web. It is not only that having an address on the system is a way to communicate effectively with your target audience, but having a home page displaying your key message is rapidly becoming an assurance that you are visible to your future deal flow.

Events

Many participants in the European venture capital community have been to the annual gathering of Gilde Investment Funds in the Netherlands or to the annual meeting of GIMV in Antwerp. A number of funds regularly organize such major events. They invite not only the investors in their funds and the chief executives of the companies in which they have invested but also prospective entrepreneurs, consultants, lawyers, accountants and fellow venture capitalists. These occasions are great places to network and they provide the organizers with valuable credibility and goodwill.

Sponsoring and gifts

Symposia, conferences and meetings of venture capitalists offer opportunities for sponsors. It all plays a role, from the delegate pack, the lunch, the key-note speaker to the gala dinner. The printed presence of the name of your company on thousands of conference folders sent around the world, or your association with a lasting memory of a gala waltzing event in Vienna perhaps, contribute to your positioning as a leading provider of venture capital. Sponsoring helps with name building, but does not communicate a specific message. Trying to be very specific or detailed in a speech at a sponsored lunch or dinner can make you the obstacle separating people from the main course or the coffee and can become very counterproductive. The art is to be short, witty and remembered.

A lavish card sent around Christmas is a way to remind colleagues, referrals and entrepreneurs of your existence. But sending a product from one of your investee companies as a gift generates goodwill, markets the products of your investee company and is a visual illustration of the kind of product you want to invest in. Over the years I have been receiving towels, rucksacks, window cleaning materials, underpants and fireworks from colleagues such as Gilde Investment Funds and Halder Investments. I believe it is a practice that should be encouraged: more than printed brochures or press releases these real-life products bring the message home in a lasting way.

Presentations

Presentations at conferences are an excellent way of conveying your message and creating visibility for your firm. Whatever the topic you are supposed to cover, you can always include an introductory slide presenting your firm and its investment strategy. But don't overdo it – the audience came to learn about the topic on the programme, not to be brainwashed by your firm's PR. More subtle and more effective is to give an interesting talk in which you refer to your own practice and experience with the subject at hand. The use of well-prepared, high-quality colour slides and proper handouts for your talk does more to make you remembered than over-aggressive plugging of your corporate message. His cartoon-based slides at the European Venture Capital Association (EVCA) symposium in Monaco made Toon Nagtegaal from Holland Ventures an instant and remembered expert in dealing with entrepreneurs.

Presentations at venture capital events are difficult because you have to impress the well-informed insiders in the business. The outside world, on the other hand, is begging for information on venture capital. We produced a standardized presentation explaining the venture capital process and addressing some key issues. That presentation has been used dozens of times, not only for guest lectures at business schools, but also for a wide range of presentations to service clubs, bank managers, lawyers and entrepreneurs. These presentations are relatively easy and always generate useful contacts and investment opportunities.

Fairs

Less obvious in terms of return on investment is participating in technology fairs and exhibitions. Certainly a presence at a fair creates visibility, but stands are expensive to build and even more expensive to man. At BeneVent Management our most successful presence at a fair was when we made our stand available to our investee companies, and we operated the bar. Like-minded entrepreneurs flocked around the PC screens and were a great source of initial contacts. However, at most fairs you might be better off touring the stands of the presenting companies, than being confined to your own patch.

Yearbooks

EVCA and most national associations such as the BVA (Belgian Venturing Association), BVCA (British Venture Capital Association), AFIC (Association Française des Investisseurs en Capital) and the NVP (Nederlandse Vereniging van Participatiemaatschappijen) publish an annual yearbook. These guides contain statistical material on the venture industry and a directory of members. It is vital for a venture capital organization to be listed in these industry references. They are widely circulated among prospective referrals and are often the reference guide from which entrepreneurs and their advisers make the first selection of venture capitalists to be contacted.

Some private initiatives, such as the *VCR Guide to Venture Capital in the UK and Europe*, try to go beyond the basic information on the venture capital funds and discuss investment strategies and past investments. It is useful to be listed in these guides, particularly because these listings usually come free of charge and anybody buying this data is at least a potential source of an investment opportunity.

As a small aside it is worth assuring that your firm is in the Yellow Pages under the right category. Some entrepreneurs are very basic in their approach to seeking equity and for them the Yellow Pages is the first place to look.

Personal contacts

In all personal contacts you convey messages, some intentional, many unintentional. Through your behaviour, attitudes, style and language you can convey positive or negative advertisements for yourself and your firm. The position you take in a board meeting of one of your investee companies is likely to have more impact than the well considered wordings of your brochure. It is in the daily reality of due diligence, negotiating, investment monitoring and value adding that you build a network and a reputation. In the trenches, under situations of severe stress and crisis, you go up or go under. Being professional, balanced and fair gives you the credibility that makes entrepreneurs, accountants and consultants refer their best friends and clients to you. It will stimulate your co-investors to invite you into their next good deal. The downside of this is that particularly larger organizations can suffer badly from the impact of the uncontrolled behaviour of one member of the team.

High level personal contacts, which are key for prime referrals and effective problem solving, have to be established in one-to-one meetings. Wining and dining are often part of the ritual of acquiring goodwill and establishing contacts with key decision makers. Memberships of the right business clubs and trade organizations are useful to build your network and to get your message around.

Serving on working committees is time consuming but it allows you to get to know your colleagues much better. I am convinced that the many committees and working groups which operate in the context of EVCA have resulted in many business links, co-investments and collaborations between investee companies.

SOURCES OF DEALS

Unsolicited contacts

As soon as your name appears in the EVCA yearbook or you have been mentioned in the press, your telephone will start ringing. Entrepreneurs in need of money manage to find your fax or e-mail number and dump unsolicited 50-page business plans overnight. The problem with the unsolicited contacts is that there is no prior quality control. You are just as likely to get the latest version of a perpetual mobile as a potential Microsoft. Larger or well established organizations get several unsolicited requests for investing per day. It is important to organize an efficient sieve at the entrance of an organization, to avoid being swamped by unwanted paper.

Direct approach

You can study industry sectors of future growth and identify the emerging companies in these sectors. From trade directories, press articles, annual reports, including those of other venture capitalists, and contacts with incubators or entrepreneurs you might identify potentially interesting companies. Before you make your approach, you should undertake a preliminary analysis of the company, find out who is who, where they come from and how their products are positioned in the market. By making the first approach to a company, you declare an interest in them. Turning them down later becomes more difficult and you will have to go beyond the standard arguments. You will also be at a disadvantage when negotiating terms because you have positioned yourself on the requesting side. The positive side of the psychology of making a direct approach is that such a sign of interest in general flatters the ego of the entrepreneur. The day he or she has to make a choice between investors, you will be at an advantage over those where the entrepreneur had to do the running.

Surfing

The development of the World Wide Web has added a new dimension to the direct contacting of emerging companies. Particularly in the IT field, information on new developments and companies is abundantly available. The much improved access to this information allows the venture capitalist to research a given area more effectively and to be better prepared before approaching a potential investee company.

Investment forums

Initially investment forums in Europe were pioneered by EVCA with the support of the European Commission. Companies from a given geographical area and/or a specific industry sector are given 15 to 20 minutes to present themselves to prospective investors. Afterwards there is an opportunity for one-to-one meetings behind closed doors. In recent years private initiative has started to take over and the Cowen and Gilde Investment Fund conference on IT, the Ernst & Young and Atlas Venture Life Sciences Conference, and the Robertson & Stephens conferences have become annual gatherings of investors and entrepreneurs. These forums can present good overviews of the latest developments in a number of areas and offer plenty of occasions for informal contact. Companies can present themselves without begging for money and investors can show an interest without commitment.

The Brussels Stock Exchange has recently created the MIM (Interprofessional Market) which is a regular meeting where intermediaries can present investment opportunities in non-quoted companies to colleague investors. It is too early to say whether this formal meeting will attract more than the deals turned down in the informal contacts.

Referred deals

Most of the better quality deals come through the referral network. According to David Silver[2] the best deals are deals referred to you by an entrepreneur whom you have financed and who wants to say 'thank you'. But before you have made entrepreneurs rich, and in addition to the entrepreneurs, a venture capitalist has to build a broad network of referrals. All the methods of communication described above can be used to address the unknown entrepreneur, but they can be applied with much greater efficiency in an indirect way by working a network of individuals and organizations that are in daily contact with entrepreneurs. These referrals can spot opportunities for equity investments and refer them to you. The standard list of referrals includes lawyers, accountants, auditors, consultants, headhunters, commercial and investment banks, merger and acquisition boutiques, incubators, technology transfer centres, chambers of commerce, leading entrepreneurs, business development departments of major corporations, etc. When presenting an opportunity to you each of these referrals has their own agenda. The auditor might be worried about her 'going concern declaration' if no additional money is raised. The headhunter might see a problem for the salary and motivation of his top candidate unless the company has more financial resources. The banker might have overexposed himself and might want to secure a bad debt. But in general the quality of the referred deals is much better than that of the unsolicited contacts. When he was at TVM (Techno Venture Management), Franz Helbig[3] pointed out that '25 per cent of the deals we see are referrals and 75 per cent are unsolicited; but over 95 per cent of the deals we actually do come from referrals'.

In a competitive environment your colleagues in the venture capital business are likely to market to the same potential sources of referrals. It is important that you communicate your key messages well to those sources and in particular that you convince them of your professional standing and integrity. They are recommending one of their clients to you and the way you handle the contact will invariably reflect on their own business relationship. Your marketing, and in particular your personal contacts and events, can help you to put yourself at an advantage over your competitors. It is more likely, however, that you will be a 'thank you' introduction because you brought them some business in the first place. Hence the lawyers, accountants and bankers which you introduce to your existing investments are more likely to bring you some good future opportunities.

Syndication

A special category of referrals are the invitations from colleagues in the venture capital industry to co-invest. In Europe around 34 per cent of all investments are nationally syndicated and 9 per cent have an international group of venture capital investors. For Waldemar Jantz[4] from TVM the most important reason for networking with other venture capitalists is deals. In his view:

Networking gives increased quality of deal flow. To syndicate deals and increase the knowledge around the table is very important, because one can be blinded, for example, by helping to establish a company and not realize that something is wrong. It is a healthy process to attract new outside investors in every new financing round, because they can help in giving a different view on our own deals. A higher leverage for deal structuring is achievable by bringing together experts from different venture funds all over Europe and including some of the knowledge and feedback from our US colleagues.

The main reason why venture capitalists invite colleagues/competitors to co-invest is very simply to make their investment less risky and more likely to yield a higher return. Hence you are either invited because you have a particular skill, industry sector knowledge, geographical presence, or reputation which will make the investment easier to monitor, faster to grow or more successful to exit; or you are invited because you are an undemanding partner who follows the lead investor blindly and has deep pockets, full of easy money.

Many invitations to be part of a syndicate are a 'thank you' for an earlier collaboration. It is in the trenches when discussing major issues at board meetings or making the required changes in companies that the difference between dependable colleagues and passengers becomes clear. It should not be a surprise that you will find the same venture capitalists in a number of deals. In working together, personal contacts become closer and more opportunities are shared. For a newcomer to the business it is a challenge to become part of the club. Suppressing your greed and taking the first step by inviting others to your best deals is the fastest road into the network.

Early stage funds

One way of assuring the right to participate in second rounds or mezzanine financing is to make investments in seed and early stage funds. Many large funds have minimum thresholds of several million ECU before an investment is considered. They find it increasingly difficult to manage a couple of ECU 100,000 in start-up or early stage companies. Here early stage boutiques, such as Capricorn Venture Partners, can play a complementary role. They provide either industry sector, stage or geographical expertise; or a combination of these. To the boutique the investment of the larger fund builds a strategic alliance which helps to ensure follow-on investments for the best of its portfolio companies. For the larger fund the boutique provides high-quality deal flow, inside information on the company before investing and a right of first refusal over the competition.

Often the deal flow of an early stage boutique is itself a source of deals for larger players. The boutique has usually a grass-roots presence in a given geographical area and receives a broad range of deals, including buyout and development capital opportunities. The deals which are outside the scope of the boutique can be of great interest to later stage players or corporations. Indeed corporate venture capital groups have a tradition of investing in funds to buy a window on emerging technologies and companies. For them investing in early stage funds is a way of buying deal flow for corporate development activities.

DEAL FLOW MANAGEMENT

The venture capital investment process is a staged process, which can best be compared with a series of sieves with finer and finer meshes. What passes through the first coarse sieve might be rejected at the second stage. Only a few jewels survive in the last sieve. The process from initial contact to closing before a notary public includes an initial evaluation, agreement on a termsheet, detailed due diligence, partnership approval and comprehensive shareholders agreement. Typically only a small percentage of the initial contacts turn into investments. Because of this high reject rate it is extremely important to manage the flow of deals and the progress through the various stages with great care. Depending on the size, geographical spread (one or more offices) and the structure of the partnership, each venture capital organization has its own particular way of handling the flow of deals.

Recording

The starting point of any deal flow management system is a database where all relevant deals are recorded and from which progress reports and statistical surveys can be derived. With the advantage of personal computers and networks any good database software can be used for the purpose of building a deal flow record. The sample deal log (*see* Appendix 1) gives an illustration of the key data needing to be captured in a deal log file for follow-up reporting and statistical analysis. At BeneVent Management we produced a weekly print-out for each investment manager showing the active deals, and then reviewed the action points in the weekly staff meeting.

Unsolicited contacts

Unsolicited requests for investing come either by phone, fax, mail or e-mail. Occasionally someone might turn up unannounced at the door of the office to grab your attention for their business. When contacted we first try to identify whether the proposal is broadly within the investment objectives of our funds or of interest to our strategic partners. Proposals which are clearly outside our scope, because of the industry sectors or the geographical area, are immediately rejected and don't get logged. All other deals are logged and an initial review is made on the basis of the written information or a telephone conversation. Around one in three deals are rejected at this first screening. A brief standardized letter is sent to confirm the decision and to thank the entrepreneur for presenting the opportunity to invest in their company.

First meeting

If a deal appears more or less interesting I prefer to invite the entrepreneur to my office for a one-hour meeting, rather than spend time reading a business plan. To Ben Rosen, the legendary lead investor in Lotus Development and Compaq Computer, the worth of a deal is usually inversely proportional to the fancifulness of the business plan. Venture capital is a people business, and hence I want to get in front of the key person as soon as possible. A one-hour meeting is just enough to get a feel for the drive and personality of the entrepreneur, the business model, the level of understanding of the customers and the upside potential of the opportunity presented. On the basis of the information received in the meeting a decision has to be made to decline the opportunity or to start detailed due diligence. After the first meeting an estimated 20 to 25 per cent of the initial contacts make it to the next step.

Confidentiality

Some entrepreneurs are paranoid about confidentiality. They propose signature of the most stringent and punitive agreements prior to disclosing any information. Because of the large number of deals that are turned down, the venture capitalist has to be careful not to be precluded from opportunities because he has evaluated a given deal. The venture capitalist should handle all the information received with the strictest confidentiality. Within this professional confidentiality it should be possible to have a first meeting with an entrepreneur. At the start of the due diligence it is customary to sign a confidentiality agreement which stipulates that the information received can only be used for the purpose of evaluating the investment opportunity, but which also restricts such confidentiality to information which is labelled confidential, which is not known to the venture capitalist and which is not in, or doesn't in the future come into, the public domain. A good example is the model 'Confidentiality Agreement' developed by the BVCA (*see* Appendix 2).

Turn down

More than 95 per cent of the deals received do not lead to an investment. Handling a turn-down, or declining to invest, is an important part of the venture capital business. The following golden rules help to reduce the negative impact of a turn-down.

◆ *Don't make an absolute statement* A turn-down by a given firm is not an absolute judgement on the business opportunity, but a decision by a particular team in the light of their investment objectives and their current situation. Maybe the funds are fully invested, but the partners keep looking at deals to preserve a presence in the market.

◆ *Say no, as soon as possible* An early turn-down is easier to accept than a break-up after a long and intense period of due diligence. Valuable time is saved on both sides by discussing key points early in the negotiations. Companies can get in serious cash flow problems if an anticipated investment does not materialize and no contingency plan is in place.

◆ *Try to be constructive and helpful* If the opportunity does not fit the investment objectives of the fund, it helps to point the entrepreneur in the direction of a suitable colleague, a bank, a consultant or any other form of help. And it helps you build your network at the same time.

◆ *Avoid making enemies* Most deals don't get done because the venture capitalist is not convinced of the ability of the entrepreneur to deliver an exiting return on the investment. Entrepreneurs don't like to be told they are not good enough, particularly not in front of their team. Bruising an ego can create life-long enemies. If a constructive discussion of the additional skills required to build the company doesn't strike a chord, forget the deal and find an excuse for not investing.

◆ *Provide feedback* If you have spent considerable time with the entrepreneur and the company, then they deserve a feedback when you decide to withdraw from an opportunity. If the deal was referred to you it is also important to inform the source of the referral about your decision and the basis for it. Making your investment criteria better understood by your referral network will improve the quality of your deal flow and avoid early disillusionment.

◆ *Return the business plan* The business plan is the property of the company. When a decision is made not to invest, all information, in particular confidential records and copies and the business plans, should be returned to the company or destroyed. It demonstrates respect for the property of the entrepreneurs and hence will earn respect, in addition to saving cupboard space.

Reporting

Deal log summaries are produced to inform the investors in the funds of the flow of deals and of the due diligence activity. Summaries of new companies can provide interesting information on new technological and market trends. Information on later stage opportunities might represent investment opportunities for strategic investors. Funds produce either descriptive lists or graphs with industry breakdown or stage distribution.

Deal flow reports are important supporting material in fund-raising, because they prove the ability of the fund adviser to get in front of the right type and quantity of investments.

CONCLUSION

The sources of deals are strongly dependent on the environment in which a particular venture capitalist operates. In general the unsolicited contacts will bring the largest numbers of deals, but they are more like a treasure hunt. One has to sift through large numbers to find the occasional jewel. The best deals come from referrals, often from shareholders, entrepreneurs, advisers and venture capitalists who owe a favour and want to reciprocate. At the EVCA Institute in Wiesbaden in November 1991 Werner Schauerte from Atlas Venture presented an interesting breakdown of their sources of business (*see* Fig. 5.1). Most successful in converting

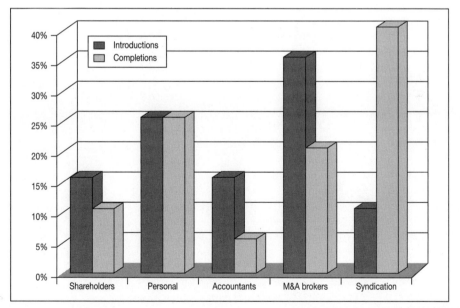

Source: Dr Werner A. Schauerte, Atlas Venture

Fig. 5.1 ♦ A breakdown of sources of business

from an introduction to a completion appear to be the personal contacts and the proposals from syndicate partners.

To get these referrals you have to communicate your key messages, build and entertain your referral network, operate professionally so that you are invited by colleagues, and be proficient in the handling of the turn-downs.

APPENDIX 1

SAMPLE DEAL LOG

Number: _____
(Can also be coded to indicate year, office or country)

Date received: _____ Initials receiver: _____

Name of company: _____

Address: _____

Telephone no: _____ Fax no: _____ E-mail address: _____

Contact person: _____ Position: _____

Stage: _____
(Seed, start-up, early, development, refinancing, mezzanine, buyout, replacement)

Industry sector:_____
(Computer related, biotechnology, see EVCA industry sectors)

Business:_____
(Narrative description of the products and the market)

Financing to date: _____ Main sources: _____

Required financing: _____ Amount requested: _____

	Last year	This year	Next year	In 3 years	In 5 years
Turnover:	_____	_____	_____	_____	_____
Profit:	_____	_____	_____	_____	_____

Reviewed by: _____
(Name of the Partner in charge of the follow-up)

Status: _____

    Initial contact   – First meeting – Termsheet   – Go-ahead   – Closing   – Turn-down

Date: _____ _____ _____ _____ _____ _____

Notes: _____

_____

_____

_____

_____

Source of deal: _____
(Unsolicited contact, direct approach, referral, advertisement)

Referral organization: _____

Contact person: _____Telephone no: _____

APPENDIX 2

STANDARD CONFIDENTIALITY LETTER

(courtesy BVCA)

[*on notepaper of supplier of confidential information, e.g. vendor or his agent*]

To: [*potential investor*]

Dear Sirs,

We understand that you wish to investigate the business of [*name of company*] (the 'company') [*and of its subsidiaries*] (together the 'Group') [in connection with [*insert nature of transaction*] (the 'Permitted Purpose')] and that you, your directors and employees, other potential syndicate members or other providers of finance and your financial and professional advisers in relation to the Permitted Purpose, (together referred to as the 'Disclosees'), will need access to certain information relating to the Group (the 'Confidential Information') [including, without limitation: …].

I   In consideration of our agreeing to supply, and so supplying the Confidential Information to you and agreeing to enter into discussions with you, you hereby undertake and agree as follows: -

    A   to hold the Confidential Information in confidence and not to disclose or permit it to be made available to any person, firm or company (except to other Disclosees), without our prior [written] consent;

    B   only to use the Confidential Information for the Permitted Purpose [provided that on being notified by us that the proposals concerning the Permitted purpose have lapsed, you may approach the Company [or its advisers] with separate proposals and we acknowledge that in so doing you may have regard to the Confidential Information provided];

    C   to ensure that each person to whom disclosure of Confidential Information is made by you is fully aware in advance of your obligation under this letter and that, in the case of other potential syndicate members, each such person gives an undertaking in respect of the Confidential Information, in the terms of this letter;

    D   upon written demand from us either to return the Confidential Information and any copies of it or to confirm to us in writing that, save as required by law or regulation, it has been destroyed. You shall not be required to return reports, notes or other material prepared by you or other Disclosees or on your or their behalf which incorporate Confidential Information ('Secondary Information') provided that the Secondary Information is kept confidential;

    E   to keep confidential and not reveal to any person, firm or company (other than Disclosees) the fact of your investigations into the Group or that discussions or negotiations are taking place or have taken place between us in connection with the proposed transaction or that potential investor/acquirers are being sought for the Company:

F that no person gives any warranty or makes any representation as to accuracy or otherwise of the Confidential Information, save as may subsequently be agreed.

II Nothing in paragraph 1(a) to (f) of this letter shall apply to any information or Confidential Information:

A which at the time of its disclosure is in the public domain;

B which after disclosure comes into the public domain for any reason except your failure, or failure on the part of any Disclosee, to comply with the terms of this letter;

C which is disclosed by us or the Company, its directors employees or advisers on a non-confidential basis,

D which was lawfully in your possession prior to such disclosure;

E which is subsequently received by you from a third party without obligations of confidentiality (and, for the avoidance of doubt, you shall not be required to enquire whether there is a duty of confidentiality); or

F which you or a Disclosee are required to disclose, retain or maintain by law or any regulatory for government authority.

III In consideration of the undertakings given by you in this letter, we undertake and agree:

A to disclose Confidential Information to you;

B to keep confidential and not to reveal to any person, firm or company (other than persons within our group who need to know, our bankers and professional advisers) the fact of your investigation into the Group or that discussions or negotiations are taking place or have taken place between us; and

C that we will not prior to [*insert date*], directly or indirectly enter into negotiations or have discussions of any kind with any other potential investors which relate to the Permitted Purpose without your prior written consent and we recognise that in reliance on this undertaking you and other Disclosees may incur substantial costs. (This relates to exclusivity and is a matter for negotiation.)

IV

A This letter shall be governed by and construed in accordance with English law [and the parties irrevocably submit to the non-exclusive jurisdiction of the Courts of England and Wales in respect of any claim, dispute of difference arising out of or in connection with this letter].

B The obligations in this letter will terminate on [*insert expiry date*].

Please indicate your acceptance of the above by signing and returning the enclosed copy of this letter as soon as possible.

Yours faithfully

On copy;

We have read and agree to the terms of the above letter.

Signed by   )
for and on behalf of)
)

Limited   )

Date: [...............]

Notes

1. Peter F. Drucker (1974) *Management: Tasks, Responsibilities, Practices*. New York: Harper and Row, 63–4.

2. David Silver (1985) *Venture Capital*. New York: John Wiley, 47.

3. Franz L. Helbig (1988) *European Venture Capital Institute*. Köln: Deutscher Wirtschafts-dienst John von Freyend GmbH, 54.

4. Waldemar Jantz, at Venture Forum Europe '93, London, 29 November–1 December 1993.

6

DUE DILIGENCE

Diederik W. Heyning
Gilde Investment Management

Introduction

The concept

The issues

The process

Conclusion

Diederik Heyning obtained his Baccalaureat in Mathematics in Paris, France and then completed his law studies at the Univesity of Leiden in the Netherlands. He is an alumnus of the PMD programme at Harvard Business School. He worked for 12 years for the English General Electric Company, briefly in the Netherlands, and later in England and France. As managing director of large subsidiaries, he gained extensive experience in the manufacture and global distribution of industrial goods. He joined Gilde in 1985 as General Partner when it was a Dfl30 mio fund learning its way into the VC industry as so many did in the early 1980s and was instrumental in the development of Gilde's activities into a number of focused funds managing over Dfl1.5 bio. Diederik Heyning actively served on the board and Executive Committee of the Dutch Association of Venture Capital (NVP) and the European Venture Capital Association. In his 12 years with Gilde, Diederik concluded over 20 deals, primarily in the ICT sector. He is currently on the board of Carmen Systems (Sweden), Janssen Pers (Netherlands), Manaus (Netherlands), PPU Maconomy (Denmark), Seagull Software (Netherlands/USA), SLP Infoware (Paris, France) and SuperNova (Netherlands/USA).

INTRODUCTION

Due diligence is a term used daily by people involved in finance or mergers and acquisitions, but it means absolutely nothing to anybody else. I have not been able to locate it in any dictionary. Its meaning of *thorough investigation* is based on the practice that *professional* contractual parties may expect from each other in a transaction involving financing or the purchase or exchange of capital stock.

For venture capitalists, due diligence can apply either narrowly to the process of verifying the data presented in a business plan/sales memorandum, or broadly to the complete investigation and analytical process that precedes a commitment to invest. This chapter will deal with the broader process. The nature of due diligence can vary widely, ranging from what is involved for a high tech start-up investment to the considerations concerning the buyout of a mature company. I will address it as a single subject, which will therefore need application to specific situations.

THE CONCEPT

The purpose of due diligence is to determine the attractiveness, risks and issues regarding a transaction. It should enable the fund managers to realize an effective decision process, optimize the deal terms, and set the stage for an effective life after investment.

For an effective decision process, venture capitalists cannot rely exclusively on the information provided by the entrepreneurs seeking funding. Venture capitalists must independently broaden the sources and scope of information. This is first because entrepreneurs must be expected to look at a business with a positive bias, and second because they do not necessarily focus on the issues that are relevant for investors. An important 'added value' for a venture capitalist to contribute is to address strategic or longer-term issues, and provide sensitivity analyses (worst-case scenarios) and strength/weakness (SWOT) analyses. These are equally essential to allow the fund managers to communicate among themselves and decide effectively on an investment.

The knowledge acquired during the due diligence process allows venture capitalists to structure a deal and cover issues in the shareholder agreement that can significantly improve the results of an investment. Identifying the most important areas of risk or upside potential and linking them to management incentives and investors' rights creates powerful tools that can be put in place only when one is aware of the relevant issues at an early stage of the negotiating process. Insight into the potential (additional) cash requirements in case of under- or overperformance can be determining factors in structuring the finance of a deal and the decision as to whether and with whom to syndicate. The information gathered during due diligence is critical in convincing syndication partners to join in a deal. They will look at the quantity and quality of the leader's due diligence as keenly as at the content of the proposition.

As venture capitalists are by definition generalists, their primary know-how is in generic issues like growing organizations, setting up distribution, preparing and realizing subsequent financings, and so forth. Due diligence is the prime occasion for a venture capitalist to become familiar with a specific industry segment, its players, jargon, yardsticks and habits. This awareness is critical in establishing a working relationship with the management of an investee company, for whom some familiarity with the industry is often an essential prerequisite for credibility, or even for just plain communication. Such industry awareness is very useful in monitoring and guiding an investee company. Over the life of an investment, it will often be critical when the time comes to identify and realize the appropriate exit. After due diligence, there is no other period that will provide both the motivation and legitimacy to go and see parties such as customers, suppliers and competitors to gain that sort and depth of knowledge.

> **PC add-on boards** are one of the fastest moving industries. The knowledge gained during due diligence on supply channels and competition enabled investors in Spea GmbH, the major European player, to identify, understand and act when the supply of critical components came under threat. The world market is divided among half a dozen fierce competitors. Investors knew whom to talk to and within a couple of months negotiated the sale of the business to Diamond Multimedia for the benefit of all parties.

THE ISSUES

The issues to be investigated during due diligence can be grouped into those determining the success of the business and those potentially threatening investors' effective share of success. I will briefly discuss the factors that *can* be of influence. Nonetheless, this comes down to a long list, requiring the user to pick and choose what is relevant to a specific case.

The three most important factors for business success are well known and are: management, management and management. And this is indeed the most important area of focus during due diligence. All checks, on which more below, will serve not only the obvious need to establish specific facts, but also – through contact with a company's environment – to get a feel for management's reputation, approach and skills. Over the period of due diligence, a picture should be formed with regard to management that above all should be *consistent*. One should never invest if there are unresolved discrepancies between various checks, the business plan and management's history, or statements and behaviour.

As the business plan is intended to describe fully all the aspects of a business, it will be the starting point and touchstone of all due diligence. Here are the issues a good business plan[1] should contain.

1   A brief background and purpose of the plan: history, current conditions, the concept, objectives, initiators and key players.

2   Description of the business products or services.

3   Description of the markets, growth prospects, competitive and other influences.

4   Summary of the technology involved, manufacturing processes, risk of obsolescence, make-or-buy options.

5   Marketing and sales strategy.

6   Organization and management, career histories, recruitment plans and strategies.

7   Financial history and projections of turnover, profits, cash flow, funding.

8   Ownership, structure, long-term contracts, financing and exit considerations.

Since due diligence is propelled by the business plan, the above outline provides a good structure for my comments on the issues to be checked.

Background

It is important to understand the *motivations* of all parties involved. This is where the background becomes important.

◆   Why is a seller selling? If the seller prefers cash instead of the shares, why should I prefer the shares instead of my cash? Is there anything the seller knows that I should know?

◆   Why is management embarking on this adventure? Are they going for capital gain or simply trying to secure a job? Based on their history, how aware are they of what they are doing?

Gilde has had poor experience with companies where both father and son(s) are part of the management. In one case, years ago, despite strong demand from all over the globe, growth was held back intentionally in order to avoid exceeding the son's management capabilities. For two years, we heard a range of arguments for delaying the hiring of a marketing person, although this was agreed at the moment of our investment. We were glad to sell back our shares at cost.

◆ Why are corporate parties involved in the deal? By necessity or opportunity? For financial or strategic reasons? What influence can we expect on operations, on further financing rounds, on exit routes?

◆ Why are other financial parties (not) involved in this round? What is the position of past or existing financiers? What are the possibilities/handicaps for syndication, further financings, hands-on contribution to realize the plan?

Products or services

It should be possible to describe simply the concept of the company's products or services, the factors that dictate their success (for instance, price competitiveness, unique features, etc.) and the benefit(s) to the end user. Why will they need it? Does it save time or money, make life easier? What alternatives are there? What happens if they do not buy it? Be wary of any proposition where you do not yourself easily understand the user benefit.

At the end of the day, it is a product's uniqueness that determines competitiveness. Make sure you understand what that is and whether it addresses a niche requirement or has potential for broad markets.

◆ How stable is the product? Is it being beta-tested or is it ready for general use? Distinguish clearly which products are *existing* and which products are *planned*. If much depends on future products, there should be a clear development plan with specifications and a timetable. Their feasibility and costs should be checked.

During a visit to Sandoz in Basle during due diligence for Uniface, it became apparent that this user was building real production applications with the first beta-test version of the Uniface software tool. To us it confirmed the market need and absence of alternatives. Uniface grew to a $100 million company in the following seven years.

◆ Cost price (not sales price!) of products invariably represents a major competitive issue. Preferably, one should check historical cost prices, although in some fast-moving industries like electronics you need to look into future cost price reductions. For early stage companies, there is no history, but often the chicken-and-egg issue of quantities versus final cost price instead. Outside expertise on industrialization, tooling costs, etc., can help to validate *structural cost price competitiveness*.

♦ Identify the proportion of the 'product' offering that in fact consists of services, as it may be determinant for the growth potential of a business. Today, for instance, a growing number of software products offer enterprise-wide solutions. This often involves major organizational consultancy to (potential) customers. Who is providing this?

Markets, growth prospects, competitive and other influences

♦ Identify the present and projected markets in terms of location (international versus local), size, growth rate, profitability, trends, etc. Identify leading companies and understand their financial (non)success. Establish industry parameters (sales per employee, output per machine, etc.) and compare them with the company's results and projections. Establish (intended) market share, and the existing demand versus supply situation. Distinguish between *free* and *captive* markets. Narrow down as much as possible the company's industry sub-segment: X per cent of 'the electronics industry' does not mean as much as Y per cent of the 'plain-paper portable fax market'.

♦ Establish a clear picture of the competitive situation both present and future. Are there any competitors enjoying more than 30 per cent market share? Is competition on a global or a local scale? Do competitors talk to each other (and the company)? Establish the position of substitute products or services. Examine the way competitive forces affect the business. Is the market ready for the product or service, or is the company ahead of the market (and spends its energy in preparing the market for its competitors)? How crucial is it that the company is or stays first in the market? Will this continue? Will/does the customer need to pay more for better?

♦ Ideally get to know not only major competitors, existing and new entrants, but also (potential) major buyers, suppliers, distribution channels.

♦ Are any buyers taking more than 30 per cent of turnover? Who are the ten biggest buyers? Are any suppliers operating a (near) monopoly? Are any distribution channels captive? Does the company have any preferred relationships? Any major changes in all this over the last few years?

In addition, establish the impact on projected sales of other possible market influences such as economic factors (inflation, recession, etc.), technological factors (new technologies), government influences (legislation, approval bodies, budgets), social factors (age, demographics, income), seasonal factors (weather, trade shows, budget cycles).

149

Technology, manufacturing processes, risk of obsolescence, make-or-buy options

Technology is often a mixed blessing. This means certain investors will only invest in non-tech, while others specifically target high tech. In all cases, it is important to establish the role and status of technology in a business model.

♦ For a buyout, technological obsolescence is a threat, since it is hard to determine in advance how much money needs to be spent on product development. It requires financial buffers, and thus limits the scope for financial leverage.

♦ For high tech firms, technology is the cornerstone of their competitive advantage and something to be managed with care. For all its far-reaching consequences, technological change is generally long in the making. It goes, with varying speed, through a series of stages before having a significant impact on the economy: scientific findings, laboratory feasibility, operating prototype, commercial introduction, widespread adoption, diffusion to other areas, significant social and economic impact.

♦ To establish the technological position of a business one often needs to look towards adjacent fields to determine likely developments. What is being worked on in the relevant research departments in universities? What is being used in more advanced industries or countries that formerly employed similar technologies? What patents are being applied for and awarded? What technological papers are being presented at conferences? What new technology is being offered (often by newcomers) at trade shows?

> **For years, technologies developed for military and space applications** have found their way into other industries. The military and NASA research labs in the USA have been a strong source of new technologies and materials. In the same vein, military research has generated a large number of high tech entrepreneurs and businesses in Israel in fields such as communications, signal processing, optical technologies and computer networks.

♦ How compressed is the product life cycle in the business sector? Does a company possess the seeds for the next generation or is it a one-shot effort?

♦ Technology is often successful in a different way than was originally expected. How broad is the applicability of a proprietary technology? What are the company's patents, exclusive rights? Who owns what? How much technology is required from others to produce? What are the chances of competitors (capriciously) claiming infringement on their patents? Is it possible or wise to buy (missing) pieces of technology?

♦ Apart from producing prototypes, how much experience in mass production is available? Is it wise to produce or to subcontract? What (tooling, industrial engineering) investment is involved in producing quantities? What time is required to get production levels up to market demand (time to market!)?

◆ For a traditional product, what is the state of the production plant? Is it likely that change in production technology will be required? Is automation required to keep costs down? Do (some) manufacturing operations have to be moved to countries with low labour costs? How much spare capacity is there (does the company operate in one, two or three shifts)? What is the size of the 'steps' to increase capacity? What will be the necessary related investment levels?

Axa Stenman BV solidly viewed itself as a Holland-based manufacturer of goods for the bicycle and building industry. Much attention was successfully paid to efficiency and automation. However, emphasis on global cost competitiveness eventually led to the establishment of manufacturing activities in the Far East and Poland, with the additional benefit of opening up new (local) markets.

◆ Environmental liabilities for the effects of production activities and chemical contamination of the soil of a production location have become major issues in certain countries. Are these a consideration?

◆ What are the options for subcontracting the manufacturing? Can the technology be sold in case marketing of the products is not successful?

Marketing and sales strategy

High tech companies are often dominated by technology focused entrepreneurs. Unfortunately, business success is often more dependent on marketing performance than product performance. Even though DOS was one of the worst imaginable operating systems, it did not prevent Microsoft from dominating the industry.

Therefore, the most important thing you should look for is *marketing awareness*. If marketing *skills* are missing, a hands-on venture capitalist can complete the team. If, by culture, management is not looking at its business through the eyes of its customers, no amount of effort can force success.

◆ Is a clear market segment targeted? What is the strategy that will support the company's strengths and exploit competitive weaknesses?

◆ What are the planned distribution channels or partnerships? Wholesale, retail, brokers, direct sales by mail order, OEMs (manufacturers incorporating the company's products), etc.? Company sales personnel, distributors or independent representatives? How will this evolve over time? What geographic roll-out is being planned? What associated costs are being projected? How does this compare to industry averages?

Insignia Solutions Ltd switched focus back and forth between OEM and direct sales over the years. The first provides funding credibility and involvement in leading edge developments but disappointing (royalty) volumes, while direct sales to end customers is a costly system to set up and can upset OEMs if done independently. Ultimately, the best result turned out to be development for and with OEMs, while keeping open the right to market directly at a later stage.

♦ What is the pricing strategy? Is it consistent with the projected quality/functionality? Is it cost-plus? Or competitorless? Based on price lists or competitive bidding? What are the planned price or discount levels for the different layers of distribution?

♦ What advertising is considered? How does this compare with industry averages?

♦ What customer credit is required for the business? What guarantees will be provided to customers?

♦ Will the company eventually *own* its end-customer base? Its own brand name? These are important exit/valuation issues.

Organization and management

Since assessing the management is the single most important item in due diligence, all other checks should contribute to this process. For a start, the professionalism (or lack of it) of the business plan is most likely to be the first thing by which an entrepreneur can be judged. Skills in formulating plans and persuasiveness in conveying it are a good dry run of what will be needed for the business to be successful.

It is preferable to fund management *teams* rather than one individual. However, all teams need a leader, and it is necessary to establish whether he or she has the energy, drive and motivating ability to lead and grow a team. Look for evidence of achievement and ambition. Characteristics of success are initiative, integrity, and commitment; plus the clear formulation of objectives and the proven ability to implement them.

Ideally an entrepreneur should combine both the technologist and the business opportunist. Unfortunately, the combination of an education in engineering and an MBA is much rarer in Europe than in the USA. In Europe, one often deals with inventors with little or no business experience, or business opportunists with insufficient substance to make a project a real success. As a consequence, it is even more important to establish that a project team contains the required marketing, technical, financial planning and control skills.

♦ Do the past achievements of team members make them suitable for the particular business? Is there individual commitment by the key people, both financially and careerwise? What is the size and source of their capital? Are they 100 per cent committed to the specific project? If not, can there be a conflict of interest? Is there the required 'fit' of the individual team members; do they complement each other; will they function to support one another and pull together rather than pull apart when things are getting rough?

◆ Is there a clear understanding of respective responsibilities and recognition of who the leader is? However painful, it is much better to have that discussion before rather than after investment. In my experience, shared ultimate responsibility (as opposed to one leader) never works; at difficult moments, it can become fatal.

In one of our UK software companies we were confronted with mutiny, two months after our investment. The ultimatum by the excellent vice-president for sales and marketing and by the also excellent chief technologist was to fire the not-so-excellent CEO or they would leave. Investors reluctantly chose not to yield to such pressure and the two left, as did the CEO shortly afterwards. It took two years to rebuild the management team.

◆ Are the salaries, bonuses, pensions and other benefits of management clear and realistic? Do the agreements with key people have clear non-compete clauses (lest you find yourself with profoundly unwanted new competitors)? Do they have the support from their home front for the demands they will have to meet from entrepreneurial challenges ahead?

◆ If a team is incomplete (for now or for later), is there a clear understanding over what positions must be filled? Is there information on potential candidates and areas of responsibility?

◆ What is the quality and ambition of second-line management? Is there scope for internal growth? How will employees share in the creation of wealth in the company (stock options, profit sharing)? What is the rationale, mechanism and cost of such programmes?

◆ What are the ideas or commitments with regard to non-executive directors? What are the backgrounds and expertise of existing board members?

◆ What external experts (legal, accounting, banking, advertising, technological) are being used? The picture provides insight not only into resources available, but also into management style and willingness to buy knowledge from elsewhere. These contacts are equally valuable as useful sources for reference checks.

To establish the scope of the organization, one should also check the property ownership, employee contracts (non-compete clauses), pension schemes and business licences (including anything bearing on environmental issues).

Financial history and projections of turnover, profits, cash flow, funding

This is the most obvious – and unfortunately often the sole – object of due diligence.

◆ What are the *assumptions* underpinning the financials? Check the consistency of financials with the assumptions (this is sometimes done by outside accountants as part of the writing of the business plan, which thus becomes 'audited' ... I like plans that have been made by the people that need to implement them).

◆ Examine (preferably audited) profit and loss (P&L) statements and balance sheets against industry comparables. Identify start-up costs. Look for unusual items in the financials, big (or very small) expenditures on capital equipment, research and development (R&D) or advertising. They can hamper the cash flow position of the company, yet are critical for long-term growth. Understand the implications of the options taken. Be sure to look for off-balance sheet commitments as well.

> **Gilde participated in the MBO of a company** active in the upgrading and prepacking of potato products. Only after the buyout, did we become fully aware of the nature and importance of the forward-purchasing commitments the company had made, and which became costly when the market turned.

◆ Look at overdue receivables. Understand the reasons (interviewing one or two can be very instructive). Look at the ten biggest accounts outstanding. Does this mean something?

◆ Work in progress (WIP) is a critical item, as its value of WIP or the shifting of a project from one year to the next will directly affect profitability.

◆ Look at systems for monitoring and planning margins, expenses and cash: all are very critical in either early stage companies or leveraged buyouts. Understand future funding requirements.

◆ Look at general and administrative expenses, marketing, R&D, depreciation, all as percentages of sales. Compare with industry averages. What are the implications?

◆ Determine the break-even level for revenues. What market share does that represent? What are the most critical items affecting break-even? Any short-cuts? (Fall-back scenarios?)

For leveraged buyouts, there are a host of relevant ratios related to leverage and capacity to meet interest and loan repayments. These should be part of the financial model used to determine and validate the deal structure. Compare them to industry averages and decide whether they are realistic.

Above all, identify the elements of growth in the business plan. Annual growth of 1 per cent each in volume, per cent gross margin and creditors, combined with

1 per cent annual reduction in inventory and debtors is a consistent recipe for a great business (and spreadsheet). Make sure you understand and agree to the feasibility of the assumptions.

Ownership, structure, long-term contracts, financing and exit considerations

These elements can be a threat to the new investors' share in the (potential) success of a business. Understand the legal form of the business and its rationale, whether partnership or corporation.

- Are there different classes of shares? What are their special rights?

- Who invested how much and when? What major changes occurred in ownership over time. Are there any other written or other commitments on stock or profit-sharing?

- Be aware of employment contracts that exceed a realistic level of remuneration or that run for a fixed period of time.

- Understand the mergers, consolidations and reorganizations the company has gone through. In case of mergers (or demergers!), distinguish the elements of growth of volume and profitability imputable to the various components of the business.

- Understand all current and planned agreements on franchise, royalty, licensing and any agreements involving exclusivity (in sales, purchasing, manufacturing, services) or in force for longer than two years. Who is the formal owner of the technology? Is the ownership free and unpledged? Can it be sold? What patents have been applied for (in what countries) and what is their status?

- Understand the existing commitments of banks and other lenders. What is their opinion on the business and attitude towards future funding requirements. What cash buffers are available? What assets have been pledged? What is the attitude of the other shareholders towards future financing rounds and dilution? Have any personal guarantees been given by management or other shareholders?

> **On the basis of its success,** one of Gilde's telecom and network portfolio companies is regularly approached as a candidate to acquire businesses with similar activities that could broaden its scope. The key manager's insistence on retaining the level of its stake in the business is a complicating factor in funding and structuring further growth.

- Finally, are there any agreements about exit? How will investors get their money out (buy back, acquisition, initial public offering on a stock market)? Do the various shareholders and management share the same agenda?

THE PROCESS

The work of a venture capital manager by nature involves the allocation of time among a number of companies deserving attention. They may be portfolio companies or new projects, and one specific project may be at issue, or many other potential deals. It is therefore important to structure and manage the due diligence process. This applies both to the internal decision process within the venture capital firm, as well as to the generation of the kind of information discussed in the previous section.

Each firm needs to establish its own practices. Our approach at Gilde is an example (*see also* Fig. 6.1). Each Monday, the partners review *fact sheets* summarizing the (prospective) business, initiators and (expected) terms related to requests received during the week. If we decide to pursue a deal, two people are assigned (on the basis of skills, interest and workload) to establish within a couple of weeks *why* we should invest or not; *what* the issues are; and *how* we are going to conduct due diligence. This is laid down in a project proposal. In practice, only one request in ten becomes a project. The discussion of the project proposal by the partners ensures that we all contribute to the substance and process of due diligence, using our collective experience and network.

New request	Active request	Project	Approved investment
300 a year < 5 days	100 a year < 14 days	30 a year 1–2 months	10 a year 2 weeks

● First analysis
● Initial issue
  identification
	● Visit to company and
	  management
	● Issue identification
	● Initial upside analysis
		● In-depth company
		  analysis
		● Market/technology
		● Determining upside
		  factors
		● Syndication
			● Terms
			● Contracts

Fact sheet	Project proposal and plan	Investment proposal	Deal

Fig. 6.1 ♦ Gilde's due diligence process

The project proposal provides the basis for the investment decisions later on, as well as the size and terms of allocated resources. Projects are discussed weekly. Typically, a partner manages one or two projects at any one time. After completion of due diligence, a project should be approved for investment on the basis of an investment proposal including – apart from the description of the business, etc. – the considerations with regard to upside, downside, deal, and plans after investment.

During the due diligence process, a lot of deals are washed out. One should therefore commit resources in steps and validate essential ingredients before undertaking major expenditures. The process involves the following stages.

1   Analyze the business plan.

2   Meet the management and visit facilities.

3   Perform desk study of markets, technologies.

4   Close deal subject to due diligence outcome.

5   Conduct detailed due diligence, involving outside experts.

Apart from these structured steps, one should grasp opportunities to read about a subject, meet people, and talk over subjects related to a project. Write down information in file notes. Discuss the status of a project with colleagues and pick their brains. Review the progress regularly and make sure to focus on the main issues. As this chapter is intended for many situations, it covers a great variety of issues. It is intended to raise awareness and serve as a checklist. However, make sure you keep seeing the wood in spite of all the trees.

Analyzing the business plan

The project has to be tested to ensure that it meets your principal investment criteria with regard to stage of investment, management, overall prospects, technology, industry sector and partners. As mentioned earlier, the quality of the business plan itself is one of the most important indicators of the management's style and professionalism. A few phone calls may confirm or invalidate the principal attractions of a proposal.

A professional venture capitalist should not invest without having carried out his or her own downside assessment of the future business prospects. The objective is that in the 'worst case' the business would still be viable and provide an acceptable return. This will often be part of a sensitivity analysis to provide insight into the business model by assessing the consequences for profit or financing requirements of assumptions such as:

◆ sales shortfall or excess or delay by 5, 10 or 20 per cent

◆ variation of gross margin percentage by 5 or 10 per cent

◆ variation of payment terms of customers and suppliers

◆ exclusion or delay of certain major (projected) contracts, or product launches

◆ changes in interest rates, and so forth.

Any business plan based on spreadsheets in which sales and margins increase materially faster than expenses and working capital is bound to show good results. The good thing about spreadsheets is that you can use them to show the effects of challenging the assumptions. The work you do with business plans will probably be cumulative and at more than one stage in the process. It would be hard to spend too much time examining what they mean for your project.

The effect of either over- or under-achievement of plans is usually an increasing requirement for cash.

Examining the outcome of a sensitivity analysis, which might be carried out with the help of outside experts, can provide an excellent framework for discussions with the management team at a subsequent stage, since the 'what if' questions reveal weaknesses and strengths of the business. In many cases, it will help in optimizing the deal structure, or lead to increasing the size of financing. Alternatively, it can result in declining a deal for lack of buffer, if a management team is not willing to accept the dilution of ownership required for adequate funding of a business.

Meeting the management and visiting facilities

Sometimes it is advisable to have a business plan presented in person to provide an opportunity to work through a plan's inadequacies. But for the sake of efficiency one should demand some form of basic outline, submitted in written form only, to determine which projects to pursue. If a business plan meets the basic investment criteria, the first action is to meet with the management team in their operating environment. The aim is to gain a limited, yet significant, under-standing of the business and management's objectives, and thus be able to propose an initial financing structure/deal and win an exclusive mandate. It is essential that the initial assessment is thorough, yet that costs are minimized. The burden of the investigation falls on the venture capital people.

On site, one should appraise the location, capacity, efficiency, quality of operating equipment and building, work in progress, raw material, finished stock and production management. Assess the management team: how do they perform under detailed questioning? Write down first impressions and review them during reference checks.

The quality of technology has to be assessed: R&D department and R&D expenditure. Likewise for marketing and sales departments. Review marketing materials and get a product demo from a regular sales person. How busy is the after-sales department? How readily available is the management reporting infor-mation. Who is and who isn't aware of the company's performance? What is the company's culture?

> **One project we looked at** years ago involved silicon wafer polishing technology, to be transferred from Florida to the Netherlands. Many impressive investors were committed to the project. When we visited the US initiator in Florida, stunning presentations were made and financial track records looked very good. It required tremendous persistence to schedule a visit to the plant, between boardroom presentations, cocktails and barbecues. The plant looked surprisingly empty and all machines were still packed in their original crates. We chose not to invest, and learned two years later that the chief executive had been arrested by the FBI for corrupt practices.

Performing desk study of markets and technologies

Parallel to the discussions with the company, one should build a reference framework by establishing data on markets, competitors, technologies, major customers and suppliers, using available market studies, databanks, press articles, annual accounts and the like. There is a surprising amount of information on all industry sectors readily accessible. Branch organizations are often a very productive source of information. The relevant details should be compiled by the venture capital executives or their internal market researchers. These data form a backdrop for evaluating the company's performance and plans. This activity will also identify potential contacts for checking and validating specific issues.

Closing the deal subject to the outcome of due diligence

The next stage of due diligence will involve numerous contacts with outside people, thus raising the costs as well as the visibility of the deal. If a project is attractive, this will become more and more clear. If there is no basic agreement with management on the opportunity and terms to invest at this point, the increase in outside interest and management's confidence that stems from further due diligence might actually complicate the closing of a deal. Equally crucial: the contacting of customers, suppliers, competitors, etc., represents commercial risks for the company that it will only wish to take if there is a framework of commitment.

Therefore at this stage there should be an agreement with management on the basic terms – valuation, size of deal, partners, rough deal structure – and it should provide exclusive rights to closing the deal for a reasonable period. Management may require a commitment from the venture capitalist to financing, subject to 'due diligence' on either all or specific aspects of a project (and possibly other conditions, such as board approval, arranging a syndicate, etc.). In any case, the venture capitalist should be free to decline a deal if any major aspect of the proposed plan is invalidated by further due diligence. As the cost of involving outside experts can be substantial, there should be clear agreement on who pays what, both if the deal goes through, and if it does not.

> **We once looked at a mechanical engineering company** building cabins for tractors. The aged owner was seeking succession and we presented the opportunity to an operational manager who was seeking a buy-in situation. Over a period of three months we put in a considerable amount of time to negotiate a deal, while the manager drafted a business plan. At the final moment, he concluded the business was insufficiently attractive. We were quite disappointed by this late defection. And we really got upset when we were presented with an invoice for 200 hours of management consultancy!

Conducting detailed due diligence, involving outside experts

Depending on the nature of a deal and critical issues identified, various outside people can be involved to validate specific aspects of a project. One group consists of experts who can be hired on a project basis, and a second group consists of the customers, suppliers, competitors, colleagues and (former) employers and employees of businesses and their initiators.

For a high tech start-up, technology experts from university departments, technology consultants, patent advisers and market research consultants may be involved.

For a major buyout, accountants, tax advisers, contract lawyers and environmental experts will most likely be employed to review past trading results, balance sheets, accounting policies, management letters, tax liabilities, employment contracts and long-term contracts. In addition, outside accountants may be involved in carrying out far-reaching sensitivity analyses.

The briefing of outside experts is an all-important matter. The specific objective and the area covered should be clearly identified, as well as the timetable, depth of analysis, level of commitment and degree of liability sought from any expert. This will avoid later disappointment where advice is either too much, too broad, too little or too narrow. Costs should be defined in advance. Briefing and final reporting should be detailed in writing. This is essential for later reference and syndication of a deal. Verbal reporting is equally important as there are often (important) things consultants will say but not write.

The best results are obtained with outside advisers if they are called in early, are kept fully aware of the due diligence process and are given full access to all relevant information. There should be interim reports to keep things on track. Ideally, there should be a level of trust and familiarity with each other's style and focus, based on earlier work together. Comments such as 'reasonable risk' and 'needs attention', are relative and it is hard to understand what they mean when you hear them from a new adviser. As venture capital by definition involves risks which cannot be fully eliminated, one should work with advisers familiar with the venture capital sector to avoid getting too much advice on the risks of equity investments as such!

The most important source of information on a company remains the people involved in its business on a daily basis: its customers, suppliers, employees, etc. Over and over again I have been struck by how keen people are to talk about their work and their companies. Anyone called on for their knowledge in a specific area is eager to talk about it. Meet people personally whenever possible. Plan in advance what you want to get out of a meeting or a call.

♦ Business and personal references can be obtained from the management of a company. Always make sure you can choose whom to talk with. Of course, most will be 'primed' for receiving a visit or a call, but with the appropriate filter one can always distil something useful, whether from a fierce competitor, ex-boss or beta-test customer. Pursue reference checks independently through your own channels to validate the picture you are getting.

♦ For personal reference checks on management, look for facts more than opinions. Establish track records in raising sales, various job functions, making moves. Try: 'Would you employ x to set up a business that ...'

♦ For reference checks on a business, ask broad questions to let the source indicate what in his or her opinion is important or relevant. 'What do you think of company xyz?' 'What would improve the product?' People do not like to criticize but do like to help. Establish whether a product is really being used in a customer's mainstream business, or just being tested. What hurdles still need to be taken if a customer is to really deploy a product? What is the time-scale? What is the cost to switch? What are the customer's economics (payback period)?

> **Recently, for the due diligence on an Israeli company** which provides graphical interface solutions for IBM AS400 computers, we spoke to its Dutch-based competitor, Seagull Software. We really learned to appreciate the strengths and weaknesses of both companies. As a consequence, we are now an investor in Seagull, and helping the company with its international expansion.

CONCLUSION

♦ Due diligence needs to be conducted in stages so as to minimize wasted time and wasted costs.

♦ Due diligence must be thorough and result in the most appropriate deal structure.

♦ Due diligence is equally essential to ensure that after the investment you can monitor an investment effectively and make sure identified weaknesses are being addressed.

Finally, rely on your partners to let you know when you're falling in love.

Note

1. Though a trifle American, a useful book is W. Keith Schilt, *The Entrepreneur's Guide to Preparing a Winning Business Plan and Raising Venture Capital*, Prentice Hall, ISBN 0-13-282302-0. Besides being good reading for venture capitalists, it is a practical tool in setting out on the right foot with entrepreneurs.

DEAL STRUCTURING
AND PRICING

Clive Sherling
Apax Partners & Co. Ventures Ltd

Introduction

Valuation

Funding requirements

Financial instruments

Other issues

 **Clive Sherling** is immediate past Chairman of the British Venture Capital Association. After graduating from the London School for Economics, Clive Sherling joined Arthur Andersen where, in 1982, he became a partner in the insolvency practice. He acted as receiver or liquidator in some of the most complex cases in the mid-1980s.

Clive Sherling joined Apax Partners as a director in 1987 and has since led investments in many financial services and consumer products companies. He plays a major role in fundraising and is the primary point of contact for investors in the Apax Partners' funds.

He is Chairman of the Football Licensing Authority, the government body responsible for supervising safety in soccer grounds and a board member of Wembley National Stadium Limited, the company responsible for the re-development of Wembley Stadium.

INTRODUCTION

Deal structuring is the organization of a business transaction which will be reflected in a legal agreement governing the relationship between the various parties who are interested in a company. A good deal structure should satisfy the objectives and balance the risk/return ratio for all parties. Generally, the best structures are simple, require minimum involvement by the lawyers, accommodate all parties and cover all eventualities.

The structure of a transaction is dependent on the legal and taxation environment of the countries in which the investee company intends to operate. This chapter ignores legal and tax issues and concentrates instead on the broader issues involved in structuring an investment. Local professional advice will be essential in any particular case to ensure that the structure developed is appropriate. The elements which are considered here include valuation, funding requirements, financial instruments and such other issues as veto rights, representation, and management requirements.

VALUATION

There is no definitive way to value a company. Its value will depend on a host of factors: the company's stage of development, the economic and public stock market environment, the company's position in its market, the prospects for the market sector in which the company operates, the likelihood that the company will need further cash to achieve its objectives, and, not least, how much competition there is among capital providers to invest in the company. Nevertheless, certain techniques provide a framework in which to consider the range in which the value of a company is likely to fall.

Stage of development

The stage of development of the company will determine how much factual information is available on which to base an analysis.

A company that is starting up will have no financial record; all it will have are projections based on what the company's management team believes it can achieve. If the company is developing a new technology or creating a new service, there may be no useful comparable companies against which to measure such projections.

Early stage companies which have developed a concept, product or service but have not yet started to market it will almost certainly be loss-making, having used up the initial capital provided by the founders. Again, the company's historic financial information will give no guidance on likely future results.

In both cases, the entry valuation will depend on qualitative factors such as the investor's return expectations, the proportion of the company that the management will give up to attract the investment and the investor's view of the opportunity for the new concept, product or service. The investor will need to analyze the product and market opportunity to establish whether the potential exists to build a large company. If the market opportunity is small, even the largest company in the market will remain comparatively small.

Additional financial information is available for more developed companies which are seeking capital to expand their businesses by opening new branches, taking on more sales or production staff, or widening their product range. The information can be analyzed and compared to other similar companies for an indication of a range of values. It will be necessary to assess the rate at which the company is likely to expand compared to its competitors, and perform the product and market analysis to establish the company's potential. The investor will also need to consider his or her own risk/return expectations, and management will need to consider the proportion of the company it is willing to sell to an investor.

If the transaction is a management buyout (MBO) or a management buy-in (MBI), the company will probably be relatively mature and have a full trading record. An investor will be able to perform quite sophisticated analysis on the company's financial performance to date and compare the historical record to management's projections. The structure of the transaction is also likely to be more sophisticated, involving debt as well as equity and possibly other increasingly esoteric instruments. The valuation will take account of the tax planning opportunities which frequently arise in such transactions. Indeed, the valuation of the company may be related to the ability to service the various instruments used and to the tax environment.

Finally, the company may be well established but experiencing difficult times. It will need turning round and the vendor will have few alternatives: failure to attract new finance may result in the insolvency of the company and the total loss of the investment. The valuation is likely to be quite low, reflecting the additional risks being taken on by the new investor.

Qualitative factors

Whatever the stage of development of the company, the investor will need to consider a number of qualitative factors.

◆ The potential for sales growth will need to be examined, covering the size of the market, the competitive position and any patent or similar protection available to the company.

◆ The investor will examine the company's forecasts in the light of this analysis to ensure that management's assumptions are compatible with the market opportunity. Particular attention should be paid to the cash flow requirements of the plan, and if further capital will be needed this should be factored into the current valuation.

◆ The investor will need to consider the likely exit time-scale, exit valuation and exit route to ensure that the company will be suitable for realization within the investor's time-scale.

These are all due diligence matters which fundamentally affect the valuation of a company at the time of initial investment.

Quantitative factors

Investor return expectations

The investor will need to determine the general level of return expectation that is appropriate given the stage of development of the company and the relative risk/reward ratio of the opportunity. In broad terms, the earlier stage the company, the higher the return expectation should be. As private equity markets have matured and become more competitive and sophisticated, return expectations have tended to drift lower. Nevertheless, as a rough guideline investors might look for the following returns:

Seed or start-up investment:	60 per cent per annum or more.
Early stage investment:	in excess of 50 per cent per annum.
Development capital investment:	35 to 40 per cent per annum.
MBO/MBI:	over 30 per cent per annum.

There are no fixed rules in this area and the investor will need to weigh up the overall risk environment surrounding the company, portfolio considerations and the degree of competition for the particular opportunity. However, since the investor can be certain that not all investments will perform according to plan, it is important not to set too low an expectation for individual investment opportunities because this will result in a poor performance for the portfolio as a whole.

Management return expectations

While the investor is considering return levels desired, the entrepreneur or management will be doing the same. In personal terms, it may be the entrepreneur's one opportunity to make a significant amount of capital, and targets will have been set accordingly. In addition, the principal driving force for entrepreneurs to set up their own companies is often the desire to be their own boss and to have control of their lives. It may be necessary, therefore, to structure the investment in such a way that the economic value flows substantially to the investor while the entrepreneur retains a majority voting position in terms of the equity.

The precise deal structure will emerge from a negotiation which reflects each party's aspirations and requirements. Differences can often be overcome by the use of financial instruments other than pure equity. However, before considering such instruments, it is helpful to agree on an appropriate method of valuing the company both at the time of investment and at the likely time of exit.

Valuation methods

Price/earnings ratio

For established companies with a reasonable track record, the most common method of valuation is to use a price/earnings (p/e) ratio. This applies a multiple to the after-tax profits of the company. Usually, the greater the company's growth expectations, the higher the multiple. For a mature company which is unlikely to grow substantially, a multiple of between 8 and 12 might be used, while a company which could grow significantly for a number of years might attract a multiple of over 20, or even over 30.

To determine an appropriate multiple, the investor should look at similar publicly quoted companies for an indication of the expected multiple at the time of exit. It will also provide a base for establishing the current valuation. In using p/e ratios, it is important to recognize that these comparable ratios relate to companies with some liquidity in their shares. It is, therefore, appropriate to discount these comparable ratios to reflect the illiquidity of unquoted shares. This discount should normally be substantial, that is over 30 per cent, and in some circumstances over 50 per cent.

Other methods

For less established companies, other measures may be relevant. In some industries, particularly in the high-growth technology related industries, companies are sold on the basis of a multiple of sales or at a price per subscriber. In other industries, net assets may be the usual measure. In some cases, for example, older basic industries with expensive but old plant and machinery, it is appropriate to look at the replacement value of the assets. If the investor is looking at a turn-around situation, the liquidation value represents the minimum price that a vendor will accept.

At the most basic level, the value of a company is the present value of the future cash flows that will be derived from owning the company. These cash flows will be generated by dividends paid on an annual or other basis, and by the capital sum realized on exit either by trade sale, flotation or liquidation. The p/e ratio is a substitute which approximates a net present value calculation.

Return ratios

Investors seek to maximize the internal rate of return on investments (IRR). The IRR is the compound rate of return of the cash flows associated with a particular investment and is the method most commonly used by investors in determining the relative attractiveness of an investment opportunity. Occasionally, other related methods, such as the pay-back period, may be used. However, such a measure makes it difficult to rank alternative opportunities effectively because it does not take into account the timing and size of the different cash flows associated with each opportunity (*see* Table 7.1).

Table 7.1 ♦ Internal rate of return (IRR)

The IRR is defined as the rate of discount which makes the net present value (NPV) of a series of cash flows equal to zero. To find the IRR of an investment project lasting t years, it is necessary to solve the following:

$$NPV = C_0 + \frac{C_1}{1 + IRR} + \frac{C_2}{(1 + IRR)^2} + ... + \frac{C_t}{(1 + IRR)^t} = 0$$

where C is the cash flow for a given period.

FUNDING REQUIREMENTS

The business plan

The first step in determining a company's funding requirement is a review of management's business plan. This should cover the following areas.

- An executive summary which should be relatively short so that a reader can obtain a basic grasp of the opportunity in a few minutes.

- Industry background, setting out details about the sector in which the business operates or plans to operate.

- Details of company strategy, covering the reasons why the company will succeed in its chosen marketplace. These will set out any differentiating factors, any legal or other protections and other competitive advantages.

- Resumés of the management's background. Management is key to all private equity transactions and the plan should set out full details of the important members of the management team, their educational background, previous experience (particularly in a similar industry) and the role each will play in the new venture.

♦ Financial history and projections. If the company is not a start-up, the plan should include the recent financial history of the company with a commentary explaining any significant variations between years. For all companies, there should be financial projections for between three and five years and a detailed explanation of the assumptions used.

The interpretation of such plans requires experience. It is not unusual for management to give optimistic financial forecasts. It is easy to underestimate both how long it will take for a new product or service to be accepted by the marketplace, however compelling the advantages, and how much it will cost to provide the service or make and deliver the product. Competitor reaction is often greater than assumed in the plan, both from existing competitors and from other new entrants if the company is entering a fast growing marketplace.

The one statement that can be made with absolute certainty is that the actual financial performance will be different from that set out in the plan. The only questions are whether it will be better or worse and by how much.

How much cash?

In the light of the business plan, due diligence and experience, the investor can determine how much cash is likely to be required by the venture. There are no definitive rules in this area, but earlier stage companies are more likely to underestimate the cash requirement because sales and costs are much more difficult to estimate than for a mature company. Therefore, the approach to deciding how much cash is required is likely to vary by stage of investment.

For early stage companies it is generally better to plan several tranches of investment to be made available on the achievement of pre-agreed milestones. These might be stages of development of a new product – making a working prototype, making a pre-production model and achieving full production – or, for a retail concept, it might be the successful operation of an agreed number of shops. It is also advisable to make provision for an unexpected follow-on requirement, although this need not be communicated to management. It is not uncommon for early stage companies to require three times or more the original investment before the business reaches maturity.

The importance of due diligence in this area cannot be understated. Apart from the competence of management, mistakes in estimating the likely cash requirements of a business are the main reason for failure of a business. Cash is the life-blood of a business and great attention must be given to determining the amount to be invested.

Having understood the base case plan put forward by management, the investor should perform extensive sensitivity analysis on the assumptions used. The investor must identify the key risks that could have a major effect on the financial forecasts and analyze the size of any such impact if the assumptions prove to be wrong. This can be fairly easy to determine, as with a measure related to sales of a product compared with budget, or more difficult, as in a business which might be exposed to factors outside its control, such as the weather, when more sophisticated analyses may be required. Statistical techniques such as Monte Carlo modelling may help determine the likelihood of the occurrence of conditions which would bankrupt the business.

It is often worthwhile to prepare an upside case and a downside case alongside the base case to set the possible limits of the range of cash required. Such modelling will help determine the amount of debt that can be carried by the business. Some considerations in this area are covered later in this chapter.

FINANCIAL INSTRUMENTS

Determining the financial structure

Having determined how much cash will be required to finance the opportunity, the investor will need to decide how this will be structured. As financial instruments have become more sophisticated, the variations have increased substantially. However, many of these instruments rely on developed financial markets.

The basic choices will include equity, quasi-equity and debt. The combination of these instruments will have an impact on the final return from an investment. Effective financial structuring will provide downside protection if the business underperforms, while retaining access to upside rewards if the company exceeds its projections.

Equity

The equity part of the financial structure of a company is most at risk. The owners are the last people to share in the assets of a company if it is sold or liquidated and have no security over any assets. On the other hand, the owners receive 100 per cent of the excess of assets over liabilities.

The equity can be defined in four different ways: common shares, preference shares, options and warrants.

Common shares

The owners of the common shares are the final owners of the business. Although many other parties, such as employees, suppliers and lenders, are interested in the financial success of the venture, their interest is usually defined by a monetary amount. The owners of the common shares will receive the excess over these defined liabilities, whatever the amount and without limit.

171

Management will wish to own the common shares. As part of the negotiations surrounding deal structuring, agreement will need to be reached on the percentage of the common shares management will be able to buy. The following factors will be taken into account.

♦ *The amount of cash management will be subscribing* It is good practice to require management to subscribe for their shares rather than be given them. The amount that they subscribe will depend on the individual's financial circumstances, but it should be significant to them without being so onerous they become afraid to take the risks inherent in any business strategy. If this amount is not sufficient to enable management to acquire the agreed proportion of their common shares, the investor will need to introduce other instruments to the structure.

♦ *An appropriate level of reward for management* This will vary on an investment by investment basis. However, the greater the risk being taken by management, the greater the appropriate rewards. For example, an individual giving up a well paid employment to start a company may merit a greater proportion of the common shares than employees who are conducting an MBO of a stable company with positive cash flow and who are putting up little cash. Each case will need to be negotiated on its merits.

♦ *Potential additional members of management* Future recruits to the management team will need to be included in the equity structure. The investors and management should agree on how to provide for future colleagues and whether the shares of such future employees will be made available by all shareholders *pro rata* or by one party alone.

♦ *Incentive arrangements* In many instances, it may be considered appropriate to provide management with the opportunity to acquire additional shares in the company if they exceed the expected plan. The structure of such an incentive plan will need to be determined at the time of investment because it will affect the proportion of the common shares that the investor wishes to obtain initially.

Preference shares

Preference shares are part of the equity of a company, but their participation in the assets and return are defined. In normal cases, they will receive back the face value subscribed. By agreement, they may receive a dividend, provided there are sufficient profits to pay the dividend. It is common to provide that any unpaid dividends will be paid at some time in the future when there are sufficient profits. It is also possible to specify that preference shares will attract a multiple of face value on the occurrence of specified events, such as the sale of a company. The tax treatment of dividends from the point of view of both the company and the investor will need to be taken into account.

Options

Options give the owner the right to acquire common shares at a specified time and price. They are often used as part of an incentive scheme for managers. For example, key managers may be given the right to acquire a number of shares in the company in three years' time at a price three times higher than the original price. This would enable the investor to achieve a reasonable return before giving up part of the equity. Options may also be used to give an investor the right to increase his or her interest in the company in other circumstances, such as the failure to achieve certain milestones.

Such instruments may allow a compromise with management over the division of the equity at the outset. Management will fully believe that its plan will come to fruition, while the investor may take a more cautious view. The equity could be divided on the assumption that the plan will be achieved, but the investor will receive options to increase his or her interest in the company if the management falls short of its plan.

Warrants

Warrants are similar to options and also give the right to acquire common shares in the future.

Quasi-equity

Two variants on the above are redeemable shares and convertible debt. Redeemable shares are usually preference shares which the company can redeem in the future, provided that it has sufficient accumulated undistributed profits. Thus redeemable preference shares might have the right to receive dividends until such time as they are redeemed by the company. This can prove attractive to the investor because it will enable a substantial part of the investment to be recovered without the relinquishment of the common shares which carry the rights to the upside potential of the company. The investor could reinvest the redeemed shares in another opportunity.

Similarly, convertible loan stock will have the right to receive interest payments from the company until such time as the loan is repaid. One advantage of loan stock is that interest is normally tax deductible and does not require the existence of profits before it can be paid. On the other hand, loan stock is shown as a liability of the company rather than as part of the equity and makes the company look less substantial to potential or existing creditors. This is particularly true if the loan stock is secured on some or all of the assets of the company which will enable the loan from the investor to rank above the claims of ordinary trade creditors. The loan might be convertible if the company is doing very well and the investor wishes to swap a fixed return for the upside potential of the common shares.

Both these instruments provide good downside protection if the company underperforms, while retaining for the investor the opportunity to share in the upside if that proves attractive.

Debt

The final element of a potential deal structure is debt, a liability provided by a lender in return for a fixed reward defined as a rate of interest. The loan can be unsecured or secured over part or all of the assets. The interest payments will usually be deductible for tax purposes and the company need not be making profits to pay the interest. The debt will usually be provided by a third party such as a bank, vendor or supplier, but could be provided by the equity investor. Obviously, the greater the amount of the investment provided by the investor in a fixed return instrument, the lower the likely overall return from the investment, unless the investor receives options or warrants in return for providing the debt. However, because debt lenders are looking for a lower return than the equity providers, it will normally be better to obtain the debt portion of the package from a lender.

The following example indicates how the various components might be used to construct a deal structure. Management are seeking to execute an MBO. The vendor is prepared to accept a price of ECU 20 million. The business turns over ECU 30 million and achieves a profit after tax of ECU 2 million. The business has no existing debt or cash. Management believe that the company will be able to make profits after tax of ECU 4 million in five years' time when the business will have cash of ECU 16 million and in total will be worth ECU 56 million. They have told the potential investors that they are able to invest ECU 250,000 between them and want to own 40 per cent of the company.

If the investor accepted these terms (option A in Table 7.2) and invested ECU 19.75 million in return for 60 per cent of the company, in five years' time he will receive back 60 per cent of ECU 56 million, that is ECU 33.6 million, which will result in an IRR over five years of just over 11 per cent per annum, while management will have converted their ECU 250,000 into ECU 22.4 million. By using some of the instruments reviewed above, this inequitable split can be altered while still allowing management to have 40 per cent of the common shares.

The first step is to pay the same price as the management for the ordinary shares (option B in Table 7.2). This is important because otherwise it is possible to arrive at a position where management make a profit on their investment while the investor makes a substantial loss. For example, in the above instance, if the company was worth only ECU 30 million in five years' time, management would receive ECU 12 million for a profit of ECU 11.25 million, while the investor would receive ECU 18 million, suffering a loss of ECU 1.75 million. Therefore, if management pay ECU 250,000 for 40 per cent of the common shares, the investor should pay ECU 375,000 for his or her 60 per cent, making a total for the common stock of ECU 625,000. The investor could now invest the remaining ECU 19.375 million in preference shares, which must be redeemed at the time of the sale of the company.

In this circumstance, if the company is sold for ECU 56 million, the investor would receive back this ECU 19.375 million plus 60 per cent of ECU 56 million less ECU 19.375 million, that is a total of ECU 41.35 million, while management would receive ECU 14.65 million. Now the investor makes a return of nearly 16 per cent, which is probably still too low.

The next step is to attribute a coupon to the preference shares of, say, 10 per cent per annum (option C in Table 7.2). Assuming that this has no effect on the exit price, the impact is to increase the investor's IRR to over 18 per cent. Management will still have converted their ECU 250,000 initial stake to ECU 9.9 million.

If the investor was looking for a greater return than 18 per cent for this transaction, options might be looked at which would increase the investor's percentage of the common stock on exit. Management may well accept these because they will have 40 per cent of the company during the period of their stewardship over it, which may achieve their non-financial objective.

Another possibility is to introduce debt to the transaction (option D in Table 7.2). With pre-tax profits of around ECU 3 million by year 2, the company could afford to pay interest on around ECU 10 million of debt and still have the interest covered around three times, that is the profit is three times the interest charge. The lender will almost certainly require a covenant from the company that interest will always be covered more than twice as well as other ratios which will have to be achieved. The introduction of debt obviously adds to the risk of the investment because failure to honour the covenants could allow the lender to take control of the business.

However, provided that all parties are prepared to accept this level of risk, the effect on the return to the investor can be dramatic. Assuming management continues to subscribe ECU 250,000 for 40 per cent of the business and the investor subscribes ECU 375,000 for 60 per cent, the investor will now need to provide only ECU 9.375 million of preference shares. If these continued to accrue dividends of 10 per cent per annum, the IRR of the investor would rise to over 25 per cent, which may be regarded as a satisfactory return for this type of transaction.

Table 7.2 ♦ The effect various types of finance will have on the eventual return to the investor

MBO company	Year 0	Year 1	Year 2	Year 3	Year 4	Year 5
Earnings before interest and tax	2.0	2.4	2.8	3.2	3.6	4.0
Interest	0.0	0.0	0.0	0.0	0.0	0.0
Tax	0.0	0.0	0.0	0.0	0.0	0.0
Earnings after interest and tax	2.0	2.4	2.8	3.2	3.6	4.0
Cash balance	0.0	2.4	5.2	8.4	12.0	16.0
Value of the company (10 times earnings before interest and tax)	20.0					40.0
Plus cash	0.0					0.0
Cost of acquisition	20.0					
Proceeds available on exit						56.0

▶ **Table 7.2** ◆ **Continued**

OPTION A	Cash	%	IRR	Proceeds
Investors ordinary equity	19.750	60%	11.2%	33.600
Management ordinary equity	0.250	40%	145.7%	22.400
Total option A	20.000	100%		56.000

OPTION B	Cash	%	IRR	Proceeds
Investors preference shares	19.375			19.375
Investors ordinary equity	0.375	60%		21.975
Investors total	19.750		15.9%	41.350
Management ordinary equity	0.250	40%	125.7%	14.650
Total option B	20.000	100%		56.000

OPTION C	Cash	%	IRR	Proceeds
Investors preference shares (with 10% cumulative dividend)	19.375			31.205
Investors ordinary equity	0.375	60%		14.877
Investors total	19.750		18.5%	46.082
Management ordinary equity	0.250	40%	108.8%	9.918
Total option C	20.000	100%		56.000

OPTION D	Cash	%	IRR	Proceeds
Bank debt (with 10% cumulative interest)	10.000		10%	16.105
Investors preference shares (with 10% cumulative dividend)	9.375			15.090
Investors ordinary equity	0.375	60%		14.883
Investors total	9.750		25.2%	29.973
Management ordinary equity	0.250	40%	108.8%	9.922
Total option D	20.000	100%		56.000

For the purposes of this example we have assumed that no interest will be paid on surplus funds and that the company is not subject to taxation.

It should be clear that the combination of the various types of finance will have a significant effect on the eventual return to the investor. The following general rules should be borne in mind.

◆ Early repayment of a substantial part of the investment has a very positive effect on the return.

◆ Never pay significantly more for the common shares than management is paying.

◆ The introduction of a yield has a positive effect on the return without necessarily affecting the exit price.

◆ Options and warrants can be used to bridge the final gap between management aspirations and investor needs.

◆ The introduction of conservative levels of debt can have a significant effect on the investor's return.

◆ Structuring will not turn a bad investment into a good one but it can mitigate the effects by providing downside protection.

Table 7.3 ◆ The sensitivity of IRR to time

The sensitivity of IRR to time can be shown as follows:				
Year	**0**	**1**	**2**	**3**
Scenario 1				
Cash flow	−10,000	5,000	5,000	10,000
Scenario 2				
Cash flow	−10,000	0	0	20,000
Both scenarios show a cash gain of 10,000 (i.e. 20,000 − 10,000), however the IRR of scenario 1 is 38.3 per cent and the IRR of scenario 2 is 25.9 per cent.				

OTHER ISSUES

Once the division of the equity has been achieved, a number of other important matters require attention. These include corporate governance issues, investor rights (particularly if the investor holds a minority of the voting shares) and control over the exit process.

The investor will want to ensure that the company in which he is investing will be managed in a proper manner from both a legal and ethical point of view. The best way to achieve this is to have board representation or the right of veto on certain key decisions.

Board representation

At the time that an investment is being made, the investor must decide whether he or she wishes to be represented on the company's board of directors, either personally or through another individual. A decision also has to be made as to whether to seek any executive responsibilities or be non-executive. A personal investor may wish to take part in the management of the company as part of the reason for the investment. However, an institutional investor is more likely to wish to take a non-executive role. The border between the two need not be absolute.

The agreement should specify how many meetings of the board will be held each year. It should also specify deadlines for the production of monthly or quarterly accounts, as well as for the completion of the annual audit.

Veto rights

It is absolutely essential to make it clear to management that they are responsible for running the company on a day-to-day basis. Effectively, they should believe that it is their company, whatever percentage of the common stock they own. However, it is also essential that the investor has control over any matters which have a major effect on his or her interest in the company. The veto rights should cover the following matters.

♦ The appointment of directors. The investor should be able to prevent the appointment of additional directors who would change the balance on the board.

♦ The issue of additional share capital, since this would dilute the investor's interest.

♦ The creation of new subsidiaries, because assets could be transferred to such subsidiaries and then sold without any control by the investor.

♦ The taking on of any debt in excess of an agreed level.

♦ The issue of a charge over any asset of the company.

♦ The licensing of any technology owned by the company.

♦ The commencement of major litigation.

♦ The establishment of a corporate pension scheme.

♦ The issue of an employment contract to the senior directors and employees, or its variation.

♦ Major related party transactions.

♦ The alteration of the company's statutes.

♦ The transfer of any shares.

Annual budget

The most effective way to influence the management is through the agreement of an annual budget. Management can then report any significant variations from the annual plan at board meetings. Through participation in the budget process, the investor can ensure that management are not diverting from the agreed strategy, are not planning to take excessive risks with the business and are continuing down a path which will lead to an eventual exit for the investor.

This process should not be taken lightly. It is not interference with management in carrying out their duties, but a key method of providing input and advice to management while continuing to look after the investor's own interests.

Control over the exit process

Investments are usually made in unquoted shares. It is wise to ensure that there will be a process enabling liquidity to be achieved for the investor's interest in the company. This is best addressed as part of the negotiation of the investment. The investor will want to ensure that management and investor share the same objectives regarding exit. In particular, it is important to be satisfied that management do not see their interest as seeking a job for life, rather than seeking to obtain a capital gain through the sale of the company. If management is planning to remain with the company for longer than the investor's timetable, this may limit the exit opportunities and value for the investor. The only exit in this case may be via a share buy back by the company. Valuation is always difficult in this situation.

Therefore, the investor should obtain undertakings regarding management's plans for exit. As a backstop, the investor may wish to secure the right to force the sale of the whole company after a period of, say, seven years if by then management has not provided an exit. This is not foolproof since it will require an element of co-operation from management at the time, but is is certainly a major step in the right direction.

While considering exit matters, the investor may seek tag-along rights to ensure that management cannot sell their shares without finding a buyer for the investor's shares on similar terms. The investor may also seek take-along rights to ensure that other shareholders can be forced to accept a suitable offer in specified circumstances.

It may be prudent to establish from the outset that the investor will not provide any warranties to a purchaser at the time of exit, simply because the investor has not the detailed knowledge of the day-to-day business. This should be made clear at the time of the investment to avoid potential conflict when the exit is being negotiated.

Management requirements

Management will also have issues that they will want addressed during the negotiation of the investment, including their annual incentives as well as exit incentives. They will also want to know about the terms of their employment and what happens to their shares if they leave the company.

Annual incentives

Management incentives can be structured in many ways. However, the objective should always be the same: the maximization of shareholder value. Incentives are usually based, therefore, on the annual budget, and they reward the achievement or betterment of the budget. The payment of the incentive can be in cash or, possibly, additional shares. It is important that short-term annual incentives do not encourage management to go for short-term growth at the expense of the long-term increase in shareholder value.

If the plan shows that the company may become tight on cash or indicates that excess inventories may cause a problem, it may be sensible to link the annual incentive to the achievement of the planned cash flow or budgeted inventory levels as well as the annual profit plan. A company making profits can still fail if it runs out of cash!

Exit incentives

The provision of exit incentives can successfully link management's objectives to those of the investor. Management's shareholding should act as a major element in bringing these objectives together, but in some cases an additional incentive may be appropriate. This is often the case when management and investor fail to agree on an appropriate split of the equity at the time of the investment. The investor might agree to give management a greater share of the upside once certain milestones have been achieved.

Any exit incentive should be linked either to exit value or, probably better, to the IRR achieved by the investor. This latter measure allows for any early repayment of redeemable shares. Management could be given an agreed number of additional shares once the investor had obtained a return over, say, 25 per cent. Alternatively, a sliding scale may be offered, whereby the higher the IRR achieved by the investor, the greater the number of shares transferred to management. This can be achieved by contract terms or through options to be exercised in defined circumstances.

Management security

One of the motivations for management to decide to run their own business is to have more control over their job security. However, an investor must reserve the right to make a change to management if the company is failing to achieve its plan and a change of management would be good for the company.

It is important that in attempting to satisfy management, the investor does not allow long-term employment contracts. If it becomes necessary to change management, the company will probably not be doing well and will not be able to afford substantial payments to employees holding such contracts. The investor will need to take local laws into account, but contracts with a notice period in excess of six months should generally be avoided.

If it is necessary to change a manager, the question of his or her shareholding will arise. In the normal course of events, these shares are to reward performance and contribution to the creation of shareholder value. If the manager has under-performed, entitlement to the shares is debatable. The position is complicated by the fact that the manager has probably paid for the shares. One way to deal with this issue is to provide that managers' entitlement to retain their shares will vest over a period of time, say, five to seven years. Therefore, if they leave after three years, they will be entitled to retain a proportion of their shares and will have to sell the remainder, normally at market price, or at cost if lower, if that was agreed at the outset.

Over recent years, the concept of a good leaver and a bad leaver has developed. A bad leaver is someone who is dismissed for fraud or other wrongdoing or someone who leaves to join a competitor. A good leaver is all other leavers. The investor might agree that good leavers could keep their vested shares and sell the remainder at market value, while bad leavers might have to forfeit their shares or sell them all at cost.

Negotiation process

This chapter covers many of the matters which will need to be discussed with management during the completion of the investment. The manner in which these negotiations are conducted may have an impact on relationships with management after the investment is made.

Management may have appointed advisers to help them. While this is probably desirable, it is important that all relevant negotiations are held directly with management rather than with their advisers. After all, it is the management and not the advisers with whom the investor will have to work for the next few years. The way in which management negotiates will give a useful insight to the investor of how well the management will look after the investor's interest after the investment has been made.

It is usually preferable to address difficult issues early in the negotiation process because leaving them until later can create tension and waste due diligence, time and cost. Even if the difficult issues cannot be resolved early in the process, so long as they are highlighted people can be considering them while other matters are resolved. It may be that as other issues are dealt with, the difficult issues are looked at in a different light and become less important.

Even when difficulties are encountered, it is important to continue negotiating until the investor is certain that agreement will not be reached. Surprisingly often, positions change as negotiations proceed and the parties adjust their expectations. In addition, once the number of issues reduces to a manageable number, it might be possible to trade individual items to enable an acceptable agreement to be reached. After all, if warring parties can agree settlements, it should be possible for most commercial differences to be resolved between parties who share a similar ultimate objective.

POST INVESTMENT – VENTURE MANAGEMENT

Toon Nagtegaal
p3 technology partners bv

Introduction

Co-operation

Policy and strategy

Information

Involvement

Adding value

Red flags

Conclusion

Toon Nagtegaal is managing partner of p3 technology partners BV, an information and communications technology venture capital firm. After graduating from HEAO Business School in Arnhem (the Netherlands), he began his career at Avra Flanges and Ringfactories BV, a family-owned company based in the Netherlands, where he worked as Managing Director from 1979 until the sale of the company in 1980. Toon Nagtegaal then joined NMB Bank and soon after became Senior Investment Manager at NMB Participatie Group. In 1987, he co-founded Atlas Venture with two other partners, where he served as Managing Director until 1990. Prior to joining p3, he was Managing Director of Holland Venture for eight years. He has also contributed his time as a board member of the European Venture Capital Association (EVCA) and as the chairman of the EVCA Conferences and Training Committee.

INTRODUCTION

This chapter is about the part of a venture capitalist's job that continues after the investment is made, after the deal is done. Post investment it's called. In my view a deal is done only when and if it is disinvested. Only then do we know if we've been successful, if we made money, if we've achieved our goals.

The previous chapters described all the activities needed to enter into a deal. It is extremely important that this work is carried out well. Mistakes made in the phase before investing have a negative influence on the venture capitalist's position in relation to an investment and finally on the results. In Chapter 7 quite a lot was directed towards the future relationship to the investment: veto rights, representation, minority protection, shareholders' agreements, management and control. It all indicates that we, venture capitalists, want to have a say in the investment after we have transferred our money. We want to be involved. Through this involvement, venture capital distinguishes itself from all other types of financing.

The question arises, why do we want to be involved and how deeply? In discussing the level of involvement, a distinction is often made between 'hands-on' and 'hands-off' types of venture capital. 'Hands-on' is often connected with early stage investments and 'hands-off' with later stage investments. The amount of risk is clearly an indicator here. Therefore part of the answer to our question is given: venture capitalists are involved in their investments to *minimize risks*.

Minimizing risks is a major task for every kind of investor. There is nothing new here. Unlike most other types of investors, venture capitalists can't withdraw their money. Bankers can withdraw their credit lines and if they do so in time, they won't lose money. Investors, playing their game on the stock market, can sell off their shares when times get rough, and the good ones even make money by doing so. For most investors, minimizing risks means being able to move the investment, to move the money to a safer place. The liquidity of venture capital investments is very low – the venture capitalist's money is normally locked into an investment for quite some time. The way to minimize the risk is through the companies invested in.

This means that the venture capitalist needs a position that carries with it an influence on the course of the investment, on the course of the business. It is also necessary to have the capacity to exercise it. Now, if this can really be achieved, the second part of the answer on why the venture capitalist continues to be involved in the investment can be given: if a venture capitalist, or other investors such as business angels, can really minimize risks, they also have the ability to *maximize returns*.

It is all about being in a position to change things regarding the investment for the better, from bad to good or from good to better. Minimizing risks and maxi-izing returns.

Again this is where venture capital distinguishes itself from other types of financing. A very important question, maybe the most important question, a venture capitalist must answer is: Am I able to minimize risks and maximize returns? Many of the answers are already given if the tasks described in the previous chapters have been carried out well. Markets and technology have been analyzed; financial engineering has been performed and an optimal deal structure achieved; a formal, legal position is assured. But there remain the more difficult questions: Do I really understand the business? Do I have affinity with the business? Is there really a basis for co-operation with the management?

'Hands-on' versus 'hands-off'

The distinction between 'hands-on' and 'hands-off' types of venture capital has already been mentioned. Especially in the early days of European venture capital this distinction was often a major point of discussion. 'Hands-on' and 'hands-off' were used to qualify the type of venture capital firm. 'Hands-off' was eventually considered not real venture capital.

Tony Lorenz describes 'hands-on' and 'hands-off' firms in his *Venture Capital Today* and identifies an 'in-between type of firm', which he calls a reactive firm. He states that the entrepreneur should carefully select a venture capital firm in this respect.

> **The entrepreneur resisting involvement** is unlikely to seek finance from a fund with a hands-on or actively supportive style and reputation. He may be able to find sources of finance from among the minority of venture capitalists who make a positive virtue of a hands-off or passive post-investment position. These funds will receive only semi-annual or annual information from the company, may have a 'reserve' right to a director and will rarely be in contact with their investees.

It is difficult to think of a situation where an illiquid investment is made and the level of interest and involvement is limited to receiving only information once or twice a year. Even quoted companies have the obligation to inform the public at least twice a year, and the more strictly regulated markets oblige their quoted companies to publish quarterly figures and inform their shareholders publicly in case of major events.

Is it the entrepreneur who determines the level of involvement of the venture capitalist? Hardly. The one who supplies the capital will estimate the risks involved and on the basis of that estimate determine which instruments for the control of those risks are needed. In cases where the venture capitalist's 'toolbox' doesn't contain the right equipment, the investment will not – or should not – be made.

In general one could say that more risks are involved in younger companies than in more mature ones. And indeed the 'hands-on' principle is mostly mentioned in connection with early stage investments and 'hands-off' with later stage. In my opinion, however, this approach is not very useful when dealing with post investment strategies. The priority is that methods should be found to minimize risks. These risks may find their origin both inside and outside the investee company. Even the investment itself might present a risk to the company and through that to the investment. A highly leveraged management buyout, for example, might get the company in question into trouble at a time when interest rates increase and investments need to be made in order to keep up with the competition. If the 'later stage' or 'hands-off' or 'passive' investor does not understand the business, because of such a low level of interest and involvement, the development of the company might be frustrated.

The common distinction between 'hands-on' versus 'hands-off' also denies one of the core elements of venture capital, be it later stage or early stage investments. I have already stated that in my view a deal is only done when and if the investment is realized. A venture capitalist is only successful if his or her investments are realized with a profit. In this most crucial part of the work it is natural to want to be involved. Moreover the venture capitalist needs to be in a position to take an action instead of just reacting or being obliged to just wait and see. The position that is meant here is one that is, first of all, legally secured. But the right to take the initiative to sell a company or ask for a listing on a stock market is of very little use if the kind of business the investee company is in is not well understood, if the present market position of the company is not known, if the present state of the organization is something the venture capitalist is not really aware of. When it comes to maximizing returns, timing of exit is often crucial – not to mention when investments are not doing well. A well-timed trade sale can make the difference between a (modest) profit or a complete write-off.

From the point of view of post investment, the issue of 'hands-on' versus 'hands-off' concentrates too much on the involvement of the venture capitalist within the investee companies. To a venture capitalist it is not the company but the investment in a company that is the instrument for making a profit, for achieving the goal. First and foremost the focus is on managing the investment. Although he or she might sometimes get into a position of co-managing an investee company, it is the investment that is of first concern. The venture capitalist manages the investment and *monitors* the company.

Investment management and monitoring

Apart from 'hands-on' and 'hands-off', the term monitoring is often used when post investment is discussed. It has already been made clear that monitoring, in the true sense of the word, cannot reflect the venture capitalist's behaviour towards the investment. The investment should be managed. But monitoring an investee company is indeed a task that has to be carried out after money has been invested by the venture capitalist.

In order to manage an investment properly it is vital to know what is going on in the investee company. The tools for monitoring are very important and will be discussed later on in the chapter. However, management, and thus investment management, goes further than just knowing what is going on, than just following or monitoring a process.

Investments are being made on the basis of best estimates of future developments. In practice things will go better or worse than estimated – certainly different. The future has this terrible tendency to surprise us, which means action. Markets change, unexpected competitors appear, new technologies are introduced, political changes may have great impact – and this is often overlooked – people change and organizations develop in new directions. Within the investee companies it is primarily the job of management to cope with this. Very often, though, they want, need or are obliged to listen to their shareholders' opinion on how to react to these changes.

For the future progress and the sake of the investment, the venture capitalist wants to be involved in the important decisions that result from changed circumstances. Involvement in this respect often means taking part in the decision-making process, or even having certain veto rights. See the contradiction: the involvement of a 'hands-off' or 'reactive' venture capitalist is limited to major decisions only – yet how can one take part in the process of taking major decisions without being fully aware of the smaller ins and outs!

The responsibility of venture capitalists towards their investee companies is great. As soon as they claim a position in major decisions they should be aware of the fact that they are actors within their own investments. It is very much like an entrepreneur who is investor and manager of the same company at the same time. For that reason I call post investment 'Venture Management'. And it is clear now that the basis for venture management is co-operation with the management of the investee company.

CO-OPERATION

It seems just too obvious, even implicit, that venture capitalists and the management of their investee companies co-operate. But is it? At least, do they co-operate well?

In 1993–4 a survey was carried out by Alex van Groeningen Management Consultants BV in collaboration with Vrije Universiteit Amsterdam on the co-operation between entrepreneurs/managers of investee companies and venture capitalists. The survey was limited to the Netherlands, but as a rather mature venture capital market it can be assumed that the Dutch market is quite representative of other European countries, now and in the future. In order to analyze the results of this study correctly, one should know that in the Netherlands in the period of the study, expansion finance counted for 50–60 per cent of the number of deals and management buyouts/buy-ins (MBO/MBIs) for approximately 20 per cent.

The survey showed that in 40 per cent of the cases the entrepreneur/manager chose the venture capitalist from whom the most value added could be expected. It was especially in start-up and expansion deals that the expected added value was the most important factor in choosing the venture capitalist. In 29 per cent of cases business was done with the venture capitalist who showed interest first. The amount of money that was to be invested and the price of it were relatively unimportant when choosing a venture capitalist.

How satisfied were entrepreneurs/managers with their venture capitalists?

- Forty per cent were non-committal
- Forty per cent were satisfied
- Twenty per cent were dissatisfied.

Furthermore:

- start-up managers/entrepreneurs were more likely than others to say that they expected and needed more support from their venture capitalists;
- expansion managers/entrepreneurs were more likely to be dissatisfied with the involvement of their venture capitalists. Most of them found the involvement limited to guarding the investment;
- MBO/MBI managers/entrepreneurs were more likely to be satisfied with the co-operation with their venture capitalists. Most of them felt properly supported;
- in more than 40 per cent of cases more capital was needed than was foreseen.

What is there to be learned from these results? First of all too many start-up and expansion managers/entrepreneurs don't get what they want from their venture capitalists – what they have chosen them for – whereas most of the MBO/MBI managers get more from their venture capitalists than they originally expected, or even expected to need. One could say, of course, that the risks involved in start-up and expansion deals are normally greater than in MBO/MBI investments: yet the co-operation with the management in order to monitor the company properly and to manage the investment should, from my perspective, be correspondingly closer. Investment management, even when it is only directed towards minimizing risks, is in too many cases failing. The tendency in the venture capital industry to concentrate on later stage deals, especially MBOs is probably a result of this.

Why are venture capitalists better at co-operating with MBO managers? Before making the final investment, the MBO manager and the venture capitalist work together very intensely. Sharing the same interest once they have dealt with their respective positions in the deal, they often fight side by side against the same 'enemy', the seller of the company. They have got to know each other very thoroughly during this period and gained mutual respect. And mutual respect is the basis for good co-operation.

How different the situation is in the case of an expansion deal. The entrepreneur built up the business from nothing to a flourishing company, with even more potential if only there was some more capital. Until the day the deal is signed there is a conflict of interest with the venture capitalist: the venture capitalist wants as many shares as possible for the money, and the entrepreneur wants as much as possible in return for every issued share, in terms both of capital and added value. Both being good at selling, they make a lot of promises – promises that in too many cases they, as the study shows, can't keep after the deal is closed. Because of their bargaining over capital and shares, it is logical that in numerous cases too little capital is invested. If there is one reason for pressure on the relationship between the entrepreneur and the venture capitalist, it is the need arising for extra capital that was not foreseen and under circumstances that are worse instead of better than forecasted by the business plan. Investing the right amount of capital is step one in investment management.

But there is more. Mutual respect is mentioned as the real basis for good co-operation. Respect is something one normally has to gain – you don't get it for free. Unlike in cases of MBOs, the expansion manager/entrepreneur and the venture capitalist had only opposing interests before closing the deal. Sure, one can, and in this case must, have respect for one's opponent, but it is something different from the kind of respect resulting from co-operation. The expansion manager (and the same goes of course for the start-up manager) and the venture capitalist start really to co-operate from the moment the deal is closed, whereas the MBO manager and the venture capitalist will already have achieved a close relationship.

So in expansion and start-up deals co-operation between management and venture capitalist has to be established after signing contracts. Expectations in this respect on the part of the managers are high. Let's have a look at the venture capitalist's work and behaviour before closing the deal. He or she has put a lot of effort into investigating product, market, technology, financial figures, organization and management. The venture capitalist will have been extremely critical, behaving in a way which will often be seen as suspicious. In many cases the entrepreneur takes this attitude for granted, being in need of the financing. During the course of discussions, respect for the venture capitalist might grow because of work thoroughly done and insights arising from a critical attitude towards all aspects of the business. This is what I meant earlier about respect for one's opponent. On this basis, the entrepreneur will have high expectations of the venture capitalist's contribution after the deal is closed.

But what happens after the deal is closed, after the contracts are signed? Does the venture capitalist go on putting that same amount of effort into the investment? Most certainly, venture capitalists have great concern about the financial figures and they are in contact with the managements of their investee companies. But are they, after closing the deal, still that well informed about products, markets, technology, etc., using sources from outside the company as well? Do they regularly speak with other people within the company apart from the management? Or do venture capitalists merely become financial 'watch-dogs' after they have invested? In that case the venture capitalist can no longer offer the same kind of critical eye as before the deal was closed. The entrepreneur will be disappointed, often even before co-operation is established. The expected 'sparring partner' will not materialize; the entrepreneur's respect for the investor will be lost. Looking at the results of the study, this is too often the case. It is bad for the entrepreneur, but even worse for the venture capitalist. Lack of good co-operation means lack of the basis for good investment management.

Information is the name of the game in my diagnosis: being informed about all the ins and outs of a company and the market in which it operates before investing, and staying informed during the course of the investment. Information is crucial for good management, as we all know, and the same goes for venture management. Before dealing with this very important part of venture management, however, we need to take care of one other important aspect of management: policy.

POLICY AND STRATEGY

The ultimate goal of every venture capitalist is to realize results that are above average and are a reflection of the level of risks taken by illiquid investments. Different paths lead to Rome. So we see venture capitalists specializing in early stage investments, typical buyout investors, venture capitalists who invest only in a certain type of industry, both in early and later stage deals, and general (often captive) funds that do everything. However, different they may be, they all have that same goal, realizing a rate of return that is higher than returns on other and less risky types of financing.

Whatever policy a venture capitalist has, it will be expressed on an investment by investment basis. For each investment this policy is signalled and a strategy laid down. For each investment the question needs to be answered: does it fit into my policy and what is the strategy that will eventually result in the expected return? The investment memorandum should give all the answers elicited by these seemingly simple questions. Does it?

It would be easy to say here that a good investment memorandum indeed does. On the other hand, I've already suggested that we can only be sure of one thing regarding the future and that is that it will be different from what was foreseen. So our strategy is based on best estimates. What do we mean by strategy in this respect?

The venture capitalist's strategy for each investment covers everything that he or she can and should do in order to minimize risks and maximize returns. Since venture capitalists can only achieve their ambitious goals by realizing investments at a profit, their strategies are completely directed towards an exit. Where and when is the predicted exit which will result in a maximum return? What needs to be done in order to get there? The investment memorandum gives answers to these questions and is in that respect comparable with the business plan of a company. It defines what actions need to be taken and what the dangers and opportunities are. The investment memorandum describes the active departure point of the investment and it should be written for this purpose, and not only as a document on which a decision is made to invest.

It therefore continues to be an important document during the course of an investment and it forms a guideline for investment management. It must be re-evaluated on a regular basis. Best practice is to do this every quarter and discuss the developments regarding the investment with the same people who were involved in deciding on the investment in the first place. The investment memorandum and quarterly statements thus form the heart of an investment's dossier.

It is important to make a distinction between developments in the investee company and the investment. The venture capitalist is interested not only in how the investee company is doing, but also in what the developments mean to his or her investment in the company. In fact, the focus of concern is the connection between developments in the investee company and its environment, and the implications for exit possibilities. To give an example. A company might lose ground in comparison to its competitors. One reaction might be to try and bring about changes in the company and/or the level of investment in order to catch up and become competitive again. But it might also be the case that, on the one hand, this would be very difficult and risky and that, on the other hand, for the time being the company still represents an interesting acquisition target because of its market position, where it is in control of valuable distribution channels. Selling the company now might be wiser, from an investor's standpoint, than trying to 'save' the company as an independent entity.

From this example we can learn that in venture management venture capitalists should be exit driven, and should be so from the start. First and foremost, they should apply their influence to make sure that the financial admin-istration of the investee company is at a level that permits a trade sale. This should be achieved very soon after having invested. Numerous potential trade sales are still being postponed or cancelled because of the status of the financial administration of a company. At their best, situations like this lead to a lower acquisition price. Where an initial public offering (IPO) is the foreseen exit route, one cannot start early enough to apply internationally accepted accountancy principles (IAAS) or US generally accepted accountancy principles (US GAAP).

It seems so obvious that venture capitalists should invest only in companies where a professionally led financial administration exists or will exist within the shortest possible time. How different reality is. In most cases where companies run into trouble, or worse, go bankrupt, financial information is unreliable and late.

Another thing we can learn from this example is that it assumes that the venture capitalist is aware of the competitive position of the investee company. As stated earlier, venture capitalists thoroughly analyze this position before investing, but it is of equal importance that they keep on doing so during the course of the investment.

Finally, the example assumes that the venture capitalist is in a position to execute a changed strategy. In situations where the venture capitalist is a minority shareholder, alone or in combination with a syndicate partner, this is not self-evident. Either the venture capitalist has the legal right to take the initiative to sell a company, even as a minority shareholder, or he or she must be able to convince the other shareholders, often including the management, that this change of strategy is best for the company and thus for all shareholders.

Being and staying informed about and by the company, is crucial for venture management and my analysis also forms the basis for good co-operation with the management of investee companies. The example does not necessarily apply just to a high-tech early stage investment, it could easily be a later stage non-tech one. In both cases information is crucial.

INFORMATION

The information we need for good venture management is in principle the same information that was needed for the decision to invest. The sources from which the information can be obtained are also the same as those in the due diligence stage: it will be supplied by the investee company and it should also be gathered from outside sources. But information alone is not sufficient – it also needs to be analyzed.

Since the information and analyses on which the investment decision was based have been set out in the investment memorandum, this document is a guideline for the type of information we need for venture management and for the way it should be analyzed. The investment memorandum also forms the basis for a comparison of estimate made in the past with the reality of the present.

Financial information

Financial information is fundamental to venture management, and of course to any type of management. It is not only important for the venture capitalist. The management of the investee company can't do without it either. It has already been said that one might take it for granted that good financial information is in place in every organization – and how different reality often is. And yes, quite often venture capitalists who ask for more adequate financial information are called 'bankers' with no feeling for the real issues of a company: 'A company is not a bunch of figures'. That is of course true, but the real truth here is that management that can do without adequate financial information is not real management!

Quite often the participation of a venture capitalist in a smaller company means a requirement for regular and standard information to be produced. It is a major obligation of the venture capitalist to ensure that after the investment is made the company will keep on producing this information. It should consist at least of the following:

♦ monthly profit and loss statements

♦ quarterly review of development, with balance sheet

♦ quarterly cash flow projections

♦ annual budgets.

These are minimum requirements. Especially for start-up companies and leveraged buyouts and buy-ins, cash is the name of the game. In those situations monthly cash flow projections are needed. In start-up businesses these requirements will put a lot of pressure on the organization. Venture capitalists too often make the mistake of being too 'soft' in this respect and accept the fact that these companies are late with their figures. There is only one solution for this problem. Investments should be made on the basis of a budget that provides for an adequately staffed accounting department, whatever the size of the company.

Management information

At least on a quarterly basis, management should report on the development of the company. This review should consist of a comparison between the financial statements and the budget and an analysis of the differences. Again, especially with smaller organizations, this will put on quite a lot of pressure. However, practice has taught that this requirement turns out to be a great help for the management of these companies. They are forced to evaluate formally the development of their business and formulate how they will react to different situations.

The report should also mention other matters concerning the development of the company. Examples are changes in the number of employees, the status of new product development, major new business prospects, major new orders and/or projects, etc. Attention should also be given to potential orders and projects that were lost. Depending on the type of business, the management should report on the backlog of orders and prospective business. This information could even be necessary on a monthly basis.

The management report should also give the view of the management on the development of the market in which the company is active. Relevant information should be given on the competition and new products, technologies and trends.

Development and changes in the management team and the second layer of management of the company, should be reported to the venture capitalist not only on a regular basis, but even *ad hoc*.

The annual accounts of the investee company are a very important category of information. They should be provided with a statement from a chartered auditor. It is preferable for the venture capitalist to have a right of veto concerning the approval of the annual accounts. The same applies to the choice of the auditor. The auditor should also supply the board and the shareholders of the investee company with a management letter. This letter will mention any shortcomings in the accounting system of the company.

The minutes of shareholder meetings and board meetings are important pieces of information for the venture capitalist as well. They should be received not too long after the meeting, especially when the next meeting is not due for a while.

Information from other sources

Before investing, the venture capitalist does not take the information supplied by the management of the prospective investee company for granted. There is no reason to change this attitude after the investment is made. The venture capitalist should continue gathering information from outside sources, on products, technologies, the market, competition and customers.

There is more than one reason for this. First, venture management like any other type of management needs to be based on the right information. Where venture capitalists are often co-responsible for a company's policy they need to take this responsibility seriously. It is only human to emphasize the information that supports one's ideas and visions, and more or less neglect information that does not.

Furthermore, venture capitalists have responsibilities towards their own shareholders. They must be supplied with information about the investments that is compiled by the venture capitalist. No venture capitalist would accept a manager hiding behind someone else in their organization. No venture capitalist is allowed to hide behind the management of the investee company. A personally informed opinion must be given about the state of affairs, the developments and the position of the investee company.

Another reason has been addressed previously. A well-informed venture capitalist will gain respect from the management of the investee company, and good co-operation will result. Based on objective information, the venture capitalist will be able to act as a valuable sparring partner for the management of the investee companies.

Organization

Information does not mean a thing if nothing is done with it. It should be properly analyzed and filed. This seems no more than obvious but it puts a lot of pressure on the venture capitalist. The amount of information that needs to be taken care of by a venture capitalist is immense and time always seems to be in short supply.

It is therefore very important to get organized. From everything that has been mentioned, it has become obvious that information is absolutely crucial for venture capital, both for making the right investment and for good venture management. One could say that the way a venture capitalist is organized in this respect is distinctive. Every venture capitalist and venture capital company will have its own policy, strategy and organization. It is not up to me to prescribe it. There are however some remarks to be made.

The information has to be standardized. The way to do this is to write quarterly reports on all the investee companies in the same format. The format of the original investment proposal should be the guideline. By doing so, the investment proposal combined with the quarterly reports represents the venture capitalist's 'official' statement on the development of the investment. It will enforce the discipline to take care of all the aspects of an investment that were considered important at the time of investing. It also makes it more feasible for the investment to be handed over to another person within the organization, if necessary.

The information gathered for one investment can be of value for another (prospective) one. Building a flexible database is therefore a great help for the information-gathering process. Especially when a venture capital company gets bigger, and even more so when it gets offices in more than one location, the importance of such a database will increase. The sources of information, which are numerous and diverse, need to be maintained.

INVOLVEMENT

I said earlier that a venture capitalist stays involved in investee companies in order to minimize risks and maximize returns. Good co-operation with the management of the investee company forms the basis for this involvement. I went on to say that being well informed is crucial for good co-operation. However, the venture capitalist also needs a formal position towards the investment, in order to be able to enforce his or her involvement. This must be regulated in the participation or shareholders agreement. In principle there are two positions that can be taken. First, a venture capitalist will nearly always be a 'preferred' shareholder, entitled by the shareholders or participation agreement to claim more rights than normally accrue to a shareholder from the articles of association of a company. Second, the venture capitalist can ask for, or require, a position on the board of a company.

The phenomenon 'board' is not as clear-cut as one would think from reading international literature or hearing venture capitalists talk about it. There is a clear difference between the Anglo-Saxon 'board' and, let us say, the continental European one. In the Anglo-Saxon environment the board is the board of directors, comprised of executive and non-executive directors. The management of the company is represented by the executive directors. The venture capitalist would typically hold a position as a non-executive director. The board of directors as a whole is the body within the company that defines company policy and will take responsibility for it.

In almost all continental European countries there is a different situation. The board that is spoken of in the corporate environment is the supervisory board, comprised of supervisors or supervisory board members only. The managers of the company, that is, one or more members of the management team, hold positions as statutory directors. The statutory director or directors define the policy of the company, and the supervisory board can in principle only approve or reject this policy. By law the supervisory board has the task of assisting and controlling the statutory director(s) on behalf of all the shareholders. The supervisory board is not usually the place to guard your specific interest as a shareholder; it is the best place to have an influence on the management of the company, to assist them and to act as a sparring partner. However, it is a definite possibility that one's interest as venture capitalist in a company is not the same as, and may even be opposite to, that of other shareholders. Such situations mostly occur when an exit of the investment of the venture capitalist seems possible, but other shareholders and management have different views about the timing and the method of exit.

So, on the one hand, the supervisory board is the right place to be to fulfil typical venture management tasks; on the other hand, taking up such a position does not mean that the venture capitalist does not require a 'preferred' shareholder's position to enforce the claims that may be needed to realize a maximum return on the investment.

It is sometimes very difficult to combine the two positions in a single person. If the venture capitalist takes a position as a supervisory board member, it is wise to have a colleague from their own firm to act as the 'preferred' shareholder. This is especially useful in meetings where topics will be raised that might result in a conflict of interest between individual shareholders and/or managers.

There might be good reasons for a venture capitalist to claim a 'board' position (either type of board) but to nominate someone to it from outside their firm. In syndicates created out of several venture capitalists, often one of the syndicate partners will take the position of board member, nominated by the others. But it also might be the case that an 'outsider', who is well known and trusted by the venture capitalist will make a better board member in a particular instance.

The biggest mistake a venture capitalist can make in that situation is to feel (partly) released from duties as an investment manager. Although many of the direct contacts with the management of the investee company can be taken over by this 'representative', it is still the venture capitalist's investment. He or she is responsible for the investment and needs to know the ins and outs of the investee company and the business it is in. The communication with the 'representative' is extremely important and should never be neglected.

Now the question arises of how deeply the venture capitalist should be involved in the investee company. The answer is as simple as it is complicated: as deeply as is needed to minimize risks and to maximize returns. This will differ from investee company to investee company and from situation to situation.

I have already said that good co-operation is the basis for good venture management, and that being well informed is the basis of that. This means that the venture capitalist's contact with the management of the investee company must be as frequent as is needed to be well informed. If the management information is not just treated as a formality, which obviously should not be the case, then there is contact at least every time the venture capitalist receives information from the management. Even if this information is clear and holds no surprises, it won't do any harm to make contact just for the sake of confirming that it has been received and, where there is good reason, compliment the management on the results achieved. Managers are human beings, aren't they? Whether a board member or not, a venture capitalist should be in contact, preferably through a meeting, at least once every quarter. Remember what I said previously about the venture capitalist's responsibility with respect to his or her own quarterly report.

Based on their 'preferred' shareholder's position, the venture capitalist will require certain rights with respect to important decisions. Especially where the venture capitalist is the most important equity financier, yet holds a minority position, veto rights over the following are normally required:

♦ appointment and remuneration of the managing director

♦ approval of the annual reports

♦ approval of the budget

♦ unforeseen investments above a certain amount

♦ establishment and liquidation of subsidiaries

♦ issue of new shares

- changing the activities of the company
- changing the articles of association.

This list is not meant to be more than illustrative. Again it is dependent on the stage of development the investee company has reached. Having claimed rights like these, however, puts a great responsibility on the venture capitalist. It cannot be stressed enough that in order to play the right role in the process of the making of these decisions, the venture capitalist needs to be well informed. It is too often the case that as a result of a lack of information, venture capitalists cause delays or completely frustrate these processes.

ADDING VALUE

In the introduction I said that if a venture capitalist is really able to minimize risks, he or she would also be able to maximize returns. Later I made a distinction between the investment and the investee company. Adding value is often mentioned in combination with venture capital. Venture capitalists should not only supply risk capital, but also add value to their investee companies.

In the survey mentioned earlier it became clear that managers/entrepreneurs indeed expect this added value from their venture capitalists and, in fact, use the expectation of added value as a selection criterion. The reason for adding value is obvious: venture capitalists want to maximize returns. How is value added?

Many of the tasks that need to be carried out for good venture management have already been described. If these tasks have been carried out well, a lot of value will already have been added to the investee company. Because of those actions the company's management information will be up to scratch. The management will have a well-informed sparring partner to discuss policy with. Venture capitalists, and not only the ones specializing in certain sectors, gain a reputation in numerous business situations. They are there not as consultants but as investors, who have their money at stake. If the business runs badly, it is not only the manager/entrepreneur who is upset, but the venture capitalist as well. This, in practice, has proved to be of great psychological importance and of value to the management and the company.

In my opinion a venture capitalist adds the most value by assisting in the creation of the best possible team to manage and supervise the investee company. Nobody is perfect and finding complementary skills and personalities within the team is the key to success, to the creation of extra value. This is not a one-time job. Organizations develop, people develop. The necessary skills and personalities in the team need to be expanded or adjusted in order to cope with tomorrow's needs. Sometimes people need to be replaced.

Management assessment is one of the major tasks to be carried out by a venture capitalist before deciding to invest. This task is not always carried out very profes-sionally. In venture management it is at least equal in importance to other tasks and yet it is too often neglected. The replacement of the top manager is mostly a reaction to poor performance of the investee company. Too little attention is given to the composition of the team at the time when the company is doing well. One of my own supervisory board members uses the term 'constructive discontent' in this regard and I think this says it all.

Venture capitalists specializing in a certain sector of industry have a particular ability to assist the management of their investee companies in specific areas of their business. Product development and marketing are examples of those areas. However, some venture capitalists tend to overestimate their abilities in this respect; at the same time they too often pay too little attention to the more general tasks described above.

RED FLAGS

Companies give hidden signals that show something is wrong. Venture capitalists should be alert to them. Some of them are:

♦ financial information is suddenly late. Quite often this is a reaction to poor, disappointing results and time is needed for 'creative accounting';

♦ the financial officer of the company is suddenly to leave the company. There might be conflict between him or her and the chief executive officer about this 'creative accounting';

♦ a change in accounting policy, especially with respect to capitalizing devel-opment or marketing costs;

♦ new, more expensive cars purchased by the management shortly after the investment;

♦ management reports that do not cover all the topics that figured in the previous ones. This often means that something is wrong in the omitted areas;

♦ a proposal to enter a new market at a moment when results in the original target market(s) are poor. This might show that the products or services do not meet the demand of the market and that management has decided to 'flee forwards' and neglect the real problems.

These signals are often culturally defined and may differ from country to country. The venture capitalist must be aware of them and develop the skills, in this respect 'antennae' to receive these signals.

CONCLUSION

An investment is only over when and if it is realized. The investing itself, putting your money into a company is only part of the game. Unlike other types of investors, venture capitalists can't move their money away from the company they have invested in. They are in there for better or worse. But unlike other investors venture capitalists are in a position to actually influence the progress of their investments.

Venture management is what I call the job of organizing this influence. Venture management goes far beyond monitoring investee companies. It is investment management, and the investee companies are the objects of investment. The requirement for venture management is, however, good co-operation with the management of these companies. For the sake of good co-operation the venture capitalist needs to be well informed. He or she needs to get information from the investee company itself and from outside sources. The same level of information is crucial for handling the investment, for having a clear view of its possibilities.

Exerting an influence on the investment, being able to minimize risks and eventually maximize returns, means involvement from the venture capitalist and adding value. For that, information is the name of the game.

GOING PUBLIC –
EUROPEAN MARKETS
AND NASDAQ

Eileen Rutschmann

E-TRASK BV

Eileen Rutschmann is the founder and owner of E-TRASK BV, based in the Netherlands, which primarily assists start-up companies in Europe with raising finance and researching and writing business cases on start-up companies, primarily in the high-tech industry, for the London Business School. In addition, E-TRASK BV is in the process of starting up an internet media company.

Eileen qualified as a Chartered Accountant in Canada with PricewaterhouseCoopers (PwC), in 1989 after obtaining an undergraduate business degree from the University of Lethbridge. In 1990 she moved to Eastern Europe living in both Budapest and Moscow for almost five years working with PwC in privatization and raising finance from western investors for former Eastern-bloc companies. In 1995, Eileen transferred to the Netherlands office primarily performing due diligence and business valuations in a variety of industries and in 1996 she relocated to PwC's London office working in mergers and acquisitions. In addition to living and working in four European countries, she has travelled to and worked extensively in numerous others including China, Thailand, the Philippines, Zimbabwe, Nigeria and the USA. In 1998 Eileen completed her M.Sc. in International Management at the London Business School where the focus of her dissertation was 'Obstacles to raising finance in the high-tech industry in the UK'.

INTRODUCTION

The initial public offering (IPO) is believed to be the holy grail of all exits because of their potential super returns. Over recent years, several European companies have decided to obtain a listing in the USA because of the high valuations and market acceptance of their products and technology. Before 1996 Europe had no equivalent liquid stock market to National Association of Securities Dealers Automated Quotation (Nasdaq) to attract European entrepreneurs to develop their enterprises[1] (EC, 1998), although European Association of Securities Dealers Automated Quotation (EASDAQ) and the Neuer Markt through its membership in EURO.NM, are developing themselves to be.

The European Union has 33 regulated stock markets and 18 regulatory organizations. This complex configuration reduces both the capitalization and liquidity for each national market and hence limits 'IPO exit' opportunities for venture capitalists and investors. The USA in comparison, has three principal stock markets (ten altogether with the US regional markets) and one national regulatory body, the Securities and Exchange Commission.

At the present time, the countries with well developed risk capital markets are principally confined to the USA. The main reason is that these markets require a large pool of suitable firms in which to invest so that investors can diversify their risk. This is not the case for many European countries because the size of their economies are not sufficiently large to support numerous newly created companies, thus the increased pressure by the European Commission to develop a pan-European market[1] (EC, 1998).

This has already started to take place in Europe by the creation of EASDAQ, a pan-European capital market for growth companies and through EURO.NM which is facilitating co-operation between some of the European markets such as the Neuer Markt and Le Nouveau Marché.

These markets were set up in response to increasing pressures from the European Union, the European Venture Capital Association (EVCA) and various financial institutions as a result of various studies performed which highlighted the rising number of European companies applying for a Nasdaq listing. Their objective is to prevent companies from relocating outside Europe to attract capital because it is generally believed that innovative companies are key components of European economies making the greatest contribution to employment and job creation.

One of the main issues posed by such companies is the difficulty in raising capital. Many studies have indicated that the lack of long-term capital for these companies has a negative effect on all European economies, jeopardizing further development in growth industries and weakening Europe's international competitiveness.

Despite some of these positive efforts, a number of regulatory and institutional barriers are still hindering development of a European-wide market which the Commission hopes will disappear over time. One positive development on this front is the recent announcement of the intended co-operation and potential merger of the London, Frankfurt and Paris stock exchanges to increase liquidity on a pan-Europe basis, although this is only relevant to large companies.

The lack of a pan-European liquid market limits IPO opportunities which therefore limits funds available to develop businesses which results in fewer businesses being started which impacts competitiveness of the country or region.

This chapter provides an overview of the listing requirements of the *London Stock Exchange (LSE), Alternative Investment Market (AIM), European Association of Securities Dealers Automated Quotation (EASDAQ), EURO.NM,* specifically the *Neuer Markt* and *Le Nouveau Marché, National Association of Securities Dealers Automated Quotation (Nasdaq)* and the London *Off-Exchange facility (OFEX)* followed by an overview of the IPO process.

Although it is not possible to draw definitive conclusions as to which is the better exchange or facility to list on because it depends upon the individual circumstances of the business, its management, its shareholders and its employees, some guidance has been provided on what to consider when choosing an exchange.

EXCHANGES: KEY TERMS

Below is a list of the more common terms which are applicable to all of the exchanges/facilities outlined in this chapter.

Sponsor/adviser

A sponsor advises a company on all aspects of going public – from assessing its initial suitability to the pricing and timing of the issue itself. Most exchanges require a company to appoint a sponsor otherwise its application will not be approved. The sponsor may be a merchant bank/investment bank, stockbroker or other professional adviser approved by the exchange or the Financial Regulatory Authority in the applicable country. The sponsor's key responsibilities include:

♦ assessing the company's suitability for flotation and reviewing its structure and capital needs

- advising the company and ensuring that its board of directors is of a structure and calibre suitable for a listed company

- advising on the method of flotation

- helping to prepare the company for flotation and helping to draft the prospectus

- pricing and underwriting the shares

- selecting the market and the syndicate.

Corporate broker

The broker may be an independent company, although integrated securities firms are able to provide both merchant banking and stockbroking services. The broker's key responsibilities are to represent the company to private and institutional investors with a view to generating a market in the company's shares and after flotation to sustain a liquid and properly informed market in its shares.

Market Maker

A market maker is a security firm that uses its own capital to buy and maintain an inventory in a specific company's stock. When a market maker receives an investor's order to buy shares in a particular stock, it sells those shares to the customer from its existing inventory. If necessary, it will buy enough shares from other market makers to complete the sale. The market maker has an obligation to be in the market with buy and sell prices at any time.

Price-sensitive information

All the exchanges outlined below require companies to notify it directly or via an Information Service of all information which is potentially sensitive to the price of its shares. Price-sensitive information typically includes changes in share-holdings of directors, directors joining or leaving the board, information on dividends, major acquisitions or disposals and significant contracts entered into and related party transactions.

Prospectus

One of the most time consuming and important tasks of obtaining a listing or 'going public' is the preparation of the prospectus. The prospectus is the standard document required by all exchanges or facilities, differing only in the extent of content required. The prospectus required for the LSE is one of the most compre-hensive and thus its contents as extracted from the LSE's Listing Rules which are based on European Community directives and are summarized below.

The prospectus includes all information which the exchanges require to be made public to investors so that they can make informed decisions and to promote investment in the company's shares.

The main components of a prospectus

♦ A declaration by the directors accepting responsibility for the information contained in the prospectus.

♦ A statement that the financial statements for the past three years have been audited. If audit reports on any of those accounts have been refused by the auditors or contain qualifications, such refusal or qualifications must be reproduced in full and the reasons given.

♦ Names, addresses and qualifications of the auditors who have audited the issuer's financial statements for the past three years.

♦ Names and addresses of the issuer's bankers, legal advisers, sponsor, legal advisers to the issuer, reporting accountants and other experts to whom statements or reports in the prospectus have been attributed.

♦ The nature and the amount of the issue, expected net profits from the issue and their intended use.

♦ A summary of the rights attaching to the shares.

♦ Fixed dates on which entitlement to dividends arise.

♦ The legislation under which the issuer operates and the legal form which it has adopted under that legislation.

♦ The date and country of incorporation.

♦ A summary of the principal contents of each material contract entered into in the past two years not in the ordinary course of business.

♦ The names of persons exercising control over the company and the names of any persons interested in 3 per cent or more of the issuer's capital.

♦ Details of the share capital of the company and any shares under option.

♦ A summary of the provisions of the memorandum and articles of association regarding changes in the capital and rights of the various classes of shares.

♦ A description of principal activities.

♦ Information about associated companies.

♦ Information on any legal or arbitration proceedings.

♦ An analysis of sales by geographic area and category of activity.

♦ Details of land, buildings and principal establishments.

♦ Information in respect of policy on research and development, number of employees, material investments in other companies.

♦ Consolidated information on the results and financial position for each of the past three years. Applicants should discuss with their financial advisers and with the Listing department of the exchange the extent of financial information that must be published.

♦ A statement by the issuer as to the adequacy of the working capital.

> ◆ Details of the issuer's indebtedness, credit rating.
>
> ◆ Names and functions of the directors and/or executive and supervisory board members.
>
> ◆ Aggregate remuneration of directors and/or executive and supervisory board members.
>
> ◆ Details of director's service contracts.
>
> ◆ Directors' interests in the company's securities.
>
> ◆ Information about risk factors.

EXCHANGES AT A GLANCE

There are pronounced country-specific differences between the markets in terms of the regulations by which they are governed, the eligibility criteria that companies have to meet and the reporting requirements to which companies whose shares are publicly quoted on these markets become subject.

The considerable diversity in the amount of information and analysis available for each of these facilities makes comparison sometimes difficult, but on a broad basis size is one of the easiest indicators, as summarized in Table 9.1.

Table 9.1 ◆ Summary of exchanges/facilities

Exchange/facility	Market capitalization (of shares) at 31 December 1998 Euro equivalent	Number of companies at 31 December 1998	Average amount raised at IPO in Euros in 1998
AIM	6.3 billion	312	6.7 million
EASDAQ	13.2 billion	39	42 million
EURO.NM (includes Neuer Markt and Le Nouveau Marché)	31.5 billion	165	32 million
Le Nouveau Marché	4.3 billion	81	12 million
LSE	6,038 billion	2,608	168 million*
Nasdaq	2,235.6 billion	5,068	44 million
Neuer Markt	26.1 billion	63	51 million
OFEX	2.84 billion	189	1 million

* includes both UK and international companies

209

Listing requirements

The listing requirements, ongoing obligations, fees and typical market profile of each of the major exchanges and off-exchange facilities for companies in Europe and the Nasdaq stock market are summarized in the rest of this chapter. The summary is not an all-inclusive and comprehensive abstract of the individual exchanges' rules and should only be used as a guideline. Since the rules of each exchange are very detailed, listing advice should always be sought through a company's sponsor.

Please note that in each case, the listing requirements were extracted from publicly available information provided by the individual exchanges/facilities.

LONDON STOCK EXCHANGE*

The origins of the London Stock Exchange (LSE) go back to the coffee houses of seventeenth-century London where those who wished to invest or raise money bought and sold shares in joint stock companies. The LSE developed as demand for new capital grew with Britain's industrial revolution in the nineteenth century.

At the end of 1998, with respect to equities only, there were 2,087 UK and Irish companies (with a total market capitalization of £1,422.5 billion) and 521 international companies with a total market value of £2,804.4 billion (total 2,608 companies and £4,266.9 billion market capitalization) listed on the LSE. The LSE attracts more foreign company listings than any other stock exchange comprising listings of shares, depository receipts and/or bonds.

There are basically three methods of flotation on the LSE, similar to all other exchanges, as follows.

1 A public offer inviting subscriptions both from institutional investors and private individuals which may be new shares issued for cash or existing shares held by current shareholders.

2 A placing whereby new shares or shares of existing shareholders are offered to the public selectively.

3 An introduction where the shares are introduced to the market and no money is raised from the public either for the company or its shareholders. To meet the requirements of an introduction, the company's shares must already be widely held and the proportion in public hands must be at least 25 per cent.

Trading in the FTSE 100 (Financial Times Stock Exchange 100 index) is conducted on the stock exchange electronic trading system (SETS). SETS is an order matching system where member firms display their buy and sell orders to the market on an electronic order book. When bid and offer prices match, they execute automati-

---

*This information is derived from London Stock Exchange copyright information and has been used with permission. However, the completeness and accuracy of such derived information is the responsibility of the publisher.

cally against one another on screen. Shares outside SETS continue to be traded under the stock exchange's automated quotations system (SEAQ). At least two market makers must be registered in each security traded on SEAQ. Those securities which are not heavily traded or for which a liquid market does not exist (for companies of a small market capitalization or few shareholders) are usually traded on the stock exchange alternative trading service (SEATS) because two market makers may not be sufficient. SEATS provides a noticeboard where buyers and sellers can display their orders. SEATS is the trading system also used by AIM (*see* below).

Settlement of all trades is primarily performed through CREST, the central settlement system for stock market transactions. The LSE strongly recommends companies apply to CRESTCo prior to trading, but only UK registered companies can have their shares settled electronically through CREST.

Listing requirements

Meeting the LSE's requirements is not a guarantee that a company is suitable for going public. Factors such as sound management, the company's position and stability in its industry, growth prospects, a streamlined operating and capital structure, and a healthy balance sheet also play a part in a company's suitability to float.

The company must also provide the LSE with a letter signed by each director confirming that the prospectus includes all the information within their knowledge (or which would be reasonable for them to obtain by making enquiries) that investors would reasonably require and expect in order to make an informed assessment of the company.

Unlike the US exchanges, the LSE does not have detailed quantitative benchmark listing requirements such as a minimum pre-tax income, minimum level of net tangible assets or a minimum bid offer. There are, however, minimum market capitalization requirements of £700,000 for shares and £200,000 for debt securities. Also, it does require a revenue earning track record of at least three years unless the company qualifies for exemption such as scientific research based companies (such as those companies primarily involved in the laboratory research and development of chemical or biological products or processes, including pharmaceutical companies and those involved in the areas of diagnostics, agriculture and food).

For those seeking exemption under Chapter 20 of the Listing Rules (scientific research based companies), the company must have conducted its activity and produced financial information for at least three years (even if it has not been revenue earning). Other conditions for listing, but not limited to, are that the company must:

♦ have demonstrated its ability to attract funds from sophisticated investors;

♦ intend to raise at least £10 million pursuant to a marketing at the time of listing;

♦ have a capitalization, prior to the marketing at the time of listing, of at least £20 million;

♦ demonstrate to the Exchange that it has achieved significant commercial milestones in its development as a scientific research based company.

Specific additional information as described in the Listing Rules may be required, for example, in respect of property companies, scientific research based companies, mineral companies, investment entities and companies undertaking major capital projects.

Fees

Application fee

The application fee is £200 which is non-refundable. In addition there is a £5,000 document-vetting fee payable in respect of any transaction, whether or not it involves the listing of any securities which requires the pre-vetting by the Listing Department of listing particulars, a prospectus, offering circular or other circular to shareholders. The fee is reduced to £2,500 for issuers incorporated outside the UK and issuers of specialist debt.

Admission fees

Table 9.2 ♦ LSE admission fees for equity securities

Market capitalization	Incremental fee per £ million or part thereof	Maximum fee
Up to £1 million	£nil	£nil
Over £1 million up to £5 million	£500	£2,000
Over £5 million to £20 million	£300	£6,500
Over £20 million up to £100 million	£200	£22,500
Over £100 million up to £500 million	£100	£62,500
Over £500 million up to £2,000 million	£25	£100,000
Over £2,000 million up to £10,000 million	£12.50	£200,000
Over £10,000 million	£nil	£200,000

Admission fees for fixed income and floating rate securities range from £4,000 to £26,500.

Annual fees

An annual *listing* fee of £3,400 is required to be paid by each issuer of equity securities listed on the LSE. In the case of equity issuers incorporated outside the UK, the charge is £1,700.

In addition to the annual *listing* fee, an annual *admission* fee is required, calculated on the scale set out in Table 9.3 below. The amount of the annual *listing* fee will be deducted from the annual *admission* fee payable by each issuer (where the annual admission fee is less than the annual listing fee, the listing fee due will be limited to such lesser amount and no further admission fee will be payable by the issuer for that year).

Table 9.3 ♦ Annual charges

Nominal value of listed securities	Upper amount of annual charge
Up to £10 million	£4,800
Up to £50 million	£8,260
Up to £100 million	£11,000
Up to £250 million	£16,520
Up to £500 million	£17,920
Up to £1,000 million	£20,660
Up to £2,000 million	£23,400
Over £2,000 million	£24,800

Where fixed income and floating rate securities only are listed, a charge of £1,220 will be made annually, unless the total nominal value of the securities is less than £250,000, in which case a charge of £610 will be made.

For issuers incorporated outside the UK, all fees are payable at half the above rates.

Ongoing obligations

All potentially price-sensitive information is required to be released to the market without delay via the Exchange's Regulatory News Service (RNS). The RNS receives, validates and then publishes/distributes the information to its subscribers.

Financial statements are also required to be issued within six months of the year-end to which they relate in compliance with UK Accounting Standards, US generally accepted accountancy principles (US GAAP) or international accountancy standards (IAS). Preliminary profit announcements of the unaudited results for the year and a half-yearly (interim) financial report must also be submitted.

In addition, directors of the public company must follow the 'Model Code for Directors' Dealings' which precludes directors from dealing for a minimum period (normally two months) prior to an announcement of regularly recurring information such as results, whether or not the information is price sensitive. It also prohibits dealing prior to the announcement of matters of an exceptional nature involving unpublished information which is potentially price sensitive.

Market profile of companies

For up-to-date information refer to the daily *Financial Times* information.

Table 9.4 ♦ Market profile of UK and international companies

	UK companies	International companies
1997 average market cap/company	£469 million	£4.2 billion
1998 average market cap/company	£682 million	£5.4 billion
Number of IPOs in 1998	69	27
Average funds raised per IPO in 1998	£60 million	£264 million

ALTERNATIVE INVESTMENT MARKET*

The Alternative Investment Market (AIM) is the London Stock Exchange's public market for small, young and growing companies regardless of where they are incorporated. Although AIM is operated by the London Stock Exchange, the market is managed by its own team within the Exchange. AIM was established on 19 June 1995 and as of 31 December 1998 had a market capitalization of £4.4 billion for 313 companies. (In comparison, the market capitalization at 30 June 1998 was £6.5 billion from 312 companies .

As with the LSE, a company must have a sponsor/adviser and broker to assist with the listing process. In fact, a company must retain the services of a sponsor and broker at all times.

Listing requirements

The requirements for admission to AIM are straightforward. Companies do not need to have reached a particular size or demonstrate a lengthy trading history. In addition, it is not required to have a certain percentage of its shares in public hands.

For companies whose main activities have been generating revenue for less than two years, directors and all employees who hold an interest of 1 per cent or more of a class of AIM securities must agree not to sell any interests they may have for at least one year from the date of joining AIM.

Every application to AIM needs to be supported by a prospectus, an application form signed by the directors, a declaration by the sponsor/adviser and a letter from the company's broker confirming its appointment.

---

*This information is derived from London Stock Exchange copyright information and has been used with permission. However, the completeness and accuracy of such derived information is the responsibility of the publisher.

Consistent with the LSE, companies can either choose to list as an initial public offering or by way of introduction where no capital is raised.

The prospectus must include the 'standard' information (similar to that required by the LSE (*see* above), but not as extensive) plus:

♦ details of all directors, including their directorships over the past five years, any unspent convictions and all bankruptcies, receiverships or liquidations of companies or partnerships where they were directors at the time or within the 12 months preceding these events, and any public criticisms by statutory or regulatory authorities;

♦ details of any party that has received fees, shares or other benefits, either directly, or indirectly, worth £10,000 or more in the 12 months prior to admission;

♦ names of shareholders entitled to exercise or control the exercise of 3 per cent or more of the votes able to be cast at general meetings, and their percentage holdings;

♦ a confirmation that the company is satisfied there is sufficient working capital in place to meet the present requirement of the company; and

♦ a notice on the first page of the prospectus drawing investors' attention to the fact that AIM is a different market from the Official List (LSE), being a market for smaller emerging companies.

The time between submission of the application and admission to AIM is normally five days. AIM can achieve this short timetable because the Exchange does not examine the contents of the prospectus – it is used primarily by the investors.

Shares are traded on SEATS. In addition, nearly 60 per cent of AIM companies are supported by two or more market makers.

Ongoing obligations

Companies listed on AIM, as already mentioned, must retain a sponsor and broker at all times, be legally established under the laws of its country and be a public company or the equivalent, publish annually audited accounts that conform to UK or US GAAP or IAS and provide interim reports (six months data), ensure that securities traded on AIM are freely transferable and require its directors and employees to comply with the Model Code.

In addition, as with all other exchanges, a company must notify the Exchange of all potentially price-sensitive information.

Fees

AIM has a very simple fee structure with just one fee required to be paid (plus VAT) as illustrated in Table 9.5.

Table 9.5 ♦ AIM fee structure

First year	£2,500
Second year	£3,000
Third and subsequent years	£4,000

The most expensive part of listing on AIM, however, is advisory fees. In the May 1997 AIM newsletter a study showed full listing costs varying from 28 per cent of funds raised to 3 per cent, illustrating that to raise less than £1.5 million rarely gives value for money. On average, however, the cost of raising cash equated to 10.6 per cent of funds raised compared to 9 per cent which is widely accepted as the norm for full listings (*see* Table 9.13, page 234).

Market profile

Almost 50 per cent of companies listed on AIM are in the services business sector which includes leisure and hotels, media, transport, etc. The next biggest sector represented is the financial services sector with some 15 per cent of total AIM companies. Of the 313 companies listed, 73 are high-tech, from the following sub-sectors: broadcasting contractors, electrical equipment, electronic equipment, engineering, aerospace and defence, information technology, medical products and suppliers, pharmaceuticals, and telecommunications. Of the companies listed, 219 had a market capitalization of between £2 million and £20 million. Only six companies had a market capitalization in excess of £100 million and 36 companies had a market capitalization of less than £2 million. In 1998, 55 companies were listed raising each on average £4.8 million.

Since AIM's launch in 1995 over 17 billion shares have been traded at a value of £4.4 billion. Money raised by new issues since that time has been over £2 billion. The average sum raised by each company in any year is £5.3 million or £4.7 million in 1998.

AIM success story

Flomerics Group plc based in Surrey, UK was founded in 1988 to commercialize computation fluid dynamics software for the thermal analysis of electronic designs. Flomerics received £300,000 as initial capital in return for a 62.5 per cent stake in 1989 by a UK venture capitalist. In 1992 Flomerics required further capital and an additional £420,000 was raised (£170,000 from employees and £250,000 from the same venture capitalist whose stake was diluted to 58 per cent). Flomerics was eventually floated on AIM in December 1995 at an initial market capitalization of £3.3 million generating an internal rate of return for the investors of 30 per cent. Flomerics' market capitalization at the end of 1998 was around £3.5 million.

EASDAQ

The European Association of Securities Dealers Automated Quotation, EASDAQ, is located in Belgium and was created as a stock market to meet the demand for capital of high-growth companies by providing a broad spread of investors within a highly regulated market similar to the Nasdaq model. The EASDAQ platform which draws upon the framework of the various European Directives as well as that of the US Securities and Exchange Commission, is designed to satisfy the needs of companies which are duly incorporated either within the Member States of the European Union or beyond.

EASDAQ provides a single governance and regulatory structure with uniform admission and trading rules designed to maintain the highest level of transparency and regulation against fraud. EASDAQ's pan-European network of investment banks, brokers and market makers helps support subsequent liquidity in trading.

By the end of December 1998, 39 companies were traded on EASDAQ with a market capitalization of Euro 13.2 billion (over twice the size of AIM at the same date). EASDAQ attracts companies from a variety of industry sectors such as engineering, electronics, information technology, biotechnology, telecommunications, automotive and leisure.

Companies which are incorporated and at any stage of development are eligible for admission to trading on EASDAQ.

Admission to trading on EASDAQ can take any one of a number of forms including:

◆ an Initial Public Offering (IPO), a private placement or a combination of the two;

◆ an IPO on EASDAQ and another market or exchange, a private placement or a combination of the two;

◆ a dual trading facility for companies with financial instruments already traded on another market or exchange, e.g. Nasdaq, which has been recognized by the Board of Directors of EASDAQ where the company is seeking to raise capital or undertake a secondary offering at the time of its admission; or

◆ a dual trading facility for companies with financial instruments already traded on another market or exchange seeking to enhance its investor base, trading hours and profile but not seeking to issue new securities or raise additional capital at the time of admission.

Listing requirements

As a first step a company should enter informal discussions with the EASDAQ Admissions Department, regardless of whether it is seeking to undertake an IPO, a capital increase or to gain a dual trading facility for its financial instruments. This admission process begins with an informal presentation of the company to EASDAQ's Admissions Department. This presentation is often made with the company's sponsor or other advisers, but is not required. The application, however, should be supported by a member of EASDAQ.

A prospectus must also be prepared and approved by the Market Authority of EASDAQ and a relevant Competent Authority.

A company completing a formal application is required to submit an Admission Agreement, a signed Application Form, and a number of supporting Admission Application documents, all of which must be in the English language.[2]

A company must be duly incorporated with total assets of at least Euro 3.5 million (US$4.2 million) and capital and reserves of at least Euro 2.0 million (US$2.4 million). These figures can take into account revenues raised in an offering. No minimum level of profitability is required.

Although exceptions are made, in general EASDAQ will consider applications from growth companies with a market capitalization, at the time of admission to trading, of Euro 40 million or more. At least 20 per cent of the capital should be publicly held and there should be a minimum of 100 shareholders.

At all times, a company must have a minimum of two market makers.

EASDAQ restricts those who owned shares at the time of listing to delay trading them for a period of at least six months.

Ongoing obligations

A company must report its financial results in accordance with either IAS, US GAAP or the standards of its home State with a reconciliation to IAS or US GAAP. Audited annual statements and quarterly unaudited reports are required to be submitted.

Fees

Application fee

The application fee is Euro 5,000 which covers the processing of the application and will be credited against the admission fee at the time of the company's admission to trading.

There are also a one-time admission fee and transaction fee as well as an annual fee as shown in Table 9.6.

In addition to the fees shown in Table 9.6 there is also an information vendor fee, such as Reuters News Network which is approximately Euro 1,000 per quarter. Also under Belgian law, prior to the first day of trading on a market in Belgium, an announcement must be placed in the Belgian financial press advising the public.

Table 9.6 ◆ EASDAQ fees

Market cap (Euro million)	Admission fee (Euro)	Annual fee (Euro)
Less than 50	20,000	7,500
50 to 100	30,000	15,000
Greater than 100	40,000	22,500

Amount raised (Euro million)	Transaction fee (Euro)
Less than 15	10,000
15 to 50	15,000
Greater than 50	20,000

Market profile

Table 9.7 ◆ EASDAQ market profile as at 31 December, 1998

Average market capitalization per company	Euro 336 million
Average money raised per company at admission	Euro 42 million
Average market capitalization at admission	Euro 167 million
Average equity issued	42.2%
Number of market makers per company (on average)	6
Average sales of companies listed	Euro 73 million

EASDAQ success stories

Innogenetics NV was founded in 1985 in Belgium and is engaged in the research, development and marketing of diagnostic products for human diseases, and in the discovery and development of therapeutic products. Innogenetics received BEF 25 million as initial seed capital from a Belgian venture capitalist and before listing on EASDAQ in November 1996, it received a further three rounds of financing. The final round of financing was mezzanine debt by a bank which provided the necessary capitalization to go public.

Innogenetics was the first company to list on EASDAQ at an initial capitalization of US$246 million. As at December 1998 it is capitalized at over US$800 million, but has seen its value reach as high as US$1.8 billion. Despite a recent slowiing down in product sales due to take-overs of its various partners, Innogenetics' revenue has more than doubled since 1997.

Orthovita, Inc was founded in 1993 by a Belgian scientist in Pennsylvania, USA to develop, manufacture and market proprietary osteobiologic bone substitutes and cements. It has recently announced approval of its fourth patent in the USA related to bioactive fibres.

Orthovita listed on EASDAQ in June 1998 and is the only US company to list on a European exchange without also dual listing on a US exchange such as Nasdaq. Orthovita's market capitalization at admission was US$111 million, but has declined to US$ 56 million (31 December 1998) largely because of deferred recognition of sales due to a voluntary product notification on BIOGRAN packaged in glass syringes. The company believes that it is in a transition period; while still continuing to generate sales from the dental market it is intensely focused on securing regulatory approvals for the orthopaedic market. As a result, Orthovita expects 1999 to be a good year.

EURO.NM

EURO.NM is a pan-European grouping of regulated stock markets dedicated to innovative companies with high growth potential. EURO.NM member markets currently include Nieuwe Markt (NMAX in Amsterdam), Neuer Markt (Deutsche Bourse in Frankfurt), Le Nouveau Marché (Paris Stock Exchange) and EURO.NM Belgium (Brussels Stock Exchange). The Milan Stock Exchange joined EURO.NM in January 1999.

In terms of total market capitalization of EURO.NM, the Neuer Markt represents around 85 cent and the Le Nouveau Marché around 12 per cent with the remaining two, NMAX and EURO.NM Belgium being relatively insignificant.

Le Nouveau Marché was launched on 14 February 1996. NMAX was launched on 20 February 1997 and the first listings took place in April 1997 and EURO.NM Belgium had its first listing in April 1997. Neuer Markt was opened on 10 March 1997 and the first two companies to list had a combined market capitalization of more than DM 600 million.

By the end of 1998, 165 companies had listed on EURO.NM with a market capitalization of Euro 31.5 billion which has increased significantly from 1997 with 62 companies and a total market capitalization of Euro 5.6 billion. Of the 165 companies listed, 81 were on the Le Nouveau Marché (Paris), 63 were on the Neuer Markt (Frankfurt), 13 were on NMAX (Amsterdam) and 8 were on EURO.NM Belgium.

The domestic markets (Neuer Markt, Le Nouveau Marché, NMAX and EURO.NM Belgium) were established to address the respective national needs, whereas EURO.NM was created to allow a European dimension and to guarantee easy access.

There is still no common European law regarding companies, no central supervisory authority and no common code of conduct for all participants. Any market therefore striving to achieve a genuinely European dimension has to be decentralized according to the principles of subsidiarity and at the same time show its unity by a high degree of harmonization and integration.

EURO.NM members have signed a Markets Harmonization Agreement which establishes rules and regulations of this European network. The agreement defines the minimum standards to be adopted by each member of the grouping. The common standards concern listing requirements for issuers, membership and market rules.

The EURO.NM framework is designed to respect each market's autonomy and initiative while ensuing the necessary degree of co-ordination and co-operation between them. By pooling resources and by utilizing existing trading systems, the markets hope to operate at marginal cost.

Listing requirements

Before listing, companies are required to present their business plan and financing scheme. Once admitted, companies are required to provide regular and adequate information for investors to monitor their performance.

Listing applications are submitted to market authorities in the country where listing is requested. Approval is based on the prospectus, a description of risk factors (if appropriate) as well as a minimum commitment of the listing adviser/ market makers of one year.

The language required for all communications with EURO.NM is English and the language of the exchange, i.e., if a company lists on Neuer Markt, all documents must also be in German, or if listing on Le Nouveau Marché, in French.

The Harmonization Agreement sets out the minimum listing requirements for those exchanges belonging to EURO.NM as follows:

- ◆ no minimum level of revenue, income or assets, but equity prior to listing should be Euro 1.5 million

- ◆ mandatory capital increase of 50 per cent of issue volume or more

- ◆ minimum capitalization of Euro 5 million

- ◆ minimum number of publicly traded shares should be 100,000

- ◆ minimum public equity offered should be 20 per cent

- ◆ lock-up period of 100 per cent shares for six months or 80 per cent for one year

- ◆ minimum one sponsor/market maker.

Ongoing obligations

Continuing obligations are straightforward and limited to publishing quarterly unaudited reports and annual audited accounts for all of the EURO.NM exchanges. These reports should be presented in accordance with International Accounting Standards or US GAAP and, if legally applicable, in the accounting standard of the respective exchange's country such as the German Commercial Code or French GAAP. If financial statements are published in the accounting standard of the country of the exchange, a reconciliation to IAS or US GAAP will be accepted.

Market profile

The average company on EURO.NM raises Euro 27.2 million at listing by issuing 33 per cent of its equity. The total capital raised by the 165 companies at the end of December 1998 was Euro 4.5 billion. Of the 165 companies listed by the end of December 1998, 67 were venture capital backed raising Euro 2.1 billion.

The average share price since listing has increased by 129 per cent and the average daily trading volume of EURO.NM is Euro 109 million.

Of the 165 companies listed by the end of 1998, 18 were dual listed with another exchange (ten with Nasdaq, two with EASDAQ, two with AIM, two with the Swiss Stock Exchange, one with the Toronto Stock Exchange and one with the New York Stock Exchange).

NEUER MARKT

The Neuer Markt, operated by the Deutsche Börse, is developing itself to become the market of choice in Europe. Since its launch in 1997 it has outgrown and outperformed almost all other exchanges. Its performance has largely been boosted by a number of large private companies seeking new sources of equity finance and high growth innovative companies. All of the companies listed on the Neuer Markt are in software, telecommunications, biotechnology, entertainment or internet commerce. In 1998, 45 companies were admitted to the Neuer Markt raising over Euro 2.3 billion or each Euro 51 million on average.

This continued explosion in growth is not expected to slow down in the near future considering that some experts estimate that there are over 2,000 corporations in Germany alone which could qualify for a stock exchange listing.

All Neuer Markt securities can be traded on the floor at the Frankfurt Stock Exchange or in Xetra, which is the Neuer Markt's automatic anonymously matching order-driven system.

Listing requirements

A company wishing to be admitted to Neuer Markt must submit an application in co-operation with a bank, financial services institution or similarly approved enterprise. The Executive Board of the Deutsche Börse AG decides on all admissions to the Neuer Markt. The admission of shares to the Neuer Markt requires the prior admission of the shares to trading on the Regulated Market (Geregelter Markt) of the Frankfurt Stock Exchange. The application for admission of shares to the Geregelter Markt may be submitted together with the application for admission of the shares to the Neuer Markt in a single document. Submission of an application for admission of shares to the Neuer Markt constitutes a waiver by the applicant of the commencement of the quotation of the shares on the Geregelter Markt.

Also, accompanying the application must be the following documents:

- articles of association or partnership agreement
- updated excerpt from the commercial register
- statutory report of incorporation of the company
- excerpts from the protocols pertaining to the relevant legal resolutions for the issue of shares
- statements on operational breakdowns, patents, disputes and cancellation of global certificates
- annual statements and reports of the company
- specification of all nominal values of shares.

In addition to the minimum admission requirements as noted above under EURO.NM, the Neuer Markt requires that every company has at least two designated sponsors or market makers to boost liquidity and every company must agree to acknowledge the take-over code. The take-over code is laid down by the German Stock Exchange Expert Committee to ensure compliance with the Rules of Conduct. It guarantees that a reasonable take-over bid is made for the rest of the shares of a company if 50 per cent of the shares have been acquired. Also, the IPO volume of at least Euro 5 million should have a par value of at least DM 500,000 and it is recommended that the amount of equity not closely held should be 25 per cent although 20 per cent would be allowed.

The issuing prospectus must be ready for public circulation in both German and English at least one working day before the admission of the shares to the Neuer Markt. The issuing prospectus is subjected to the German prospectus liability law and must be approved by the Admissions Board and the Deutsche Börse prior to admission.

Fees

Admission fees range from Euro 1,000 to over Euro 10,500 depending upon the size of the issue. Annual fees for services rendered by Deutsche Börse are DM 15,000 or Euro 13,000. For those companies incorporated outside of Germany, the fees are reduced by half.

Neuer Markt success stories

AIXTRON AG was listed on the Neuer Markt in November 1997. Its share price has increased by over 428 per cent (at 31 December 1998) since listing while consolidated profits have doubled since that time. Of the companies listing on the Neuer Markt in 1997, AIXTRON is in the top five performers.

AIXTRON was founded in 1983 in Aachen, Germany and is now the world's leading manufacturer of MOCVD equipment for the production of compound semiconductors. AIXTRON's customers include AT&T, Lucent Technologies, Alcatel, Motorola, Siemens and IBM to name a few.

Mobilcom of Germany, a telecommunications company has seen its share price increase by over 3,300 per cent (31 December 1998) since listing on the Neuer Markt in 1997. Mobilcom operates in Germany's highly competitive telecoms market and believes to have taken 9 per cent market share since inception.

TelDaFax, a German telecommunications company is the only company which has listed on both Neuer Markt and Easdaq. The French company Chemunex, which is engaged in micro-biological testing systems, has also listed on both Le Nouveau Marché and EASDAQ. TelDaFax's share price has increased by over 8 per cent (31 December 1998) since listing in July 1998. Chemunex has had less success, but is in an industry which has long lead times.

LE NOUVEAU MARCHÉ

Le Nouveau Marché is operated by the Société du Nouveau Marché (SNM). An admission committee decides on the listing or delisting of financial instruments on the Nouveau Marché subject to the minimum listing requirements being met as set out under EURO.NM.

In 1998, 43 companies were admitted to the Nouveau Marché each raising on average over FF 80 million or over Euro 12.2 million at listing. In essence, Le Nouveau Marché is interested in companies with expected annual growth rates of at least 20 per cent.

Shares are traded in Le Nouveau Marché through a central electronic order book and by market making via the floor.

Listing requirements

In addition to the listing requirements set out in the EURO.NM harmonization agreement, applications for listing should include:

◆ the company's Articles of Association;

◆ certification of approval of its programme of activities, where such approval is required;

◆ certification, where applicable, of its authorization to be a member of a regulated market, issued by the *Conseil des Marchés Financiers*;

◆ for applicants established in another Member State, certification that the *Comité des Établissements de Crédit et des Entreprises d'Investissement* has received notification of their right of establishment or freedom to provide services in France;

◆ a description of the nature of the proposed activities;

◆ the amount, composition and breakdown of ownership of its capital;

◆ the composition of the Board of Directors or governing bodies;

◆ a list of internal rules and regulations, if any;

◆ a description of the technical resources and personnel that will be allocated to member functions;

◆ a written promise to sign the membership agreement drafted by SNM;

◆ a written promise to abide by the exchange's rules and their application provisions.

As with all the other regulated exchanges, a prospectus must also be submitted.

Fees

Le Nouveau Marché's fees are expressed as a percentage of the capital raised with respect to admission fees and as a percentage of the market capitalization in the first year of listing with respect to annual fees as shown in Table 9.8.

Table 9.8 ♦ Le Nouveau Marché's fee structure

Capital raised in millions of Euros	% Admission fee
5–7.5	0.5
7.5–15	0.4
15–30	0.3
30–75	0.2
More than 75	0.1
Issued share capital in millions of Euros	**% Annual fee***
Less than 3.8	0.5
3.8–7.5	0.1
More than 7.5	0.02

*A minimum of Euro 4,500 applies

Nasdaq

The National Association of Securities Dealers Automated Quotation, Nasdaq, is the largest electronic, screen-based market in the world with the capacity to handle share volume in excess of 1 billion shares a day. It was created in 1971 to match the demand for capital by high growth small and medium-size companies with the public interest in wanting to own stock in rapidly growing companies. In 1998 5,068 companies were traded on Nasdaq with a combined market capitalization of over $2,589 billion (slightly more than the value of UK listed companies on the LSE). Of the 5,068 companies traded, 441 were non-US based. In 1998, Nasdaq raised more than 25 times the capital raised on EASDAQ, EURO.NM and AIM combined for new listings.

Known for its innovative, leading-edge growth companies, Nasdaq has two tiers: the Nasdaq National Market, with Nasdaq's larger companies whose securities are the most actively traded and, the Nasdaq SmallCap Market, with emerging growth companies. Each tier has its own set of financial requirements that a company must meet to list its securities.

Nasdaq is the market of choice for US based public companies by nearly 2:1 over New York Stock Exchange and is the leading American market for non-US listings. The Nasdaq market is distinguishable from other traditional markets because of its structure based on multiple competing market makers and advanced technologies.

Table 9.9 ◆ Nasdaq National Market listing requirements

Requirements	Initial listing 1*	Initial listing 2*	Initial listing 3*	Continued listing 1 & 2	Continued listing 3
Net tangible assets[1]	$6 million	$18 million	N/A	$4 million	N/A
Market capitalization[2] Total assets Total revenue	N/A	N/A	$75 million or $75 million and $75 million	N/A	$50 million or $50 million and $50 million
Pretax income (in latest fiscal year or two of last three fiscal years)	$1 million	N/A	N/A	N/A	N/A
Public float (shares)[3]	1.1 million	1.1 million	1.1 million	750,000	1.1 million
Operating history	N/A	2 years	N/A	N/A	N/A
Market value of public float	$8 million	$18 million	$20 million	$5 million	$15 million
Minimum bid price	$5	$5	$5	$1	$1
Shareholders (round lot holders)[4]	400	400	400	400	400
Market makers	3	3	4	2	4
Corporate governance	Yes	Yes	Yes	Yes	Yes

* Listing 1, 2 or 3 is a means used by Nasdaq to emphasize that there are different types of companies, based on their financial profile, which are suitable for listing on Nasdaq.

[1] Net tangible assets means total assets (excluding goodwill) minus total liabilities.

[2] For initial or continued listing under option 3, a company must satisfy one of the following to be in compliance: 1 the market capitalization requirement or 2 the total assets and the total revenue requirement.

[3] Public float is defined as shares that are not held directly or indirectly by any officer or director of the issuer and by any other person who is the beneficial owner of more than 10 per cent of the total shares outstanding.

[4] Round lot holders are considered to be holders of 100 shares or more.

Table 9.10 ♦ Nasdaq SmallCap Market listing requirements (which also apply to all non-Canadian foreign securities and American Depository Receipts)

Requirements	Initial listing	Continued listing
Net tangible assets[1]	$4 million	$2 million
	or	or
Market capitalization	$50 million	$35 million
	or	or
Net income (in the latest fiscal year or two of last three fiscal years)	$750,000	$500,000
Public float (shares)[2]	1 million	500,000
Market value of public float	$5 million	$1 million
Minimum bid price	$4	$1
Market makers	3	2
Shareholders (round of lot holders)[3]	300	300
Operating history[4]	1 year	N/A
	or	
Market capitalization	$50 million	
Corporate governance	Yes	Yes
ADRs (American Depository Receipts), rights and warrants[5]	100,000	N/A

[1] For initial or continued listing, a company must satisfy one of the following to be in compliance: 1 the net tangible assets requirement (net tangible assets means total assets, excluding goodwill, minus total liabilities), 2 the market capitalization requirement or 3 the net income requirement.

[2] Public float is defined as shares that are not held directly or indirectly by any officer or director of the issuer or by any other person who is the beneficial owner of more than 10 per cent of total shares outstanding.

[3] Round lot holders are considered to be holders of 100 shares or more.

[4] If operating history is less than one year, initial listing requires market capitalization of at least $40 million.

[5] For foreign listings only.

Ongoing obligations

Tables 9.9 and 9.10 which summarize the listing requirements give details of the continued listing requirements. In addition, companies must file annual audited reports and interim quarterly reports.

Nasdaq National Market fee structure

There is a one-time initial listing fee of $5,000 which includes a non-refundable $1,000 application fee.

Other entry and annual fees are based on the company's total shares outstanding (TSO) for all classes of stock listed on the Nasdaq National Market, excluding convertible debentures, according to the fee schedule below. In the case of an IPO, the fees are applied to the TSO reported in the company's final prospectus and in the case of the annual fee, the TSO reported in the company's latest filing on record at year end will be used.

Annual fees for the listing of additional shares are $2,000 or $0.02 per additional share, whichever is higher, up to a maximum of $17,500 per action.

Table 9.11 ♦ Nasdaq National Market fee structure

Based on total shares outstanding	Entry fee ($)	Annual fee ($)
Fewer than 1 million	29,525	10,710
1+ million to 10 million	33,750–70,625	10,960–12,960
10+ million to 20 million	73,875–90,000	17,255–18,755
20+ million to 50 million	90,000	22,795–26,625
50+ million to 100 million	90,000	32,625–43,125
More than 100 million	90,000	50,000

Nasdaq SmallCap market fee structure

There is a one-time $5,000 company listing fee, $1,000 of which is also non-refundable as an application processing fee.

Other entry fees are variable per each class of security as follows:

◆ all equity securities – the greater of $1,000 or $0.001/share, not to exceed $5,000;

◆ convertible debentures – the greater of $1,000 or $50 per million dollars face amount of debentures, not to exceed $5,000.

The maximum entry fees to be paid per issuer cannot exceed $10,000, inclusive of the $5,000 original company listing fee.

Annual fees are the same for each issuer at $4,000 for the first class of securities and $1,000 for each subsequent class of securities. There is no maximum amount for annual fees.

Annual fees for the listing of additional shares are $1,000 or $0.01 per additional share, whichever is higher, up to a maximum of $7,500 per action.

Nasdaq market data

Nasdaq lists more IPOs than any other exchange in the world, far exceeding its US rivals. In 1996, one of Nasdaq's best years, 680 companies were listed at a value of $24.5 billion. In the same year, only 88 companies were listed on the New York

Stock Exchange at a value of $11.9 billion and 18 companies were listed on the American Stock Exchange at a value of $510 million.

Since 1996, the number of listings on Nasdaq has declined. In 1997, 494 companies were listed (a decrease of 27 per cent) at a value of $19.4 billion (a decrease of 21 per cent). In 1998, only 273 companies have listed raising $13.8 billion (a decrease of 29 per cent compared to 1997) or $50 million each. This decline in the number of listings impacts the option to exit by IPO for many companies because it may be an indication of worsening market conditions which limits the size of funds which can be raised.

Table 9.12 ♦ Market profile of the average company

	Nasdaq SmallCap (millions) 31 Dec 1998	Nasdaq National (millions) 31 Dec 1998
Assets	$348.3	$650.8
Revenues	$258.4	$295.7
Equity	$118.9	$180.8
Net income	$5.1	$9.9
Shares outstanding	8.1	21.5
Public float (shares)	5.7	14.4
Market value	$25.4	$662.0
Number of market makers	8.1	11.5
Average share price	$3.15	$30.82

Nasdaq success stories

There are numerous Nasdaq success stories especially in light of the surge in high-tech stocks over the past year such as INTEL, Microsoft, Cisco Systems, Dell Computers, Sun Microsystems and even the newer additions of Amazon and E-Bay. For instance, Microsoft's share price almost doubled in the six months following summer 1998. This environment has made it attractive for European companies to seek listing on Nasdaq.

Some successful examples to date are: ARM Holdings plc based in Cambridge, UK which design high performance, low cost, power efficient risc microprocessors and which has chosen to list via ADRs on Nasdaq in April 1998 and has seen its share price increase by over 50 per cent since; and Lernout & Hauspie, a Belgian company developing voice recognition software which has also seen its share price triple since listing in 1997 on both EASDAQ and Nasdaq. Lernout & Hauspie's market capitalization is currently in excess of US$1.6 billion.

OFEX

OFEX is an off-exchange share matching and trading facility established by J. P. Jenkins Limited in 1991 to enable London Stock Exchange member firms to deal in the securities of unlisted and unquoted companies. Securities traded on OFEX are not quoted or dealt in on the London Stock Exchange or subject to its rules. The facility is operated by J. P. Jenkins Limited in conjunction with Newstrack Limited. J. P. Jenkins is the only market maker in the majority of shares traded on OFEX and thus has a position from time to time in the shares traded on OFEX. Newstrack Limited is a sister company to J. P. Jenkins Limited and provides a screen-based company information service for OFEX securities. It disseminates OFEX and other client company information including fundamental data, price information and announcements via Bloomberg, Primark (formerly Datastream/ICV) and Reuters electronic information services. In addition all OFEX prices are published daily on the Newstrack/OFEX internet site (www.Newstrack.co.uk and www.Ofex.co.uk).

The OFEX trading facility has historically catered for a range of differently capitalized companies, from £600 million down to as little as £100,000. The constituent OFEX companies themselves cover a wide range of sectors, and include football clubs, regional brewers, high tech and biotech, media, engineering, property and so on.

OFEX was initially considered a direct rival to the London Stock Exchange's AIM, but it cannot be compared to the AIM because it is not a 'market' regulated by the LSE, but purely a mechanism for trading off-exchange. OFEX primarily attracts companies that require smaller amounts of capital which are predominantly raised from private investors. OFEX is basically a source of 'retail venture capital' for young companies and a stepping stone along the route to a more senior market.

Private investors wanting to trade in securities on OFEX must do so through a stockbroker regulated by the Financial Services Authority (FSA). Unlisted and unquoted shares are defined by the FSA as 'non-readily realizable investments' meaning that such shares can become illiquid at any time.

Listing requirements

A company making an application to join OFEX must do so through a sponsor/corporate adviser who must be regulated/authorized in the conduct of investment business. It is not mandatory for an OFEX company to appoint a stockbroker but companies may find this desirable, particularly if they are planning to move to a more senior market in the future.

Consistent with stock exchanges, companies can apply for an OFEX facility via an introduction (where the company does not have a funding requirement and will trade existing shares) and by way of a fund-raising through a public offer or private placing of shares.

To apply via an introduction, a company must, through its adviser, submit the following documentation:

♦ audited report and accounts covering the last three years (the most recent of which should be free of audit qualifications), or a business plan for companies with a shorter track record;

♦ memorandum and articles of association which must be free of any restrictions relating to the transfer of shares;

♦ declaration of business activities from each director of the company;

♦ OFEX completed company information questionnaire;

♦ OFEX and Newstrack agreements; and

♦ details of any agreements which are central to the business of the company.

A company intending to apply for an OFEX facility in conjunction with a fund-raising is required to have public limited company ('plc') status which allows shares to be traded and submit a prospectus.

Ongoing obligations

OFEX requirements for continuing obligations on the facility are not as stringent as for companies whose shares are listed on a regulated market, however, there is an OFEX Code of Best Practice which requires companies to disclose information to investors and Newstrack, in particular, in relation to price-sensitive information.

There are no minimum or maximum limits on capitalization for entry and there is no minimum limit in the amount of shares in public hands.

Fees

There is an application fee of £1,000 (+VAT for UK companies) and if the application is successful, there is an annual fee for the Newstrack information service of £3,500 (+VAT for UK companies).

Market profile

As noted, OFEX attracts a wide range of companies from established family-owned concerns to fast-growing technology companies and 'start-up' businesses. Companies typically include family-owned, which may benefit from the higher rates of inheritance tax relief available for unlisted securities, companies seeking to qualify for Enterprise Investment Scheme relief, companies with few share-holders and those which are the subject of management buyouts and buy-ins.

As at 31 December 1998 there were 189 companies traded on OFEX with a combined market capitalization of £1.99 billion. The market capitalization for the end of the year has fallen by some £810 million from the July 1998 total of £2.8 billion, largely because nine OFEX companies with a combined market capitalization of £822 million were the subject of takeover bids between those dates. In any given month, on average, the total percentage of securities traded is 50 per cent.

GOING PUBLIC: IPO PROCESS

There is considerable diversity of the IPO process within Europe, therefore the IPO process outlined below is primarily that of the USA. Many of the key features characteristic of the process in the USA apply at least in principle to the European markets (Bygrave, 1994).[3]

After the company has approved the decision to pursue an IPO, the process begins with the issuing company selecting advisers such as one or more investment banks and a law firm. The issuing company typically uses its existing auditors to help prepare the registration documents or prospectus to verify the financial information contained within. A registration statement is filed with the exchange authorities which contains information on the company and the offering. The key aspects of this document, including the financial statements, are printed as a prospectus which is used to sell the shares in the company.

Refer to chapter 10 for more details regarding the valuation or pricing of the IPO and the investment bank's role in stimulating demand in the company's shares.

The investment banks underwrite the offering, that is in effect, undertake to purchase the stock in the offering at an agreed price and bear the risk of its resale. In practice, this underwriting commitment is not made until the investment bank has obtained indications of interest from prospective buyers and a price linked to the level of demand can be determined. Once a valuation of the company is determined and supported informally by investors, an IPO discount is typically applied to the valuation (about 10–15 per cent) to assure that the market will purchase the shares.

The size of the offering is the next critical step in the IPO process. Typically, the larger the offering the better, because it provides increased liquidity in the market and the costs of carrying out the IPO will be proportionally smaller. Of the shares in the offering, the shares sold by selling shareholders, as distinguished from new shares which will bring additional capital into the company, will typically not exceed one third to one half of the size of the offering (Bygrave, 1994).[3] This reassures investors that the present shareholders (management and/or venture capitalists) have enough confidence in the company to want to retain a substantial part of their ownership.

Sale of shares in the offering is usually divided so that one third or more is placed in a so-called 'institutional pot' for sale to institutions sufficiently active in the IPO market so that their trading behaviour can be readily predicted (Bygrave, 1994).[4] The remaining free shares in the offering is allocated among underwriting syndicate members, a significant portion of which is also sold to institutional buyers. If the issuing company and the investment bank has done a good job positioning the company and convincing the investment community that the suggested price range for the shares are good value, orders for purchasing the shares will typically be several times the available shares for sale in the offering. In such cases, buyers' original orders are cut back to the extent necessary to match supply and demand.

The lead investment bank (or main underwriter) is usually granted an option to sell additional shares equal to 15 per cent of the shares shown as available for sale in the offering (known as the 'green shoe'). The purpose of this option is to allow the investment bank to oversell the offering. The investment bank can then supply the shares oversold from shares purchased in the market in the early hours of trading after the offering is effective or from the 'green shoe'. This permits the investment bank to act as a buyer immediately following the offering which helps support the share price and push it in the desired upward direction.

The price paid by buyers of the shares is a gross price which includes compensation to the investment banks or brokers used to help sell the shares. The issuing company, typically from the net proceeds, must pay all other expenses such as lawyer and accounting fees, filing fees, etc. The compensation to the investment banks or sponsor is approximately 5–8 per cent of the gross price of the IPO, depending on the total value of the stock offered for sale. It is now more common for accountants and lawyers to quote their fees, similar to investment banks, as a percentage of the amount of funds raised, as opposed to a fixed fee.

Table 9.13 ◆ Average expenses of an IPO

Amount of funds raised (in millions of Euros)	5m	10m	20m	50m	100m
Less: Fees to investment banks, sponsor	360k	700k	1,400k	3,200k	6,000k
Accountants, lawyers	120k	200k	400k	1,200k	2,300k
Other (i.e., admission fees, printing prospectus, etc.)	20k	100k	100k	100k	150k
Net proceeds to company (millions of Euros)	**4.5m**	**9m**	**18.1m**	**45.5m**	**91.85m**

The proceeds which go to the investment bank generally comprise three components: 20 per cent as a management fee, 60 per cent split among all those who sold the shares and 20 per cent to cover underwriting fees. The latter 20 per cent underwriting fee can be used to help stabilize the shares once the offering is effective, to create demand for the shares if necessary and/or to hold the trading price at or above the offering level. The investment bank typically agrees to be the issuing company's market maker to help create demand in the stock for either an indefinite or definite period.

The fees investment banks charge to take your company public and/or to provide broking services are believed by some to be astronomical. Considering that there are very few poor investment bankers and even after factoring in the risk they assume, the fees appear to be somewhat of an anomaly. What is more surprising is that these high fee structures have survived for so long. One company in California, EOffering, is hoping to change all that by providing underwriting services online for IPOs in the US$25 million to US$50 million range. They expect to drop the underwriting fee to about 4.5 per cent. Whether EOffering or similar other companies such as WIT capital succeed in shaking up the traditional investment banking marketplace still needs to be seen because the incumbent players will certainly not sit back and watch their profits erode.

The last role the investment bank plays is to provide the company with quality research coverage which is used to stimulate trading in its shares. The research analyst is a vital spokesperson for companies in their first few years of trading on the market.

To keep the IPO market healthy, investment banks usually deliberately employ techniques to encourage demand in shares in the market immediately after an IPO. Two of the more common ploys used by investment banks are:

◆ over-stimulate demand and then promise their best customers an allotment on the condition that they make a commitment to purchase the remainder of their order in the aftermarket;

◆ penalize customers who sell their shares immediately after the offering by taking back a broker's underwriting commission (Bygrave, 1994).[3]

Despite this, market forces tend to take over and the price of the majority of new listings eventually starts to fall relative to the general market.

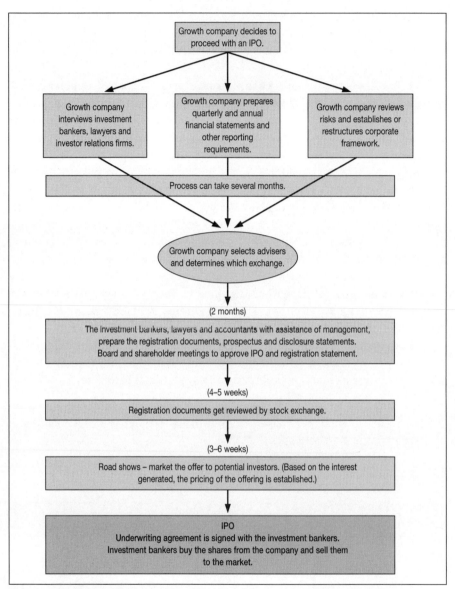

Fig 9.1 ◆ The IPO process

GOING PUBLIC: WHICH EXCHANGE?

As one can see, not all stock exchanges or off-exchanges are the same, varying considerably by listing requirements, ongoing obligations and market profile. It is difficult to ascertain which exchange to choose because it depends on your company's individual circumstances, but in essence, one should choose an exchange which enhances the value of your stock by creating an attractive market for it.

One of the ways an exchange can do this is through market makers. The more market makers used to trade in your company's stock, the greater the available capital is to support trading in your stock. The greater your company's stock is traded, the more liquid it is, thus increasing its value. The number of market makers used should be an important consideration for small companies which do not have large market capitalizations or a large number of shares widely held, both of which also increase liquidity. The greater the number of market makers used also decreases volatility in your company's stock (large blocks can be traded without impacting the share price significantly) which gives investors confidence, a key element of efficient markets. Competition is also increased, the greater the number of market makers used, which should provide price efficiencies to investors. The number and quality of analysts following your company's stock are also vital in enhancing the quality of an exchange.

Other criteria to focus on when choosing an exchange are:

◆ how your company's cost of capital will be affected;

◆ how easy it is to raise additional capital;

◆ the valuation obtainable;

◆ its ability to generate name recognition and credibility;

◆ its ability to develop a critical mass of listed firms;

◆ the level of admission and ongoing fees; and

◆ the service level of the exchange itself in terms of supporting your company with its new responsibilities as a public company.

For fast-growing innovative companies hungry for capital, the LSE is probably not an option since it caters primarily for larger and more mature enterprises. Although it exempts certain scientific-based companies from some of its listing requirements which is an added advantage for those companies with a limited financial history, new admissions may be more heavily scrutinized by comparison with one of the other major European exchanges. AIM appears to have the least stringent listing requirements next to OFEX. EASDAQ, the Neuer Markt and Le Nouveau Marché are similar in their listing requirements and admission processes. Nasdaq, like other US exchanges also has stricter listing and higher disclosure requirements. The intensity of the disclosure requirements, however, can sometimes provide a certification of a company's quality levels when such quality is not easily determinable.

Excluding the largest companies on Nasdaq and the LSE, admission fees for these exchanges/facilities range from Euro 1,400 to Euro 150,000 and annual fees range from Euro 5,000 to Euro 19,000. Although EASDAQ is one of the most expensive exchanges to be admitted on, new listings on average raise sums (Euro 42 million) comparable to Nasdaq (Euro 44 million). Nasdaq however, lists more companies than all the other exchanges reviewed above combined, largely due to the size of the US market. Depending upon the capital raised and the market capitalization of your company in the first year of listing, Le Nouveau Marché can also be quite expensive.

Of the exchanges reviewed in this chapter, the Neuer Markt comes only second to the LSE (UK companies only), in terms of average capital raised (Euro 67 million versus Euro 85 million). In comparison to EASDAQ, the fees charged by the Neuer Markt make it good value.

AIM is the least expensive exchange to list on (next to OFEX), although the small sums of capital raised make the advisory fees significant in relation to the listing fees.

The amount raised at admission and the fees charged, however, should not be the only deciding factors when choosing an exchange. Its performance, in terms of generating interest in the shares of the underlying companies, is also important. In this respect, the Neuer Markt out-performed all other exchanges in 1998 increasing by over 174 per cent compared to Nasdaq increasing at close to 40 per cent. EASDAQ also performed very well in 1998 increasing by over 72 per cent. In comparison to the other exchanges the Nouveau Marché performed modestly, increasing at only 26 per cent whereas AIM had a dismal year, decreasing by 19.2 per cent.

Liquidity is another measure used to evaluate an exchange's performance, typically calculated by dividing monthly trading turnover in value by market capitalization. In this respect, both EASDAQ and Neuer Markt are comparably liquid between 1–1.5 per cent, but the Nouveau Marché averaged around 4 per cent near the end of 1998, largely due to its low market capitalization.

Contacts

LONDON STOCK EXCHANGE
www.londonstockex.co.uk

Telephone:	44-(0)171-797-1000
Fax:	44-(0)171-797-3043

London EC2N 1HP
UK

AIM
www.londonstockex.co.uk

Telephone:	44-(0)171-797-4404
Fax:	44-(0)171-797-4063

London EC2N 1HP
UK

EASDAQ
www.easdaq.be

Brussels

Telephone:	32-(0)2-227-6520
Fax:	32-(0)2-227-6567

56 Rue de Colonies, Bte 15
Koloniënstraat 56, Box 15
B-1000 Brussels
Belgium

London

Telephone:	44-(0)171-489-9990
Fax:	44-(0)171-489-8880

Warwick House
65-66 Queen Street
London EC4R 1EB
UK

EURO.NM
www.euro-nm.com

Brussels

Telephone:	32-(0)2-509-1388
Fax:	32-(0)2-509-1342

Palais de la Borse
B-1000 Brussels
Belgium

London

Telephone:	44-(0)171-556-7887
Fax:	44-(0)171-556-7557

75 Canon Street
London EC4N 5BN
UK

Neuer Markt
www.neuer-markt.de

Telephone:	49-(0)69-2101-5100
Fax:	49-(0)69-2101-3961

Le Nouveau Marché
www.nouveau-marche.fr

Telephone:	33-(0)1-49-27-1606
Fax:	33-(0)1-49-27-1323

Nasdaq
www.nasdaq.com or www.nasdaq-uk.com

Telephone:	44-(0)171-374-6969
Fax:	44-(0)171-374-4488

Durant House
8/13 Chiswell Street
London EC1Y 4XY
UK

OFEX
www.ofex.co.uk

Newstrack Limited

Telephone:	44-(0)171-488-3334
Fax:	44-(0)171-481-4045

Lloyds Court
1 Goodman's Yard
Tower Hill
London
E1 8AT

References

Bygrave, William D, Michael Hay and Jos Peeters (1994), *Realizing Investment Value*.

EASDAQ web site, 'www.easdaq.be' and EASDAQ information package, Brussels.

EURO.NM web site, 'www.euro-nm.com' and EURO.NM information package, Brussels.

European Commission (April 1998), *Risk Capital: A key to job creation in the European Union*.

European Venture Capital Association, *Private Equity Guidebook Central & Eastern Europe*.

London Stock Exchange (June 1998), *A Guide to Going Public*.

London Stock Exchange (August 1997), *AIM: A guide for companies*.

London Stock Exchange (December 1998), *AIM newsletter*.

London Stock Exchange (May 1997), *AIM newsletter*.

Nasdaq web site, 'www.nasdaq.com' and Nasdaq information package.

Neuer Markt web site, 'www.neuer-markt.de'.

Newstrack Limited (April 1998), *The OFEX Trading Facility*.

Nouveau Marche, Le web site, 'nouveau-marche.fr'.

Ofx (December 1998), *Monthly review*.

Notes

1. European Commission (April 1998), *Risk Capital: A Key to job creation in the European Union*. Financial Times/Pitman.

2. A dispensation can be received, under special circumstances, to submit the admission and application forms in a language other than English.

3. Bygrave, William D., Hay, Michael and Peeters, Jos (1994), *Realizing Investment Value*.

4. Ibid.

10

QUOTATION

AS AN

EXIT MECHANISM

Pierre-Michel Piccino
Baring Private Equity Partners

Aleksander Kierski
AIG-CET Capital Management

Introduction

Issues to consider for a successful IPO

Desirability of a quotation

Selecting advisers

IPO process

Pierre-Michel Piccino joined Baring Venture Partners in 1987. For 14 years he was with Du Pont de Nemours International SA, where he held various positions in sales, marketing and general management; his final post was as manager of the Europe and Middle-East Packaging Division. Previously, he spent four years at the Batelle Research Institute in Geneva. He has a degree in mechanical engineering from the École Polytechnique in Lausanne. He is the chairman of the supervisory board of Gemplus Card International SCA, a world leader in the manufacturer of smart cards. He is also director of Pandora Investment (Luxembourg), Ipsos Holding (France), France Telecom Network Services (Switzerland), Mimetics SA (France) and Pixtech Inc., which is quoted on the Nasdaq.

Alexander Kierski is Chief Investment Officer of AIG New Europe Fund, a USD 317 million private equity investment vehicle for Central Europe. Previously he was with Baring Private Equity partners for eight years, where he was a Partner responsible for investments in Western Europe. Formerly, he was with Arthur Andersen where he provided operational reviews, financial audits and litigation advisory services to a range of clients in the financial services industry. In addition, he worked for two years at Postech S.A., a start-up company, where he was responsible for the development of two software applications for the retail industry. These applications were subsequently sold to a cash register manufacturer of international standing. He graduated from the University of Sydney with a computer science and physics degree and holds an MBA from the Business School of Lausanne.

INTRODUCTION

An initial public offering (IPO) is one of the most significant events in the evolution of a company and represents a major accomplishment on the path to finding a full or partial exit for the venture capitalist. Being publicly owned will allow the company to be part of the 'A' league of established businesses, where it will reap great rewards and face new opportunities. The challenge of achieving a successful IPO and maintaining the attractiveness of the company to the financial community over the long term is not an easy task and it has to be carefully prepared and managed.

One of the key reasons for a company to be listed on a stock exchange is that it enables it to raise significant and cheaper funds (at a higher valuation) than from any other source. In most venture capital backed companies, an IPO is undertaken to raise money for a capital increase (called primary) to finance development, and in some cases to sell existing shares (called secondary) so as to provide liquidity for existing investors. The IPO establishes an independent or third party market value for the company which enables the full exit (over time) of the venture capitalist at market prices. Having public status enables the company to provide major incentives through stock option plans in order to attract and retain employees. In addition to the financial aspects, the IPO provides high visibility and media coverage for the company as a result of the reporting requirements and reports made by investment banking analysts.

A successful IPO requires the total dedication and commitment of the management team since they will be the driving force behind the process. Selecting the advisers, restructuring and due diligence and preparing the prospectus and the road show can take months and have an impact on day-to-day operations. Marketing the company and maintaining its attractiveness to investors will result in higher visibility and pressure on the management team for growth in earnings per share (EPS), a challenge they might not have faced while the company was privately held.

ISSUES TO CONSIDER FOR A SUCCESSFUL IPO

There are four questions that need to be answered when evaluating a potential IPO.

1 Is the company ready for an IPO?

2 How will the company be valued?

3 What will be the size of the offering?

4 On what stock exchange and when should the offering be made?

These questions are normally addressed during the first presentation or 'beauty parade' of potential investment bankers to the company, when the investment banks will sell themselves as to their performance, research expertise and placement capacity. Decisions will be taken on the four issues during the adviser's meeting with management, with the final pricing of the offering determined just before the IPO.

Is the company ready for an IPO?

A company's preparedness is paramount to a successful IPO. The management must be committed, understand the responsibilities which flow from being a quoted company and be confident that they can deliver to market expectations.

The readiness of a company to undertake an IPO also depends on the visibility and stability of its long-term financial model. Companies that are profitable have already proved the business case and can relatively easily countenance future financial visibility. The seasonality of the business has to be well understood since it affects the quarterly growth model. Stability of management and operations as well as the potential of the product and technology development are also important.

The company as an individual entity or group of entities should be easily comprehensible to its potential investors as this will provide confidence, so it is preferable to have a clear corporate structure, without intermediary or subsidiary companies with minority investors, preferential ownership, special share rights and control agreements.

The financial department must be equipped to provide ongoing financial reporting and other company information to comply with requirements, providing annual accounts, quarterly statements and, especially, achievable forecasts to the investment bankers in a timely manner.

Valuation

A successful IPO requires a pricing that strikes a balance between the immediate needs of the issuer and selling shareholders and their medium- and long-term interests. In an ideal IPO scenario, the share price will rise significantly within the first months of the offering and then stabilize and increase proportionally to the results of the company. This scenario will secure the support of the investor community.

The valuation of a company is driven by the demand for its shares. Thus the investment bankers will have to establish a marketing strategy and identify target investors to maximize this demand. The marketing strategy is composed of the following internal factors:

◆ *Positioning of the company in the market to obtain comparable company valuations* The positioning of the company is important as it will classify its given sector of the industry. Comparable companies from this sector will be used by the investment bankers to arrive at valuation benchmarks based on price-earning ratios, sales multiples, long-term EPS growth estimates and financial models (such as EBIT – earnings before interest and tax – margins and sales growth).

◆ *'Story' on the company's growth prospects and ability to convince investors that growth is sustainable* In most emerging companies the story behind the company is critical as it will give it uniqueness and facilitate a successful IPO at an attractive valuation. In general, the marketing strategy for the story focuses on the huge market opportunity, the company's leadership position in the market and the industry, its technology, time to market advantage, as well as any other particular features. A significant support to the 'story' is the company's current financial visibility and performance. For emerging companies which are unprofitable a good marketing strategy will permit it to capitalize on large future valuations at the time of the IPO.

The more unique a company's positioning and story the more impact they have on its IPO valuation. Europe and the USA have considerably different approaches to the valuation methodology for emerging companies. In Europe valuations are primarily based on historical financial performance; in the USA, valuations are heavily based on future growth and earnings potential.

◆ *Stability of growth* The IPO valuation will also have to take into account the long-term growth prospects to guarantee a stable and consistent value increase. Thus the IPO will have to be priced reasonably to be in line with the EPS growth prospects and equity story.

Based on the positioning and equity story the investment bankers arrive at an estimated p/e ratio. The p/e ratio multiplied by the net income (historic or future, depending on the timing of the IPO), result in the equity value range to which is applied an IPO discount (between 10 and 15 per cent). The IPO discount is applied so that there is reasonable assurance that the market will purchase the shares.

◆ *Public market value versus merger market value* There are two different values that a market could apply to a company: the public market value and the merger market value. The public market value is dictated by the company's financial performance and expectations. The merger market value takes into account the control aspect, which in most cases commands high premiums due to potential takeover bids. Before an IPO, the company's management, board of directors and shareholders should define whether they intend to have a tightly controlled ownership structure or specific share rights to prevent a takeover, or whether they will allow market forces of supply and demand to dictate ownership. In Europe many quoted companies have implemented anti-takeover measures which have reduced volatility and liquidity in these stocks. The control premium value cannot be taken into account when evaluating the value of the company; it should be treated as potential upside.

Size of the offering

The size of the offering should be balanced between the amount of money the company needs, the liquidity in the market and the dilution impact on future EPS. On average, the larger the offering the better, as this will provide sufficient liquidity in the market and the costs of carrying out the IPO will be proportionally smaller.

External factors

There is an issue as to critical mass and liquidity. The size of the offering has an impact on stock liquidity and potential price volatility. The IPO offering has to be large enough to attract long-term institutional investors, and thus provide enough liquidity (number of shares) for them to buy and sell without substantially moving the price of the stock. Small IPOs tend to be more volatile and are more narrowly distributed among investors.

Internal factors

The primary/secondary mix has to be decided. The capital requirements of the company should be the first consideration. Generally, investors prefer IPOs which fund business growth opportunities, although purely secondary issues can be successful when there is strong justification for the exit (spin-off, etc.); otherwise shareholders will be seen as baling out of the company. In emerging companies purely secondary IPOs are rare since the company needs capital to grow and investors are aiming to take advantage of the growth opportunities for their capital. The secondary component may be a substantial part (say, 50 per cent) of the offering depending on the positioning of the company and the nature of the investor. In emerging businesses it is preferred that founders, managers and employees do not sell at the IPO offering. However, if justified, it is accepted by the investor community.

The size of the primary offering should take into account dilution and EPS growth, as the forecasts should be consistent with the company's story. A primary component that is too high could increase dilution to such an extend that EPS growth will fall below levels acceptable to the market, which will undermine the pricing fundamentals. Many IPOs reduce primary sales to decrease dilution and maximize EPS growth in order to have a second primary offering at a higher valuation.

Stock exchange and timing

The obvious choice for a stock exchange listing is the company's home market where recognition is highest. Over recent years several European companies have decided to obtain a listing in the USA, with an international tranche primarily in their home country. This is chiefly driven by high valuations and market acceptance of their products and technology.

The state of the market has a great influence on the success of the IPO and on obtaining a high valuation. Demand for new issues changes over time, so that it is difficult to pick the ideal time-frame. Delaying or stopping the IPO is expensive and can be disappointing to the company. However, if the state of the market is weak, the company can arrange a small offering and follow it up with a larger one once market conditions improve and a higher valuation is achieved. It is wise to plan an offering when few issues are being marketed and following good annual or quarterly results.

DESIRABILITY OF A QUOTATION

Going public offers both the managers and the venture capital shareholders great benefits. However, once public, their challenges and priorities in the short and long term differ from when they were a private company. An IPO should generate large amounts of capital for the company's development, provide potential realizations and third party valuations, which benefits both groups.

Management's perspective

The considerations for management fall under a number of headings.

Prestige and credibility

Achieving a successful and highly visible offering will bring prestige and credibility to the company and its management. This will have commercial impact on clients, suppliers and corporate partners. In most cases it announces the emergence of the company from a venture capital stage. However, the visibility can also be a disadvantage since competitors will be fully aware of the company's performance and consistently poor results could damage the company's reputation with the investor community and the public.

Market for equity capital

Equity financing, because of potentially high IPO valuations, could prove to be cheaper than debt financing, increasing the company's network, improving gearing ratios and avoiding any drain on cashflows. Depending on the company's performance, capital markets will enable it to raise equity capital on further occasions for internal or M&A activities.

Partial realization for management

Management and employees can realize some of their holdings at the IPO, which will represent substantial personal wealth creation.

Dilution of control

Management's control over the company after the primary issue and subsequent issues will be diluted. Decisions that were once taken by a small group of people will have to be taken by a larger board of directors, and major decisions will involve the public shareholders. In order to retain equity control within the company, management will be in favour of creating a group of core shareholders who are likely to demonstrate long-term support and confidence in the company and its management.

Incentives for employees

The quotation will create an instrument for tangible management and employee incentives; it will also be a tool to attract new employees. Thus, before the IPO, management normally proposes a new stock option plan for existing and potential employees.

Demands on management's time

An IPO and ongoing reporting requirements will represent additional costs and take up a large amount of the management's time.

Short-term performance pressure

Demand for the company's stock will be judged on the basis of the company's quarterly performance. Thus there will be enormous short-term pressure on the management to deliver consistent and smooth growth, in comparison to a private company where emphasis is primarily on long-term market share/product objectives and annual profit performance.

Disclosure and loss of privacy

The company and management will have to provide disclosure on share ownership, salaries and benefits, conflicts of interest and potential lawsuits. All lawsuits or potential lawsuits, whether material or not, should be settled so that they cannot affect the offering.

The venture capitalist's perspective

The particular considerations for the venture capitalist include the following.

Sell at IPO or at second offering

In most IPOs, the venture capitalists get the opportunity to sell part of their holding, and a follow-on secondary offering will be planned to sell the remaining part if the company's stock performs up to expectations. It is important to make the right decision as to whether to sell at the IPO, and if so how much: while the IPO value may have taken four to six years to achieve, the value of the holding can double or triple over the year following the IPO. Historically a second offering has always outperformed the IPO in value. This is a tricky judgement for the venture capitalist to make as a belief in the performance of the business must be measured in relation to investment bankers' expectations, the volatility of the market, which is out of the venture capitalist's control, and the resulting time-frame of a potential second offering.

Lock-up period

After the IPO, investors are subject to a lock-up period during which shares cannot be sold. Subsequently shares can be sold in low proportions, depending on liquidity. This makes it a time-consuming process to liquidate the holding.

Control premium

A holding giving control dictates a premium, so that a significant percentage of the company should be in the hands of the public and the shareholder structure should be transparent, with no shareholder having a preferential position that could inhibit a takeover bid.

SELECTING ADVISERS

A key step in a successful IPO and the long-term quotation viability of the company is selecting the right advisers. The most important advisers are the underwriters/investment bankers, as they will guide the company through the whole process. Advisers coming second are lawyers, accountants and investor relations firms.

Underwriters/investment bankers

The selection of an underwriter/investment banker should not be based purely on its suitability for the task of quoting the company on the stock exchange, but also on its long-term commitment and ability to market the company. The investment banker's track record for listing similar companies is important because it establishes its credibility in the marketplace.

Listed below are other issues to consider when making a selection. They are in no particular order of importance; however, for small and emerging companies, research and industry knowledge and long-term commitment are critical because these will bring quality and credibility to the marketing of a company.

Track record

The investment banker should demonstrate a track record of listing companies in the same industry, with a similar size of offering and distribution capability, and with good aftermarket support and capital appreciation over the long term. The company should also examine the short-term aftermarket performance of past pricing. If the price dropped significantly after the listing, then the IPO was overvalued and the public overpaid; if the price increased sharply after the listing, then the IPO was undervalued and the company's shareholders suffered an unnecessarily high dilution. A good history of aftermarket performance gives the investment bank an advantage in selling the IPO. The company should evaluate the quality and quantity of research coverage by the investment bank, as well as its relationships with institutional investors.

Research capability and industry knowledge

For emerging companies, research and aftermarket support by the analysts is the most important differentiator between the investment banks. The investment bank's analysts have to understand and share the vision of the company, provide a high degree of support on a regular basis and have credibility in the marketplace. Analysts' periodic reports help position the company and communicate the company's story to the investment community. They are also the best equipped to evaluate and explain a momentary weakness in the company's performance. Furthermore, investment banks who focus on a given sector or industry are more likely to have greater access to institutional investors and to be investors themselves.

Market strategy and distribution capability

The investment banker will have to position the company in order to obtain comparable valuations but will also use the positioning and story behind the company to launch a market strategy that will maximize demand from investors. In general, underwriters want to make the offering large enough to accommodate institutional investors, since they represent the largest investor group and thus are the key to a successful IPO. Retail investors and international investors are secondary. Investment bankers will target institutions that focus on the given industry and try to achieve a broad placement among leading institutional investors.

An investment banker should be selected in the light of its distribution capability, domestically and internationally: that is, managing a syndicate and achieving access to the target investors (institutional and/or retail). A syndicate is normally created to assure distribution. This normally consists of 20 to 50 firms, depending on the size of the offering. The syndicate will enable the distribution to reach a group of investors which is diverse in terms of size, location and focus.

Market-making capability

The company's investment bankers typically undertake to be its market maker, in other words, to participate actively in the trading of the company's stock on their own account and thus provide liquidity. To evaluate commitment to market making, an analysis should be obtained of the positions held by the investment bank in the companies that it took public.

Breadth of services

An investment bank should not only provide IPO services, but also be there to underwrite follow-on equity offerings, arrange debt financing and provide treasury and cash management advice, M&A and other financial services. Once the relationship with the investment bank is established, it should be leveraged to provide additional services after the IPO.

Long-term commitment

To guarantee long-term commitment, the advisers have to see the company as a valued client. An adviser should be chosen whose core business is listing companies of similar characteristics and market making on the same stock exchange. A small, emerging company is less likely to get attention and long-term commitment from an adviser who is part of a large financial group. However, it makes sense for emerging companies to appoint two investment banks, one for its distribution capabilities and the other for research and industry knowledge.

Lawyers

The company's legal counsel will draft and review the prospectus, provide advice on shareholder structure, IPO litigation risks and disclosure requirements. A law firm should be chosen that has relevant industry knowledge and a track record in IPOs.

Accountants

The company's auditors should be selected on the basis of their experience in international accounting standards, GAAP and domestic standards, and tax matters for publicly listed companies. Industry experience concerning specific accounting regulations is helpful but not necessary. Accountants with an international reputation will certainly enhance market confidence.

Investor relation firms

Investor relation firms are important before and after the IPO. They should not only provide mandatory information requirements, but also articles and interviews in the press. This can significantly increase awareness of your company and its business, thus boosting investor and public confidence. As this is an ongoing process, a choice may be made to manage this activity inhouse instead of subcontracting it. Investor relation firms should be hired some time before the IPO in order to generate public interest through media coverage of the company's products, history and potential.

IPO PROCESS

The duration of the IPO process is mainly dependent on the time needed to prepare the company and the registration requirements of the stock exchange. The whole process as listed below should not take less than three months.

The decision to proceed (several months)

The board of the company takes the decision in principle to raise funds through an IPO. The company interviews investment bankers, lawyers and investor relations firms. It prepares quarterly and annual financial statements, as well as any other reporting information. It reviews potential risks, restructures or organizes mergers of entities so as to simplify the company's structure, and it assesses potential litigation and tax liability.

Company selects advisers

The advisers agree terms and conditions with the company and draw up a timetable. Due diligence is started by the advisers.

Registration statement (two months)

The investment bankers and lawyers, with the assistance of the management of the company, prepare the registration document, prospectus and disclosure statements. The board of directors and shareholders' meeting approves the IPO and registration statement. These documents get reviewed by the stock exchange governing body, typically within a month. Any comments from the governing body are responded to.

Road show (three weeks)

Investment bankers together with management market the offering to potential domestic and international investors. Based on the interest generated, the pricing of the offering is established.

IPO (one day)

With pricing and date for the offering being fixed, the underwriting agreement is signed with the investment bankers. The investment bankers buy the shares from the company and sell them to the market.

11

BETTER EXITS

John Wall and Julian Smith
PricewaterhouseCoopers

John Wall is the Regional Senior Partner for PricewaterhouseCoopers Corporate Finance and Investment Banking. He has extensive experience of the venture capital industry and has been lead adviser on many acquisitions, disposals and complex fund raising projects during his career as a corporate finance adviser.

John is a frequent conference speaker in Europe and a past member of the Exits Committee of EVCA giving specialist advice on venture backed disposal mandates.

Julian Smith spent seven years in corporate finance at Pricewaterhouse-Coopers in London, including a secondment with HSBC Private Equity, specializing in buyouts and exit advice, including the buyout and subsequent exit of CentreWest London Buses. He now specializes in transport sector transactions and has recently joined the team advising the British Government and London Transport on the raising of £8 billion for capital investment in the London Underground Public-Private Partnership.

Foreword

This special paper, written by John Wall and Julian Smith of PricewaterhouseCoopers was commissioned and edited by the Exits Committee of the European Venture Capital Association (EVCA). The role of this committee is to stimulate exit[1] opportunities for venture backed companies. Its composition is set out below.

The committee requested Price Waterhouse Corporate Finance to carry out a survey of the practical experience of major European venture capital funds in exiting their investments with a view to establishing what steps can be taken to improve exit performance. Thirty venture capitalists were interviewed representing 14 countries in Europe. This paper presents the findings of the survey and gives advice to venture capitalists on how the problems identified in the survey might be resolved or reduced in order for them to achieve a significant improvement in exit performance and therefore investor returns.

Membership of the Exits Committee
Chairman: Mr Diederik Heyning, Gilde Investment Fund (NL)
Members: Mr Daniel Janssens, EC-DG XIII (L)
               Mr Philip Vermeulen, GIMV (B)
               Mr John Wall, Price Waterhouse (GB)
               Mr Ian Riley, BC Partners (GB)
               Mr Pierre Riels, Sofinnova SA (F)
               Mr Erkki Kariola, Start Fund of Kera (SF)
               Mr Waldemar Jantz, TVM (D)
Secretary: Mr Serge Reicher, EVCA

INTRODUCTION

European venture capitalists are better at *investing* than *exiting*. Consequently there is a significant overhang of investee companies waiting to exit. The Price Waterhouse Corporate Finance survey found that:

◆ European venture capitalists regard IPOs as the ideal exit, and consequently do not devote enough attention to trade sales;

◆ financial buyers are not taken seriously by most venture capitalists;

◆ many exits are by buy back, though this is often not anticipated at the outset of the deal;

◆ many venture capitalists do not plan for exit from the date of investment;

◆ most venture capitalists do not market their investments widely enough, and many do not make full use of intermediaries to help them;

◆ members of management are often an obstacle to a profitable exit.

This paper therefore discusses how exit performance could be improved by:

◆ focusing more attention on alternatives to IPO;

◆ planning exit from the beginning of the investment;

◆ preparing adequately for trade and financial sales;

◆ making effective use of the buy back[2] option;

◆ wider marketing of businesses for sale;

◆ using intermediaries when needed;

◆ getting the support of management for the venture capitalist's exit intentions.

THE INVESTMENT OVERHANG

A comparison of the level of exits with the level of new investments for venture backed companies in Europe indicates that there is a significant overhang of investee companies waiting to exit. In other words, venture capitalists appear to be better at *investing* than they are at *exiting*! The current European venture capital portfolio, totalling ECU 25.1 billion at the end of 1995, equates to eight years of divestment activity, whereas the venture capitalists we interviewed had a normal target life for their investments of between three and six years. More importantly, given that the majority of large investments (greater than ECU 50 million) exit relatively early, the position must be significantly worse for smaller deals. There clearly is a problem in achieving exit within an acceptable timescale and for that reason this survey was undertaken.

The annual survey of EVCA members indicates that by far the largest number of exits takes place by trade sale. The only exception was in 1994, when IPOs had a particularly strong year and overtook trade sales in terms of value, though not number, *see* Fig. 11.1.

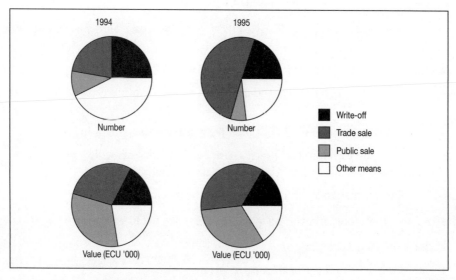

Fig 11.1 ♦ European venture capital exits by route

Source: EVCA

THE SURVEY

Coverage

Thirty venture capitalists were interviewed representing venture capital funds in 14 countries throughout Western and Central Europe. The funds chosen had investment portfolios of at least ECU 100 million and were judged by EVCA to be a representative sample of the venture industry in Europe. The survey covered the following issues.

♦ The record of venture capitalists in achieving exits.

♦ The significance of price compared to other factors in deciding on exit.

- The advantages and disadvantages of different exit routes.
- How proactive venture capitalists are in planning exits.
- The steps taken by venture capitalists to prepare their investments for exit.
- Marketing to trade buyers.
- The use of intermediaries or advisers.
- The role of management.

This was a survey of attitudes, not outcomes, and it covered a heterogeneous industry. Statistics would not be meaningful or representative; the results are therefore reported using the words of the interviewees and, while the answers are inevitably subjective, they have been edited to give a representative overview of the European exit market.

Exit record

The exit experience of venture capitalists varies greatly from country to country and from one institution to another; the most significant factor in this variation is the degree of maturity of the venture capital market in each country. During the survey two types of venture capital investor were clearly distinguishable, although the majority of venture capitalists combine some of the features of each type.

The pro-active investor

The pro-active venture capitalist prefers to buy a business as a principal and then incentivize management by stock options or otherwise. He generally plans the exit from day one and is motivated exclusively by cash returns or internal rate of return (IRR) in determining the exit route.

The passive investor

An alternative approach is to act as a passive investor, generally with a minority stake. The passive venture capitalist often invests on a longer term basis with no specific exit route in mind, relying on an annual dividend to provide his return. Very often his only exit route is by means of a redemption or buy back of his investment by the management or co-shareholder. He operates in a younger venture capital market, often with few other players, and is concerned about the reputation of both his institution and the venture capital 'industry' in general and may therefore choose not to maximize returns if this would require an exit route, such as a trade sale, which would not be welcomed by management.

Reasons for failing to exit

Seventy per cent of the venture capitalists interviewed said that they had at some time experienced difficulties in exiting their investments. The following reasons were identified as the causes of their problems:

◆ stock market sentiment

◆ lack of institutional buyers for IPOs

◆ lack of trade buyers for a particular investment

◆ unco-operative management or co-investors

◆ due diligence results

◆ poor performance by the business.

Many of these problems could be avoided or their effects reduced by proper planning of the exit from an early stage in the life of an investment. For example, the problem of market sentiment or a lack of institutional buyers of stock could be dealt with by having a contingency plan for a trade exit as an alternative. A lack of trade buyers does not arise overnight, and therefore a company with a properly planned exit route would identify such a problem and enable the venture capitalist to search for alternative buyers outside the sector or market concerned or to consider the possibility of financial buyers.

It is true that management often have a vested interest in keeping their jobs and may therefore obstruct a trade sale. However, the venture capitalists with a successful exit record have been able to motivate and incentivize management or their co-shareholders to work with them for common goals.

If new information at the due diligence stage causes a buyer to withdraw, this often indicates that the process could have been better managed. Such information should certainly not come as a surprise to the vendor if the business has been properly prepared for exit and therefore there is no reason to surprise the purchaser – unless it is a deliberate tactical reason! Generally however, a smooth exit process should avoid the purchaser being derailed by surprises which put a successful outcome at risk.

Poor business performance is perhaps the one issue which cannot easily be addressed by exit planning; however, the effects can be minimized by correct timing of the exit – and this does depend on planning.

Despite widespread problems, many of the 'pro-active' venture capitalists claimed a high rate of success, while most of the 'passive' investors did not.

Exit consideration – is price the only issue?

Most venture capitalists view price, or their IRR, as the overriding factor determining their approach to exit:

'Price is the only issue.'
'No other factors – IRR only.'

Where other factors were mentioned, it was often because of their impact on the IRR:

'Relative certainty of it happening; nature and style of consideration.'
'Timescale. No warranties.'
'Liquidity, tax considerations.'

In contrast, some of the passive venture capitalists have other factors to consider, often driven by their own status or ownership:

'We don't invest only to make money. We are generally the principal banker so the price on exit is only one part of the discussion. The final goal is customer loyalty for the branch, as long as we make money.'
'The future of the company is important; we want it to prosper after our sale.'
'We are the only active venture capital house. We would not like to leave behind a dissatisfied entrepreneur.'

EXIT ROUTES

Trade sales and IPOs

The two most common exit routes for venture capitalists are sale to a trade purchaser and IPO. Venture capitalists have strong views on the advantages and disadvantages of each.

IPO – The Holy Grail?

Advantages

- ◆ higher price?
- ◆ favoured by management
- ◆ can be a dual track approach – may provoke a trade bid
- ◆ share in future growth of the business from retained shares.

Disadvantages

- ◆ higher cost than other routes
- ◆ is it really an exit? The lock up agreement prevents an initial 100 per cent exit
- ◆ continued shareholding carries a risk that gains may not be realized and venture capitalists lose the special rights they have in a private company
- ◆ many European markets are illiquid
- ◆ the message has to be simple and attractive to a large number of investors
- ◆ not an option for many small companies.

261

The venture capital world's view of IPOs is summed up by:

'You get the best price if the market is strong – it also flushes out the trade buyers.'

IPOs are the venture capitalist's 'Holy Grail'; they are seen by many as the ultimate exit, to which all aspire, because of the super returns they have sometimes produced and because they allow management to stay in charge. However, the reality is that many more investments exit by trade sale.

The disadvantages of IPOs, particularly in Continental Europe, are summed up by the statement:

'You can only sell 10 to 20 per cent (of the company's shares) and then you have to wait two years – fewer and fewer companies are going to the market.'

The lock-up agreement which requires a venture capitalist to retain a significant investment, if not its whole stake, in order to inspire confidence in institutional investors, means that an IPO is not always an exit.

Since the survey was carried out, the French market has improved, as the following examples indicate, however, public markets are inherently cyclical, and most other countries in Europe have not experienced the same improvement.

Case study – Aigle

Apax Partenaires held an 85 per cent stake in this manufacturer of outdoor clothing. It was floated in October 1994 with a capitalization of FF 450 million but due to general sentiment in the market, only 20 per cent was passed on to new shareholders, with the vendors retaining a majority.

Case study – Européenne d'Extincteurs

Européenne d'Extincteurs was a publicly quoted manufacturer of fire extinguishers, with a capitalization of around FF 400 million, in which Credit Lyonnais had a 65.1 per cent shareholding. It was being prepared for sale to a strategic purchaser but the public market strengthened and CL therefore sold their entire shareholding in 10 per cent parcels to institutions in June and July 1996.

Where only a small share is sold, a good exit price may mean nothing if the price in the market falls before the venture capitalist is able to sell the remainder; some investors therefore prefer the certainty of the trade sale process.

The strongest argument for IPOs is the idea that the preparation required, particularly in marketing, often leads to a pre-emptive trade bid, thus enabling the venture capitalist to achieve the best of both worlds. However, the other side of this coin is that proper investigation of the opportunities for a trade sale, and proper planning of the process, might well have revealed the same purchaser and saved some of the legal and professional costs associated with a flotation.

Trade sale – the second best route?

Advantages

- ◆ Buyers may pay a premium for synergy, market share or market entry.
- ◆ One hundred per cent cash exit and therefore certainty, subject to warranties, indemnities, escrows[3] and deferred consideration.
- ◆ Cheaper than an IPO.
- ◆ Faster and simpler than an IPO.
- ◆ Only option for some small companies.
- ◆ Need to convince only one buyer – rather than the whole market.

Disadvantages

- ◆ Often opposed by management, who lose their independence.
- ◆ There are few trade buyers in some countries.
- ◆ Most venture capitalists will not give warranties to purchasers.

The most commonly identified disadvantage of trade sales, particularly in smaller European countries, was:

'More difficult to do trade sales than flotations – there are not a lot of obvious buyers.'

But it was also noticeable that many venture capitalists do not attempt to identify overseas, non-sector or financial buyers – thereby somewhat limiting their chances of success.

There was a majority view that trade sales are quicker and easier than IPOs, with dissent only from those who experienced difficulty finding buyers. The real debate was on prices achieved:

'(Trade sales are) the best value – the buyer knows what he is buying and there is only one buyer to negotiate with.'

However, the negative quotes about trade sale prices need to be seen in the context of the number of venture capitalists who do not market their investments fully when they come to sell!

Sales to financial buyers

The overwhelming majority view on exit by sale to other venture capitalists, or by secondary buyout, was:

'Not attractive. If I can't make money, how can they?'

Sales to other venture capitalists – venture capitalists' concerns

♦ Third best option on price (due to purchaser's high IRR requirement).

♦ Management would have divided loyalties during the sale process, and therefore the buyer would have better information than the vendor.

♦ The price impact of the buyer's concern that the vendor may have managed the business for short term cash gain.

However, there was some recognition that certain situations present opportunities for financial buyers:

'We were approached by a venture capital house and we were surprised to see anyone had an interest in taking (our investment) on.'

but these sometimes arise from emotional, not economic, reasons.

'(A financial sale) would mean we were less successful than envisaged, but you can get tired of an investment.'

Opportunities for financial purchasers[4]

♦ Transition from early to later stages of development 'provides an independent valuation when a capital increase is required'.

♦ Refinancing at the end of a closed end fund.

♦ Need by the owning venture capitalist to realize a gain (for tax or reporting reasons).

♦ 'A way for management to stay in when an IPO is not an option.'

♦ Venture capitalists may attribute a higher value to a high cash/low growth business than a trade buyer would.

♦ Enables a business to releverage.

♦ Breakdown in relationship between management and investor – 'The buyer may be a better owner for the company.'

The low number of sales to financial buyers seems to be more a result of mutual suspicion than business logic. Given the increasing number of businesses now being bought from corporates by financial buyers, one would expect to see the same trend in venture capital disposals. The trend in corporate disposals is partly driven by venture capitalists' willingness to accept lower IRRs than was formerly the case. Given the high leverage applied to venture capitalist purchases, which reduces the average cost of finance, there is no reason why a venture capitalist buyer should not match a trade bidder when there are no synergies or other special factors to be considered. One venture capitalist said: 'There are some businesses which should be in a permanently leveraged state.'

An example is United Texon which was a £75 million management buyout (MBO) from Emhart of the USA in 1987. Flotation in London was planned for 1994 but cancelled in favour of a sale to Apax for £131 million, which included the refinancing of £90 million of debt.

In this case some of the original investing funds were nearing the ends of their lives. The refinancing led by a new investor provided an independent valuation and this facilitated a transfer from one fund to another within the same house without any risk of favouring one fund over another. By the same token, an ongoing participation by the vendor can help to inspire confidence in a financial buyer and it seems that a large number of sales to financial buyers involve some retained stake.

A few other positive examples came to light through the survey:

'We got a good price on X, a retailer – it was an unpopular business – an MBO was the best option and management wanted to stay in.'

'It allows you to turn over your investments. Our most recent exit was the second MBO for the business (and we helped finance it) – it gave management the majority stake they wanted and crystallized a 22 per cent IRR for us (which we could only recognize on a disposal).'

Share buy backs

Buy back or redemption by co-investors or management has historically been a common exit route for passive investors, and for all venture capitalists when other routes fail.

This is often a result of poor performance leading to a lack of interested buyers, or else a consequence of the management or majority owners of smaller businesses refusing to accept a sale to a third party. It is surprising that many venture capitalists have not felt able to include standard buy back terms in their investment agreements, although the survey indicated that these are becoming more and more common. The principal objection is that a predetermined formula may mean that the exit price is effectively capped even if the business is worth more.

'Buy backs are the second most common exit route. We have no standard clause because this would put an upper limit on the sale price – management want it both ways.'

There is little doubt that a buy back is the least favoured exit route, short of insolvency, simply because the lack of competition and the buyer's strong position result in a poor sale price for the exiting investor. Venture capitalists are realists, however.

'Creates an opportunity when one would not otherwise be available. We always insist on having some sort of anti-embarrassment clause where management intends to stay in. We did a deal earlier this year for which management received a bid two months after buying us out!'

'A buy back gets the investment off our books and out of the statistics. We may get the opportunity to buy it back again at a lower price.'

'It is more difficult than a trade sale because they have to find the money. There is a lot of discussion about value.'

'For a bad investment it is the only way out. In one case management made an offer and it required a painful negotiating process to get us a 20 per cent return – but there was no alternative acceptable to management.'

The approach to exit – planning or reaction?

We asked all the interviewees whether their approach to exits was proactive or reactive. The majority regarded themselves as proactive and supported this assertion with comments like these:

'We are proactive – we decide to get rid of a company and then work on it. We have given up planning exit from Day 1 because it always turns out to be different from what we expect. Very often the technology and the market develop differently from expectations.'

'Proactive – we look at the business and say "Good time to sell", and start the process.'

In our view this does not constitute a truly proactive approach. However, some people are genuinely proactive.

'We plan before entry. After two years we plan ahead based on performance and market windows, although we are not "market timers".'

'We always discuss exit openly with the founder when we make the investment. Sometimes the operating plans take into account what is required for exit.'

But at the other end of the scale are the following comments.

'Reactive – the co-shareholders or directors approach us. A lot of clients would not come to us if we planned exits in advance.'

'Our companies are always for sale – price dependent.'

In general it seems that the commonest approach is to regularly review the portfolio, keep an eye open for potential buyers, and identify opportunities as they arise. In our view there is scope for improving exit performance by better planning of the exit process for each investment from Day 1.

The sale

Preparation for sale

The venture capitalists who focus on IPOs were generally agreed on what preparation is necessary, in terms of presentation, to achieve a successful exit.

'Professional product brochures. Three years ago we started sending financials to the press. Annual reports are consistent and accessible.'

Other issues included the quality of management, consistent company performance, reporting systems and legal structure.

While it was noted that these things were also useful for a trade sale, and this is shown by the popularity of a 'twin track' approach, the general view was:

'With a trade sale you have what you have – but hopefully you have done the right things'

… which implies that it is only at the point of exit that the venture capitalist starts to think about the preparation which should already have been done!

Given the short timescale, often less than a year, which venture capitalists allow for planning trade exits, it is not surprising that less attention is devoted to preparation than is the case for IPOs. Nevertheless, it is self-evident that more effort devoted to preparing businesses would assist the sale process.

Perhaps contrary to public perception, the majority of venture capitalists were opposed to the idea of managing the business strategically with a view to maximizing exit opportunities and proceeds. They generally believe that it is wrong to jeopardize the long-term prospects of a business for short-term gain, either because a buyer might realize what had happened and adjust the price accordingly, or because they are genuinely concerned for their reputation.

'We wouldn't manage for the sake of exit.'

'We just try to make the business as presentable and successful as possible.'

'We don't normally adjust strategy – but exit is always in the back of the mind, for instance, when an investment decision has to be made we ask to what extent

it will add value. We may not embark on major new investment because we may not recover full value.'

A small minority of venture capitalists are prepared to determine strategy according to exit requirements. Most commonly this involves making acquisitions in order to be the right size for flotation. For example:

'We have strategy discussions, and we may say (about a proposal): "This might be attractive in profit terms but will not make the company big enough for an IPO".'

'The public market tends to reward a growth story.'

In preparing for a trade sale, other factors come into play as size is less significant:

'Be clear about the strategy – choose one which might make the business attractive to a competitor.'

'We had a choice of a non-exclusive export licence or an exclusive one. Management tried to make it non-exclusive but we prevented this because it might have put off a trade buyer.'

'We are a small country; the cost of building overseas markets is high so we focus on one or two to show the potential to a trade buyer. This is partly aimed at exit but is also the right thing for the company.'

Marketing the business to trade buyers

Practice varies between those venture capitalists who market their exits widely, and those who rely on their contacts in the industry.

'The market is inactive so we have to be active. We consider who would be the best buyer in the world and approach two or three.'

'The worst thing is to get into a one horse race.'

'All things being equal, yes, we market widely. Sometimes values can be eroded by wide marketing so we might just talk to one or two. Depends how much of the business is proprietary and the impact this has on value.'

'We are on the board so we know who the competitors are – who would fit strategically.'

'Yes – we or the board know them. But more and more we are using professional intermediaries.'

'We know most of the companies (who would be interested). We have not looked overseas because we have not had time.'

'We know who will buy. We don't look outside our own country. In our sort of business it is traditional to sell to a regional or national buyer. We know that UK financial buyers are interested but it is important that the deal is accepted by the other owners and staff, who are often nationalistic and afraid of foreign buyers.'

The majority of venture capitalists took the view that buyers would generally be found from within their investment's own sector and country. This clearly excludes any strategic purchaser who might pay a premium to establish himself in a new market, and possibly puts a cap on the price which can be achieved. Most venture capitalists seem to be put off marketing by the resources required and the risk of breaking confidentiality. Many preferred advisers to be paid by the acquirer.

It was surprising to discover that many venture capitalists appear to be 'satisficers' rather than 'maximizers':

'Sometimes we don't market widely if we can achieve our hurdle IRR for the particular investment – but in one case we went around the world to do that because we knew exactly which biotech companies had a good fit.'

Case study : Non-sector buyer – Elddis Caravans

Elddis Caravans was the UK market leader in the manufacture of touring caravans. It was a management buyout backed by Northern Venture Managers and Price Waterhouse advised on the sale. We analyzed the UK, European and North American markets for caravans and found that they were mainly supplied by domestic manufacturers. We saw an opportunity to sell the business either in Continental Europe or in North America and targeted all the main producers, making presentations in France, Germany, Canada, New York and California. The obvious buyer was Fleetwood, a billion dollar turnover manufacturer of recreational vehicles based in California, who had European expansion plans. Thor in New York and Firan in Montreal were in similar position.

In addition to a strategic search with Elddis for buyers in the caravan business we searched for contacts through the Price Waterhouse Corporate Finance network. Our London office identified a company called Constantine, who were previously in shipping related activities and then property development and had substantial cash on their balance sheet but lacked a core trade. They had no existing interest in caravan manufacturing but were interested in any transport related companies. It was Constantine who bought the business at a premium price.

The use of intermediaries to advise on exit

Venture capitalists seem to be divided in their views on advisers. We observed five different approaches to using intermediaries:

'We always use an external adviser.'

'We use intermediaries 25 per cent of the time – if you have an interesting asset it sells itself.'

'We have our own in-house M&A section – not sure they are specialist but they say they can do it and it is difficult to go outside unless other investors request it or we have to market internationally.'

'We talk to some of the larger M&A houses – they act for the buyer.'

'We do work ourselves. We are thinking of using intermediaries more and more, especially for companies which have been in the portfolio too long.'

Regardless of individual approach it seems that there is an increasing tendency to use advisers.

'More and more they earn their fees.'

'Advisers focus on one job while we are often taken out of the process by another crisis.'

Where external advisers are used, they may be investment banks, M&A (mergers and acquisitions) specialists or the corporate finance departments of the major accounting firms.

Venture capitalists look for a number of different strengths when selecting advisers:

♦ contacts

♦ ability to market discreetly

♦ industry sector knowledge and deal experience

♦ independence

♦ resources

♦ ability of individuals

♦ enthusiasm and commitment to the job

♦ nature and size of investment.

Many people appoint advisers they know and trust; others prefer a 'beauty parade' as a means to make the adviser work hard.

The role of the adviser may vary from a simple search for acquirers to including the preparation of an information memorandum and leading or hand-holding in the negotiations. Occasionally the adviser will be invited in at an early stage to advise on strategy.

When asked how advisers add value to the exit process, venture capitalists mentioned a number of areas.

'Confidentiality – they judge who to trust.'

'Open up connections we do not have.'

'Buyers people didn't think about.'

'Resources and manpower.'

'Geographical coverage, for instance, Asia and North America.'

'Good quality information memorandum; acquirers are busy – they will read it quickly and form a view.'

'It is useful in negotiations to have a party in between that you can shout at – you can't yell at the purchaser.'

'They have the time to get a better price.'

The role of management

The exit decision often revolves around management. Even if they do not have voting control, their role puts them in a strong position.

'Anyone who says management isn't critical to a float is crazy; and they can muck up a trade sale pretty badly.'

'You cannot sell if management doesn't want to.'

Many of the proactive investors make detailed arrangements with management from day one regarding decisions on exit, and some will only invest if the management team shares their exit goal. By contrast, life for others is more difficult.

'They (management) try to resist exit as much as possible.'

'We never get them to agree at the point of entry. Their goal is to expand – not to sell.'

THE NEED TO IMPROVE EXIT PERFORMANCE

The survey confirmed that the majority of European venture capitalists have difficulty in exiting some of their investments.

Clearly, there are cases when these difficulties are due to factors beyond the venture capitalist's control, but the survey revealed that there are many aspects of the exit process where venture capitalists have influence and can take steps to improve exit performance:

◆ use of alternatives to IPO

◆ planning exit from Day 1

◆ adequate preparation for trade and financial sales

◆ proper use of the buy back option

◆ effective marketing

♦ use of intermediaries when needed

♦ getting the support of management.

These issues, and the action venture capitalists can take, are considered below.

HOW TO IMPROVE EXIT PERFORMANCE

Planning exit from the point of entry

Exits need to be planned. Even those venture capitalists who take a long-term view need to consider what will happen when the business is no longer performing as originally expected, when they get tired of management, or when their funds are no longer needed for the development of the business.

Before making an investment the venture capitalist should consider the following issues, as part of their due diligence process.

♦ What will be the exit route?

♦ Who will buy the business?

♦ Is the business strategy the right one to bring about the desired exit?

♦ Is the structure of the business appropriate for a straightforward exit? (If not this should be addressed in the business plan.)

♦ Is management keen to exit? If not:

    – can they be incentivized?

    – how can the venture capitalist's interests be protected?

Focusing management on exit

If management are not keen to consider exit under any circumstances, it may not be in the venture capitalist's interests to do the deal.

One approach might be to ask them to consider:

♦ what would happen to the business in the event of retirement/death/illness;

♦ whether it might at some point be in the interests of the business to involve a trade partner;

♦ whether they are ever likely to want a change of investor or to buy back the venture capitalist's share (using surplus cash).

Whatever the plans, it is in management's interests to create a high quality business which gives them the option of selling it at some future point. They should therefore consider the exit options now. Often it may be found that this subject is best dealt with through management's financial or legal advisers to avoid the venture capitalist worrying management by giving the impression of being too focused on exit. This may also be the best approach at the point when the venture capitalist wants to achieve an exit.

If management are agreed that exit is the aim, they can be incentivized by means of shares, share options and bonuses to ensure that their goals coincide with those of the investor. Incentivization will not work unless the management are agreed on the principle of exit. The effectiveness of incentivization by equity stake can sometimes be increased by using a ratchet,[5] although it is important that the ratchet is based on targets meaningful to the investor. For example, it would not be appropriate to agree a profit based ratchet if the venture capitalist was most concerned about the final purchase price or IRR. IRR-ratchets are complicated but may ensure that management and venture capitalist have the same interests. It should be stated however that deals are often best kept simple especially as no ratchet mechanism can cater for all circumstances.

The survey results indicated that more and more venture capitalists were including buy back clauses as standard in their investment agreements. This gives them the ability to force an exit if the business does not perform to expectations. Some venture capitalists still believe that their clients will not accept this, and there was a concern that any price based formula acts as a cap on value.

Structuring the investment as a combination of fixed term loan (or preference shares) and equity shares – the traditional UK approach – can avoid or reduce this problem, subject to local tax and legal constraints, by providing for repayment of the majority of the venture capitalist's investment after a few years, without requiring the sale of equity shares. This combination also means that the venture capitalist has an incentive not to force repayment unless this is in the interests of the business because the value of his or her equity shares would be reduced.

Which exit route?

The venture capitalist needs to know which exit route he or she is aiming for at the point of investment. This is not however, an irreversible decision. Some of the most successful exit performers seem to be those who aim for an IPO and use this as a means to encourage pre-emptive trade bids.

The message from the survey, and from actual exit performance, is that trade sales[6] should often be regarded as equal or preferable to IPOs, but that they require the same degree of planning.

In the current market financial bidders should be taken seriously. They are often prepared to go through a bidding and shortlisting process in the same way as a trade bidder, though they require more time to get to know the industry.

Case study: Betonson

Betonson is a Dutch manufacturer of prefabricated concrete products including piles, water mains, floors and concrete elements for bridges and viaducts, which was owned by a syndicate of eight venture capitalists. Price Waterhouse Corporate Finance advised the syndicate and the company on the disposal in February 1996.

Initially, the likely bidders were expected to be a number of international building material producers not yet present or active in the Netherlands; however, some of the bidders turned out to be those with established Dutch operations. The eventual purchaser was Van Nieuwpoort Beheer BV, a major supplier of aggregates, who wished to avoid the loss of a key customer if a new owner were to switch purchases to their own group suppliers.

In the end, skilful negotiations with all parties resulted in Van Nieuwpoort offering a price significantly in excess of initial expectations, clearly as a defensive move. Management welcomed the acquisition by Van Nieuwpoort because it preserved their business and avoided integration into another manufacturer.

Managing the business for exit

Many venture capitalists are opposed to managing a business solely with a view to maximizing the chances of and proceeds from exit; they prefer business decisions to be made in the long-term interests of the business itself, although it is acknowledged that, at the margin, they might, for example, not make a large capital investment if they were about to sell their stake.

Despite these concerns there are many aspects of strategy and day-to-day management where the thought of exit may lead to decisions which are in the interests of the business – decision making may, for example, be quicker and more focused if management is working towards a set timescale.

Some of the issues which management and investors should address during the life of their investment are set out in the table below. This approach should lead to a more straightforward exit process and an increased number of unsolicited offers.

Exit checklist – things for management to consider to enhance the business and make exit easier

Strategy

♦ Have one!

♦ Try to achieve a consistent growth record.

♦ Reflect exit plans in the timing and choice of strategy options.

- ◆ Ensure that new opportunities are being created as old ones are realized – to ensure that growth continues.

- ◆ Remember that competitors may be the likely purchasers – they will pay more for a business which can be merged to provide profit improvements. If they do not buy, their interest will increase the price.

PR/marketing

- ◆ All achievements should be reported in trade and financial press.

- ◆ Results and new orders should always be announced.

- ◆ Remember that advertising and marketing does not just sell the product – it may help sell the business.

Financial statements

- ◆ Accounts should look professional and be well presented from the first year.

- ◆ They should be informative, and reflect the strategy of the business – they are not just a legal requirement.

- ◆ Ensure they are consistent from year to year.

Reporting systems

- ◆ Management of the business and exit are both facilitated by reliable, timely and relevant management information.

- ◆ These requirements should be addressed from Day 1.

Legal structure

- ◆ Keep it simple. If it is not, simplify it while there is time.

- ◆ Avoid minority stakes which do not have a strategic purpose – or try to eliminate them prior to exit. One single shareholder can hold up the whole process.

Management

- ◆ Ensure the team is balanced, experienced and of a high calibre.

- ◆ Do not allow gaps to develop.

- ◆ Plan for succession.

- ◆ Ensure they can individually demonstrate a successful record at exit.

How to get value from trade and financial sales

The disadvantages of trade sales raised by venture capitalists were:

- ◆ lack of trade buyers

♦ lower price than an IPO

♦ requirement for warranties.

It is worthwhile addressing these issues because trade sales can be quicker and easier than IPOs, they may attract a premium, and the only alternative may be a low value buy back offer.

The importance of adequate planning and preparation has already been mentioned. Combined with a proper marketing campaign and good publicity from Day 1, this should enable a lack of buyers and therefore the low price expectancy to be overcome. This lack of buyers is often perceived rather than real – but it is necessary to look outside the sector and country of the investment and an intermediary may be needed to do this. It is surprising how often a marketing campaign produces buyers who were not on the original list of interested parties. Price can often be increased by ensuring adequate information is available and by providing warranties to cover areas of uncertainty. Preparation of an information memorandum is a worthwhile discipline as it exposes weaknesses in the business before they are discovered in due diligence, thereby avoiding aborted deals.

Practice on warranties varies immensely from one country and venture capitalist to another. Some venture capitalists have a fixed policy of never giving warranties while others are more flexible.

Those that take the narrow approach need to recognize that they will sometimes lose value as a result because the price will be discounted. When they sell by IPO, they often have no choice but to retain shares in order to support the price; they should regard warranties in a similar light, except that in the latter case they are in control and have received the cash.

Conversely, it should be recognized that warranties are intended to deal with a situation where the vendor is reasonably certain of the facts (for instance, title, audited figures) and wishes to reassure the purchaser – he or she therefore does not expect to have to pay a significant claim and, by giving a warranty[7] realizes full value for his or her investment. If this is not the case then it might be preferable to deal with the risk by an adjustment to price which might avoid the vendor suffering the entire cost. Warranties should always be limited in time and value with a minimum threshold to avoid small claims.

An alternative to providing warranties is deferred consideration.[8] This can be structured to provide participation in any future upside, similar to an ongoing shareholding, in contrast to warranties which are generally given in respect of issues at the date of sale. The disadvantage of deferred consideration is that the vendor has no control over the outcome.

An indemnity[9] should be avoided unless it relates to a matter for which the vendor accepts liability, but where the amount is unquantified, such as historic tax liabilities, and it is therefore necessary to avoid complicating the sale. Nevertheless, if there is a low risk of payment being required, it will often be appropriate to insist that the vendor takes the risk as this will not have a significant impact on value.

If the purchaser has concerns about the vendor's good faith or financial position, then an escrow deposit may be an effective means of adding credibility to the warranty. However, if it is expected that a large part of it will be utilized, then it might well have been worthwhile to make a corresponding, but smaller reduction in price.

THE APPOINTMENT OF ADVISERS

The survey identified an increasing trend towards the appointment of advisers to act for the company or venture capitalist investor on disposal.

An adviser or intermediary may not be needed if the vendor receives a world-beating unsolicited offer, and the vendor has the resources and experience to maximize the value of the offer. It is often the case however that the value of an unsolicited offer from a keen bidder can be increased by introducing competition through a formal sale process.

Do I need one?

The venture capitalist who is deciding whether to appoint an adviser for a particular sale, should ask the following questions.

◆ Do I have the time and resources to do the job in-house without being distracted by more urgent tasks?

◆ Do I and the management know of all potential buyers, including overseas and non-sector?

◆ Is it acceptable for the initial approach to buyers to be open, thereby revealing which business is for sale (since they can find out which businesses I own)?

◆ Do I have an objective view of the value of the business?

◆ Will management/partners accept my advice as independent and impartial?

If the answer to one or more of these questions is 'No', then the appointment of an adviser should be considered. Venture capitalists' views of what is required of an adviser, and how to appoint them are set out in *The use of intermediaries to advise on exit* at page 269.

How do I pay them?

The effectiveness of an adviser is influenced by their fee structure. It is normal practice to pay a percentage of the consideration as a way of incentivizing the adviser to achieve a sale and maximize the price. This approach is increasingly being modified to increase its impact.

A fixed element to the fee can help to ensure that the adviser devotes sufficient time to upfront tasks such as the preparation of an information memorandum. Without this, the time investment by the adviser may be very high in relation to the incremental consideration which a high quality memorandum might achieve. The retainer may therefore be in all parties' interests; however, there is an alternative view that the adviser will not work so hard if their pay does not depend entirely on results. Any retainer should be deductible from, rather than in addition to, the final success fee to ensure that the variable fee is high enough as a percentage of proceeds to provide sufficient incentive.

It is more and more common to pay a higher percentage success fee on a margin of proceeds over a certain level as a super incentive to 'go the extra mile'. Since the vendor would not otherwise receive these proceeds, a high marginal percentage is easily affordable. The threshold may be set based on the values estimated by advisers when competing for the mandate. It was traditional to use the 'Lehman scale'[10] of decreasing percentages but this is less common now because with a small marginal benefit to the adviser from any increment in the sale price, it is clearly less effective as an incentive.

How to keep it confidential

One of the chief concerns expressed about M&A advisers was the risk of information leaking.

In practice, leaks arise more often due to gossip in an industry (regardless of confidentiality agreements) than from the adviser who will be acutely conscious of the need for secrecy.

Maintaining confidentiality depends on having the right attitude. The venture capitalist should emphasize its importance at the beginning of the process, use a codename in all correspondence, and if necessary request that the M&A adviser limits knowledge to those of his or her staff actually working on the job. Naturally confidentiality letters should be used, but these are difficult to enforce and rely on the co-operation of the other party. Commercially sensitive information should not be released, even with a confidentiality letter, where it would damage the business if the deal is aborted.

Notes

1. *Exit*

   The sale of an investment.

2. *Buy back*

   The repurchase by management or the majority investor of the venture capitalist's stake in a business.

3. *Escrow account*

   A deposit held by lawyers as security for warranties.

4. *Financial purchaser*

   A venture capitalist or similar investor who purchases a business as principal. For the purpose of this text the term includes a secondary management buyout.

5. *Ratchet*

   A mechanism, usually contained in a shareholder agreement, which transfers shares from an investor to the management if the business achieves certain targets.

6. *Trade sale*

   The sale of a business to an industrial purchaser.

7. *Warranty*

   A guarantee by a vendor of certain facts relating to a business being sold, actionable by the purchaser in the event of breach.

8. *Deferred consideration*

   A portion of the purchase price which is payable at some future date, often subject to certain conditions.

9. *Indemnity*

   Agreement by the vendor to reimburse certain future outgoings relating to the business.

10. *Lehman scale*

    Scale of disposal advisers' fees based on transaction size, as follows:

Sale proceeds	Incremental percentage fee
£1–2 million	4 per cent
£2–3 million	3 per cent
£3–4 million	2 per cent
Above £4 million	1 per cent

12

INTERNATIONAL
SYNDICATION

Michiel A. de Haan
Atlas Venture

Michiel A. de Haan is the founder and one of the general partners of Atlas Venture, an internationally diversified venture capital company, currently managing $400 million from offices in Europe (Amsterdam, Munich, Paris) and the USA (Boston). He is a board member of several portfolio companies in the life sciences industry and board member of the European Life Sciences Partnering Foundation; European Technologies Holdings NV (chairman) and Advanced European Technologies NV (seed capital funds advised by Technology Holding in Munich); Parquest Venture Partnerships (an Anglo-French venture capital fund). He is also a past chairman of EVCA; a member of EVCA's Market Development Committee and its liaison with international venture capital organizations; and a member of the Corporate Finance Committee of the Council of the Netherlands Industrial Federations VNO/NCW.

INTRODUCTION

Syndication, or sharing an investment with a professional colleague, is one of the most complicated and challenging parts of the venture capital business. It brings to all the other aspects which make our profession complex the need to handle relationships with colleagues in often turbulent company situations and with large financial consequences at stake. Syndication is not like a gentle outing in a rowing boat for two on quiet water. It is more like a survival trip on a raft on the Colorado river with ten people on board. A mistake by any one of the ten is decisive for the fate of everyone. While the risk is high, the reward is: financial success by adding high value through intensive support in all areas of entrepreneurship.

Simply put, syndication means the sharing by venture capitalists of an equity position in a venture-backed company. The more equal or similar the position is in economic and legal terms, the more appropriate and meaningful the phrase syndication and syndicate partner becomes. In practice the positions of venture capitalists involved together in an investee company can differ considerably, as will become clear in this chapter.

Subjects to be discussed are the various reasons to syndicate, the way this could occur in the different life phases of a company and, finally, key points which apply whenever international syndicates are formed.

Good investor relations and the sudden takeover

A large Dutch company was taken over by the management. The lead investor had structured the entire deal and had looked for partners for a syndicate for the done deal, so as to share the risk. The lead investor itself took the biggest stake and also acquired a seat on the board. The management too – naturally – had an interest. Further partners were found, including an English venture capitalist (because of intended flotation on the English stock exchange), and two Dutch venture capitalists, one of them Atlas Venture. From the outset the management had made great efforts to keep all members of the – rather large – syndicate well-informed with regard to the way matters were progressing. This was achieved by means of periodic reporting and by well-prepared and informative shareholders' meetings. This gave rise to a high level of mutual trust, the value of which is proved by the following incident.

▶

▶

> The company had the opportunity to realize a profitable takeover, but in order to do this it had to make very quick decisions. However, at first sight the price was rather high. Under normal circumstances a syndicate would have found decision making with a time limit difficult to accept. The first reaction would have been: 'Have they gone completely mad!' Valuable time would have been lost in calling the management to book. But in this case the atmosphere was so co-operative that the syndicate partners quickly agreed on the figures and, in spite of the high price, recognized that the purchase was nevertheless sound. Rapid decision making was therefore possible and the acquisition turned out to be a success. The company's good investor relations proved to be worth the trouble.

WHY SYNDICATE?

For a venture capitalist there can be various grounds for not participating alone in an enterprise. These vary from reasons connected with strategic and financial aspects to psychological reasons.

Synergy

One important reason for syndication is that by participating together, internal contacts are created between venture capitalists which can be useful to both parties. In this way international networks of venture capitalists are formed with specializations in various areas. One of the most significant challenges in the world of venture capital is the assessment and handling of uncertainties in order ultimately to optimize the risk/reward ratio. Bringing in expertise from many sides can create a synergy effect. The ability to acquire additional expertise in a specific area may even be the most decisive reason for joining a syndicate. After all, many venture capital investments involve businesses that are breaking new techno-logical ground. For this reason it is good for both venture capitalists and companies if the former, through their participations, are able to acquire an extensive orientation and build up a depth of expertise by joining in various ventures in one specific area, for example life sciences or information technology.

Apart from this, it appears that a single leader usually emerges within the syndicate, for example the one with the greatest expertise, or the one who is committed for the largest amount. In practice, in the largest syndicates, the smaller participants are unusually quite happy for a major participant to come forward as leading investor. Nevertheless, decision making continues to require precision. For example, who takes the decision when a key position is to be filled such as that of financial director? What happens if the leading investor is opposed by other participants? Certainly during the unstructured starting phase, while responsibilities have not yet been established by written agreement, this can sometimes mean management with daggers drawn.

Risk sharing

The sharing – and thereby reducing – of financial risk can also be a reason for syndication. This reason was deliberately not the first to be mentioned. Of course, what matters is the net result, but in the philosophy of professional venture capitalists this is attained by adding value over a wide area.

The sharing of risks can make sense when relatively large sums are involved. In start-ups, in particular, the risks are high, and the characteristic of risk-bearing capital is quite simply that in failure no money can be claimed back. This is in contrast to bank credit, where the bank is in most cases a preferential creditor. Participations in various ventures also means that profits are spread. The creation of more exit options (selling the participation at the right moment) results in a more stable and broader flow of income.

We are talking about risk sharing here instead of risk spreading because of the fundamental differences that exist in risk perception between banks and investment companies. The former are primarily loss oriented in the financing of an enterprise; they want to be as certain as possible that an enterprise is able to fulfil its interest and redemption obligations. The return of the enterprise is not allowed to fall below that level. Their profit comes mainly from the interest margin and partly in a risk premium. A venture capitalist is there to increase the value of the enterprise as much as possible for the shareholders (after all, the venture capitalist is a shareholder too). Efforts are aimed at a value increase at the moment of selling of at least two to three times the purchase price, but preferably much higher – five to ten times.

There is no such thing as easy money

One narrow escape dating from the early days of Atlas Venture (at the beginning of the 1980s) was participation in a company which was prominent in its own field. The company had plans for quotation on the stock market within the foreseeable future, but the founder/major shareholder wanted to get out before then because his capital was needed somewhere else. Because of this he agreed to a certain discount on the value of the company. Therefore a bridging loan was required for a certain period. 'Easy Money' thought a number of large banks, as did Atlas Venture, who also put money into it. One of the banks extended a substantial loan as well as a small share of venture capital. As soon as the major shareholder realized his assets, all the skeletons began to fall out of the cupboard. What's more, the market also started to turn against us. The company hit financial problems, and when that bank suddenly started to behave not as a member of a syndicate but as a provider of loan capital, and demanded extra financial guarantees from the shareholders, the atmosphere was ruined for good.

▶

▶

In retrospect it is easy to reconstruct the points at which such tensions could have been foreseen. The syndicate members saw participation purely as an attractive investment; they did not participate so as to produce additional value. Furthermore the role of the bank – providing loans as well as share capital – was, to put it mildly, unclear. It had never had to assume the potentially conflicting role of provider of share capital as well as loan capital. With great effort, and thanks to a market upswing, the enterprise did ultimately stay afloat. Atlas Venture sustained no loss through the participation, but that's about all that you can say. There's no such thing as easy money.

Better division of tasks

A third reason is that by working together tasks can be better divided. As noted earlier, a professional venture capitalist is not just a money lender who, after the participation, hangs around in passive anticipation. Depending on the development phase of the company, the venture capitalist operates very much as co-owner or as director. This is, of course, because the professional venture capitalist not only has in-depth financial knowledge, but has also built up know-how concerning the company, its products and technology, and the market in which it operates. Thus with one syndicate partner, for example, guidance could lie more on technological aspects, while with another the accent could be on financial guidance.

It is also possible to achieve a good division of tasks through geographical distribution. For a wholly European venture capitalist, for example, it could be advisable to look for a partner with business interests in the USA, thereby bringing in transatlantic experience.

Bringing in objectivity

The fourth reason is that the presence of several venture capitalists can have the effect of introducing objectivity. It so happens that participation in companies often occurs at a phase when the entrepreneur/founder, or the entrepreneur/owner(s) and descendants of the founder, are still very closely involved with the company. As a rule, participation by a venture capitalist is the first opportunity for co-owners with a certain level of authority to come into the company from the outside. And that again at a stage when radical changes will take place, such as accelerated expansion or additional growth, moving towards more openness in relation to a future quotation on the stock exchange. These developments often have emotional connotations for the owner, so the presence of more than one venture capitalist brings an objectivity which ensures rational decision making by all concerned. Of course great care must be taken to ensure that decision making by a larger number of participants does not get bogged down in the formation of alliances, and the politicizing of differences of opinion.

One question always arises in the building up of a syndicate: what is the optimum size? In fact there are no rigid rules here. With too many participants there is the risk that they will get in each other's way. Furthermore, there is no guarantee that everyone will make the effort they committed themselves to. Among eight oarsmen there can always be one or two who do not perform at their best without the others noticing. And for another thing, if everyone has a hand in the decision-making process, it is certainly no guarantee that the optimum decision will be made: too many cooks can spoil the broth. Many psychological aspects come into play in deciding on the composition and size of a syndicate: mutual trust, daring to delegate to one another, mutual respect and working together. Members of a venture capital syndicate are all embarking on an exciting adventure together. This demands that mutual relationships will also be able to survive crises successfully.

The syndicate leader as holding director

A former family business, prominent in the industry, has via an investor buyout become the property of a group of shareholders of various kinds. One section of the group consists of so-called informal investors, prosperous people who participate in companies with their private means; another section is a group of professional venture capitalists, among them Atlas Venture. In order to realize an effective yield for the shareholders, it was decided to form a holding company bringing in 100 per cent of the company shares, with the members of the syndicate being shareholders of the holding. The leader of the syndicate fulfills the function of (unpaid) director of the holding. In this way he is able to keep an eye on, and has an influence on, the day-to-day business of the company. He is also the first-line contact person for the shareholders. What this represents is a formalized syndicate leadership. In addition, the shareholders also hold two of the five seats on the board. One of them is an Atlas investment manager. This method of working is proving to be very effective. Through the holding the shareholders produce their added value to the standard of the working company. The holding provides for collaboration and co-operation without having to seek separate contact with all shareholders. And via the meetings of the board of directors they are able to be the sounding board and the judges of management decisions.

ADVANTAGES FOR THE INVESTEE COMPANY

Involvement with a strong syndicate yields three important advantages for an investee company.

1 The company is able to make maximum use of any available external specialists in the areas of financing, technology, marketing, international networks, etc. In short, business development capability is enhanced.

2 A strong syndicate is a good guarantee for the availability of possible supplementary financing for further expansion.

3 The company itself is immediately assured of a positive reputation on financial markets. 'Being carried' by a syndicate of prominent venture capitalists often means a springboard to financial markets.

SYNDICATION AND THE DEVELOPMENT PHASE OF THE COMPANY

There are many times when venture capitalists are able to combine forces: the start-up phase; at a 'done deal'; and at a second or later round of financing. These rounds can occur at later development stages of the company, for instance, for further expansion or for management buyout. Every phase has its own specific features. Remember, though, we are talking about financing rounds here. These are connected with the development phases of the company. Nevertheless it is important to discuss these phases separately, because this will provide insight into those times when (additional) capital is required.

Example 1 ♦ Development path of a modern information technology company

Phase of the company	*Market position and financing source*
Research/ideas development	Originating mostly from people active in large information technology companies
Knowledge protection/patents on software, mostly fairly limited (copyright)	Early company formation
Development of own knowledge base/product First so-called beta/version	First round financing Atlas Venture
Established production/marketing Further series/applications	Second round financing Atlas Venture
International strategy and first partnership with multinational information technology companies; so-called Original Equipment Manufacturer (OEM) and Value Added Reseller (VAR) contracts	Acknowledged as technology leader Large capital injection Participation of co-investors

---

Accelerated international market penetration: Europe and USA	First profitable year
Accelerated growth in turnover: Greater than100 per cent	Market leader/breakthrough; Nasdaq quotation
Consolidation rapid growth: Greater than 30 per cent	Minimum of six months after listing Atlas Venture allowed to start selling its shares on the stock market. Total exit generally lasts another year because of strict regulations.

Example 2 ♦ Development path of a modern life science company

Phase of the company	*Market position and financial source*
Research/ideas development	Source: universities/technology centres
Knowledge protection/patents	Early company formation
(Laboratory) proof of principle	First seed capital Atlas Venture
Development of own (protected) knowledge Technique → molecule → drug	Start financing Government technology subsidies
Recognition by pharmaceutical multinational Major research financing for developing new drug First phase drug approval process by regulatory authorities	First large injection of capital together with other venture capital firms
Clinical (patient) trials on effectiveness, side-effects, etc. Second phase approval process Marketing agreements with pharmaceutical industry Government marketing approval	Second large injection of capital by venture capital and industry Quotation on Nasdaq or London Stock Exchange

PHASES IN FINANCING

Start-up

In the start-up phase in a high-tech sector possibilities for syndication are limited. This is usually a matter of intensive co-entrepreneurship of the venture capitalist, and this requires such thorough expertise and deep commitment that effectively, intense participation by more than one venture capitalist is not so likely to occur. In this phase decision making can require a high level of agreement and it is primarily a question of teamwork rather than of structured decision-making processes with different roles for decider and judge. In addition, management and control have not yet crystallized into a structure of separate bodies for shareholders and (non) executive board.

Later rounds

Particularly in the USA, a so-called 'management committee' is often set up for fast growers, a forerunner of a full board. The venture capitalist is usually chairperson of the board. As well as the owner/founders, this board may also include non-executive board members. The existence of a platform of this sort allows a full management board to be built on it at a later phase, possibly following the entry of other venture capital companies.

During this phase, the role of the venture capitalist develops from co-entrepreneurship to management monitoring, not so much taking decisions personally as evaluating decisions and providing a sounding board for management. Of course, this transition is always a very gradual process.

Conflicting relationships and delayed decision making

For five years Atlas Venture had been the only external shareholder in a technologically advanced company which, in itself, was a promising enterprise. However, as a result of the stagnating economy and unsuccessful management the company had developed problems. Solutions were sought by changes in the directorship and by extra capital injections. In the end Atlas considered the participation too great in relation to the risk; it went in search of a second venture capitalist, so that together they could keep the company afloat and turn it back into a flourishing concern. A syndicate partner was found and Atlas and this partner both took up an interest of 49 per cent. A plan was developed for improving the situation. It included once again the replacement of some of the management. As it happened, there was a special relationship between the management of the syndicate partner and the management of the company. In spite of the fact that the syndicate partners both recognized the need for radical decisions, this relationship was a considerable obstacle. At one stage the syndicate partners actually agreed that the company could not survive in its current form, yet no final decision followed and as a consequence Atlas had no other choice than to withdraw unilaterally and to allow itself to be bought out.

'Done deal'

The leading investor may have reasons to look for a number of participants from whom only a limited contribution in a particular target area is expected. For example, the contribution may be in financing technology (risk sharing) or regional distribution.

In a similar 'done deal' situation, it is often no longer possible for new participants to immerse themselves deeply in the subject. In this case it is a question of whether there is sufficient trust in the leading investor, or whether the participants themselves are already well versed in the technology and market of the venture concerned.

Generally speaking, only the smaller venture capitalists will be prepared to subscribe to a done deal. The bigger ones are usually only willing to act as leading investors.

Management buyouts

A syndicate can still continue to add more participants until a late phase – at a management buyout, or reasonably close to a planned market quotation. This usually happens for reasons of financial engineering, for example to optimize the financing structure. Participation does not have to be through share capital *per se*, but can also be through (partial) granting of a subordinated loan (mezzanine financing). The role of the venture capitalist syndicate is then to bring in high quality financial expertise in order to create, through financial engineering, the most favourable starting point possible for the further development of the company. This might be for autonomous continuation under the current management, or for the bigger step of an Initial Public Offering (IPO) and quotation on a stock exchange.

Figure 12.1 gives an insight into the development of an investee company and the financial phases involved.

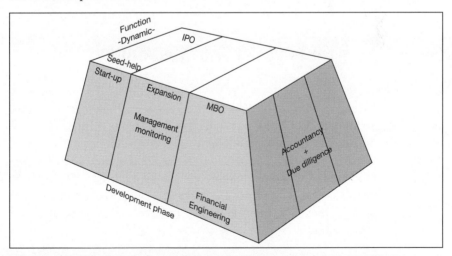

Fig. 12.1 ♦ The financial phases involved in the development of an investee company

Subsyndicates

Subsyndicates may be formed for financing in later rounds. This enables the authority of the existing syndicate to remain as flexible as possible. Although the decision making, newly entering group can appoint a representative to the original syndicate, the latter must have their proxy.

TYPOLOGY OF VENTURE CAPITALISTS

From the foregoing it follows that venture capitalists can find themselves in various positions, depending in part on the development phase and the financing phase of the investee company. For instance a syndicate could comprise of the following:

◆ *venture capitalist A* founding investor, chairperson of the board, holds significant stake (more than 15 per cent) through founder shares and all subsequent series of shares ('rounds');

◆ *venture capitalist B* founding investor, no board seat, holds significant stake (more than 15 per cent) through founder shares and all subsequent series of shares;

◆ *venture capitalist C* came in at third round, no board seat, holds small stake (less than 2 per cent). Did not join in the last two rounds after becoming negative about the company when in went through a period of problems;

◆ *venture capitalist D* came in at last ('mezzanine') round before the company's planned move to go public. Holds medium-size stake of 10 per cent. Has board seat because of absolute size of the investment (more than $5 million).

THE PROCESS OF SYNDICATION

When forming a syndicate, it has to be established that the members are genuinely prepared to work together. In addition, it is important that everyone is open as regards their intentions and objectives. There must be clear understanding in advance as regards the different roles: which member is to be the leader and which institution – rather more specifically, which investment manager – is to be the spokesperson through whom decisions will be taken within the syndicate. This creates total clarity for all concerned and prevents the risk that syndicated members, intentionally or unintentionally, may be played off one against the other.

Dealing with international cultural differences

Three partners owned a flourishing company in the information technology sector. The company was (and still is) established in Belgium, a neighbour of the Netherlands (one of the home countries of Atlas Venture) and, as far as business culture is concerned, rather different. In time two of the partners wanted to find a way out and to realize the increased value of their shares, achieved as a result of three years' hard work. In that period they had managed to triple the turnover of their company.

The third partner wanted to go on with the business and therefore needed money for the buyout of his two co-owners. Atlas Venture was prepared to take an interest because of its expertise in the area of information technology. However, this was only on condition that a local venture capitalist participated as well, in order to be sure of optimum communication, and to overcome the many differences in business culture. A local syndicate participant was indeed found and as matters progressed this proved to have been a good move. Thanks to the presence of the local partner, impending tensions within the company were recognized early, were discussed immediately in association with the syndicate, and were resolved. In this way the business was able to continue to prosper. Recently it was sold for a good price to a British company quoted on the stock exchange. Atlas Venture continues to maintain good contacts with the management.

Syndication, particularly when the members of a syndicate are in different countries, demands that great attention is paid to mutual communication. Suitable arrangements must be made concerning procedures, as well as associated practical issues such as contact times, taking into account time differences, and travel. In addition there must also be a degree of openness which allows all members to make their own contributions. With international syndicates, cultural differences make this something that requires particular attention. Finally, it is important to set up a well-structured schedule beforehand, and for the syndicate to stick to it.

Important points for potential partners

Potential partners in a syndicate, particularly an international syndicate, should bear in mind the following.

◆ A lead investor who wants to form a syndicate will always try to depict the investing company as favourably as possible to potential syndicate members. Nevertheless it is important to provide as honest a picture as possible, so that no hidden flaws come to light later within the syndicate.

◆ When putting together a syndicate it is important to clarify that members are also ready and able to participate in the second, third and fourth rounds of financing. Venture capitalists need cloth to spare in their financial jackets. If the necessary means cannot be acquired in a later round, there is a risk that a company will be forced to sell before coming to full maturity, or will even be compulsorily sold.

♦ Apart from the availability of sufficient financial capacity, the investment policy of the syndicate members (time-frame, dividends, etc.) must also be clear from the start.

♦ Sometimes problems arise within syndicates because the members fail to acknowledge one another's professionalism sufficiently. Periodic evaluation concerning (the appreciation of) every member's contribution can prevent this. This evaluation can also include an assessment of how far the various members have fulfilled their commitments. The point here is that all concerned have the shared objective of creating value. For this purpose it is important that the available expertise within the syndicate is recognized and utilized.

♦ The syndicate members must have enough scope for the execution of due diligence and the maintenance of contacts with the investee company. This, of course, without causing too much disturbance to production processes within the company.

13

'BUSINESS ETHICS' –
A VERY TRICKY
SUBJECT!

Michael Denny
Northern Venture Managers Ltd

 **Michael Denny** has been the executive chairman of Northern Venture Managers Ltd since 1988. Educated at Eton College, he trained in marketing with Procter & Gamble Limited, then ran his own private industrial holding company. He joined the National Enterprise Board as North-East regional director in 1981 and was managing director of Northern Investors from 1984 to 1988. He was a member of council of the British Venture Capital Association from 1987 to 1992, and chairman of the Association in 1990–1. He is a non-executive director of Northern Investors Company PLC, Northern Venture Trust PLC, Northern 2 VCT PLC, Postern Fund Management Limited and Gap Fund Managers Limited.

INTRODUCTION

Whatever the past history, we all – either individually or corporately – have our own views as to what is acceptable behaviour and what is not (or, as some might say, what we can and can't get away with!). At its simplest, this is the subject.

The concept of business ethics probably has its origins in the ancient system of barter, which existed before money was even invented. In order to survive, people exchanged goods for goods, and this process represented the earliest business transactions known. In order to strike a deal both parties to the transaction had to be satisfied that they had received equal value for what had been given, and so the concept of morality, fairness and behaving properly when conducting transactions became a desirable standard.

Money was not invented until about 700 BC, and with it gradually came the concept of profit. The prime function of money was to act as a common denominator, which not only enabled a value to be placed on goods and services, but also represented a universal means of exchange; and of course it was much more efficient than barter. Throughout history, people have therefore striven to act properly in their business dealings. Exhortations to be good and fair, instead of evil and unjust, have also been heavily influenced through the ages by religion and the teachings of various churches.

THE NEED FOR BUSINESS ETHICS

Let us start with the view that the profit motive is an acceptable and even desirable objective of economic activity. The macro-assumption is that market forces of supply and demand will establish a price mechanism and the driving motivation of management will be profit. While the profit motive through market forces is paramount and appears to have survived better than centrally planned economies, the most advanced societies in reality contain a mixture of profit motivation and government spending: the simple fact is recognized that private sector activity will not take on certain projects if sufficient return on capital, or profit, cannot be achieved on an acceptable time-scale.

The sum of all business activity can therefore be measured in millions of business transactions which represent billions of ECUs, and a code of business ethics (be that formal in law or informal in practice) is essential to demonstrate fair dealings and proper accountability, and to minimize the risk of fraud.

Trust

The whole principle of ethics centres on the single word 'trust'. Indeed, by the seventeenth century, the London Stock Exchange used the maxim 'My word is my bond' as its mark of respectability. At its beginnings 350 years ago, the embryo insurance business was transacted at the Lloyds coffee shop in the city of London; its motto was and remains *'Fidentia'* – roughly translated it means 'of utmost faith (or trust)'. In simple words these institutions say: 'Trust me!' Quite simply, to do business, people have to trust each other and that brings us right back to the world of business ethics.

Professional bodies

In the USA and the UK it could be argued that the backbone of business ethics is represented in the professions, where individual men and women take special training and, through testing examinations, become members of professional bodies – such as architects, lawyers, accountants and engineers. These professional bodies – particularly in the UK – are very long established and often exist under a Royal Charter.

Throughout the world, such professional bodies often became recognized as 'The Establishment' and as the source for laying down codes of conduct and ethical guidelines which have to be followed by members. Enforcement is usually by standing disciplinary committees, who have the authority to expel members for serious breaches of conduct. Such expelled members can actually lose their livelihood and be shunned by society for falling short of the conduct expected by their professional body, which is founded on the principle of creating a bond of trust with society itself.

Building 'best business practice'

To supplement professional bodies, European countries have developed formidable legislation for dealing with investment business and licensing fit and proper persons to conduct that business. In addition, trade associations have been established – such as the British Venture Capital Association (BVCA), which was set up just ten years ago. That initiative was continued later by the European Venture Capital Association (EVCA). This is all part of a process of building on 'best business practice' in each country. Establishing rules on business ethics is part of that process.

ETHICAL ISSUES FOR INVESTORS IN CENTRAL AND EASTERN EUROPE

We all acknowledge that the whole area of business ethics is a tricky subject, but there are some basic issues that should be considered in the context of the venture capital community – be that in London, Paris, Prague or Budapest.

It is not easy to be an investor in Central and Eastern Europe. Some of the reasons are obvious, others less so. Some of the problem areas are:

♦ lack of reliable financial information

♦ lack of management skills

♦ limited access to/availability of other sources of finance

♦ limited knowledge of the investment process

♦ limited understanding of equity investment

♦ limited identifiable 'exit' routes.

Questions to ask

This list may also act as a reference point for matters of business ethics. For example: is it ethical for an investment manager to use clients' money to finance the borrowing of investee companies – just because today some of the banks (and other financial institutions) in Central and Eastern Europe are still reluctant to lend to the level that the manager thinks they should? In other words, was your investment firm actually set up to be a bank? Remember to whom the investment manager is responsible! What was the firm set up to do? Are you an investor or a lender? Venture capitalists should not end up financing the 'bank's risk' (if it goes right you will gain no extra reward for your client; but if it goes wrong, you have just lost more money than you needed to by compounding the risks). Stick with the 'equity value' risk. Good investment managers find that that is quite enough of a risk to manage. At this time it is anticipated that it is very difficult to bring banks and other financial parties into investment deals. As a result, this is probably the most dangerous area of potential risk to investment funds presently operating within Central and Eastern Europe.

Another question might be: is it ethical to expect your clients to put up more money for no additional equity reward? Again this might be by way of, say, a subordinated loan in order to save an investee company from failure, or to retain employment in a depressed area. Will it be good money (your client's) after bad (the lost earlier investment)? Will a further round of financing add to the projected internal rate of return (IRR) of the fund or are you just putting up more money with no real thought for any additional benefit that could accrue to your client? Please remember that the second round of finance is always the most dangerous type of investment activity. The interests of the parties are then not without conflict and/or pressure.

Conflicts of interest

This line of thought leads on to discussion of the vexed issue of 'conflicts of interest'! Let's start with an easy one. Who is the client? Who does the venture capitalist actually work for? Who is paying the salary bill? Is it the investee company or the sources of the capital to be invested? Once one begins to think through the proposition, most people will conclude that it is the investors who pay. They are the sources of capital, the shareholders – but even this most funda-mental truth is all too often forgotten!

To do deals, we need to talk to introducers. You know the type! 'Psst, have I got a good deal for you!' Of course, we need these connections, but investment managers also need to be careful. What do these introducers want in return? The answer is quite simply fees and favours. So the investment manager should beware of corporate financiers bearing gifts. The key point to be remembered is that the interest of the promoters of deals is not the same as that of the investors. There can be massive conflicts of interest.

The issue is about short-term versus long-term rewards. The tell-tale difference in approach is simply the desire for income versus capital. The promoters look for reward by fees, rather than by sharing in any capital gain actually achieved. Capital gain is the investor's reward. Corporate finance is a necessary short-term parasite on the back of the long-term investment world. Corporate finance pays well and earns huge fees, but it is not about selecting investments; and watch out for the new hybrid promoters/introducers, who are looking for a free equity ride as part of their introductory fee! A simple rule is that no person can serve two masters. So again the investment manager must ask, 'Who is paying whom?' It is no good going back to the promoters after a deal has gone sour and complaining that you were misled (and, what's more, that you paid a huge fee to them for intro-ducing the deal too!). In short, by then, it's far too late. Never assume. Assumption can be a very dangerous thing. Don't take short-cuts. *Caveat emptor.* That is what the investment managers are paid to do – bluntly, they are paid to get it right. That is what the due diligence process is all about.

What about directors' interests – directors on the board of a fund; directors on the board of investee companies; directors on the board of a management company. Could there be conflicts of interest? Directors are meant to contribute to the affairs of a business and not just act as representatives of others or to sit in meetings as some sort of police! A director is meant to be responsible for just the company on whose board he or she sits. A director can't really act for two or more companies in any relationship chain. Venture capitalists need to be sure to wear the right hat whenever they sit at the corporate table.

Nepotism and insider trading

What about nepotism – both political and social? It happens all over the world. It might gain you, or colleagues, some short-term benefit to back a particular company because of some political (or even commercial) benefit; but sooner or later that decision will begin to cast its shadow over you. By then it will be too late to change things or wish that you hadn't made the investment. Investments must be made on the merits of the case and people should be employed and/or promoted on achievement – and not just because of 'connections'.

Look out for insider trading: could there be personal gain either to one of the fund management's team or perhaps to a director of the investee company (and remember that the 'gain' could be financial or political)?

If I, for example, suggested that one of my managed funds should invest money in a company in which I (or a member of my family) have an interest, we all know that that idea wouldn't work. We know that it wouldn't be right! Indeed, we know that however much I might seek to hide the facts of the transaction, the deal would inevitably become public knowledge. People would complain – particularly my shareholders. I would lose both my reputation and my livelihood! It may not be fraud but such a transaction could hardly be classified as ethical.

Be open and honest

Another business ethics issue is the need for 'transparency' in all transactions. Again the question is one of who is working for whom and for what reward. Beware of all close relationships – be open and honest. A good rule is to 'hide nothing' and when in doubt to 'disclose everything'.

Venture capitalists should therefore ask if a proposed action might violate any legal or moral rights held by any individual or group. It is a fact – too often forgotten – that in the case of business ethics there is only a down-side. If things go right, that was always expected; but if things go wrong, then the balloon really goes up!

What about fund managers drawing fees from the fund and charging investee companies additional fees for monitoring, arranging or even nominating one of its employees to become a director of the investee company? Is that ethical? Is it 'upfront'? Did the investors in the fund know that this might happen? What is the agreed method of operating? Who should receive the fees? Should it be (a) the employee of the management company – personally (as a bit of extra income); (b) the management company; or (c) the fund? After all, the investment manager should always remember that the fund's money is the shareholders' money and that it was that money that made the deal possible.

And what about those fund managers who set up funds, say, 18 months ago and are drawing large fees but seem to be making no investments? It is hardly fraud but is it ethical? Many investors believe that managers should rush out and build portfolios within a certain time. They don't like managers sitting on their cash (they can do that themselves). Which is the more ethical approach? Personally, I am very nervous about putting pressure on fund managers to invest. I would rather investors were told the truth – that it takes time to build up a venture capital portfolio. The strike rate may only be 3 per cent of all enquiries received, and each investment executive employed can probably achieve only two sensible new investment completions in any one year, and that's in the West. So what might be reasonable in Central and Eastern Europe is perhaps only one!

Then there are syndications – are you syndicating 'risk' or 'quantum'? Do your investors know why you accepted or sold down a syndication? There is a type of investment executive who is very much transaction driven. Executives like this feel inadequate if they are not dealing! If bored, they will often seek out other people's higher risk deals for their own portfolios (and hope for the best!) – or worse still, accept reciprocal syndications without properly assessing the type of risk being offered in that deal. If you are going to syndicate, do make sure that the risks are comparable and understood by the investors whose money you are paid to look after.

Cartels and price protection arrangements

What are the issues when investee companies are part of a cartel and/or price protection arrangement? Are they legal in your country, or is the business artificial and actually dependent on fixed prices to survive? This is not just an Eastern European question. In the West, the European Union is trying to stamp out price fixing, but interestingly it is often governments which try to keep prices either low or artificially high (with subsidies or charges) to buy votes (particularly in the more depressed areas). Examples might be in agriculture, steel-making, shipbuilding, and of course in the provision of national airlines! At a lower economic level, the European cement industry is presently under a cloud for operating a 'high price' cartel. The European Union is trying to stamp out this unacceptable and unethical business practice.

Fraud and corruption

Then we come inevitably to fraud and corruption. We all know that, as a minimum, bribery is out! That is obviously unethical, but there are many less blatant types of persuasion or influence, such as entertaining, presents in kind and subjection to political pressure.

Again, some rules that may help. My advice is to beware of the role of publicity seekers (try to remember just who is helping whom). Don't put yourself in the position of being entertained beyond that which is normal, and don't become beholden to other parties who may have other agendas. Nice photographs of you having a 'lovely time with Sophie or Stephen' in some low-down night-club may be jolly good fun at the time, but could be used for blackmail and lead to corruption at a later date. Sadly, it is so easy to be led astray. Remember the only real news to a journalist is 'bad news'!

We must also look at the ethics of the way a company undertakes its business – within the law as an absolute requirement, even if it might be more profitable outside it. The question of proper bookkeeping (one set of books or three!) needs to be properly addressed. Nobody likes paying tax but taxes are part of the rule of law and it is just not worth trying to beat the system. Of course, it is wholly reasonable to set up legal structures to minimize tax (such as offshore trusts or using up special tax allowances). It is also sensible to lobby for changes to the country's tax regime.

OTHER LEGAL AND MORAL ISSUES

There are many other 'legal and moral issues' connected to business ethics. For example, do the proposed actions conform to accepted legal and moral standards? Is the way you are acting the way you would wish to be treated yourself? Can you find other ways of getting around the problem without breaching these ethical questions and still be able to do business? You may find your independent outside or non-executive directors useful in helping you solve some of these tricky problem areas.

Then consider the ethical questions surrounding the security of information given by potential investee companies. You may sign their letters of confidentiality but do they offer any protection? Of course, you need the information since you can't work without it. However, if you divulge any of it to a third party, you may, at the very least, be accused of behaving 'badly', of having poor business ethics. At worst, you could be breaking the law and be subjected to a claim for damages. Whatever the facts of the case, your reputation will take a knock and you will gradually find that your deal flow will dry up as people hear that you are not to be trusted. So it all comes back to this word 'trust'.

The same arguments apply to the safety of clients' money and of investee company share certificates – just remember that neither belong to you, the investment manager!

There are 'compliance procedures', and the investors themselves need to be sure that there are proper regulatory authorities and penalties.

There must be proper 'corporate governance'. This means that investment managers need to remember that all investment decisions are ultimately about people. Managers must therefore take references (a lot!); they must check personnel histories for inaccuracies; and they must use their local contacts to check out backgrounds thoroughly.

Investors must satisfy themselves that there are proper and effective internal control procedures. There must be regular contact with investee companies. If you don't visit and take an interest in the investee company, the owner/manager will assume you don't care and will ignore your interests – and may even try to find ways of eliminating the value of your client's investment. There is a real need for regular reporting and proper monitoring, and that means actually attending board meetings on a regular basis.

MAINTAINING BUSINESS ETHICS

The following are some useful tips.

♦ Don't set targets in investee companies that are simply 'too difficult' to attain. It leads to creative accounting and worse! Employees fearful of under-performance may begin to falsify statements to protect their position. It may even lead to fraud, simply because people – rather than admit failure or simple underperformance – will sometimes then set out to mislead lenders, investors and trade creditors. If caught, they will probably end up blaming the investors for being unreasonable in the first place!

♦ Establish a proper understanding of each investee company's activities and *modus operandi* prior to investment – put the understanding in writing (possibly within the legal agreement). Make sure you know what the real purpose of the investment is and make the company's directors stick to that plan. You don't want any sudden changes of direction after the investment. A new plan needs a new decision process!

♦ Make use of subscription agreements and other legal documentation. Can the company's articles of association help the investor? Don't assume – check it!

♦ Internal audit systems – what can be done to keep the fund 'clean'? There is the same need for regular reporting and regular board meetings within the management company and/or the fund as for investee companies. After all, there should be no difference in attitude between investors in the fund and the fund itself when it is an investor in companies.

♦ Employ staff who are qualified and of good quality, keep training them, keep them interested and busy (idle hands lead to mischief!); make examples of anybody caught behaving in an unacceptable fashion. Use publicity to deter – don't try to hide the problem.

♦ Use non-executive directors, not as 'police' but to add commercial value to investee companies. Will you or your colleagues actually try to stop a fraud – particularly if that action might lead to personal difficulties for you? You might even lose your job! In my opinion, two non-executives are probably better than one.

◆ If you find something horribly wrong, be aware of whether you actually go to law to settle the dispute. Know if there is a real law and whether it will work.

Administration of funds

To safeguard assets against fraud, investment funds need to be administered and accounted for in a disciplined framework, which within the venture capital industry would include the following.

◆ A process of due diligence to check out the commercial viability of opportunities – as mentioned before, don't assume and don't take short-cuts!

◆ Investment decisions to be made by a duly authorized board of directors, all of whom should have had relevant training and experience and be independent of the managers.

◆ Board representation on investee companies – the need to keep in touch.

◆ Post-investment monitoring of business performance – do it properly and take an interest or else! Remember that if you don't take an interest in the companies that you invest in, they will gradually start to take less interest in you and less interest in your interests.

◆ Awareness of when an action of the company is irregular and/or inconsistent with past performance, or when a particular group is benefiting unduly (or being victimized?). Then a decision can be made as to whether you can or should try to interfere.

CONCLUSION

Business ethics is a grey area. In its broadest sense it consists of 'doing the right thing', 'behaving properly' and 'conducting oneself in a proper manner'; it implies honesty, trust and good intentions.

Essentially, however, the maintenance of acceptable business ethics rests with the individual and his or her attitude to morality, fairness and justice. The effectiveness of the individual is supported and enhanced by government legislation, professional bodies, trade associations and corporate organizational structures. Good ethics is good business, and responsible management will prosper by looking after employees, suppliers and customers, as well as making a profit for shareholders.

14

RETURNS ON VENTURE CAPITAL

William D. Bygrave
Babson College

William D. Bygrave, MA, D.Phil. (Oxon.), MBA, DBA, is the Frederic C. Hamilton Professor for Free Enterprise and Director of the Center for Entrepreneurial Studies at Babson College, Visiting Professor at INSEAD (The European Institute of Business Administration), Special Professor at the University of Nottingham, and Visiting Professor at the London Business School.

As an academic, he teaches and researches entrepreneurship, especially financing of start-up and growing ventures. He spent the 1992–3 academic year at INSEAD where he introduced an MBA course Entrepreneurial Finance and led a Pan-European team from eight nations that studies entrepreneurs' attitudes toward realizing value and harvesting their companies. One of the outcomes of that research was the initiative that led to the founding of EASDAQ.

He is author of *Venture Capital at the Crossroads*, with Jeffry Timmons; and editor of *The Portable MBA in Entrepreneurship*, *Frontiers of Entrepreneurship Research*, and *Entrepreneurship Theory and Practice*. He has served on the review boards of three entrepreneurship journals. He was director of the annual Babson College – Kauffman Foundation Entrepreneurship Research Conference in 1994 and 1995.

As a practitioner, William D. Bygrave founded a Route 128 venture-capital-backed high-tech company, managed a division of a NYSE-listed high-tech company, co-founded a pharmaceutical database company, and was a member of the investment committee of a venture capital firm.

INTRODUCTION

The principal factor that drives the venture capital industry is the financial return on the money invested in portfolio companies. When returns are high, venture capitalists and their investors are ecstatic and money is bountiful, but when returns are low, they are gloomy and money is scarce. But what determines the returns?

Since its beginning in Boston, Massachusetts in 1946, the US venture capital industry has gone through several high–low cycles. It is now clear to most observers that the success of the US venture capital industry is linked directly to the health of the National Association of Securities Dealers Automated Quotation (Nasdaq) small capitalization market. When the Nasdaq small-cap market is booming, it is relatively easy for venture-capital-backed companies to float initial public offerings at high valuations, which enables their venture capital investors to realize substantial returns. This means that the institutions and individuals that invest in venture capital funds get a good return on their money, which makes them more willing to put additional money into venture capital funds.

True, the flows of venture capital are influenced by other factors such as the capital gains tax, pension fund regulations, new technologies, and government policies, but the biggest factor by far is the health of the initial public offering (IPO) market. Even if a successful venture-capital-backed company does not go public but instead is acquired by another company, its valuation is generally determined by the valuation of comparable companies that are public.

In this chapter, we will discuss the rates of return that investors expect from venture capital, look at the actual returns, examine how those returns are affected by the market for IPOs, and explore the financial profiles of venture-capital-backed companies that went public in the period 1994–7, which was a period of unprecedented prosperity for the venture capital industry.

EXPECTED RATES OF RETURN

Entrepreneurial folklore says that professional venture capitalists do not invest in a company until their rising greed overcomes their declining fear. Put differently, it means that they do not put money into a company until they are convinced that there is a reasonable probability that the potential financial returns measure up to the risks. As a rule of thumb, it means that they expect to get a return of between five and ten times their initial investment in about five to seven years. In an ideal case, the company will grow rapidly and float an initial public offering of its shares within five years of the first venture capital investment.

Common shares are the riskiest equity in a company – none more so than shares in a young, private company. Besides the fact that common shareholders stand last in line to get paid when a company fails, investment in a private company lacks liquidity because there is no public stock market where the shares can be readily traded. But there are many other risks to contend with. Consider the financing of Apple Computer. Steve Jobs first approached a professional venture capitalist in the autumn of 1976. At that time, the company was selling Apple I microcomputers to hobbyists. The total market for microcomputers was minuscule; and no company had a commercially viable product. What's more, Jobs and Stephan Wozniak were college dropouts with modest work experience. The venture capitalist turned them down because Jobs and Wozniak were neophyte entrepreneurs without significant management experience with an introductory product in an embryonic market. At the venture capitalist's suggestion they approached Mike Markkula, a semi-retired Intel veteran, who made an angel investment in Apple and brought much needed management savvy. The company introduced the Apple II in 1977. Next year, when Apple sales were annualizing at about $10 million the first professional venture capital was invested. By then the infant microcomputer industry, propelled by the VisiCalc spreadsheet, was no longer exclusively the domain of nerds; early adopters were actually using microcomputers for real business applications.

When venture capital was invested in Apple, the management risks, market risks and technological risks, although still high, were much lower than they had been 18 months earlier, and they were outweighed by the potential financial returns. How do venture capitalists evaluate those risks and what kind of returns do they expect from the companies in which they invest?

First and foremost, venture capitalists invest only in companies with first-class entrepreneurial leaders in markets that are big enough for a company's sales to grow to at least $50 million with pre-tax profit of 20 per cent within five years. Experience shows that a company like that will be able to go public, or bought by a larger company, and will return five to ten times the venture capitalist's original investment. A tenfold return in five years yields an annual rate of return of 58 per cent, and a fivefold return yields 39 per cent, which are within the range of satisfactory risk-adjusted returns.

Next, venture capitalists hedge their bets by staging the financing in more than one round. Suppose an early-stage company projects that it requires $8 million of equity financing before it will be able to go public; if a venture capital firm decides to invest, it will usually split the financing into two rounds of say $4 million each.

Provided that the company meets its projected sales and profit milestone with the first round of $4 million, the venture capitalist will almost certainly want to invest the second $4 million. Typically, if the first round is sold at $1 per share, the second round will be about $3 per share. Hence, with two rounds of financing, the company sells only 5,333,333 shares (4 million plus 1,333,333) to raise $8 million rather than 8,000,000 shares if it had raised all the financing in one round. However, in the event that the company falls hopelessly short of its milestone, the venture capitalist most likely will not invest any more money, and in the worst case will be prepared to write off the first $4 million. So by staging the investment, the venture capital firm hedges its risk, and the company, provided that it meets its projections, reduces the number of shares that it sells. If this were a real-world case, it's likely that the venture capitalist would syndicate the deal with two other venture firms, because another way that venture capitalists manage their total financial risk is by investing in a portfolio of different companies.

Finally, venture capitalists reduce their financial risk by purchasing convertible preferred shares, which give them very specific rights and preferences compared with holders of common shares. The final investment agreement can run to two hundred or more pages but the key provisions of the agreement are summarized in a term sheet of a few pages. Those provisions protect the venture capitalist's investment in the event of both negative and positive future events. The venture capitalists have rights to convert preferred shares to common shares, dividend rights, redemption rights, registration rights, protection from ownership dilution in a recapitalization, rights to maintain *pro rata* ownership in future rounds of private financing, and rights to approve the issue of any equity security, the liquidation of the company, and the acquisition of or investment in another company. They also have ways of controlling the company through both ownership of equity and seats on the board of directors. If they hold 51 per cent of the common shares, they have outright voting control. Although they initially might not have a majority of the board seats, they have the right to appoint a majority of the board of directors if specified negative events happen. In addition, the term sheet places significant requirements on the management and employees of the company. These include issuing timely annual audited financial statements and monthly or quarterly unaudited statements, non-compete agreements, key person life insurance, a stock vesting agreement that any employee who leaves prematurely has to sell a portion of his or her shares back to the company at their nominal price, an agreement that while the company is private any employee cannot sell shares to a third party without first offering them to the preferred shareholders, a limitation on the stock option pool, and limits on managers' salaries.

Due diligence, financial prudence and legal agreements notwithstanding, it is impossible to eliminate the risk inherent in equity investing. In general, investments in younger companies are riskier than those in older ones because they have shorter track records and investments in them have to be held longer. Hence, venture capitalists classify companies according to their stage of development. A seed-stage company is one with not much more than a concept; a start-up company is one that is already in business and is developing a prototype but has not sold it in significant commercial quantities; a first-stage company has developed and market-tested a product and needs capital to initiate full-scale production. Second-stage, third-stage and mezzanine financing fuels growing companies; and bridge financing may be needed to support a company while it is between rounds of financing, often while it waits to go public. The younger the company, the greater the risk, and the higher the expected return. The expected annual return declines from about 80 per cent for seed-stage financing to about 30 per cent for a third-stage financing (*see* Table 14.1).

Table 14.1 ◆ Expected returns on venture capital equity investments

Stage	Expected annual return
Seed	80%
Start-up	60%
First-stage	50%
Second-stage	40%
Third-stage/Mezzanine	30%
Bridge	25%

It is the expected returns combined with the valuation of the company that determine the price per share a venture capitalist will be willing to pay to buy equity in the company. Since venture capital is invested in growing companies, the venture capital firm wants to know what the value of the company is likely to be at some future time when it can sell its investment and realize a capital gain. It estimates the valuation of the company at some future date then discounts it back to its present value.

Here is a simplified illustration of the most commonly used method. A one-year-old company is seeking $4 million of start-up financing. Its projections show that it will have earnings (net income) of $10 million five years in the future. The venture capital firm believes that the company can have an IPO in five years and the price to earnings (p/e) ratio will be 20. Thus, the future total valuation of the company will be $200 million (20 × $10 million). The venture capital firm wants a 60 per cent rate of return; so the present value of the company is $19.07 million [$200,000,000/(1.6)^5]. Hence, for an investment of $4 million, the venture capital firm needs 21 per cent [($4/$19.08)*100] of the company's equity to achieve a 60 per cent return. There are huge uncertainties in that computation: the earnings are only projections; even if the company achieves its projections five years hence, it might not be able to go public if the market for IPOs is in a slump; and who is wise enough to foresee what the p/e ratio will be five years in the future?

Fig. 14.2 ♦ Percentage equity required to yield a 60 per cent annual rate of return on a $4 million investment

Holding period (in years)	Future valuation of the company (million)				
	$40	$80	$120	$160	$200
2	26%	13%	9%	6%	5%
3	41	20	14	10	8
4	66	33	22	16	13
5	NA	52	35	26	21
6	NA	84	56	42	34
7	NA	NA	89	67	54
8	NA	NA	NA	NA	86

Table 14.2 shows how the percentage ownership required to yield a 60 per cent return on a $4 million investment varies with the future valuation of the company and the holding period. It contains some simple messages for entrepreneurs seeking venture capital. First, they should think big enough when making their projections because the greater the future valuation of the company, the less equity they will have to sell to raise their venture capital. Second, they should propose an early public offering, because the shorter the expected holding period for the investment, the less equity they will need to sell. Third, they should grow their companies as big as possible before raising venture capital, because the longer they wait, the lower the required rate of return and the shorter the holding time to harvest the investment. In this example, if the company were a first-stage instead of a start-up investment, the required rate of return would be 50 per cent instead of 60 per cent, and it might be ready to go public in four years instead of five. Hence, the company would need to sell only 10 per cent of its equity instead of 21 per cent.

Target annual returns that can go as high as 80 per cent seem to be outrageously exorbitant to neophyte entrepreneurs. But they have to keep in mind that returns from good investments have to compensate for losses on bad ones. In a successful venture capital portfolio, out of every ten investments, two will make or exceed the target rate of return, two will be total write-offs and the remaining six will range from the 'living dead' where the companies never get big enough for a significant harvest to the 'walking wounded' that need refinancing if they are to have a chance of making it. The average annual returns on US venture capital since the birth of the professional industry in 1946 have been in the mid-teens, which suggests that this industry is not making excessive returns on a risk-adjusted basis. Indeed, some financial observers might argue that the returns are not adequate compensation for the risk involved.

HISTORICAL PERSPECTIVE FROM THE USA

Before 1985, when Venture Economics began to collect data that enabled it to calculate the returns on venture capital funds, the actual returns were shrouded in secrecy. The industry abounded with anecdotes and hearsay. For example, everyone knew about American Research and Development's (ARD) investment in Digital Equipment Corporation (DEC). It was part of the folklore of the industry. Even if the amount invested varied from $60,000 to $70,000 and the amount returned in about 12 years varied from $500 million to $600 million depending on who recounted the tale, the annualized rate of return of 130 per cent or there-about is the stuff that legends are made of (Bygrave and Timmons, 1992).[1] But the reality was that, even with as spectacular an investment as DEC in its portfolio, ARD's annualized rate of return for the 20 years 1946–66 was only 14 per cent (Rotch, 1968).[2] In 1966, of course, the value of its investment in DEC was still growing. By the late 1970s, when DEC had been harvested and ARD had become part of Textron, ARD's annualized rate of return fell into the single digits (Gervirtz, 1985).[3]

Two of the best-known private venture capital firms are Bessemer Securities and Hambrecht and Quist. According to Poindexter, Bessemer reported a 17 per cent compound rate of return for the period 1967–74, and Hambrecht and Quist, a 15 per cent compound rate of return over several years to 1972 (Poindexter, 1976).[4]

Most tests on venture capital profitability have used small samples of publicly held Small Business Investment Companies (SBICs). A study of 14 public venture capital firms found the rate of return to be 11 per cent, on average (Faucett, 1971).[5] Hoban (1976)[6] constructed a portfolio composed of 110 actual venture capital investments made by four different venture capital firms in 50 different companies during the period 1960–8. The four venture capital firms were a publicly held SBIC, a private partnership, a private corporation owned by a wealthy family and a subsidiary of a large bank holding company. He found the gross (before management fees and income taxes) annualized rate of return of the portfolio to be 22.9 per cent for the period to the end of 1975. Poindexter gathered data from 29 publicly held firms consisting of 26 SBICs and three companies investing in venture capital. The geometric mean of the annual rate of return for the 29 firms over the period 1961–73 was 11.6 per cent. Over the same period, Poindexter found that the annualized rate of return of the Standard and Poor's 500 was 7.1 per cent (Poindexter, 1976).[4] It is worth noting that rates of return for the sample of venture capital firms depended strongly on the calendar period over which they were computed. For example, it was 10.7 per cent for the period 1961–6, 31 per cent for 1967–71, and 1.2 per cent for 1972–3.

Martin and Petty (1983)[7] analyzed the performance of 11 publicly traded venture capital firms, of which all but two were in Poindexter's sample. They computed the compound rate of return on the publicly traded stock of those 11 firms for each of the six years 1974–9. The average rate of return on the publicly traded stock of the 11 venture capital firms over that period was 27 per cent. Unfortunately, Martin and Petty's rate of return on publicly traded stock was not the actual rate of return on the firm's venture capital investments. The two should not be compared because there may be little or no relationship between their values at any one time. For example, Arthur D. Little, former chairman of Narragansett Capital Corporation, which was in both Poindexter's and Martin and Petty's samples, stated that in the mid-1970s Narragansett's share price fell to 80 per cent below the book value of the assets in its portfolio (Wayne, 1988).[8]

A study by First Chicago Investment Advisors used a method similar to Martin and Petty's to study the rates of return of public venture capital companies from 1959 to 1985. The compound annual rate of return over the 26-year period was 16 per cent (Ibbotson and Brinson, 1987).[9]

It is not easy to get the data needed to calculate the actual rates of return of venture capital investments – not even for publicly held funds such as Poindexter's sample of 29. Poindexter commented that it was an arduous task. To get the actual rate of return, it is necessary to dig into the financial statements in annual reports and 10Ks to get operating expenses, interest expenses, income dividends, capital gains dividends, operating expenses, interest expenses, net assets, long-term debt and net worth. Those numbers must be adjusted to allow for any additional public offerings and stock splits. The reliability of the net asset figure may be questionable because most of its value resides in a fund's portfolio. The value of that portfolio is an estimate of the current market value of the companies in the portfolio, and most of those companies are private.

Poindexter surveyed 270 venture capital firms that managed the bulk of the domestic venture capital pool. He estimated that the respondents who supplied rate-of-return data managed one third of the domestic pool of venture capital. They were asked to estimate their firm's compound rate of return since inception. The mean of the estimated rates of return of the 59 firms was 13.3 per cent, with a range from 35 per cent to –40 per cent (Poindexter, 1976).[10]

Here is a summary of the historical perspective:

1 the compounded return on venture capital seems to have been in the teens – probably the mid-teens – from the inception of the industry to the early 1980s; and

2 there were wide swings in the annual returns from lows of a few per cent to highs exceeding 30 per cent.

ACTUAL RETURNS

As stated previously, when Venture Economics began its rates of return database in 1985, the actual returns of venture captial funds were a secret that was closely guarded by each venture capital firm. Traditionally, venture capital partnerships did not – and to this day still do not – publish their rates of return. However, the raw data needed to compute the returns was available from the limited partners who invest in venture capital funds.

The US venture capital industry is dominated by venture capital partnerships composed of limited partners and general partners. The limited partners provide the money and the general partners provide the management. Venture capitalists in one venture capital firm may be general partners in several partnerships under the management umbrella of that firm. Some of the older venture capital firms manage half-a-dozen or more partnerships. In return, the general partners receive an annual management fee and a share of any profit that the partnership makes. The general partners' annual management fee is usually 2–3 per cent of the paid-in capital, and the general partners' share of the profit, known in the industry as the partners' carried interest, is usually 20 per cent; the other 80 per cent goes to the limited partners. Partnerships generally have a ten-year life, which can often be extended.

When a new partnership is formed, the money committed to the partnership is paid in several instalments (takedowns) over the first two or three years. The general partners send reports and financial statements to the limited partners, usually quarterly. From those financial statements, limited partners can calculate their share of the book value of the partnership (the residual value). The residual value consists of any uninvested capital and the estimated partnership's share of the value of portfolio companies in which the partnership has invested. When a company in the partnership's portfolio goes public, the limited partners may receive their share of the stock in that company, although the venture capital partnership sometimes holds back stock for a period before distributing it. That is called a distribution. It is usually valued at the offering price per share of the public offering. Besides stock, there may be other distributions such as cash from trade sales and dividends.

The algorithm for computing the internal rate of return (IRR) is fairly simple in principle. The residual, the distributions and the takedowns are each reduced to their present value on the date of the first takedown. A distribution of D dollars has a present value of $D/(1 + IRR/100)^t$, where IRR is the annualized internal rate of return, and t is the time in years from the date of the first takedown to the date of the distribution. The present values of a takedown of T dollars and a residual of R dollars can be computed the same way. The value of IRR is computed by finding its value when the present value of the takedowns equals the present value of all the distribution plus the present value of the limited partner's share of the residual.

At the end of a partnership's life, all its investments have been realized and distributed net of annual management fees and carried interest to the limited partners. Thus, a limited partner can compute its net IRR, or what is called a cash-on-cash return, because it knows how much cash it paid into the partnership and how much cash and/or liquid assets it received in return. This is called the cash-on-cash return or net return. However, it is not possible to compute a 'pure' cash-on-cash IRR before a partnership is liquidated because some of its investments have not yet been realized and their residual value is not precise. Hence, the computation of interim returns are less precise than pure cash-on-cash. Both the US National Venture Capital Association and the European Venture Capital Association have set out guidelines for valuing unrealized investments (e.g., *Venture Capital Journal*, June 1990[11]; EVCA, 1996[12]). Venture Economics, which has published US venture capital returns annually since 1988 in its *Investment Benchmarks Report*, and in collaboration with Bannock Consulting began publishing European returns in its *International Investment Benchmarks Report* in 1997, reports net returns.

RETURNS IN THE USA

The cumulative returns of 783 private equity partnerships formed between 1969 and 1996 are shown in Table 14.3. The IRRs are the net returns to the limited partners from the date of inception of each fund to 30 September 1997. This data set comprises 601 venture capital funds and 182 buyout funds. The pooled return is the IRR on the total pool of capital. The pooled return is higher than both the median return and the average return, because the amount of capital per fund is not evenly distributed among the funds. Half the capital is in relatively few very large funds, which in aggregate produce substantially higher returns than the other half that is in relatively many small funds. Likewise, the median return is lower than the average return. The average IRR for all the venture capital funds is 14.3 per cent, which is consistent with the historical returns that were discussed earlier in this chapter. Returns of buyout funds reported in Table 14.3 are noticeably higher than the returns on venture capital. It is important to note that the upper quartile return is substantially higher than the average (5.0 percentage points) and the median (8.9 percentage points). At the end of the chapter, we will compare the performance of venture capital funds with the public stock markets.

Table 14.3 ◆ Cumulative net IRRs of US limited partnerships equity formed 1969–96 from inception to 30 September 1997

Type of fund	Number of funds	Cumulative IRR (%) from inception to 30 September 1997			
		Pooled	Median	Average	Top quartile
Venture funds	601	15.3	10.4	14.3	19.3
Buyout	192	21.0	14.5	16.1	24.6
All private equity	**793**	**17.7**	**11.5**	**14.7**	**20.1**

Source: Venture Economics

When the venture capital funds are agglomerated according to the stage of development of the companies in which they invest (Table 14.4), early-stage funds have outperformed balanced funds, but have underperformed later-stage funds. Finance theory predicts that early-stage funds should have returns greater than later-stage funds, because the earlier the stage, the greater the risk, all other things being equal. But that ignores the mechanics of the venture capital investing. Looked at it simplistically, a venture capital investment in a later-stage company is more certain because the company has been in business longer and has a history that can be examined. What's more, a later-stage investment is usually realized sooner than an early-stage investment. And of course, unlike public markets where the stocks are freely traded and there is an abundance of public information, venture capital is invested in private companies whose shares are not traded on public markets. Hence, it is no great surprise to find that the returns on venture capital funds appear to defy finance theory.

Table 14.4 ◆ Net rates of return for US private equity funds to 31 December 1997

Type of fund	Number of funds	IRR (%) for time period ending 31 December 1997				
		1 year	3 years	5 years	10 years	20 years
Early/seed focused	220	33.8	48.9	31.1	18.3	17.8
Balanced	343	22.6	37.3	25.3	14.9	13.8
Later-stage focused	58	41.4	42.7	37.0	23.9	NA
All venture funds	**621**	**29.5**	**41.2**	**28.1**	**16.7**	**15.4**
Buyout funds	211	22.1	21.3	21.7	19.9	21.2
Mezzanine debt	35	10.3	13.9	15.1	10.7	11.1
All private equity	**867**	**24.0**	**27.1**	**23.7**	**18.0**	**17.1**

Source: Venture Economics

Besides the stage of the companies in which a venture capital fund invests, the year in which the fund begins investing can also affect the returns. As Bygrave (1989)[13] demonstrated by analyzing the returns of funds that commenced operations between 1978 and 1983, the returns varied according to vintage. He found that the IRR of each successive vintage from 1978 to 1983 declined. This is reflected in Table 14.5, which shows the cumulative returns by vintage from 1980 to 1997. Caution is needed when interpreting the IRRs for young funds that are only a few years old because venture capital funds are ten-year limited partnerships that invest most of their funds over the first four years and realize most of those investments in the later years of the fund. Some observers think that it is unrealistic to publish returns until funds are at least four years old. Nevertheless, the trend in early returns of a given vintage is often an indication of the trend in later returns that can be expected from that vintage. This is clearly demonstrated by comparing the IRRs of the 1978–82 vintages when they were one, two and three years old (Bygrave 1989)[14] with the returns when they were mature (Table 14.5). The explanation for the decline in the returns of the 1978–82 vintages is that the annual flow of new venture capital increased almost twentyfold from $170 million in 1979 to $3.4 billion in 1983. That sudden flood of new capital meant that more and more new venture capital partnerships were started, many of them with relatively inexperienced venture capitalists. It also meant that there was intense competition when it came to investing in portfolio companies. A common complaint at the time was that there was too much venture capital chasing too few deals in which the money could be invested. The intense competition among venture capitalists for deals caused pre-money valuations of companies to increase. Also the pressure to invest combined with the inexperience of many of the venture capitalists resulted in too many investments in marginal companies.

As the amount of money flowing into the industry levelled out after 1983 and then steadily declined from $4.2 billion on 1987 to $1.3 billion in 1991, returns by vintage trended upwards. Of course, those returns were boosted considerably by a hot IPO market that made realizations increasingly plentiful as well as more and more bountiful. The IPO market began to heat up 1991 and became white hot in 1996. Since the 1996 peak, the market has cooled off.

Over the period 1993–8 – somewhat like the 1978–83 period – there has been another rapid increase in the amount of venture capital from $2.5 billion in 1993 to $17.8 billion in 1998. Once again, some venture capitalists are grousing that too much money is chasing too few deals. Pre-money valuations have increased, and the amount of money invested in each deal has increased from about $2.2 million in the early 1990s to more than $4.0 million in 1997. It seems inevitable that the returns will decline, especially if the IPO market remains as cool as it was in the first nine months of 1998. Perhaps we are already glimpsing this impending decline because the early returns of the 1996 and 1997 vintages have dropped noticeably from the returns of the 1994 and 1995 vintages.

Table 14.5 ♦ Performance of US venture capital funds by vintage

| | Quartile performance by vintage year | | | | | | | | | | | | | | | | | |
| | Cumulative net IRR as of 31 December 1997 to limited partners of venture capital funds formed in: | | | | | | | | | | | | | | | | | |
	1980	1981	1982	1983	1984	1985	1986	1987	1988	1989	1990	1991	1992	1993	1994	1995	1996	1997
Maximum	50.3	25.4	13.5	41.5	25.5	28.3	25.6	31.5	42.6	56.2	75.1	32.1	106.3	90.5	89.3	257.5	223.9	101.9
Upper quartile	19.3	13.1	8.9	9.8	11.4	16.5	12.8	17.4	21.6	20.5	32.9	23.0	37.9	26.5	35.2	34.4	14.7	14.2
Median	13.9	10.1	4.9	5.0	5.4	10.4	7.1	11.4	9.5	9.4	17.5	15.7	17.4	12.7	19.0	25.0	-0.5	-3.1
Lower quartile	13.0	-0.2	-0.8	0.4	2.7	2.1	4.4	3.1	3.2	2.1	6.3	1.3	11.2	5.5	12.7	10.1	-11.1	-20.8
Minimum	-1.9	-3.3	-19.1	-11.4	-18.4	-41.5	-2.3	-37.8	-10.7	-9.1	-3.2	-11.3	3.2	-8.3	-20.8	-3.7	-71.0	-89.7

Source: Venture Economics

In summary, the actual cumulative returns on venture capital funds confirm the historical perspective, the median returns are in the teens but they are subject to cyclical swings that take them from the single digits to the high teens. The upper quartile is substantially higher than the median, ranging from the high single digits to the high thirties. Later in this chapter we will examine what drives venture capital returns and causes their cyclical swings.

EUROPEAN RETURNS

In contrast to the USA, before 1996, there was a dearth of information on the performance of European venture capital funds; and the scant information that was available was not a valid representation of the industry as a whole. With the tremendous growth of the European venture capital industry, there was increasing need for the European industry to follow the lead of the US industry and encourage the systematic collection and publication of returns data. In response to this need, the European Venture Capital Association initiated and the European Commission sponsored a study by Venture Economics and Bannock Consulting that was published in 1996 as the first *European Private Equity Performance Pilot Study*.[15] Subsequently, Venture Economics and Bannock Consulting published the *1997 Investment Benchmarks Report: International Private Equity*,[16] which focuses on the performance of venture capital and private equity capital in Europe and the UK.

Table 14.6 ◆ Cumulative net IRRs of European mature private equity funds from inception to 31 December 1996

Type of fund	Number of funds	Cumulative IRR (%) from inception to 31 December 1996			
		Pooled	*Median*	*Top quartile*	*Top Quarter*
Early stage	27	5.7	4.5	13.0	27.2
Development	60	7.3	5.4	13.3	18.7
Buyout	67	17.6	15.5	25.2	41.9
Generalist	48	19.4	1.3	7.9	22.9
All private equity	**202**	**18.6**	**6.6**	**17.4**	**29.1**

Buyout funds 1980–94. All other funds 1980–92.
Generalists include one very large evergreen independent fund.
The 202 funds were composed of 106 focused on the UK, 21 on France, 8 on Spain, 4 on Germany, 4 on Italy, 5 on the Netherlands, 51 on several countries and 3 on other countries.

Source: 1997 Investment Benchmarks Report: International Private Equity, published by Venture Economics

The cumulative net IRRs for European private equity funds from inception to 31 December 1996 are shown in Table 14.6. There are two cautions:

1 more than half the funds concentrate in investing in the UK; and

2 the data include one huge evergreen generalist fund – indeed, so huge that it makes the pooled IRR for generalist funds much greater than the top quartile IRR.

The pooled returns of the early-stage funds and the development funds are 5.7 per cent and 7.3 per cent with the median returns at 4.5 per cent and 5.4 per cent and top-quartile returns at 13.0 per cent and 13.3 per cent. Hence the 'classic'[17] venture capital returns are substantially below the US venture returns (Table 14.3). However, the European buyout returns are comparable with those in the USA. Because the pool of European buyout and generalist funds combined is much greater than the pool of early-stage and development funds combined, the returns on all private equity in Europe is comparable with the returns of all private equity in the USA (Table 14.3).

The pooled European returns broken down into time periods of one, three, five and ten years, all ending in 31 December 1996 are shown in Table 14.7. These can be compared with the US returns by time period in Table 14.4, with the caution that the European time periods end on 31 December 1996 whereas those in the USA end in 31 December 1997. Again, just as with the comparison of overall returns, the early-stage and development funds in Europe performed substantially below 'classic' venture capital in the USA for all periods. The European industry performed exceptionally well for the one-year period ended 31 December 1996, with returns of 47.7 per cent for early-stage funds and 19.3 per cent for development funds. For the same period the US venture funds returned 40.1 per cent, broken down by early-stage 43.5 per cent, later-stage 32.1 per cent and balanced 40.6 per cent. The ten-year returns on European buyout funds and all private equity are comparable with those in the USA.

Table 14.7 ♦ Net rates of return for European private equity funds to 31 December 1996

Type of fund	Number of funds	IRR (%) for time period ending 31 December 1996			
		1 year	3 years	5 years	10 years
Early stage	27	47.7	16.4	12.5	6.5
Development	60	19.3	15.8	9.5	7.9
Buyout	67	32.7	20.1	16.5	18.0
Generalist	48	24.2	11.1	13.5	21.2
All private equity	**202**	**27.0**	**13.6**	**13.8**	**18.5**

Buyout funds 1980–94. All other funds 1980–92.
Generalists include one very large evergreen independent fund.

The 202 funds were composed of 106 focused on the UK, 21 on France, 8 on Spain, 4 on Germany, 4 on Italy, 5 on the Netherlands, 51 on several countries and 3 on other countries.

Sources: 1997 Investment Benchmarks Report: International Private Equity

UK RETURNS

The British Venture Capital Association (BVCA) in conjunction with The WM Company and Crossroads Management (UK) Limited publishes the returns on UK venture capital funds. The returns are for independent venture capital funds (unquoted funds managed by venture capital firms) that invest primarily in the UK. The results are shown on Table 14.8, which shows the returns for 152 independent funds that manage £4 billion of capital, estimated to represent 98 per cent of the capital raised over the period 1980–97. Although many of these funds are included in the European returns (Tables 14.6 and 14.7), the UK data set is more comprehensive and does not include one huge evergreen generalist fund. There is one caution: the UK returns are for the period ending 31 December 1997 whereas the European returns are for the period ending 31 December 1996.

Table 14.8 ◆ Net rates of return for UK private equity funds to
31 December 1997

Type of fund	Number of funds	IRR (%) for time period ending 31 December 1997			
		1 year	3 years	5 years	10 years
Early stage	17	14.5	22.9	21.3	8.2
Development	38	30.6	24.4	25.4	9.2
Mid-MBO	32	19.1	25.2	27.5	15.7
Large MBO	33	20.8	33.9	35.7	19.7
Generalist	32	20.6	25.6	20.9	10.2
All private equity	**152**	**21.0**	**29.6**	**29.3**	**14.6**

Development includes expansion and small MBOs with less than £2 million of equity invested.
Mid-MBO includes equity investments of 2–5 million.
Large MBO includes equity investments over £5 million.

Source: British Venture Capital Association

In general, the UK returns on their own (Table 14.8) have surpassed the European returns and the UK returns combined (Table 14.7). Hence, the returns on the European funds excluding the UK funds are in general lower then the UK returns. The one exception appears to be the one-year return, but they should not be compared because the UK returns are for 1997 and the European returns are for 1996.

The UK buyout and overall returns are in general comparable with the US returns. But as with the European funds, the returns on early-stage and development funds are below the returns on early-stage and later-stage US funds.

THE IPO MARKET AND VENTURE CAPITAL RETURNS
IN THE USA

As was noted at the beginning of this chapter, the health of the small-capitalization stock market is a powerful force on the venture capital market, because when the small-cap stock market is doing well, it is relatively easy to realize an investment in a successful company with a flotation. We will now examine the relationship between the small-cap stock market and the returns on venture capital.

In Fig. 14.1, the difference between the ten-year return on small-cap stocks and the S&P 500 stocks is plotted on the left-hand axis over the period 1974 to 1989. The top-quartile annual return on US venture capital funds is plotted in the right-hand axis over the same period. This demonstrates very clearly that there was a close correlation between the health of the small-cap stock market and the annual returns on venture capital. When the returns on small-cap stocks peaked in 1983, the IPO market also peaked. That facilitated the flotation of 121 venture capital companies, which at the time was a record number venture-capital-backed IPOs in any one year. Not surprisingly, with so many successful realizations, venture capital annual returns also peaked in 1983.

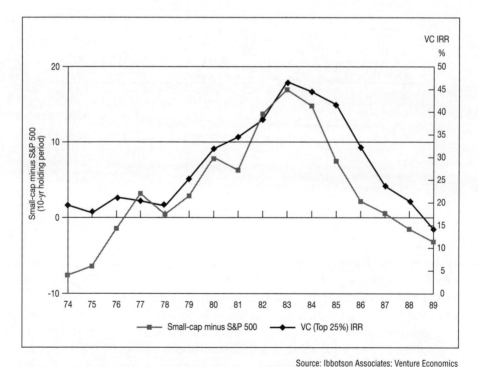

Source: Ibbotson Associates; Venture Economics

Fig. 14.1 ♦ Small-cap minus S&P 500 venture capital returns

A more direct causal relationship between US venture capital returns and the IPO market is demonstrated in Fig. 14.2. Here, the venture capital annual returns are plotted on the right-hand axis over the period 1985 to 1997, while the total amount of money raised by venture-capital-backed IPOs is plotted on the left-hand axis.

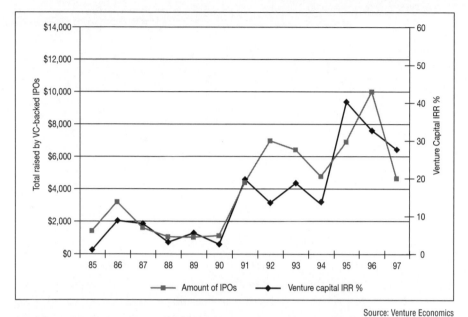

Source: Venture Economics

Fig. 14.2 ◆ Venture capital annual IRR versus total raised by VC-backed IPOs

The annual number of venture-capital-backed IPOs and the average offering size are plotted in Fig. 14.3. It was not until 1991 that the annual number of IPOs exceeded the 1983 peak. And it was not until 1991 that the venture capital annual return was again above 20 per cent. Annual returns were above 50 per cent in 1995 and 40 per cent in 1996 when the annual number of IPOs and the average offering size set back-to-back records.

An IPO is not the only way for a venture capital fund to have a successful realization. Another method is via a trade sale. In the case of stellar performers, a trade sale (also called an acquisition or merger) sometimes realizes a higher value than an IPO. However, on average, the valuation realized with a trade sale is substantially less than the amount realized with an IPO as can be seen in Fig. 14.4, which plots the valuations of IPOs and acquisitions from 1993 to 1997 in the USA. Hence, a venture capitalist's favourite realization is an IPO. So in general, when the small-cap market is favourable, an IPO is the most frequently used realization route and venture returns are higher; conversely, when the small-cap markets is unfavourable, a trade sale is often the most frequently used realization route and returns are lower. This is shown clearly in Fig. 14.5, which plots the annual number of IPOs and acquisitions over the period 1980 to 1997. From 1984 to

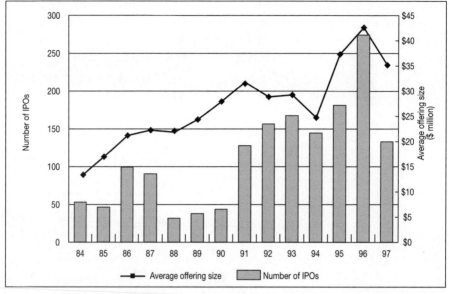

Source: Venture Economics

Fig. 14.3 ◆ Venture-capital-backed IPOs 1984–97

1990, there were more acquisitions than IPOs and annual returns were below 10 per cent. And from 1991 to 1997, there were more IPOs than acquisitions and annual returns were above 10 per cent rising to almost 50 per cent in 1996. Thus there is compelling evidence that venture capital returns are closely linked to the IPO market. We will now examine the characteristics of venture-capital-backed IPOs.

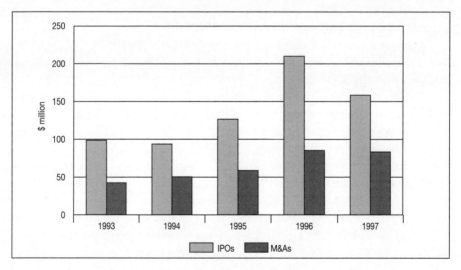

Source: Venture Economics

Fig. 14.4 ◆ Average valuations of VC-backed IPOs and M&As 1993–7

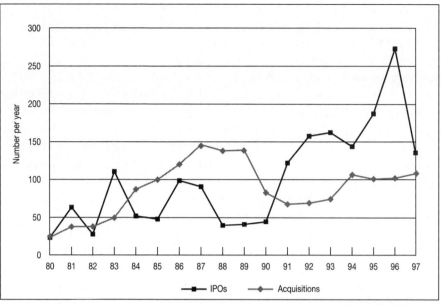

Fig. 14.5 ♦ Number of IPOs and acquisitions of venture-capital-backed companies

Characteristics of IPO companies in the USA

Trade books, textbooks and scholarly literature prescribe profiles of the 'ideal' company for a venture capital investment, e.g., *The Portable MBA in Entrepreneurship* (Bygrave 1997),[18] *New Venture Creation* (Timmons 1994)[19] and 'Opportunity Recognition: The Core of Entrepreneurship' in *Frontiers of Entrepreneurship Research 1987* (Timmons et al. 1987).[20] In general, the prescriptive profile was for a high-tech company, regardless of the industry segment. The basic premise underpinning this profile is that the 'ideal' company will be able to float a firm commitment IPO with a prestigious underwriter less than five years after the first venture capital has been invested, or be acquired at a valuation comparable to what would have been realized through a public offering. The evaluation criteria spelled out in these profiles appear to be based on anecdotal evidence from venture capitalists themselves rather than on systematic empirical studies of actual deals.

In a recent study, Bygrave et al. (1998)[21] studied the actual profiles of successful venture-capital-backed high-tech companies and compared them with the profile of the 'ideal' company that seems to have evolved from prescriptive wisdom. They examined venture-capital-backed companies that have gone public on the Nasdaq with firm commitment offerings by reputable underwriters. This group was chosen because they were among the cream of the crop of venture capital investments: they were the investments where the venture capitalists had realized a successful harvest. Granted, as was noted in the previous section, initial public offerings (IPOs) are not the only way for venture capitalists to realize a good return on their investments – trade sales may be just as rewarding, or sometimes even more so. However, studies have shown that on average IPOs produce a higher return than other harvests (Khoylian 1988,[22] Bygrave and Timmons 1992,[23] Fineberg 1997[24]). What's more, companies that have firm commitment IPOs with reputable underwriters are generally considered to be successful investments by their venture-capital backers. Hence, by examining IPO prospectuses, Bygrave et al. (1998)[25] were able to look at the profiles of venture-capital companies that were successful investments. To look for the effects of the stage of the industry life-cycle, they deliberately chose an industry at an early stage, the Internet, and one at a later stage, semiconductors. They also chose industries that they considered to be at intermediate stages, software and computer hardware.

They examined 122 venture-capital-backed high-tech companies in four industry segments that floated firm-commitment initial public offerings on the Nasdaq during the period January 1994 to July 1997. There were 24 Internet companies, 59 software companies, 25 computer hardware companies and 14 semiconductor companies. They examined market/industry, technological, operating and financial criteria of those companies. Market/industry criteria included market size, market growth rate, market share, distribution channels and life-cycle stage of the industry segment. Technological criteria included uniqueness of the product or service, patents and copyrights. Operating and financial criteria included annual revenue, growth rate, profit margins, cash flow, time to profitability, return on assets, return on equity, price-to-earnings ratio, time from the first round of venture capital to the IPO and times return and internal rate of return on the first round of venture capital.

The results of the analysis with all industry segments – Internet, software, hardware and semiconductors – agglomerated together are shown in Table 14.9: Marketing and operations, and Table 14.10: Finance and investment. Median values are shown in Tables 14.9 and 14.10 rather than mean values because the distributions are skewed. Column 3 of each table lists what the prescribed wisdom says are the most desirable characteristics for a venture capital investment – the so-called high-potential venture – and column 4 lists the least desirable character-istics – the so-called low-potential venture. The prescribed wisdom is taken from *New Venture Creation*[26] and *The Portable MBA in Entrepreneurship.*[27]

Marketing and operations for all companies, Table 14.9

The median profile of the companies in the data set was close to the prescribed high-potential profile when it came to market size ($1.3 billion versus 0.1–1 billion), market growth rate (32 per cent versus 30–50 per cent), and stage of the industry segment (2 versus 1 and 2), but appeared to be way off in market share (2 per cent at time of IPO versus more than 20 per cent in five years) and annual growth in sales (48.8 per cent versus 15–20 per cent). The median gross margin was well above the prescribed figure (60.6 per cent versus more than 40 per cent, but the net income margin was well below (1.7 per cent versus more than 10 per cent). The actual annualized sales revenue and annualized net income were also well below the prescribed levels.

On three criteria, the actual median profile fitted the prescribed low-potential rather than the high-potential profile: a market share of 2 per cent was substantially below the 'less than 5 per cent' figure for a low-potential; a time to break-even just of five years was longer than the minimum cutpoint of four years prescribed for a low-potential; and a return on equity of 7.6 per cent was well under the 'less than 15–20 per cent' for a low-potential.

Table 14.9 ◆ Marketing and operations of all venture-capital-backed public companies

Marketing and operations	Medians	Prescriptive wisdom	
	All industries	High-potential	Low-potential
Market size	1.3 billion	$0.1–$1.0 billion	<$20 million or >several $billion
Market growth rate	32.0%	30–50%	<10%
Market share	2.0%	>20% by year 5	<5%
Stage 1–4, 1 = infancy, 4 = late (median)	2	1 and 2	3 and 4
Stage 1–4 (mean)	2	1 and 2	3 and 4
Year started	1988		
Annual sales growth trend (all years)	42.3%	15–20%	<10%
Sales growth trend (12 months)	48.9%	15–20%	<10%
Annualized sales revenue	$23,792,000	$50,000,000	
Gross margin	60.6%	>40%	<20%
Profit margin	1.7%	>10%	Low
Net income (last year)	$200,204		
Net income (last quarter annualized)	$1,412,000	$5,000,000	
ROA	1.0%		
ROE	7.6%	>25%	<15–20%
Years to breakeven [1]	4.98	1.5–2	>4
R&D ratio	17.7%		
Number of employees	130		

[1] Includes only companies that have broken even

329

Finance and investment for all companies, Table 14.10

From the venture capitalists' viewpoint, the actual profile spectacularly exceeded the specifications for a high-potential venture: IRR of 145.3 per cent versus more than 25 per cent; time from first venture capital investment to initial public offering of 2.57 years versus less than five years; and a p/e ratio of 50 versus 20.

Table 14.10 ♦ Finance and investment for venture-capital-backed public companies

Finance and investment	Medians	Prescriptive wisdom	
	All industries	High-potential	Low-potential
IRR	145.3%	>25%	<15%
Return on investment multiple	6.94		
Years from 1st VC investment to IPO	2.57	<5	>10
Time from incorporation to IPO	7		
Price/share 1st round of VC	$1.31		
IPO price	$12.00		
P/E ratio	50	20	5
Size of IPO	$27,000,000		
Market capitalization after IPO	$100,687,163		

For purposes of comparison, there were 655 IPOs on the Nasdaq in 1996, for which the average IPO price was $10.84, the average size of the IPO was $35.2 million, and the average market capitalization after the IPO was $120.5 million (source: Securities Data Company).

Grouping by industry segment

Up to this point, the data have been analyzed with all 122 companies agglomerated together. When they are separated into their industry segments, the profiles are very different (Tables 14.11 and 14.12). The industries are arranged from left to right by the increasing maturity of each segment in Tables 14.11 and 14.12. The mean for the stage of the Internet companies was 1.26, software 1.76, computer hardware 2.12 and semiconductors 4.00. The industry segments are positioned according to the means of their stages on a product life cycle curve in Fig. 14.6.

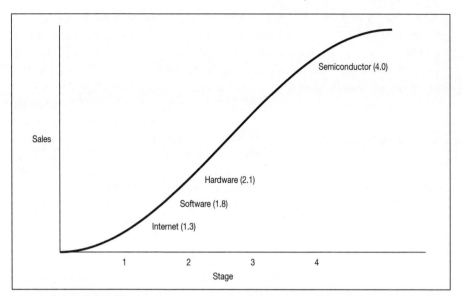

Fig. 14.6 ♦ Product life cycle curve showing industry segments positioned according to the means of their stages

Market and operations for each industry segment, Table 14.11

The median market size of $259 million for the Internet companies fell within the prescribed range of $100 million to $1 billion for a high-potential; the software and hardware medians were somewhat above the top end of that range; but the median for semiconductors placed it firmly in the prescribed low-potential category. The Internet and hardware market growth rates of 135.7 per cent and 37.5 per cent exceeded the high-potential minimum of 30 per cent but the software and semiconductor rates of 23.5 per cent and 15.5 per cent fell short of the high-potential minimum. Perhaps what was most startling about the market criteria was that not one of the median market shares for the four industries came close to the prescribed 'more than 20 per cent by year 5' for a high-potential. Indeed, all four market shares placed them firmly in the 'less than 5 per cent by year 5' prescribed for a low-potential.

The operating results of the companies showed that the sales growth medians of all four industries were above the 15 per cent threshold for a high-potential. With the Internet growing fastest at 93.3 per cent and semiconductors slowest at 30.1 per cent. But not one of the sales revenue medians reached the $50 million level specified for a five-year-old high-potential; the $39.9 million median for semiconductors came closest to being a high-potential; while the $9.7 million for the Internet was the furthest away. When it came to profits all segments exceeded the minimum of gross margin 40 per cent for a high-potential, but all fell short of the net income margin of 10 per cent. With net income loss of a whopping 36.7 per cent, the Internet median was definitely a low-potential. And although not

331

nearly as bad as the Internet, the net income margin for both the hardware (–0.5 per cent) and software (3.4 per cent) placed both in the low-potential category. Only the median for semiconductors (7.9 per cent) approached what was expected for a high-potential. With such dismal net income margins, it was no surprise that the return on equity classified all but the semiconductors as low-potentials. Finally, the median time to breakeven of the companies for which that information was available was way longer than the two years for a high potential and consistent with four years or longer for a low-potential.

Table 14.11 ♦ Marketing and operations of venture-capital-backed public companies by industry segment

Marketing and operations	Medians			
	Internet	*Software*	*Hardware*	*Semiconductor*
Market size	$259,000,000	$1,150,000,000	$1,400,000,000	$13,600,000,000
Market growth rate	135.7%	23.5%	37.5%	15.5%
Market share	1.2%	2.5%	2.7%	0.2%
Stage 1–4, 1 = infancy, 4 = later (median)	1	2	2	4
Stage 1–4 (mean)	1.26	1.76	2.12	4.00
Year started	1992	1987	1988	1984
Annual sales growth trend (all years)	87.0%	54.3%	55.7%	24.7%
Sales growth trend (12 months)	93.3%	45.9%	54.3%	30.1%
Annualized sales revenue	$9,720,000	$23,396,000	$27,268,000	$39,940,000
Gross margin	72.7%	75.6%	39.1%	42.2%
Profit margin	–36.7%	3.4%	–0.5%	7.9%
Net income (last year)	($2,414,530)	$308,000	($639,000)	$1,495,000
Net income (last quarter annualized)	($3,462,921)	$1,644,000	$2,140,000	$3,226,000
ROA	–85.7%	1.3%	–6.4%	6.9%
ROE	–64.5%	5.3%	16.5%	24.4%
Years to breakeven [1]	4.00	5.00	4.80	5.00
R&D ratio	27.0%	18.4%	14.5%	14.6%
Number of employees	124	134	92	213

[1] Includes only companies that have broken even

Finance and investment for each industry segment, Table 14.12

The financial returns of all industry segments except semiconductors considerably exceeded the expectations of venture capital investors for a high-potential. What's more the semiconductor companies almost met their expectations. In all segments the p/e ratio was bigger than the prescribed threshold of 20. It was worth noting that the Internet companies went public slightly less than one year after their first round of venture capital.

Table 14.12 ◆ Finance and investment for venture-capital-backed public companies by industry segment

Finance and investment	Medians			
	Internet	Software	Hardware	Semiconductor
IRR	506.9%	124.8%	148.0%	30.5%
Return on investment multiple	7.16	6.67	10.71	4.94
Years from 1st VC investment to IPO	0.96	2.53	4.04	5.00
Time from incorporation to IPO	5	8	7	11
Price/share 1st round of VC	$1.25	$1.50	$1.13	$2.79
IPO price	$14	$12	$10	$11
P/E ratio	70	54	32	26
Size of IPO	$34,000,000	$27,600,000	$22,320,000	$29,130,000
Market capitalization after IPO	$163,488,290	$105,510,812	$89,244,768	$77,468,542

IPO summary

There was no one set of specifications that was a unique prescription for a venture-capital-backed company – not even when there was considerable latitude in the specifications. The quantitative criteria in that specification were contingent upon many factors. However, the industry segment and its life-cycle stage stand out as critical components. It was clear that the quantitative criteria for an Internet company were quite different than those for a semiconductor company.

The performance criteria that define a high-potential company were contingent on the expectations of the future performance of the market. Of the four industry segments, the Internet was both the youngest and the fastest growing. Indeed, it was growing so fast that predictions about the size of that market were continually being revised upward. In 1996, market researchers were predicting that the total value of electronic commerce transacted over the Internet – so-called e-commerce – would be perhaps $10 billion by the year 2000. By 1998, e-commerce was already running at a rate that topped $10 billion annually, and John Chambers, the CEO of Cisco Systems, was predicting that the total value of e-commerce could exceed $1,000 billion by 2001. It was expectations of explosive growth of e-commerce that were driving a frenzy of entrepreneurialism and investment, and explains why the actual values of many criteria for Internet companies were so different from those prescribed for a high-potential.

The Internet companies were still below the inflection point on the life-cycle curve where increasing returns and positive feedback economics prevail (Arthur, 1994[28] and 1996[29]). In contrast, the semiconductor companies were at a late stage in the life cycle where decreasing returns and negative feedback economics dominates. As expected in a late-stage industry, the semiconductor companies were the slowest growing of the four segments. That was why the investors required larger sales revenue and higher profitability at the time of a public offering for a semiconductor company than an Internet company, but placed a lower p/e ratio on the stock.

VENTURE CAPITAL RETURNS AS AN ASSET CLASS

As more and more money is being invested in venture capital funds it is apparent that investors regard it as a separate asset class. We will now see how it compares with other asset classes. In Tables 14.13 and 14.14, the returns on US venture capital are compared with the returns on publicly traded stocks and mutual funds. We selected 1995 as a benchmark year because US venture capital returns set an all-time record (Table 14.13), with the overall one-year return topping 50 per cent for the first time ever. The early-stage return was 51 per cent and the late-stage return was 56 per cent. These returns were very impressive, but so were the returns in the US public stock markets with the S&P 500 returning 37.6 per cent for the same period.

Table 14.13 ♦ Returns on US venture capital funds and public stocks
'1995 Was An Excellent Year'

	Returns are annualized IRRs for the specified period			
	Venture capital	**S&P 500**	**Fidelity select mutual funds**	
	(700 funds)		*Computers*	*Electronics*
To 31 Dec., 1995	1-year	1-year	1-year	1-year
Early-stage	51.0%	37.6%	51.8%	69.0%
Late-stage	56.0%			
All VC funds	**50.7%**			

Sources: Venture Economics; Fidelity Insight

To compare the returns on venture capital with public stocks, we have selected two Fidelity select mutual funds that specialize in investing in the same industry sectors as venture capital funds: computers and electronics. In 1995, the one-year returns of Fidelity select computers and electronics mutual funds, excluding transaction costs, were both higher than the overall return on venture capital (Table 14.13).

A similar comparison of venture capital returns with S&P 500 and the Fidelity Select Computers and Electronics returns through to the end of 1997, both short term and long term, are shown in Table 14.14. We see that the one-year overall return on venture capital was less than the S&P 500 return but was much higher than both the Fidelity Select Computers and Electronics returns. The overall five-year return on venture capital at the end of 1997 was 28.1 per cent, which was higher than the S&P 500 return of 20.3 per cent and the Fidelity Select Computers return of 24.7 per cent but lower than the Fidelity Select Electronics return of 32.5 per cent. For the ten-year returns to 1997, the overall return on venture capital was 16.7 per cent compared with 18.1 per cent for the S&P 500, 19.2 per cent for Fidelity Select Computers and 23.0 per cent for Fidelity Select Electronics.

In general, Tables 14.13 and 14.14 show that late-stage venture capital funds outperformed not only early-stage funds but also the stock market, both short term and long term.

Table 14.14 ♦ Returns on US venture capital funds and public stocks '1997 Was A Good Year'

	Returns are annualized IRRs for the specified period			
	Venture capital	**S&P 500**	**Fidelity select mutual funds**	
	(621 funds)		*Computers*	*Electronics*
To 31 Dec., 1997	1-year	1-year	1-year	1-year
Early-stage	33.8%	33.6%	–2.9%	10.3%
Balanced funds	22.6%			
Late-stage	41.4%			
All VC funds	**29.5%**			
To 31 Dec., 1997	5-year	5-year	5-year	5-year
Early-stage	31.1%	20.3%	24.7%	32.5%
Balanced funds	25.3%			
Late-stage	37.0%			
All VC funds	**28.1%**			
To 31 Dec., 1997	10-year	10-year	10-year	10-year
Early-stage	18.3%	18.1%	19.2%	23.0%
Balanced funds	14.9%			
Late-stage	23.9%			
All VC funds	**16.7%**			

Sources: Venture Economics; Fidelity Insight

The performance of UK venture capital funds is compared with the stock market in Table 14.15. Care has to be taken in comparing the UK with the US returns because the US funds are only 'classic' venture capital whereas the total for the UK funds includes both 'classic' venture capital (early-stage and development funds) and buyout funds. The UK early-stage and development returns underperformed all the FTSE indices – All Shares, 100, and Small-Cap – over the ten years ended 31 December 1997, but outperformed all FTSE indices over the five years ended 31 December 1997. The one-year development return beat all three FTSE indices, but the early-stage returns beat only the FTSE Small-Cap index. Buyout funds beat all three FTSE indices over both the five-year and ten-year periods. Somewhat like the US funds, returns on UK development funds were higher than returns on early-stage funds. We have not compared the returns on the European venture capital fund with stock market indices because, as we have already noted, UK funds preponderate in the European set of venture capital funds for which we have returns data.

Table 14.15 ♦ Returns on UK venture capital funds and public stock markets

	Returns are annualized IRRs for the specified period ending 31 December 1997			
	Venture capital	FTSE all-share	FTSE 100	FTSE small-cap
	(152 funds)			
To 31 Dec., 1997	1-year	1-year	1-year	1-year
Early-stage	14.5%	23.6%	28.7%	9.1%
Development	30.6%			
Mid-MBO	19.1%			
Large MBO	20.8%			
Generalist	20.6%			
Total	**21.0%**			
To 31 Dec., 1997	5-year	5-year	5-year	5-year
Early-stage	21.3%	16.6%	17.2%	14.8%
Development	25.4%			
Mid-MBO	27.5%			
Large MBO	35.7%			
Generalist	20.9%			
Total	**29.3%**			
To 31 Dec., 1997	10-year	10-year	10-year	10-year
Early-stage	8.2%	15.7%	16.7%	12.4%
Development	9.2%			
Mid-MBO	15.7%			
Large MBO	19.7%			
Generalist	10.2%			
Total	**14.6%**			

Source: British Venture Capital Association, May 1998

CONCLUSION

The 1990s have been a spectacular era for venture capital in the USA and in Europe. Returns rose to dazzling heights, with the annual return peaking at above 50 per cent in 1995. New commitments of money to US venture capital funds increased from $1.3 billion in 1991 to $10 billion in 1997 to almost $18 billion in 1998. We saw a similar pattern in the 1980s: returns rose to a peak around 40 per cent in 1983, money flooded into the industry, returns declined, and then the flows of venture capital ebbed. It remains to be seen what will happen to the returns in the late 1990s–early 2000s as a result of the torrent of venture capital in 1997 and 1998. The effect on the returns will depend on two factors:

1 will venture capitalists be able to find enough companies in which to invest at reasonable pre-money valuations?; and

2 will the Nasdaq small-cap market be favourable for IPOs by venture-capital-backed companies when it is time to harvest those investments?

Perhaps we are already seeing the softening of the US returns in the data presented in this chapter (Tables 14.4, 14.5 and 14.14). Pre-money valuations of companies have increased substantially, which means that the returns on the venture capital invested in those companies will decline unless the size of the realizations increases, or the time to realization decreases, or both. The IPO market turned less favourable in the middle of 1997 (Fig. 14.3) and stayed that way through the first three quarters of 1998. Rather than increasing, the IPO valuations decreased in 1997, as did trade sale valuations (Fig. 14.4). What's more, the ratio of IPOs to trade sales realizations is declining, which in the past has been a harbinger of declining returns.

The UK venture capital returns over the five years ended 31 December 1997, much like the US returns, were excellent. As in the USA, money has flooded into UK funds, with a record £6.5 billion of new capital committed for future venture capital investments in 1997. And just like the US industry, we may be seeing a softening of the returns (Tables 14.8 and 14.15).

It seems that venture capital investors are satisfied if they get a premium over the stock market of at least 400 basis points (four percentage points) to compensate for the increased risk. That is 400 basis points over the S&P 500 Index in the USA or the FTSE All-Share Index in the UK. They certainly achieved such a premium over the five-year period ended 31 December 1997. If venture capital returns drop over the next five or so years, and stock market returns fall at the same time, the flows of venture capital should hold up provided that venture capital continues to produce a return premium over the public markets. But if there is a catastrophe in the capital markets caused by the collapse of one or more international markets, or if the Internet investment bubble, which has been inflated to explosive size, bursts with a thunderous bang, investors may shy from small-cap stocks. If that happens, it will be difficult to float IPOs; venture capital returns will be unsatisfactory; and the industry will suffer.

As we complete this chapter, it remains to be seen what will happen to venture capital returns over the next five years. But we do know that the returns are cyclical. It seems unlikely that returns over the next five years will be as spectacular as over the five years ended in 1997. However, as a result of excellent returns in the 1990s, venture capital is now firmly established as an asset class. Katie Cattanach, Managing Principal of Sovereign Financial Services, said this about the US industry in 1998:

> ... by the early 1990s, the term [venture capital] was part of the standard asset-allocation lexicon. In the mid-1980s, institutions talked of 3 per cent to 5 per cent allocations, whereas today, they talk of 5 per cent to 10 per cent allocations, although the larger figures are for the private equity class as a whole.

And Clive Sherling, Chairman of the BVCA Investor Relations Committee, commenting on the *1997 Performance Measurement Survey* of independent UK venture capital funds, said:

> The BVCA believes that this survey demonstrates that there is a role for venture capital in any balanced portfolio.

Bibliography

Arthur, W. Brian (1994) *Increasing Returns and Path Dependence in the Economy*. Ann Arbor Michigan, University of Michigan Press.

Arthur, W. Brian (1996) 'Increasing Returns and the New World of Business,' *Harvard Business Review*, July–August.

Bannock, G. and Partners (1991) *Venture Capital and the Equity Gap*. London: Graham Bannock and Partners.

Bannock Consulting, Venture Economics and EVCA (1997) *European Private Equity Performance Remains Strong at 19%*. News release, 5 December.

Boylan, M. (1982) *What we know and don't know about venture capital*. American Economic Association Meetings. 28 December 1981. National Economist Club, 19 January 1982.

British Venture Capital Association (1988) 'UK venture capital funds show significant and repeated out-performance of UK pension fund assets' BVCA press release, 14 November.

Business Week (1988) For venture capitalists, too much of a good thing, 6 June, p. 126.

Bygrave, W. D. (1997) 'How the venture capitalists work out the financial odds' in Birley, S. and Muzyka, D. F. *Mastering Enterprise*. London: Financial Times/Pitman, pp. 82–6.

Bygrave, W. D. (ed.) (1997) *The Portable MBA in Entrepreneurship*. 2nd edn. New York: John Wiley & Sons, Inc.

Bygrave, W. D. (1989) *Venture Capital Investing: A Resource Exchange Perspective*. Doctoral dissertation, Boston University.

Bygrave, W. D., Hay, M. and Peeters, J. B. (eds.) (1994) *Realizing Investment Value*, Financial Times/Pitman.

Bygrave, W. D., Johnstone. G., Lewis, J. and Ullman, R. (1988) 'Venture Capitalists' Criteria for Selecting High-Tech Investments: Prescriptive Wisdom Compared with Actuality' in Reynolds, P. D. et al. (eds), *Frontiers of Entrepreneurship Research 1998*.

Bygrave, W. D. and Stein, M. (1989) 'A time to buy and a time to sell: A study of venture capital investments in 77 companies that went public' in Churchill, N. C., Katz, J., Kirchhoff, B., Vesper, K. and Wetzel, Jr. W. (eds), *Frontiers of Entrepreneurship Research*, pp. 288–303.

Bygrave, W. D. and Timmons, J. A. (1992) *Venture Capital at the Crossroads*. Boston, MA: Harvard Business School Press.

Davis, T. J., Jr and Stetson, C. P., Jr (1985) 'Creating successful venture-backed companies' in Pratt, S. E. and Morris, J. K. (eds), *Pratt's Guide to Venture Capital Sources*. 9th edn. Wellesley Hills, MA: Venture Economics.

European Commission (1996) Directorate General XIII-D, European Private Equity Performance Measurement Pilot Survey, Technical Report. Luxembourg.

EVCA 1992 Yearbook: *Venture Capital in Europe*. Zaventem, Belgium: EVCA.

EVCA (1998) *New Pan-European Performance Study*. Europe Private Equity update, EVCA No. 9, Special Edition, January.

EVCA (1996) 'European Private Equity Performance Measure Pilot Survey' in *Technical Report*, December.

Faucett, R. B. (1971). *The Management of Venture Capital Investment Companies*. Masters thesis, MIT.

Fineberg, S. A. M&A (1997) 'Values Soar While Sales Dip', in *Venture Capital Journal*, 37 (4), 31–2.

Fineberg, S. (1998) 'Flirting with $10 Billion' in *Venture Capital Journal*, February, 24–8.

Fineberg, S. (1998) 'Venture Capital Financings Reach Another High' in *Venture Capital Journal*, July, 37–40.

Fineberg, S. (1998) 'Fund-Raising Blitzes In First Half' in *Venture Capital Journal*, August, 38–40.

Fineberg, S. (1988) 'Venture Investing May Be Headed for a Plateau' in *Venture Capital Journal*, November, 42–4.

Forbes. (1988) 'Too much money, too few deals', 7 March, p. 144.

Foster, S. (1997) Venture 'IPO Volume Dives. The relative weakness of the small cap...' in *Venture Capital Journal*, August, 42–5.

Gannon, M. (1998) 'Half Empty or Half Full? IPOs fall again...' in *Venture Capital Journal*, August, 41–4.

Gevirtz, D. (1985) *The New Entrepreneurs: Innovation in American Business*. New York: Penguin Books, New York.

Hoban, J. P. (1976) *Characteristics of Venture Capital Investing*. Ph.D. Dissertation. University of Utah.

Ibbotson, R. G. and Brinson, G. P. (1987) *Investment Markets*. New York, N.Y.: McGraw-Hill, 99–100.

Ibbotson Associates, *SBBI 1991 Yearbook*.

Keeley, R. H. and Turki, L. A. (1992) 'New Ventures: How Risky Are They?' in Churchill et al., (eds.), *Frontiers of Entrepreneurship Research 1992*. Wellesley, MA: Babson College.

Khoylian, R. (1988) *Venture Capital Performance*. Needham, MA: Venture Economics, Inc.

Kozmetsky, G., Gill, M. D. Jr. and Smilor, R. W. (1984) *Financing and Managing Fast-Growth Companies: The Venture Capital Process*, Lexington, MA: Lexington Books.

Levering, R., Katz, M. and Moskowitz, M. (1984) *The Computer Entrepreneurs*. New York: NAL Books, p. 457.

Martin, J. D. and Petty, W. P. (1983). 'An analysis of the performance publicly traded venture capital companies' in *Journal of Financial and Quantitative Analysis*, 18(3), 401–10.

Morgenson, G. and Ramos, S. (1993) 'Danger Zone' in *Forbes,* 18 January, 66–9.

Morris, J. K. (1985) 'The pricing of a venture capital investment' in Pratt, S. E. and Morris, J. K. (eds), *Pratt's Guide to Venture Capital Sources*. 9th edn. Wellesley Hills, MA: Venture Economics, 108–11.

Neidorf, S.(1998) 'From Molehill to Mountain. VC Gets Bigger...' in *Venture Capital Journal*, October, 33–7.

PC Week (1987) Sevin Rosen, 'Venture capitalists to call it a career'. 2 July, 125–32.

PC World (1988) 'Playing the ponies'. January, 110–14.

Poindexter, J. B. (1976) *The Efficiency of Financial Markets: The Venture Capital Case*. Ph.D. Dissertation. New York University.

Reyes, J. E. (1997) 'Venture Returns Hit 40 % Again' in *Venture Capital Journal*, October, 52–5.

Reyes, J. E. (1998) 'European Private Equity Performance Continues to Show Strong Results' in *European Venture Capital Journal*, February/March, 20–1.

Reyes, J. E. (1998) 'Venture Capital Performance Takes a Breather' in *Venture Capital Journal*, July, 44–6.

Rotch, W. (1968) 'The Pattern of Success in Venture Capital Financing' in *Financial Analysis Journal,* 24 (Sept–Oct), 141–7.

Ruhnka, J. C. and Young, J. E. (1991) 'Some hypotheses about the risk in venture capital investing' in *Journal of Business Venturing*, 6 (2), 115–33.

Sahlman, W. A. (1989) The changing structure of the American venture capital industry. Paper presented at the National Venture Capital Association Meeting, Washington DC, 10–12 May.

Sahlman, W. A. and Stevenson, H. H. (1986) 'Capital market myopia' in *Journal of Business Venturing* 1(1), 7–30 (Winter).

Soja, T. A. and Reyes, J. E. (1990) *Investment Benchmarks: Venture Capital*. Needham, MA: Venture Economics, p. 191.

Stevenson, H. H., Muzyka, D. F. and Timmons, J. A. (1986) 'Venture capital in a new era: A simulation of the impact of the changes in investment patterns' in Ronstadt, R. et al. (eds), *Frontiers of Entrepreneurship Research*. Wellesley, MA: Babson College, 380–403.

Timmons, J. A. (1994) *New Venture Creation*. Irwin, Homewood, IL.

Timmons, J. A., Muzyka, D. F., Stevenson, H. H. and Bygrave, W. D., (1987) 'Opportunity recognition: the core of entrepreneurship' in *Frontiers of Entrepreneurship Research 1987* Babson College, Wellesley, MA, 109–23.

US Congress (1984) Study by the Joint Economic Committee. *Venture Capital and Innovation* by R. Premus. December.

Vachon, M. (1993) 'Venture capital reborn' in *Venture Capital Journal*, January, 32–6.

Venture Capital Journal, October 1982, 8–10.

Venture Capital Journal, July 1984, 4.

Venture Capital Journal, June 1990, 1–2.

Venture Capital Journal, February 1993, 30–5.

Venture Capital Journal, March 1993, 21.

Wall Street Journal (1988) 'Recent venture funds perform poorly as unrealistic expectations wear off. 8 November, 1988, B2.

Wayne, L. (1988) 'Management's tale' in *New York Time Magazine,* 17 January p. 42.

Wells, W. A. (1974) *Venture Capital Decision Making*. Ph.D. dissertation, Carnegie-Mellon University.

Notes

1. Bygrave, W. D. and Timmons, J. A. (1992) *Venture Capital at the Crossroads*. Boston, MA: Harvard Business School Press.

2. Rotch, W. (1968) 'The Pattern of Success in Venture Capital Financing' in *Financial Analysis Journal* 24 (Sept–Oct), 141–7.

3. Gevirtz, D. (1985) *The New Entrepreneurs: Innovation in American Business*. New York: Penguin Books, New York.

4. Poindexter, J. B. (1976) *The Efficiency of Financial Markets: The Venture Capital Case*. Ph.D. Dissertation. New York University.

5. Faucett, R. B. (1971). *The Management of Venture Capital Investment Companies*. Masters thesis, MIT.

6. Hoban, J. P. (1976) *Characteristics of Venture Capital Investing*. Ph.D. Dissertation. University of Utah.

7. Martin, J. D. and Petty, W. P. (1983). 'An analysis of the performance publicly traded venture capital companies' in *Journal of Financial and Quantitative Analysis*, 18(3), 401–10.

8. Wayne, L. (1988) 'Management's tale' in *New York Time Magazine*, 17 January, p. 42.

9. Ibbotson, R. G. and Brinson, G. P. (1987) *Investment Markets*. New York, N.Y.: McGraw-Hill, 99–100.

10. Poindexter, J. B. (1976) *The Efficiency of Financial Markets: The Venture Capital Case*. Ph.D. Dissertation. New York University.

11. *Venture Capital Journal,* June 1990, 1–2.

12. EVCA (1996) 'European Private Equity Performance Measure Pilot Survey' in *Technical Report*, December.

13. Bygrave, W. D. (1989) *Venture Capital Investing: A Resource Exchange Perspective*. Doctoral dissertation, Boston University.

14. Ibid.

15. European Commission (1996) Directorate General XIII-D, European Private Equity Performance Measurement Pilot Survey, Technical Report. Luxembourg.

16. Bannock Consulting, Venture Economics and EVCA (1997) *European Private Equity Performance Remains Strong at 19%*. News release, 5 December.

17. The term 'classic' venture capital was coined by Bygrave and Timmons (1992) to distinguish investments in seed-stage, early-stage, startup-stage and expansion-stage companies from investments in mature and declining companies such as buyouts. Hence, in the European classification scheme, early-stage and development investments are 'classic' venture capital.

18. Bygrave, W. D. (ed.) (1997) *The Portable MBA in Entrepreneurship*. 2nd edn. New York: John Wiley & Sons, Inc.

19. Timmons, J. A. (1994) *New Venture Creation*. Irwin, Homewood, IL.

20. Timmons, J. A., Muzyka, D. F., Stevenson, H. H. and Bygrave, W. D., (1987) 'Opportunity recognition: the core of entrepreneurship' in *Frontiers of Entrepreneurship Research 1987*, Babson College, Wellesley, MA, 109–23.

21. Bygrave, W. D., Johnstone. G., Lewis, J. and Ullman, R. (1988) 'Venture Capitalists' Criteria for Selecting High-Tech Investments: Prescriptive Wisdom Compared with Actuality' in Reynolds, P. D. et al. (eds), *Frontiers of Entrepreneurship Research 1998*.

22. Khoylian, R. (1988) *Venture Capital Performance*. Needham, MA: Venture Economics, Inc., p. 6.

23. Bygrave, W. D. and Timmons, J. A. (1992) *Venture Capital at the Crossroads*. Boston, MA: Harvard Business School Press.

24. Fineberg, S. A. M&A (1997) 'Values Soar While Sales Dip', in *Venture Capital Journal*, 37 (4), 31–2.

25. Bygrave, W. D., Johnstone. G., Lewis, J. and Ullman, R. (1988) 'Venture Capitalists' Criteria for Selecting High-Tech Investments: Prescriptive Wisdom Compared with Actuality' in Reynolds, P. D. et al. (eds), *Frontiers of Entrepreneurship Research 1998*.

26. Timmons, J. A. (1994) *New Venture Creation*. Irwin, Homewood, IL.

27. Bygrave, W. D. (ed.) (1997) *The Portable MBA in Entrepreneurship*. 2nd edn. New York: John Wiley & Sons, Inc.

28. Arthur, W. Brian (1994) *Increasing Returns and Path Dependence in the Economy*. Ann Arbor Michigan, University of Michigan Press.

29. Arthur, W. Brian (1996) 'Increasing Returns and the New World of Business,' *Harvard Business Review*, July–August.

EPILOGUE

Dr Jos B. Peeters

Going by the title of this book you might hope that having come to the end of it you are now a full professional and are assured of making millions by being one of the most astute venture capital operators. You might be disappointed, the wisdom of business school gurus and the shared experience from seasoned colleagues will guide you, but your key factor for success will be your ability to partner with some of the most exceptional entrepreneurs and to get your timings right. To guide you further in this process, in particular when you are investing in technology-based growth companies, I would like to offer the following 'Ten Commandments'.

1. 'Invest to exploit business opportunities, not to develop technology or science.'

The development of basic science and technology is nearly impossible to manage. Fundamental developments are unpredictable in cost and time and often the results prove difficult to protect and to keep outside the public domain. Invest only if there is a business opportunity, when you can see a clear way of exploiting a technological advantage or a scientific discovery. Do not invest for the excitement of new, ground-breaking science.

2. 'Back teams that are, or have the potential to become, the intellectual leaders in their market' – Prof. Gary Hamel.

Professor Gary Hamel, an expert in revitalizing large corporations, states that only companies and corporations that can position themselves as the intellectual leaders in their market today can become the market leaders of tomorrow. Only entrepreneurs who have a superior insight in their business today and in the driving forces in the market and the technology have the potential to become the significant players of tomorrow.

3. 'Do not invest in people that do not pass the Paul Bailey humour test or who are driven by greed or a mania for control.'

The late Dr Paul Bailey, a partner with the former BBHQ (now BPEP), had a very simple test. If an entrepreneur does not laugh at least three times in the first half-hour of the first meeting, then do not invest. If he or she has not enough sense for relativity or for real life then he or she most likely doesn't have enough common sense to build a business. If an entrepreneur has a track record for being overly greedy or is obsessed by control, whatever contract you sign with him, whatever good intentions there might be at the start of the relationship, sooner or later you will be put in a corner. Do not expect people to change their attitudes.

4. 'Remember the boiled frog syndrome. Love is a dangerous investment adviser.'

To understand what happens with your attitude towards an investment opportunity you have to study frogs. If you take a frog and throw him in a jar of boiling water, the frog will react immediately and jump out. However, if you put a frog in cold water and heat the jar gradually you will boil the frog to death. He will adapt his senses and he gets killed without noticing it. Don't go native; don't fall in love with your investments to the extent that you become insensitive to the writing on the wall.

5. 'Time your investments to survive the chasms in the technology adoption life cycle and don't count on your friends to bail you out.'

Read *Crossing the Chasm* from Geoffrey Moore. The chasm, a time of great despair, between the technology enthusiasts and visionary early adopters and the mainstream pragmatists, who are not comfortable with the immaturity of the solutions offered, is real and expensive. Keep enough powder dry because you might find it very difficult to raise additional money in this phase of development.

6. 'Don't get sunk in black holes for money, cut your losses early and invest your time in potential successes.'

One of the major difficulties of technology investing is to decide when to stop pouring money into a company. Which is the last million that will reach the turning point? Some analysis shows that any investment beyond 1.4 times the amount initially planned was not worth doing. Cut your losses early and invest your time in your potential winners.

7. 'Adopt a highly focused investment strategy and stay with it.'

As in any business, focus is part of the success. Having a clear idea of what you want to do and what you do not want to do is not only time efficient, but it is also very effective in building your image in the market and in attracting the kind of deals you want. Changing a strategy en route nearly always means that you have to write off a number of previous investments.

8. Keep your decision lines short, the probability of making the right decision is equal to one half – Prof. Neil Churchill.

Making decisions on technology-based investments requires a lot of judgement and this judgement is hard to convey in write-ups and should not be expected from complete outsiders to the investment. Professor Neil Churchill coined this golden rule that the probability of making the right decision is equal to one divided by two to the n power, where n is the number of decision-making layers.

9. 'Always keep the door in sight, exits do not happen automatically, have the power to get out.'

The venture capital business is about buying reasonably cheap, adding value and selling at a good price. Investing is relatively easy, working with a company is more complicated, but it is not over until you have returned money to the investors. Exits have to be worked on, they don't come automatically and timing is of the essence. But remember that you cannot lose by selling at a profit and that it is better to sell before the top than once you are over it and everybody is running for the door.

10. 'Have a local presence, a strong link to the USA and a global network.'

Be local and think global. Technology-based venture capital is a pedestrian business. It is a grass roots business. You have to be close to your investments, be able to go there regularly and at short notice. Hence a local presence is essential. But with the depth of their venture capital industry, the sophistication of their specialist investment banks and NASDAQ as the prime public market for growth companies, the USA will continue to be the dominant force in technology investing. An understanding of this environment is mandatory to be successful in Europe. With the fast developments in India, Latin America, the Far East and the Pacific Rim, intelligence on these markets is no longer a luxury for technology companies in Europe.

Conclusion

You will see exiting opportunities and commit minor or major sins against these commandments. If you get your timing right and there is enough greed in the markets you might even realize excellent returns. But if the going gets tough you might, as I have many times, regret not having been more religious.

GLOSSARY

AFIC   Association Française des Investisseurs en Capital

AIFI   Associazione Italiana degli Investitiori Istitutionali nel Capitale di Rischio

AIM   Alternative Investment Market

ARD   American Research and Development

BTU   Beteiligungskapital für Technologieunternehmen

BV   Dutch private limited liability company

BVA   Belgian Venturing Association

BVCA   British Venture Capital Association

BVK   Bundesverband Deutscher Kapitalbeteiligungsgesellschaften

CEO   Chief executive officer

CFC   Controlled foreign corporation

DEC   Digital Equipment Corporation

EASDAQ   European Association of Securities Dealers Automated Quotation

EBIT   Earnings before interest and tax

EIS   Enterprise Investment Scheme

EPS   Earnings per share

ERISA   Employee Retirement Income Security Act

EURO.NM   Pan European group of regulated stock markets

EVCA   European Venture Capital Association

FCPI   Fonds Commun de Placement Innovation

FCPR	Fonds Commun Placement à Risque
FSA	Financial Services Authority
FTSE 100	Financial Times Stock Exchange 100 index
IAS	International accountancy standards
IPO	Initial public offering
IRR	Internal rate of return
LSE	London Stock Exchange
MBI	Management buy-in
MBO	Management buyout
MIM	Meeting of the Interprofessional Market
Nasdaq	National Association of Securities Dealers Automated Quotation
NMAX	Nieuwe Markt Amsterdam
NV	Dutch public limited liability company
NVP	Nederlandse Vereniging van Participatiemaatschappijen
OEM	Original equipment manufacturer
OFEX	London Off-Exchange facility
PFIC	Passive foreign investment company
P&L	Profit and loss
PLC	Public limited company
R&D	Research and development
RNS	Regulatory News Service of the London Stock Exchange
SBIC	Small business investment company
SCR	Sociétés de Capital Risque
SEAQ	Stock exchange automated quotations system
SEATS	Stock exchange alternative trading service

SETS   Stock exchange electronic trading system

SMEs   Small and medium-sized enterprises

SNM   Société du Nouveau Marché

TBG   Technology Participation Society

TSO   Total shares outstanding

TVM   Techno Venture Management

UBTI   Unrelated Business Taxable Income

US GAAP   US generally accepted accountancy principles

VAR   Value added reseller

VCT   Venture Capital Trust

WIP   Work in progress

INDEX